ONE
CAME BACK

{UN REVENANT}

May you enjoy many
happy hours with
Rémi Trembleay

Margaret

Cher Hector,

J'espère que mon
travail de traductrice
te plaira ! Amitiés
bien vives. Claire
Quintal

ONE CAME BACK

A FRANCO-AMERICAN CIVIL WAR NOVEL
by
Rémi Tremblay

translated by
Margaret S. Langford

Professor of French and Franco-American Studies
Keene State College
Keene, New Hampshire

in collaboration with

Claire Quintal

Founding Director Emerita
French Institute, Assumption College
Worcester, Massachusetts

Images from the Past
Bennington, Vermont

⚜ ⚜ ⚜ ⚜ ⚜ ⚜ ⚜ ⚜ ⚜ ⚜ ⚜ ⚜ ⚜ ⚜ ⚜ ⚜ ⚜ ⚜

1 2 3 4 5 6 7 8 910 XXX 08 07 06 05 04 03 02

First edition

Library of Congress Cataloging-in-Publication Data

Tremblay, Rémi, 1847-1926.
    [Revenant. English]
    One came back: a Franco-American civil war novel /
  by Rémi Tremblay translated by Margaret S. Langford
  in collaboration with Claire Quintal.
    p. cm.
  ISBN 1-884592-22-8 — ISBN 1-884592-09-0
    1. United States—History—Civil war, 1861-1865—Fiction. I. Title.
PQ3919.T7 R413 2002
843'.8--dc21   2002001913

Copyright 2002 Margaret S. Langford
Published by Images from the Past, Inc.
P.O. Box 137, Bennington, Vermont 05201
www.ImagesfromthePast.com
Tordis Ilg Isselhardt, Publisher

Printed in the United States of America

Design and Production: Ron Toelke Associates, Chatham, NY
Printer: Thomson-Shore, Inc., Dexter, MI

To Robert "Steve" Langford

my in-house Franco-American

folklorist and consultant

CONTENTS

❧ ❧ ❧ ❧ ❧ ❧ ❧ ❧ ❧ ❧ ❧ ❧ ❧ ❧ ❧ ❧❧ ❧ ❧ ❧ ❧

List of Illustrations	x
Foreword	xi
Acknowledgments	xvii
Introduction	1

One Came Back
Part One: A Country Boy Goes to War

I	An Act of Desperation	15
II	Léon Duroc	17
III	Poor and in Love	20
IV	A Declaration of Love Followed by an Explanation	22
V	A Reconciliation before Parting	26
VI	The Conspiracy	28
VII	The Trap Snaps Shut	31
VIII	The Rescue	34
IX	The Enlistment	36

Part Two: From the Wilderness to Petersburg

X	The 14th Regular United States Infantry	38
XI	Back and Forth	42
XII	Eugène Leduc	46
XIII	Guerrillas	50
XIV	From the Frying Pan into the Fire	52
XV	Back to the Regiment	55
XVI	Léon's Anguish	57
XVII	Single Combat	59
XVIII	Meanwhile, Back at the Plantation	62
XIX	Two against Five	64
XX	The Battle of the North Anna	68
XXI	A Few Skirmishes	71
XXII	The Battle of Cold Harbor	75
XXIII	Incidents and Accidents	80
XXIV	Two Predictions	84
XXV	Mortally Wounded	87

Part Three: Meanwhile, Back in Québec

XXVI	Meanwhile, Back in Pingreville	91
XXVII	It Just Goes to Show…	95
XXVIII	A Letter from Léon	99
XXIX	Louise in Despair	102
XXX	That Worthy M. Grippard	105
XXXI	Phantasmagoria within Reach of the Working Poor	108
XXXII	Phantasmagoria Put to the Test	111
XXXIII	Among Friends	117
XXXIV	Phantasmagoria Reviewed, Corrected, and Considerably Augmented	121
XXXV	The So-Called Ghost's Ultimatum	125
XXXVI	Our Old Acquaintances from Montréal and Pingreville	129

Part Four: A Wandering Canadian

XXXVII	Before Petersburg	133
XXXVIII	A Mine Explosion	138
XXXIX	The Sutler	143
XL	Jeff Davis's Promises	148
XLI	Making a Promise Is One Thing; Keeping It Is Quite a Different Matter	151
XLII	Serving the Confederacy	154
XLIII	A Wandering Canadian	157
XLIV	Where a Certain Infantryman Becomes a Cavalryman	160
XLV	His First Riding Lesson	163
XLVI	Where a Certain Cavalryman Becomes an Infantryman Once Again	167
XLVII	The Wanderings of a Prisoner of War	170

Part Five: Prison Life

XLVIII	Castle Thunder	173
XLIX	An Unfortunate Encounter	176
L	The Horrors of Libby Prison	179
LI	You Can't Get Enough of a Good Thing	185
LII	Hunger Is a Bad Advisor	188

Part Six: Desertion

LIII	Paroled	191
LIV	Adventures and Misadventures	195
LV	Under Guard	201
LVI	Back to Annapolis	205
LVII	The Knights of the Guardroom	209
LVIII	Back to New London	212
LIX	To Each His Own	215

Part Seven: One Soldier Comes Back from the War

LX	A Visit to Pingreville	218
LXI	Ah, the Good Old Days When I Was a Deserter	221
LXII	Ghosts in Difficulty	225
LXIII	An Important Deposition	229
LXIV	An Eventful Life	234
LXV	An Unexpected Encounter	238
LXVI	The Dead Man's Fiancée	241
LXVII	A Family Put to the Test	245
LXVIII	Someone Really Does Come Back	249
LXIX	Two Brothers in Arms	252
LXX	Epilogue	255

One Came Back: A New Translation and New Edition

A Note from the Translators	260
One Came Back, Un Revenant, and *Back from the Grave*	261
The 14th Regular U.S. Infantry and Rémi Tremblay's War Record	262
Abbreviations	264
Notes	265
Selected Franco-American Centers and Institutes	292
Bibliography	293
Biographies	297

List of Illustrations

Rémi Tremblay   xviii

Battle of Cold Harbor, Virginia, June 1, 1864 —
The Eighteenth Corps driving Longstreet's forces from their
first line of rifle pits.   76-77

Battle of Petersburg, Virginia, June 16, 1864 —
Eighteenth Corps carrying a portion of Beauregard's line.   136-137

Explosion of the mine before Petersburg.   140-141

Soldiers in camp visiting the sutler's store.   146-147

Interior of Libby prison, Richmond, Virginia,
with prisoners from General Lee's army confined after the surrender.   182-183

In the trenches before Petersburg.   196-197

FOREWORD

A Unique Civil War Novel

One Came Back is the first known published English-language translation of the Civil War novel *Un Revenant*. Part autobiography, part melodramatic love story, *Un Revenant* is the work of Rémi Tremblay, published in Montréal in 1884. It is the story of two adventurous, underage French Canadians — Léon Duroc and Eugène Leduc — who enlist in the Union army. Both young men fall in love; both their situations appear hopeless.

Tremblay knew about the United States and the War Between the States. Having moved from Québec to New England with his family, he had lived in the mill towns of Fisherville, Massachusetts, and Woonsocket, Rhode Island, before enlisting in the 14th U.S. Infantry Regiment at the age of sixteen. As a Union soldier, he fought in the battles of Spotsylvania Courthouse, Wilderness, Cold Harbor, and Petersburg. Here he was captured and was interned at the infamous Libby prison in Richmond. Having survived the ordeal, Tremblay fled to Canada — which made him a deserter, like his hero Eugène Leduc. Nevertheless, he was not later deterred from returning periodically to the United States where, despite his lack of formal education, he worked as a journalist and, eventually, as editor of a Franco-American newspaper in Fall River, Massachusetts.

Of the two romantic tales, the more important is played out in the province of Québec, Canada, in and around the city of Montréal. It is the story of Léon Duroc and Louise Latour — the Romeo and Juliet of another age, seemingly doomed to an impossible love. Driven apart as they are by the forces of evil, their love, nevertheless, survives the greatest of torments — death itself — for Duroc is reported killed in battle. On the other hand, Eugène Leduc's brief encounter with the adolescent beauty from Louisiana, Hélène Duchâtel, is, in some respects, even more hopeless. Not only do they meet on Confederate soil, but Hélène is already engaged to another, a Confederate officer! Will their love, seen only fleetingly in each other's eyes, ever find mutual expression?

No wonder this story has been described as the *Gone with the Wind* of the French language. The elements are similar: forced marches, carnage, valor, inhumanity, destruction, and death on the one hand; love, hope, passion, deception, faithfulness, and fulfillment on the other. Yet, because the author was both a participant in the war and a French Canadian, his perspective is unique in Civil War literature. Opposed as they are to slavery and therefore to the ideals of the Confederate cause, his heroes are, nonetheless, critical of Northern mores and often sympathetic to the refined ways of Southern gentility.

Tremblay's "Epilogue" adds another dimension to the tale, one having little to do with the story. The novel concludes with a defense of Franco-Americans. The exodus of from one to one and a half million French Canadians to New England and northern New York in the late nineteenth and early twentieth centuries has remained to this day largely unnoticed by official histories of the United States.[1] But, in Tremblay's time, these emigrants were often labeled traitors by government and ecclesiastical officials back home in Canada. The author, who had personally experienced the immigration and the scorn, would use his novel to set the record straight.

The story line
Did Rémi Tremblay have literary or journalistic sources for his tale of a returning soldier? Homer's *Odyssey* could have served as a model for Léon and Louise. Odysseus too went off to battle. Making his way home from Troy despite formidable obstacles, he found his beloved — and ever-faithful — Penelope surrounded by suitors.

From "real life," Tremblay knew of the adventures of Major Edmond Mallet, a Franco-American from Oswego, New York. Mallet served with the 81st New York Volunteers. Like Tremblay, he fought in the Battle of Cold Harbor, Virginia (June 1–12, 1864), in which some 19,500 Northern soldiers alone lost their lives. Among these were reportedly "hundreds" of young Canadians. Mallet, seriously wounded at Cold Harbor, was left to die on the battlefield. The Oswego newspaper reported his death. But, in a development strangely similar to Duroc's in *One Came Back* and reminiscent of Samuel Clemens's words that the news of his death had been "greatly exaggerated," Mallet lived to tell the tale. Tremblay dedicated his poem "Le Drapeau du 14e" to Mallet. The Mallet-Tremblay correspondence in the 1880s reveals their cordial relationship.

Tremblay as storyteller, journalist, and moralist
Tremblay's story opens "It was a cold, rainy May night in the year of Our Lord 1864." Not exactly an eye-catcher for avid twenty-first-century consumers accustomed to dazzling effects lest they pick up another book or hit the remote. Yet, methodically, in a pace definitely consistent with that of his contemporaries, the storyteller sets the scene. Translated into cinema, the technique could be made to work: as the credits roll, we see the fog, the rain, the darkened streets, the carriages before the luxurious house, the distraught young man, the policeman, the water. We sense the unfolding drama. The man jumps. The credits end. Dissolve. It would appear that Tremblay's telling is, after all, quite modern.

He also writes like a journalist — which, of course, he was. Tremblay's novel first appeared in weekly installments; in Franco-American newspapers serialized fiction was the rage. As to Tremblay's audience — a North American French-reading public — he had to take them from something they knew, Montréal, and something they understood, love and despair, to his real subject, the Civil War. He undoubtedly also wanted to sell his product; and so, in the style of the day, he offered his readers a melodramatic soap opera awash not only with passion (within limits acceptable to religious and moral sensitivities), but also with the latest science and technology.

Yet, one cannot but sense that the story Tremblay really wants to tell is that of his war experiences. At times, the account of life in the Union army could have been the work of a reporter living on the front lines, penning his reports by night and sending them off by courier or telegraph for appearance in the next day's gazette. He names towns, soldiers, officers, and military units; he describes rations, marches, and camps; but he especially captures the sights and sounds of war: bombs, bullets, armies with bayonets drawn, blood, and all the horror of an ineluctable charge to oblivion. But, just as in contemporary media accounts — written or televised — the scenes don't necessarily hold together. What is the point of the encounter between Leduc and the "big Irishman"? The description of these two men taking time out to fight each other as they approached the Confederate army does little for the main plot. Had Tremblay seen — or experienced — such an event? It does make for a good tale, however, when writing for people who had their own gripe with the Irish in the mills of New England. The novel is not a model of political correctness.

And that raises the issue of Tremblay's actors. Are they type characters? The names of the French-Canadian characters would seem to suggest so. Then why not the Americans? Perhaps the play on words in English would have been lost on the readers. The Québécois bad guys are Bagoulard (fast-talking pork-barrel politician), Bohémier (the "Bohemian" type), Grippard (*grippe-sou,* avaricious), and Brindamour (an ironic "bit of love"). But the good guys are Latour (suggestive of strength), Labonne (good), Leduc (the duke), and, especially, Duroc (of stone). If Tremblay's storytelling is at times journalistic, his character portrayal has the feeling of a morality play.[2]

Style: proverbs, irony, jokes, and science

One thing this novel is not: stylistically boring. There is a new twist at every turn of the page. Sometimes objective as Eugène Leduc's treetop description of the battle raging in the plain, the story at other times becomes wholly personal. When the good people of Baltic, Connecticut, put up the money to pay the train fare home for the now-defecting Leduc, the former Union soldier promises to repay them in prayer. And again the novel takes on a very autobiographical tone: "The masses have long since been said," Tremblay informs the reader, "but the soldier they returned home to his family feels that he can never repay the debt; on his behalf, we can assure them that he will be eternally grateful."

Nor does Tremblay shy away from making his personal opinions known, his favorite tool being the proverb. "Virtue is its own reward," he reminds us. And the pithy instruction continues: "The more miserable the man, the more miserable everybody wants to make him. The better off he is, the better he is treated." "In a small town, everyone knows his neighbor's business better than his own." "Wealth excuses many crimes." He even has a maxim about maxims: "Nothing is handier than a maxim if you have money." *Sayings of Chairman Tremblay?*

Close on the heels of the pithy saying is Tremblay's use of irony. "Such honest behavior could not go unrewarded," he writes, referring to a theft. "People will perhaps admire his honesty, but they'll never forgive him his poverty." "When need be, M. Latour knew how to use a double standard." His lashing spares neither European, American, nor Canadian. "We aren't any better than other nations...but those whose countrymen have done everything they could to corrupt our political and business mores shouldn't be the first to throw stones at the Canadian people when they see one of us do cynically in the light of day what the Europeans have taught us to do secretly." "No laws or regulations can withstand the almighty power of money, that god worshiped in every country in the world and especially in the United States!" And for the French Canadian: "Like them [the Americans], we have our charlatans here — our religion peddlers, our conscience dealers, our overrated reputations, and our idols with feet of clay. We bow down before the golden calf as much as they do, and, if we can't surpass their servile admiration for gilded vice, the honest man convicted of the crime of chronic and inveterate poverty is much more deeply despised here than he is in the United States." Tremblay moves easily from reporter to autobiographer to satirical columnist.

Sometimes he tests the limits of the reader's imagination. Two examples come to mind. The descriptions of *phantasmagoria* are questionable both in their science and in their enactment. Of course, just as in the case of Jules Verne, what would have been technologically crude in his day would have no problem being staged today. Then there is Eugène's Leduc's ability to replicate accents. With hardly any schooling in his native French and only a short time in the United States, could this sixteen-year-old really have become so accomplished a linguist? Novels do require a voluntary suspension of disbelief.

The Langford translation and the NMDC reprint

Tremblay loves to play with words, but his word jokes don't always work in English. That alone makes the translator's job difficult if not impossible. When Brindamour is caught with the convex mirror, he responds, "Ce n'est pas le miroir qu'on vexe." How to render that in English and keep the joke? To her merit, Professor Langford has come as close as possible: "This isn't the 'vexed' mirror" (Chapter xxxv). At other times, the play on words is simply impossible to render. Such is the case of *élargis* (early in Chapter LIII) meaning both paroled and fattened up. This time the translator has simply avoided the play on words; some things defy translation.

Also important to note here is the fact that Professor Langford brings to her task a dual competency: French linguistic ability on the one hand and a knowledge of things French-Canadian and Franco-American on the other. Her insights into North American French culture result from years of professional commitment and from personal experience. Undertaking this translation took foresight, pursuing it demanded courage, accomplishing the task required both skill and love.

This translation builds on the work of the National Materials Development Center. From 1975 to 1982 the center published roughly one hundred items — books and audio-visual materials — on or by Franco-Americans. Especially noteworthy in this undertaking are the ten-volume anthology *Littérature franco-américaine de la Nouvelle-Angleterre* and nine nineteenth- and twentieth-century Franco-American novels which, up until that time, had long been out of print. Tremblay's *Un Revenant* was one of those novels. Professor Langford brings this effort another step forward by making one of these classics available to an even larger reading public.

French Canadians and Franco-Americans in the Civil War

Estimates of the number of French Canadians who participated in the War Between the States range from 20,000 (Roby) and 30,000 (Chartier) to 45,000 (genealogical source). Historian Robert E. Chenard of Waterville, Maine, addresses the issue of one local participation. "The small village of Waterville furnished 525 soldiers, one of every eight of its citizens or about one third of its adult men, during the Civil War. In 1860, Waterville had a population of only 4,420, with French-Canadian descent, a total of 855 households. Sixty of these soldiers were of French-Canadian descent, representing a proportional share of Waterville's Franco-American population in this conflict."

The best known, perhaps, of all French-Canadian participants in the Civil War was Calixa Lavallée. Born in Québec, Lavallée lived for many years in the United States, first in New Orleans, then in Massachusetts, where he died and was buried — before being exhumed and buried anew in Canada. A musician, he enlisted in the 4th Rhode Island where he became a bandleader. But Lavallée is especialy known as the composer of the Canadian national anthem, "O Canada."

Parting notes

That a soldier presumed dead should return from war is something of a literary *lieu commun* based on reality. The following story from a recent newspaper article offers just one example. The *Herald News* of Fall River, Massachusetts, reported that, to mark the eightieth anniversary of the end of World War I, France honored American veterans of that conflict by bestowing the Legion of Honor upon them.

Among them was Franco-American Edmond Forcier, then aged 103. It seems that Forcier, wounded in the battle of Château-Thierry, was believed dead. Military authorities notified the family, and a funeral was held at the Saint-Jean-Baptiste Church. Several days later, the deceased Forcier was found recovering in a military hospital.

Tremblay was ahead of his times. His parting words in *One Came Back* are, "In a forthcoming work, whose title has not yet been chosen, perhaps we'll give the reader further news about some of the characters...." *One Came Back II?*

Julien Olivier
Folklorist, writer, and journalist
Barrington, New Hampshire

ACKNOWLEDGMENTS

Principal readers and consultants
Julien Olivier, Franco-American author, journalist, folklorist, raconteur; Robert Fournier, Société historique franco-americaine, Suncook, New Hampshire; Christopher Kusack, Professor of Geography, Keene State College, Keene, New Hampshire; James Smart, Professor Emeritus of History, Keene State College, Keene, New Hampshire.

Contributors, readers, and consultants
Terry Borton, Director, The American Magic-Lantern Theater, Boston; Paul Chassé, Professor Emeritus of French, Somersworth, New Hampshire; Mervyn Heard, phantasmagoria expert, Exeter University, Exeter, England; Michael Hurt, Historical Society of Cheshire County, Keene, New Hampshire; Louis Brossard, Professor Emeritus of American History, Montréal; Monique Lebrun-Brossard, Professor of Linguistics, Université du Québec à Montréal; Gloria Friedman, Art Historian, Franklin Pierce College; David A. Keough, The U.S. Army Military Institute, Carlisle Barracks, Pennsylvania; Peggy Partello, Librarian, Mason Library, Keene State College; Brian C. Pohanka, Historian, The 5th New York Volunteer Infantry, Alexandria, Virginia; Allan Rumrill, Historical Society of Cheshire County, Keene, New Hampshire; Patrick Schroeder, Historian, The 5th New York Volunteer Infantry, Daleville, Virginia; Richard E. Sommers, The U.S. Army Military History Institute, Carlisle Barracks, Pennsylvania; Frederick Wolf, Professor of Physics, Keene State College, Keene, New Hampshire.

Libraries, archives, centers, and organizations
The Bibliothèque Mallet, Union Saint-Jean-Baptiste, Woonsocket, Rhode Island; Le centre de recherche et civilisation canadienne-française (Université d'Ottowa); the Société historique française; The Civil War Collection, Mason Library, Keene State College; The Franco-American Center, Manchester, New Hampshire; The Franco-American Center, University of Maine at Orono; The Historical Society of Cheshire County, Keene, New Hampshire; The men of the 5th New Hampshire, Keene, New Hampshire; The U.S. Army Military History Institute, Carlisle Barracks, Pennsylvania.

A very special vote of thanks to Images from the Past: Tordis Ilg Isselhardt, publisher; Sarah Novak, editor; and Ron Toelke and Barbara Kempler-Toelke, designers.

Rémi Tremblay

INTRODUCTION

Boys Into Men:

Rémi Tremblay and the American Civil War

Following the successful serialization in its newspaper, the *La Patrie* press of Montreal published *Un Revenant* in book form in 1884. Why then, twenty years after Tremblay's war experiences? Perhaps, in his thirties by then, he was thinking of other veterans who also had crossed the border in their teens to enlist in United States regular and volunteer units. Of the thousands who enlisted (with various estimates of their number ranging from 20,000 to 45,000), 14,000 died (Brossard and Lebrun-Brossard, *Le Forum*, vol. 27, 6, 1999, p. 25). For these men and their survivors, this foreign war was still very much a reality in the 1880s. Some still had not resolved pension issues. Others, like Tremblay, still feared repercussions from old desertion charges. Action taken by the United States government in March, 1889, providing a mechanism for soldiers charged with desertion to clear their records, tells us how prevalent this fear was.

A survivor of the battles of the Wilderness, Spotsylvania, and Cold Harbor, of the siege of Petersburg, and of the infamous Libby prison, Tremblay never forgot his war experiences or his regiment: the 14th Regular United States Infantry. *Un Revenant* forms an integral part of a very intriguing chain of events in the author's life: his father's participation in the rebellion of 1837, a French-Canadian independence movement; his own efforts to expunge desertion charges from his record; his request, through Congress, when the United States entered World War I, for permission to complete the remainder of his term of enlistment; and his restatement of his military career in his autobiography, *Pierre qui roule,* only a few years before his death.

A cursory look at Rémi's chronology would suggest that his Civil War adventure was quickly over — only a few months out of a lifetime spanning almost eighty years. Yet, from his infancy, Rémi's life had prepared him for those crucial months with the 14th Regulars which would shape his existence until the day he died.

He was born on April 2, 1837, in Saint-Barnabé, Comté de Saint-Hyacinthe, Québec. As a child, he heard many tales of men fighting for their beliefs from his father, François-Xavier Tremblay, and his two uncles, who had fought at Saint-Denis in the 1837 Papineau rebellion (Santerre, p. 235; *Pierre qui roule,* pp. 23-28).

We know that he attended the village school in Sainte-Victoire and read the same texts as his noble hero Léon did. Here he first learned English: a boy of Irish descent from Montréal had come to the countryside to improve his French; Rémi and his new friend exchanged French and English lessons. When Tremblay was twelve, he emigrated with his family first to Fisherville, Massachusetts, then to Woonsocket, Rhode Island, where they found work in the mills. He related this experience both in *Un Revenant/One Came Back* and *Pierre qui roule*. Like many boys of his age, Rémi worked in the mills with other family members. His English improved (*Pierre qui roule*, pp. 55-56). By the time he had spent a few months in the army, he could speak the language fluently (*One Came Back*, Chapter XII).[1]

At sixteen had he mastered the language well enough to imitate accents and dialects with the same facility as his alter ego Eugène? Whatever the case, in later years Tremblay demonstrated his English proficiency both as translator and journalist. He even drafted an unpublished English translation of *Un Revenant*, now reposing in the archives of the Centre de recherche et civilisation canadienne-française. An examination of this interesting document, discovered by Dr. Claire Quintal, has enriched the *One Came Back* translation and annotations.

Tremblay keeps telling us why he joined the Union army. In 1861, Rhode Island volunteers, having survived the Battle of Bull Run, paraded through the streets of Woonsocket upon their return at the end of their three months' enlistment (*Pierre qui roule*, p. 75). Young Rémi, now fourteen years old, is dazzled by the sight of these men in uniform. The pages of *One Came Back* record his two fondest wishes: to fight beside brave men like these and then, perhaps, find a way to fight for France. Sadly, he realized he would have to join the Foreign Legion rather than the regular French army to do so (*One Came Back*, Chapter II). French Canadians, so says Tremblay, have no flag to call their own. He doesn't relish the idea of fighting for the English. At any rate, he must put off his plans for a while. At fourteen he is too young to be a soldier. Shortly afterwards, the Tremblays make the arduous trip back to Québec by horse and wagon.

Why and how did young French Canadians enlist in the Union army? For how long? What was their training like? How did they get to the battlefield? Seemingly *One Came Back* provides a very realistic picture. Times were hard. Men of all ages needed to provide for their families as best they could. Moreover, glowing accounts of heroic adventures on the battlefield inspired dreams of glory. Tremblay researchers, military records, and Rémi's own testimony as well show us that young men were constantly bombarded with news about the war. In *One Came Back*, Duroc read glorified battle accounts in the Montréal newspapers; Leduc marveled at the Rhode Island volunteers returning from the first Battle of Bull Run in a parade through the streets of Woonsocket. And we know from *Pierre qui roule* that Eugène's experiences are Tremblay's. The same work also states that Rémi had read letters to his father from a young soldier friend of the family, Louis Menon. Later, unexpectedly, Rémi met him at a Union army camp, a circumstance that bears a striking resemblance to Eugène's encounter with Léon. Could there be some connection between Menon's life and the fictional Léon Duroc?

While many young men might have been tempted to join the Northern army just for the glory of it, they also could have found the financial incentives equally compelling. As the war progressed, bonuses were offered just for enlisting; also, some American families "bought" replacements to keep their fathers, sons, and husbands from the carnage. Linking the two motives, Tremblay hints that valiant young Canadians might very well have had noble reasons for being bounty soldiers. And the honorable Léon enlists to make good M. Latour's stolen $1,000.

Once decided, all found it easy to enlist. Léon took the train to Rouse's Point, New York, just over the border from Québec. Would-be soldiers also could get there on foot. Rémi, like his hero Eugène, walked there from Contrecoeur, just outside Montréal, via Chambly and St. Jean. When he arrived hungry and footsore on Sunday, November 7, 1863, a recruiting officer made sure he got a good meal and a place to stay until Monday, when he was promptly sworn into the 14th Regular U.S. Infantry. Like Eugène, Rémi is underage.

His enlistment papers bear the signatures of two "guardians" who swear that he is of age and fit to serve. Many others like him joined the army even though they were underage. Some placed a paper bearing the number "eighteen" in their shoes so that they could swear they were "over eighteen." Height requirements had been lowered. Five feet three inches tall, Rémi/Eugène was just tall enough. And, while the enlistment for regulars had been three years, Rémi's papers show him agreeing to enlist for five.

Once sworn in, what happened next? Eugène's and Léon's experiences seemingly illustrate what occurred at two different moments during the war. Like Rémi, Eugène then goes through two month's training at Fort Trumbull before being marched into battle (*One Came Back,* Chapter XII).

The next eighteen months for the 14th U.S. Regulars find Rémi/Eugène fighting in some of the Civil War's bloodiest battles (Wilderness, Spotsylvania, North Anna, Cold Harbor). At the siege of Petersburg, he witnesses the disastrous mine explosion. And, by his own admission, his service is punctuated by several fugues. Subsequently captured, he was sent to Libby prison. Were it not for his last escapade following his release on a prisoner exchange, we might not know as much about his war experiences as we do. And Tremblay's military career did not end with the Civil War. Like Eugène, after earning his certificate from the Montréal Military School, he fought in the Fenian wars.

Other sources complete his biography for us. In 1867, he married Julie Lemery of Woonsocket, Rhode Island.[2] They had three sons: Emile (1873-1901), Eugène (1876-1904), and Jules (1879-1927). Their places of birth reflect Tremblay's life on the move in Québec: Stoke, Sherbrooke, Montréal. Following Julie's death in 1896 he married Alida Charlebois, on August 31, 1897 (Chassé, p. 62). He became a successful journalist, editor, translator, poet, and novelist. He wrote several travel books, four volumes of poetry, and two novels. *Un Revenant/One Came Back* (1884) is for the most part the autobiographical account of his Civil War experiences. The 1923 *Pierre qui roule: Souvenirs d'un journaliste (A Rolling Stone: Memoirs of a Journalist)* is also autobiographical. *Contre le courant,* a second novel based on his European travels, remained unfinished at his death.

Seemingly his frequent use of pseudonyms in *One Came Back* is not at all unusual. He borrowed his own son's name, Eugène, for his picaresque hero. Eugène, in turn, borrowed other names in the course of his escapades: Kelly, Washington C. Joslin, and James Randall. During his prolific career Tremblay showed a predilection for using pseudonyms himself. In his biographical sketch of Tremblay, Cyrille Felteau lists the following: Bistouri, Père Louison, Fanfan Mimiche, Mio Zotis, Quéquienne (his pseudonym in *Pierre qui roule*), K. Rosine, Sévère Sansfaçon, and Vicomte de Blague-Fort (Felteau, p. 182).

Always on the move, Tremblay worked as a journalist on both sides of the border and traveled through Europe. He died on January 30, 1926, in a hospital in Pointe-à-Pitre in Guadeloupe where he had gone because of his failing health.

Tremblay spent eighteen months in the army — not a long time in a seventy-nine-year life span. Yet, during that time, he lived through some of the bloodiest Civil War battles and survived six months in the infamous Libby prison. He would come back again and again to these experiences in his writings, in addition to *Un Revenant:* in his arguments with the Protestant clergyman Narcisse Cyr about his (Tremblay's) war record (Chassé, p. 55); his correspondence with Major Edmond Mallet concerning his desertion and his brother-in-law's war pension (Mallet-Tremblay correspondence, 1885-1887; Bibliothèque Mallet, Union Saint-Jean-Baptiste, Woonsocket, Rhode Island); the poem "Le drapeau du 14e," dedicated to Major Mallet (*Coups d'aile et de bec,* 1888); and his autobiography, *Pierre qui roule* (1923).

When the soldier leaves the war, does the war leave the soldier? And how can he make his friends and family understand? Most of Tremblay's observations fall into these broad categories: the coming of age of the new recruits, heroism, desertion, the sounds of battle, the prisoner's life, the soldier's life, and the soldier's return. But does he create a unified novel? Yes, say Professors Brossard and Lebrun-Brossard.

Un Revenant/One Came Back: **historical novel and autobiography**
Tremblay critics all agree that *Un Revenant* records the author's Civil War experiences. Yet some have criticized the novel's structure; for example, Léon disappears from the narrative, only to reappear at the end. Professors Louis Brossard, an American history specialist, and Monique Lebrun-Brossard, linguist, lay these criticisms to rest in their incisive joint analysis "*Un Revenant,* roman historique ou autobiographie?" (*Le Forum,* vol. 27, no. 5, pp. 14, 22; no. 6, pp. 17, 25, 29; vol. 28, no. 1, pp. 22, 32). Yes, the novel is both historical and autobiographical. It begins the saga of Tremblay's adventures which are concluded in his autobiographical novel *Pierre qui roule.* It is unique. Eugène is at the same time Rémi and a historical/sociological type: the prototypical young

French Canadian of the 1860s. As is appropriate, we follow the hero's adventures.

And Léon? Forty chapters take place during the later years of the war (1864-65); the rest are divided between Montréal and Pingreville. During the first eight chapters we follow the adventures of Léon Duroc who, we have every reason to believe, is the author's alter ego. The next seventeen take us from Fort Trumbull to Petersburg. Chapters eleven and twenty-five prove particularly important. Léon and Eugène meet in the eleventh chapter. In the twenty-fifth chapter Léon is reported dead. The next eleven chapters take place in Canada. Should we be bothered by this shift? On the contrary. In keeping with the novel's socio-historical character, these chapters show us what is happening back at home while young men are off fighting.

Building on the Brossards' analysis, we add the following: *Un Revenant* is also a *roman à clef*. Charles Auguste Grippard, the villain who ruins the Latours' fortunes, is none other than Louis-Adélard Senécal, the notorious war profiteer profiled in *Histoire de la Presse* (Felteau, vol. I, pp. 137-145). Like Grippard, he went bankrupt just after the end of the war only to begin again. In the 1880s, he was once again a successful financier and politician. In a particularly virulent pamphlet entitled the "La caverne des quarante voleurs" (The Cave of the Forty Thieves), Wilfrid Laurier, the great French-Canadian statesman, characterizes Senécal as the bandit chief whose motto is "Je pose zéro…et je retiens tout" – "I invest nothing… and I keep all the profits" (p. 141). Contemporary readers would have appreciated his caricature in *Un Revenant*.

Three chapters before the end of *Un Revenant,* Duroc reappears. Recognizing that this technique could be criticized, professors Brossard and Lebrun-Brossard maintain that this reappearance effectively links the two story lines. The novel's structure is perfectly in keeping with the *roman d'aventures:* a young man seeking his fortunes returns home at the end of his adventures. Léon's reappearance saves the day.

The new recruits' coming of age

Unlike Eugène, Léon gets little preparation for life on the battlefield. After three days of hasty training at Fort Trumbull, the depot for the 14th Regular U.S. Infantry in New London, Connecticut, he is off to war. As his troop train speeds toward the Potomac, Léon soon begins to realize that the war is like nothing he has ever heard of, read about, or imagined. Yes, blond misses do wave their handkerchiefs at the passing train. But as soldiers arrive in Washington, the mood is somber. No bands play, no flags wave. The pieces of the picture fall into place bit by bit as the soldiers come closer to the battlefield. Leon's group consists of new recruits, veterans just released from the hospital, and others back from leaves. From Washington the troops take an idyllic steamship ride down the Potomac which ends in brutal reality as they disembark at Belle Plain Landing in Virginia. Through Leon's eyes we see wounded from the Battle of the Wilderness boarding as the fresh troops disembark. Eugène can't help turning away at the sight of one poor soldier with an exit wound through the back of his neck. He's forced to keep his mouth open as "a kind of bloody, straw-colored fluid" oozes from it (*One Came Back,* Chapter x).

After camping for the night at Belle Plain Landing, the next morning the fresh soldiers march toward the front. The Battle of Spotsylvania is already under way. First, they see what is left of the Wilderness battlefield. Charred tree trunks and blackened and bullet-riddled trees extend as far as the eye can see (*One Came Back,* Chapter x). Anderson's regimental history of the Fourteenth reports that the body of one Lieutenant Tom Collins, presumed burned in the conflagration, was never recovered (p. 600). Shortly thereafter, the new recruits hear the sounds of war for the first time. As many veterans report, these sounds are constant, terrifying, and inescapable. Tremblay describes the harsh, strident whistling sound the mortars make (*One Came Back,* Chapter x).

Finally Léon, the raw recruit, previews his future transformation. In camp he encounters a compatriot: Rémi/Eugène. At seventeen, Eugène is already a battle-hardened veteran. Rémi describes Eugène as he himself must have looked at that time: hardly more than a boy, five feet three inches tall, bright-eyed, intelligent, sturdy. This young man has already earned the respect of his fellow soldiers. With seven months' service behind him, he has already served longer than many of the older men. They all call him "Frenchy" (*One Came Back,* Chapter xi). Léon, though just about the same age, still looks and reacts like a raw recruit. Brave and noble though he is, he has not yet undergone the same trial by fire as Eugène. Is Tremblay thinking of his own unexpected meeting with Louis Menon as he shows us Léon's encounter with Eugène? He doesn't tell us. Whatever the case, their long conversations during quiet moments in camp show the pleasanter side of the soldier's life.

Here Léon's arrival in camp allows us to see how army life has already changed for Rémi/Eugène. Sometime in July during the siege of Petersburg, Léon is wounded. Despite his pleas, Eugène is refused permission to accompany his friend to the hospital. A few days later, Léon is reported dead. Léon's absence from the narrative occasioned by his supposed death during the siege of Petersburg marks an equally important stage in Rémi/Eugène's evolution. With Léon no longer at his side, Rémi/Eugène has no one to restrain his impulsive behavior. Seemingly our hero's various fugues result from boredom, impatience, and an innate restlessness linked with a romantic desire to serve in the French army. When his noble companion (his social conscience) "dies," he acts on his impulses.

With Léon to caution him, would Eugène have deserted from the regiment during the siege of Petersburg? Or escaped from the Confederates to begin his wanderings through Virginia and Kentucky, and have been recaptured and incarcerated in Libby prison? Hearing the news of his friend's death, Eugène feels his conscience has just died. The narrator comments, "If Léon had stayed by his side, his advice would certainly have persuaded him to avoid the many impulsive acts which caused him so many setbacks later on" (*One Came Back,* Chapter xxv). Tremblay looks back on all of Eugène's adventures with a compassion and understanding for his hero — and himself.

Heroism

Rémi/Eugène's accounts of heroism make us wonder why more soldiers didn't die on the battlefield. He went off to war in search of glory. Now and then he found it. Wherever possible, he demonstrates his sometimes reckless courage. We are told that he and Léon don't "salute" the bullets as they pass. That is, they don't jump and they don't move out of the way. And even brave men tend to jump when they hear the bullets whistling by. As Tremblay says, "'Saluting' a bullet doesn't necessarily prove you're afraid; however, not 'saluting' clearly demonstrates that you're not afraid and that you have nerves of steel besides" (*One Came Back,* Chapter XXIII).

One of the most dramatic demonstrations of Eugène's valor comes at the Battle of Cold Harbor. He and the others with him are cut off. They have been waiting for the order to retreat to the second entrenchment line only a half mile away. The order hasn't come. Tremblay brings to life Anderson's terse description of the prevalent confusion on that day (Rodenbough, p. 601). An unknown number of Confederates lie in wait somewhere in the wood.

The regimental flag must be preserved at all costs. Thirty brave men deploy to form a color guard. We hear the men's concerns. The commanding officer, Captain McGibbon, fears what will happen if he falls once again into Confederate hands. The sergeant, suffering from an old leg wound, reluctantly agrees to pass the flag to Léon if they are challenged. Suddenly we hear the rebel challenge, see ten Federals running, the bullets riddling the flag and cutting the staff in half as they carry it away. Then, in a clearing the men catch sight of the 5th New York Zouaves holding a small plateau. Léon cries, "Rally round the flag, boys!" The four remaining Federals — Léon, Eugène, a young second lieutenant, and Lieutenant McGibbon — gather around the tattered remains of their regimental flag. Following this dramatic moment, the color guard joins the rest of the battalion, now consisting of only a hundred men, who are making their stand in a thicket to the left of the Zouaves (*One Came Back,* Chapter XXII).

All of this is true, Rémi states in his letter transmitting the poem "Le drapeau du 14e" to Major Edmond Mallet. Mallet, he adds, will remember what the fighting was like on that day. In his retelling of the flag incident in *One Came Back,* Rémi slightly alters the cast of characters: Léon replaces Sergeant La Belle; Eugène is, of course, Rémi.

As we know, Léon is wounded and subsequently reported dead in July, 1864, during the siege of Petersburg. Of course this false information provides a convenient mechanism to link the melodrama unfolding back home in Montréal to Léon's unexpected return from the dead later on just in time to confound the villains and reclaim his fiancée.

The soldier's life

Civilians dream of glory on the battlefield. Here men dream of being adequately clothed, sheltered from the elements, eating when they are hungry, and resting when they are tired. Tremblay does show us such interludes. There are quiet moments as soldiers talk in the rifle pits or around the camp fires. When the sutler's tent is open for business, a fighting man can buy about anything his heart desires: eggs, butter, new boots, books to read, a hat to replace his army issue (*One Came Back,* Chapter XXXIX).

Yet Tremblay repeatedly brings us back to the common soldier's trials and tribulations. Whether in camp, on the march, or in prison, life is hard. New recruits go on the march laden with food, clothing, and all sorts of equipment. Veterans carry little with them. Many throw away ill-fitting shoes and go barefooted. Frequently they march into the night and camp without lighting campfires for fear of revealing their position to the enemy. "The exhausted soldiers stretched out on the ground fully dressed with their loaded rifles under their heads; sometimes they slept in the mud despite the pouring rain beating down on their faces" (*One Came Back,* Chapter XI).

They received food for three days at a time: sugar, hardtack, and bacon. When supplies were cut off, these rations had to last five or six days. Rémi describes the feel of marching for endless miles through enemy territory. Where are the men going? Somewhere. When will they get there? Sometime. Now they are simply tired, hot, weary, and on the move.

In Tremblay's description of camp life during the siege of Petersburg the reader sees how pleasant their existence could have been if the men hadn't been worked constantly and deprived of sleep. "Often...a soldier relieved of guard duty at nine o'clock in the morning would have to go out at noon to work in the trenches under enemy fire" (*One Came Back,* Chapter XXXVII).

Soon Rémi will show his readers what happens to Eugène in Libby prison. Was Rémi himself first imprisoned in Richmond toward the end of July, 1864, only to escape to wander through the countryside as Eugène does? Was he then, like his hero, imprisoned for a second time following the Battle of Saltville in October? Whatever the timing, Rémi was there — his military records include the slip of paper showing he was exchanged at Aikens Landing on February 7, 1865.

Desertion

Although Rémi/Eugène frequently refers to himself as a deserter, only one charge of desertion remains on his military record: his escape while under guarded escort on the way to Fort Trumbull at the war's end. The army acknowledges that he was a prisoner of war, captured at Weldon Railroad and released in a prisoner exchange. It does not, however, excuse the Fort Trumbull episode.

We find one additional reference to Tremblay's connection with the U.S. military. When the United States entered World War I, Tremblay attempted to rejoin the American army — on the grounds that he had never completed his enlistment. Near the end of his life, Rémi still cherished his young man's wish to fight against France's enemies. His offer was refused (*Pierre qui roule*, p. 224).

The sounds of battle

Tremblay introduces the unrelenting sounds of battle as replacements move through the blackened fields left after the Battle of the Wilderness. Men marching into battle should expect the shelling; elsewhere, Tremblay shows us that the noise, shelling, and slaughter can intrude even into the soldier's most peaceful moments. One day, during the siege of Petersburg, we find Eugène hurrying to prepare his coffee before night falls and the campfires must be put out. Fires at night can provide enemy gunners with excellent targets. Both armies have superb artillery, Rémi tells us. In fact, he says, some mortars can shoot projectiles weighing up to six hundred pounds. While this might be a slight exaggeration, we do know that a mortar nicknamed "The Dictator" could shoot a two-hundred-pound projectile. Once again Tremblay describes the terrible whistling sound. The large projectiles sound like locomotives rushing toward the soldiers. At night it looks like "a ball of fire jerkily making its way up into the firmament" (*One Came Back,* Chapter XXXVII). Eugène narrowly escapes death as a fragment blows up his campfire.

The prisoner's life

Rémi's eyewitness report of life in Libby is unforgettable. In a sense, the prisoners are fortunate. This isn't Andersonville. They have a roof over their heads, running water, and primitive toilets. However, many die because of the crowding, lack of clothing, poor food, fevers, and dysentery. As he enters Libby, Eugène gives a false name. He's afraid of being recognized. When roll is called and when the rations are divided, he answers to his pseudonym, Washington C. Joslin. Interestingly enough, an officer by the name of George C. Joselyn, of the 15th Massachusetts Volunteer Regiment, would have been released from Libby on a prisoner exchange shortly before Rémi's incarceration. Did Tremblay, like his hero Eugène, actually meet Colonel Joselyn? He remains silent on this point. Whatever the case, Tremblay leaves us this graphic description of men receiving their meager rations:

> The three or four hundred prisoners held in each room were divided into squads of sixteen men. Each squad leader divided the four loaves of cornbread, each one weighing about one pound, into sixteen exactly equal parts. When the loaves had been divided in this way, he asked the assembled men if they were satisfied with the allotments. As long as there wasn't unanimous agreement that all the portions were of equal size, he had to take a crumb from one portion to add to another until everyone was satisfied. Then one of the men took the booklet containing the names of all the men in the squad and turned his back to the sixteen rations laid out on the floor. Anoth-

er man put his hand at random on one of the rations and asked:

"Whose is this?"

"John Smith's," said the man with the booklet as he made a mark by the aforesaid John Smith's name.

"Whose is this?" repeated the first man as he pointed out another ration.

"Washington C. Joslin's," said the man with the book, without looking, always keeping his back turned to the rations and checking off the names as each man got his share.

And so it went until the last name on the list had been called out. To further insure that the guarantee of impartiality was even more complete, the two distributors were chosen on the spot to make it practically impossible for them to have an understanding beforehand (*One Came Back,* Chapter L).

Eugène, like Rémi, spends the winter of 1864 in Libby prison. As was the case in other prisons, speculators in Libby managed to live well while others struggled to survive from day to day. Some had greenbacks, though this was nearly impossible given the close searches each newcomer underwent. By bribing the guards, these speculators managed to smuggle in goods: wheat bread, cornbread, and tobacco — primarily chewing tobacco. Many of the men gave up smoking for chewing — possibly to stave off hunger pangs. The speculators also made a profit from bargaining for cornbread rations.

What do the men eat? Their primary food is poor cornbread, supplemented now and then by bones with little or no meat on them. The lucky recipient of a bone would crack it open, eat the marrow, and then make a thin soup out of the remainder. Sick men fortunate enough to receive castor oil as medicine drank it directly from the bottle. Eating and keeping warm become the prisoners' two major preoccupations. Crowded, barely having room enough to lie down, with nothing more than ragged uniforms to protect them from the cold, they sleep "spoon style" on the bare floor. When the Sanitary Commission representatives arrived on New Year's Day, each man received a blanket. However, the blankets immediately became barter items. Eugène forms a blanket corporation with a Philadelphian and a German. He becomes the sole proprietor of the assets when the other two starve to death.

While the speculators remain sleek and fat, other men become parasite-ridden, walking skeletons. Even with running water available, starving men are not inclined to remove their rags in the winter cold to wash. Despite the cold they must have been tempted from time to time to do so. Revealing a bit of prison humor, Tremblay talks about lice so big that they can pick their teeth with bayonets. Prisoners so inclined, says Tremblay, can saddle, mount, and ride them at a gallop around the prison.

When a prisoner exchange is finally arranged, only the weakest are released. The speculators don't qualify. Eugène, thanks to a recent cornbread feast, almost doesn't look sickly enough. Nevertheless, he succeeds in joining the group. After a few weeks' recuperation at Camp Parole, he deserts while on leave. Recaptured, he escapes from the guard taking him to prison at Fort Trumbull and makes his way back to Canada.

By the time Eugène/Rémi leaves Libby prison, he has undergone a dramatic transformation. In the spring of 1865 we find Eugène steaming down the James River in the company of other released Union prisoners. He and his comrades have gorged themselves after months of deprivation. Three prisoners die from overeating. The *City of New York*, originally destined for civilian passengers, is, as Eugène tells us, a magnificent boat. Its ornate saloon with glistening mirrors and velvet-covered furnishings draws the young soldier in. Barely seventeen years old, Eugène hasn't seen himself in a mirror for six months. Suddenly he starts, for he is staring at a horribly emaciated stranger. Dirty, wearing a tattered uniform, the long-haired bearded soldier is covered with lice. Realizing he's staring at himself, he bursts into tears (*One Came Back*, Chapter LIII).

After a few weeks' rest and recuperation at Camp Parole in Maryland, the apparition will look like a human being again. And, as the title indicates, Eugène (Rémi) does go home — like a ghost (*un revenant*) come back from the grave. He has been in the Union army for eighteen months.

When Rémi/Eugène is released from Libby prison he has experienced the worst of what the Civil War has to offer: battles, life on the march, life as a fugitive, life in prison. By the time his thirty days' leave is over, Lincoln is dead, Richmond has fallen — it is all over. Like many men at that time, he deserts.

The soldier's return

Rémi's biographers pass quickly over what happens to him as he returns to civilian life. Yet this transition time deserves particular attention. *One Came Back* follows the process step by step. After the thrill of his successful escape and the joyful reunion with his family, Eugène experiences the shock of returning to civilian life. Other young men his age have permanent jobs. The tradesmen in the vicinity are not hiring. He can find only temporary, seasonal work. While his parents are simply glad to see that their son has returned safely, neighborhood gossips can't understand why he has come back without a cent. He must be "a spendthrift, a good-for-nothing, a ne'er-do-well" (*One Came Back*, Chapter LXI). While others have been in school or learning a trade, Eugène has learned to "endure fatigue and handle a rifle very well" (*One Came Back*, Chapter LXI). Eugène/Rémi resolves once again to act boldly (even rashly). If he can't find a steady job, he'll cross the border and turn himself in as a deserter at Fort Montgomery. Convicted deserters can look forward to twenty to twenty-five years at hard labor on the Dry Tortugas. The Dry Tortugas have long been part of Eugène's flight fantasies. While he was with the Fourteenth, he had imagined the Dry Tortugas as a step, albeit a risky one, toward his dream of fighting one day with the French army. Ships on their way to the continent might stop there. A bold prisoner could smuggle his way aboard. Now he sees the prison island only as a deserter's final desperate destination.

Eugène's definitive return to civilian life comes about in a most surprising way. Fort Montgomery is deserted. Only a kindly old sergeant remains on guard. Everything has changed. No one, not even the army, is interested in him. The old sergeant gives him some fatherly advice: "If there isn't any work on the other side of the border, there should be some on this side. Try looking and you'll probably find something. No one will give you any trouble provided you keep your secret. They're not looking for deserters like they used to. Go on, promise me you'll give up your deplorable plan" (*One Came Back,* Chapter LXI).

We know that, like Eugène, Rémi did survive the war. Both briefly pursued military careers in Canada. Neither ever joined the Foreign Legion. Why, then, does Tremblay focus on these few brief months? Why does he publish a novel rather than write his memoirs? And this, twenty years after the fact? Does he need the distance in time and the comfort of a fictional framework to write his eyewitness testimony of these horrible events? Whatever the case, by 1865, eighteen months in the 14th Regular U.S. Infantry have transformed Tremblay. In the end, like his hero Eugène, he is no longer an adolescent. At age seventeen, he is a veteran, a man. And like many veterans of other wars, his experiences remain as real and immediate to him as an old man as they were when he lived them for the first time.

Margaret Langford
Keene State College
Keene, New Hampshire

CHAPTER I

AN ACT OF DESPERATION

I t was a cold, rainy May night in the year of Our Lord 1864. A heavy shower had cleaned the sidewalks and diluted the street mud. Water streamed down the sidewalks and gurgled ominously as the sewers swallowed it up. That night the moon hadn't obliged the city and the Municipality of Montréal had grudgingly allowed the lamplights to be lit — much to the aldermen's regret, though they were ever solicitous of the welfare of their constituents.[1] It was about 1:30 in the morning. A light rain, not quite a London fog, not quite an all-out shower. The few passersby, out late by choice rather than by necessity, shivered. Two carriages waited in front of a luxurious house with one room brilliantly lit. Although several of the best families lived in that house on the rue Saint-Denis, the room in question served as a gathering place for some high-society gamblers. Had it been situated in that part of the city known as Faubourg Québec, it would have been called a dive, a gambling joint, or even something worse, but of course in this aristocratic district it had to have a more respectable name. Consequently, its regular clientele had dignified this room by calling it the Saint Fortunatus Club — an act which would have scandalized that holy man who, had he been consulted, never would have agreed to be the patron saint of such a dissolute den.

Indeed, although nothing more reprehensible than their unfortunate passion for gambling could be held against most of this club's habitués, as in all groups of this sort, it also numbered among its members a few wily confidence men all the more dangerous because they had succeeded in fabricating reputations for honesty as well established as they were ill founded. The patrons played for high stakes and, while the most cunning managed to make money at the expense of the others, the existence of this association had already caused the demise of many fortunes, jeopardized several commercial establishments, and paved the way for the impending downfall of a great many more.

Suddenly the door to that establishment burst open. A visibly distraught young man rushed out and hurried down Saint-Denis Street. Gradually, however, he slowed down. At Craig Street he turned around, came back as far as the house he had just left, then, after hesitating for a few seconds, he went back down the rue Saint-Denis once again.[2]

At the corner of Dorchester Street, a policeman stood motionless under a lamplight. He had noticed the young man's comings and goings and wondered what on earth he could be doing out walking back and forth on a night such as this. Sensing that the guardian of the peace might question him about his nocturnal wanderings, the stranger decided to beat him to the punch. He went up to the policeman, asked him for directions to Commissaires' Street, and then went off in the direction indicated.

A spectator seeing his face in the flickering flame of the next lamplight could have guessed that he had just made a sudden but drastic decision. The young man quickened his pace. Sobbing and muttering to himself, he proceeded down the street between the church and the Bonsecours market. Oblivious of the mud, he crossed the space separating the wharves from the retaining wall, ran to the end of one of the piers, and stopped, seemed to falter for a moment, then, overcoming his hesitation, he crossed himself.

"Farewell, Louise!" he cried.

And he threw himself into the waves.

The sound of the body falling into the water was echoed by another shout.

A deep voice rang out, calling: "Hey there, boys! Come over and help me. A man is drowning!" At that, a tall athletic man plunged into the water.

A rowboat with two oarsmen equipped with a lantern soon appeared on the scene and, after two or three unsuccessful dives, the stalwart boatman finally reappeared, swimming vigorously, with an unconscious body in tow, holding the head above the water. The others hurriedly pulled the inanimate form into the boat.

The rescuer swam to shore.

CHAPTER II

LÉON DUROC

Who was this young man the worthy boatman had just snatched from the jaws of death? How had this believer — the sign of the cross made as he flung himself into the water testified to his faith — reached the point of seeking refuge from the slings and arrows of fortune by committing suicide? Why — at an age when everything seems rosy, when the future seems full of those wonderful possibilities that the young persist in believing will happen despite what those who have lived longer have experienced — why had he come to drown all the golden dreams he must have made, all the hopes of his adolescent heart, along with his life, in the waters of the Saint Lawrence? Because in the last three days he had seen all his dreams of happiness topple like a house of cards. The sweet dream he had been living had just vanished in the face of heart-rending reality. With all his wonderful plans in ruins, he foresaw only one future: a life filled with shame and dishonor.

Orphaned when he was twelve, Léon Duroc had had to accompany an uncle, who had taken him in, down to work in the American factories. For three years he had lived, worked, and eaten with his young cousins. His mother had seen to it that he received a good elementary schooling at the village school; at twelve he could spell and had mastered the elements of grammar and, although he didn't know it then, this gave him an undeniable advantage over a great many lawyers, writers, and statesmen from his country. He had read *Le Miroir des âmes, Geneviève de Brabant, Les quatre fins de l'homme, Le Pensez-y bien,* and *L'Instruction de la Jeunesse,* in addition to his text-books, of course. He knew by heart quite a bit of *Le Cantique de Marseille, the Lyre-Sainte, and the Cantique des Missions.*[1] He had perused some song collections over and over again and had heard that there were such things as newspapers.

In spite of his learning, or perhaps because of it, Léon didn't take to factory work. Since he applied himself, he soon learned to read and write English correctly and, when his uncle brought him back home three years later, he spoke the language quite fluently. A handsome boy, with an open countenance, intelligent and distinguished looking, he had little difficulty finding a position as a clerk with a rich merchant in Pingreville, formerly a village, which, no longer satisfied with being just a town — with its population of six thousand souls, two newspapers, and a great many inns — had sought and received permission to call itself a city.[2]

Duroc learned his new job quickly. Honest and dedicated, attentive to his customers, he deserved the confidence of his employer, M. Latour, who, in addition to feeding and lodging him, paid him a modest salary.

M. Latour was an orderly, economical man of strict morals who dedicated the few rare moments his business allowed him to the pleasures of home and hearth. A complete slave to the wishes of Mme. Latour, a charming woman with a mind of her own — and who knew how to use it — the worthy tradesman would not for anything in the world have dared disagree with his better half. He was prosperous. She wanted him to become rich. Thanks to a few fortunate business speculations, in two years' time he had become rich. Had she ordered him to be witty, he would have managed to obey her, much to the surprise of everyone who knew him. She was his second wife and he was infatuated with her, so people said. A little bit too much so, added the gossips.

Mme. Latour was a pretty brunette — still young, romantic for show, coquettish for vanity's sake, and ambitious because of her convictions. She was not wicked. She was just scatterbrained. Hard work and a few tribulations might have made a good-hearted woman of her. A life of ease and time spent reading romantic novels had turned her into a featherbrained china doll. Her forced sentimentality was ill adapted to her husband's rather practical cast of mind. A down-to-earth and pragmatic tradesman, his only fault lay in his simple-minded adoration of her. He did not for a moment think of following his wife's imagination by hopping on a cloud in search of the impossible dream. While Madame practiced her smiles, invented provocative winks, and constantly courted compliments from the countrified dandies of her acquaintance, the head of the house saw to it that she lived in the lap of luxury while, at the same time, increasing the dowry of his daughter Louise, his child by his first wife.

When Léon Duroc came to work for M. Latour, he was barely fifteen; at that time little Louise, aged thirteen, was finishing her studies at the local convent school. A beautiful child, the loss of her mother had made her much more serious than children her age usually are. She was very talented and excelled in all the arts and sciences taught at the institution where she spent ten months of the year, appearing very rarely and then only briefly at her father's home except at vacation time. Since the death of her mother, whom she had dearly loved, Louise had showered upon her father all the love of her affectionate nature.

We hardly need add that M. Latour loved her dearly in return. She was the living image of his departed companion with whom he had enjoyed a kind of happiness that he dared not compare with the one the second Mme. Latour was giving him at present. He liked to remember those ten years of financial straits, battling against poverty — a battle he had won thanks to the active, energetic, and devoted assistance of his courageous companion.

Just when she could have begun to enjoy this affluence, won at the expense of so many sacrifices and hard work, death had come to snatch her away from her loving husband and child. And now another lounged on the beautiful furniture — each piece the fruit of that devoted woman's privations — all now belonged to someone who had never done a thing to earn the right to a life of ease. So goes the world. *Sic vos, non vobis,* etc.[3]

M. Latour's first wife had known and loved him when he was young. She had been devoted to him, had helped him through the first stages, always the most taxing, on the difficult road which leads to a fortune. The second had married him because she found him to be as rich as he was bald. The momentum was there, the first step had been taken. Wealth and M. Latour's baldness had both increased rapidly in the preceding two or three years, so much so that that his purse had fattened just as his hair was thinning out. The second Mme. Latour found him laughable and considered him as her banker rather than as her lord and master.

As for him, he loved her with that blind and unreasoning love remarried widowers usually shower on their second wives when they are by far the younger of the two spouses. Of course he had loved Louise's mother, but she had never been the recipient of all the consideration and lavish attention he proffered his new companion. Did he hope that all this kindness would make her forget their age difference? Perhaps, but in the meantime, although the new Mme. Latour had no intention of setting her cap for someone else, she was, nevertheless, much more interested in pleasing the young men-about-town than the man who had given her his name.

CHAPTER III

POOR AND IN LOVE

éon Duroc had been in M. Latour's employ for almost three years. Louise had completed her studies and had returned home. A dark-eyed blonde, her type of beauty was as rare as it was charming. Léon had become a strapping fellow with black curly hair and the hint of a downy brown mustache decorating his upper lip. Living under the same roof, it was natural enough for these two innocent young people to develop a closeness which soon, without their realizing it, evolved into a deeper and more tender feeling.

Although Mme. Latour was excessively cordial toward him, Léon didn't even bother to notice. In vain did his employer's wife bestow upon him her sweetest smiles, her most studied looks; he had eyes just for Louise, and was happy only when he had the pleasure of seeing and talking to her.

Mme. Latour had passed along some novels to Léon — some of which were quite racy. He had read them in his spare time without attaching too much importance to the situation. He was surprised that Mme. Latour could feel any sympathy for the floozy heroines and dissipated heroes of her favorite books, but this did not in the least move him to throw himself at the feet of the romantically inclined wife of his employer. Had he been foolish enough to do so, the coquettish Mme. Latour, rather than encourage him, would have given him a lecture on morality, all the while rejoicing to herself at her success. His indifference to her advances ruffled her pride. She had wanted to try out the charm of her seductive powers on him. The attempt had failed, causing her some vexation, which she nevertheless managed to hide.

At first she had told herself Léon was a great big ninny who could not be tamed, then she thought she had seen Louise and Léon exchanging secret glances that she found to be more eloquent than they should have been. With the blind rage of a woman scorned, she resolved to spy on them to find out if her suspicions were well founded. She had made up her mind to thwart, if need be, the dreams of happiness she believed the two young people were beginning to entertain.

From that moment on, she took perverse pleasure in doing everything in her power to put them at odds with each other, and began looking for a young man for Louise. She gave parties and soon several suitors had become rivals for the honor of courting the lovely young girl. Louise encouraged no one, but the attentions of these young men brought Léon back to reality.

Up to that time, he had been telling himself that the passion he felt for Louise was nothing more than sincere friendship. Now, all of a sudden, he was surprised to find that he didn't like seeing her being admired and sought after. For the first time, he realized that the idea of her belonging to another would make him the most miserable of men, so he concluded, and rightfully so, that he was hopelessly in love. Should he repeat to Louise the confession he had just made to himself? First of all, did Louise love him? Yes, probably — like a sister loves her brother, but even if she experienced more tender feelings toward him, even if, beyond his wildest hopes, he could be certain she loved him, he would have suffered in silence rather than let her think he was after her fortune.

What was he, after all? A simple clerk earning a very modest salary. He was eighteen years old. He would need at least ten years to get established. Louise was sixteen. Even if she had been poor, he would perhaps still have hesitated to ask her to marry him immediately and to share his life of privation. Under no circumstances would he ever have suggested putting off marriage for ten years while waiting for him to become prosperous. He loved her for herself as much as for what she meant to him, and he would not for the world have wanted her to have to make even the slightest sacrifice on his behalf. He saw her as being rich, young, fawned upon, able to make a very advantageous match at any time, and he reproached himself, almost as if it were a crime, for the frustration he felt when he saw her courted by the wealthiest and the most distinguished young men in Pingreville society.

And now that he saw all these obstacles placed between him and the only possible road to his happiness, he realized — too late, alas — that he loved Louise with all the passion of a first love. Like another Ixion chained to fortune's fatal wheel, he felt condemned to be driven perpetually onward with no possible hope of achieving that happiness which had just appeared before him shimmering, like a mirage.

He kept saying to himself: "I'll forget." He thought he heard a voice answering him: "No, you won't forget. Drag your ball and chain along behind you, you prisoner of love; that will teach you to let your heart rule your head. Either you'll marry Louise or you'll spend the rest of your life pining for her."

Marry her! Was it that easy? Was it even possible? Oh, those long sleepless nights he spent turning the sharp dagger piercing his heart!

"If only I dared hope she loved me," he kept repeating to himself. "If she were poor or if I were rich, I'd have asked for her hand right away. My lowly station in life makes it my duty to remain silent." And he began pretending to be cold and distant in her presence.

But Louise, for her part, not knowing what caused this coldness, felt hurt. Mme. Latour took advantage of this misunderstanding to try to make Louise think less highly of Léon. She went about her task with too much zeal. Without meaning to, she would make things turn out far differently than she had intended.

CHAPTER IV

A Declaration of Love
Followed by
An Explanation

I t was Louise who forced a showdown. Though he tried to mask his inner turmoil, Léon had not completely managed to hide his feelings. With the intuition of the woman who loves and feels loved in return, Louise had guessed that Léon was struggling to hold back a confession which seemed always to be on the verge of escaping from his lips. One day when they were alone together she said to him point-blank: "Léon, did you know there is serious talk of marrying me off?"

"So soon?" Léon had answered, turning frightfully pale.

"So soon! But you're forgetting that I am no longer just a little convent school boarder. I'm over sixteen years of age already and it is right and fitting I should be thinking about my future."

Louise had taken great pains to sound playful, but her feelings ran much deeper than she wanted to show. Léon's own feelings had not escaped her notice.

"Aren't you going to congratulate me?" she added after a pause.

"Pardon me," stammered Léon, "I congratulate you with all my heart. I hope you will be happy. As for your future husband, whom I don't have the honor of knowing well, but whom I think I've seen here, he doesn't need my best wishes to assure his happiness with you. I assume it's M. Lavergne?

"Yes, it seems he's the one they want me to wed."

"He will be a charming husband — he is rich, handsome, elegant — you must love him a lot."

"You're certainly a strange one! I haven't yet said if I've agreed to marry him. As for me, I won't get married unless you're at my wedding."

"No, thank you! I've often played supporting roles, but if it were up to me, you'd only see me play the lead."

"Aren't you the ambitious one! And what role should we give you then?

"The husband's role; I won't accept any other."

"You'll come to my wedding, I tell you. You'll play the lead, since you insist."

"Ah, Mademoiselle, please forgive me. This is all my fault; I've gone too far. I wanted to seem lighthearted and I told you a very serious truth, though I pretended to be joking with you. Now you are going on in the same vein and I'm tempted to take what you just said seriously. Please, let's not carry this any further. Don't give a poor wretch false hopes — that would be too cruel! Louise! I had vowed to carry my secret to the grave; and now I've let it slip out in spite of myself. I love you and I'll never love anyone else but you. For a long time I tried to deceive myself. It wasn't until last Sunday that I realized I could never pluck you out of my heart. The heart-rending grief I felt when I learned you were to be married opened my eyes. I feel I'll never get used to the idea of seeing you belong to another; and yet, since I understand all too well how different our stations in life are, I would never dare ask for your hand. You're old enough to be married; as for me, I will have to wait for at least ten years before I can think about marrying. You are rich and I would not for anything in the world have you think I am after your dowry. Even if you loved me, a happiness I dare not hope for, I would not ask you to refuse an excellent match to wait until Lady Luck decided to make our situations in life more evenly matched. Get married if you want, I won't complain. My wishes for your happiness will follow you wherever you go. If you do marry, I myself will never marry.

"I have already told you how fervently I worship the memory of my departed mother. You know that I never knew my poor father. You are aware yourself what a hold memory, like religious belief, has on us. I know with what tender reverence you remember your deceased mother. So you'll understand how bittersweet the memory of your adorable face will be for me. As for you, if you have ever felt some affectionate tenderness for me, please tell me so, for that would enrich my collection of precious memories that will be my only lot here on earth. But what an egotist I am. I'm talking about myself when I should be thinking of you. When are you getting married?"

"Whenever you like."

"You're still making fun of me."

"Not at all. You say you love me. I'm offering you the leading role at my wedding and leave it to you to choose the day. It seems to me that I've gone just about as far as the rules of decorum governing persons of my sex permit."

"Louise! Are you really serious? Am I awake? No! That would be too much happiness! Do you really love me? Me? You prefer me to M. Lavergne?"

"First of all, I don't love M. Lavergne. As for you, you big ninny, do I have to get down on my knees and tell you I love you? Surely you've already guessed as much."

"Good God, what have I done to deserve such happiness? Louise! I've hardly slept a wink for eight days. I was about to go crazy. I had become so used to regretting my lost happiness that it had become an obsession. In fact, last night I got up and composed a sonnet I had no intention of showing anyone. Here it is. Please excuse the craftsmanship. But in it you will find expressed the feelings I have just been sharing with you. Now that I know you love me I'm the happiest man in the world. You say I should set the date for our wedding. That will be when I can provide you with a comfortable living. As for your dowry, you can keep it until I can match it with an equal amount resulting from my work and savings. But here's the sonnet I have been telling you about."

Louise then took the paper he handed her and read the following sonnet out loud:

> *What I will never say, not even to you*
> *Louise, I put on this page so white,*
> *For a long time you've made me blue*
> *But I called it friendship soft and bright.*
>
> *Alas, true love imposed its law.*
> *Forlorn, I dreamed and woke up Sunday.*
> *That fatal love filling me with awe,*
> *Fell like an avalanche suddenly.*
>
> *Wealth between us puts a barrier*
> *Poor and beginning a sorry career*
> *Should I intrude when you live happily?*
>
> *I in unhappy love persist.*
> *And hiding secret thoughts insist*
> *On adoring hopelessly and silently.*[1]

"So you're a poet too, my dear Léon, all the more reason to love you!"

"I'm in love, and what lover hasn't massacred the language a little while trying to write poetry? I'm more of a lover than a poet. I managed to forget all about that a moment ago. I was drunk with too much happiness. Now I remember my lover's role well enough to ask you to seal our gleeful bargain with a kiss."

He had taken Louise's hand and put his left arm around the blond girl's slender waist. Far from resisting, she raised her crimson lips to his without prudishness, and their lips mingled in a long, chaste kiss — the betrothal kiss.

At this very moment M. Latour burst into the room. Louise and Léon looked aghast.

"What does this mean?" M. Latour's voice boomed out.

"Please excuse me, sir," Léon answered. "We just got engaged and…"

"Ah! Engaged, are you? Louise, go to your room. As for you, young man, pack your bags and get out of here at once. Engaged! Children! And penniless children at that! M. Duroc, if you are counting on my daughter's dowry, you should know she's a minor and that she won't get anything before she is of age, and, as far as that goes, you wouldn't get it even if she were of age."

"I don't need your dowry and I have not yet asked you for your daughter's hand."

"No, but you have just kissed her. Don't say another word; if you do, my hand will kiss your fine mustache; then we'll be able to say you've kissed everyone in the family."

Léon turned pale.

"M. Latour," he answered calmly, "I'm ready to explain myself if you want. I asked your pardon, but I'm not a slave and your threats don't frighten me. I've always respected you, but I warn you, if you dare raise a hand to me I'll defend myself; I won't need anyone to help me out."

M. Latour realized he had been a bit hasty. He had always liked Léon. Besides, Léon was a strapping fellow and his determined demeanor showed he wasn't a man to be crossed. So M. Latour just shrugged his shoulders and Léon went off to pack his belongings.

CHAPTER V

A Reconciliation
Before Parting

It so happened Mme. Latour had half-heard Léon's declaration of love while peeking through the keyhole. Tiptoeing away, she had gone off to warn M. Latour and, creeping silently back, they had both arrived just in time to witness the scene which had so irritated the tradesman.

Louise had run off sobbing to her room where first M. then Mme. Latour went to talk to her. M. Latour wasn't completely sure what tack he should take. He had gotten over his first feelings of anger; besides, he was more upset with Léon than he was with Louise.

"So you're engaged now, Mademoiselle," he said as he entered the room. "And I suppose I don't have anything to say about that?" Then, softening his tone, he added, "Tell me, daughter, whatever possessed you to listen to this young nitwit's twaddle?"

"Father, I didn't want to hurt you; I believe this is the first time I've displeased you since I reached the age of reason, but don't be angry with Léon; he isn't a nitwit; on the contrary, his behavior is beyond reproach. He's been avoiding me for several days. He's been pining away because of me and he would never have told me he loved me if I hadn't made him."

"So you ran after him. In my day, young women weren't so brazen."

"I understand how much my behavior must appear unseemly to you, but I love Léon and I found a way to come right out and tell him so because I realized he felt his poverty stood in the way of our love."

"And you thought it did not? Do you think I've worked hard all my life just so I could find you a penniless husband, a husband you will have to support?"

"You know very well that Léon is much too proud to accept my dowry before he's made something of himself. He's sober, steady, and hard-working. When you married my mother, you weren't rich, but didn't you manage to make her happy just the same?"

"Yes, that's true. But your mother was not accustomed to living in luxury like you are. With your fortune and your beauty, you can make a good match. What you two think is a lasting love is just an infatuation. You're still very young and you'll both get over this before long."

"Never. What good is my fortune if it stands between me and my happiness? Oh, father! You could help Léon make his way in life. In a few years, with your help, he could set himself up in business. We're not in a hurry to get married. I'll wait until he's ready."

"So be it! I'll let you keep your illusions, but I hope you'll both get over your infatuation. I've just thrown Léon out. I'm sorry he's leaving since I must admit he's a good employee, but the way he answered me proves that he would be a difficult son-in-law and perhaps a brutal husband. You can see that after the scene I've just witnessed he cannot stay in my employ."

Mme. Latour, who had remained silent up to that point, believed it to be her duty to intervene: "Perhaps you've been a bit harsh, *mon ami,*" she said. "Just think: if Léon decided to tell people why he left, everyone in town would be talking."

"But I can't very well say that I'm sorry."

"No, but you could keep him here until you get someone to take his place and he finds a job somewhere else. He hasn't left yet. Go speak to him and try to make your peace with him."

The very next instant M. Latour went up to Léon, who was busy closing his bags.

"M. Duroc, I was a bit sharp, I must admit. I believe you to be enough of a man of honor that you won't whisper sweet nothings to my daughter without my permission. Consequently, I'm asking you to delay your departure for a fortnight. For my daughter's sake as well as your own, nothing about this incident must get out."

"Since you've just thrown me out, I'm leaving. As for the rest, don't worry; no one will know I've had the honor of being thrown out by you under such happy circumstances."

"You're not going to leave now. I need you. I've always been interested in your future. My daughter loves you or thinks she loves you. If that love can stand the test of time and absence; if, for your part, you prove yourself worthy of her, I'll try to find ways of helping you to make your way in the world. I'll write to my friends in Montréal and I'll try to get you a good job there. Does that suit you?"

"I can't thank you enough! You're worthy to be Mlle. Louise's father. Please forgive my hasty words a moment ago. Go ahead and hit me; I won't even think of defending myself! In fact I wouldn't have defended myself a moment ago — in spite of what I said. I would have remembered in time that you are my beloved Louise's father."

"Fine, fine. You can tell her all that if and when you earn the right to call her your wife."

CHAPTER VI

THE CONSPIRACY

Two weeks later, Duroc left Pingreville to go to Montréal. M. Latour had strongly recommended him to the owner of a prosperous wholesale establishment. In addition, he had entrusted Léon with the sum of $1,000 which he had instructed him to deposit in the People's Bank to redeem a note about to come due in a few days.

Those two weeks had seemed very short to the young couple. On two or three occasions they had managed to see each other alone and renew their vows. Mme. Latour had redoubled her efforts to win over Léon, but he had not paid the slightest attention to her sentimental posturings. As he was leaving, she kissed him goodbye under the pretext that he was just like one of the children; Léon took advantage of the situation by kissing Louise without the slightest protest from M. Latour, who was present. In short, everyone had ended up by treating Léon as if he were indeed Louise's fiancé and not at all a stranger.

When he got to Montréal, Léon first registered at the Hotel Canada, then went to the store where he hoped to be employed. The owner being out of town, our young man went back to the hotel where he found M. Grippard, a merchant he had often run into at M. Latour's.[1]

M. Grippard had many business dealings. He was a "promising" merchant. Rumor had it that he was very rich and that he handled a lot of money, although everyone remembered he had been quite poor a few years earlier. He owned sawmills, steamboats, and did a great deal of buying and selling of grain. He inspired a great deal of confidence in M. Latour, who had frequently held him up to Léon as a model of hard work and activity.

Léon told M. Grippard he hoped to go to work for Pincemaille and Co. and, proud of the confidence his former employer had placed in him, he added: "Since you know Montréal, no doubt you can tell me where People's Bank is located. I have to go there to deposit $1,000 in M. Latour's account."

"Certainly, but the bank is closed now; you'll have to wait until tomorrow."

An attentive observer could have noticed a greedy glint in M. Grippard's piercing gaze as young Duroc confided in him.

"Please excuse me for a moment; there's someone I have to see," the tradesman said, bowing; then he went up the stairway leading to the first floor.

Let's follow him to his room; the scene we're about to see would have opened Léon's eyes if he had been there to witness it.

M. Grippard rang a bell. A bellboy appeared.

"Are Messrs. Bagoulard and Bohémier still in the lounge?

"Yes, sir."

"Tell them I want to see them here immediately."

"Very well, sir."

A few moments later, two young men crossed the room's threshold. Both were thin and pale. One wore his hair long and had a very tiny mustache. Tall and slender, he seemed to be some twenty-odd years old. The other was short, frail, bent over and, though he was barely twenty-six years of age, looked like a little old man.

"What'll you have?" asked Grippard.

"Intoxicating liquor," answered young Bohémier.

"Brandy forever!"[2] exclaimed Bagoulard, shaking his head to toss back a rebellious lock of Absalom-like hair.

"Three cognacs," said Grippard to the bellboy, who went out immediately. "My young friends," Grippard said as soon as he left, "a windfall has just landed in our laps. Imagine a naive young country boy with $1,000 in his pocket and who's boasting about it. Somebody should borrow it from him."

"We'd be very happy to be your co-signers," Bohémier hastened to say in a comic tone of voice which made the others laugh.

"If it were just an ordinary loan, I would not be in need of your services," said Grippard. "What's most bothersome is that this young man doesn't want to lend money that doesn't belong to him. M. Latour of Pingreville, his former employer, has entrusted him with depositing this amount in the People's Bank."

"So what you want is to force him to loan the money?"

"Yes and no. Shush! Here's the bellboy. Let's get rid of him; then we can continue our conversation."

After tossing his cognac down in one gulp, M. Grippard paid for the drinks and, when the bellboy had left, lowered his voice as he continued: "Bagoulard and I will take him to the Saint Fortunatus Club. We'll run into Bohémier there. We'll try to get the country boy to play with us. If he does, so much the better. If he doesn't, I'll find a way to borrow the $1,000 for a play that Bohémier must win; then I'll find I don't have any money and naturally he'll just have to wait until I'm ready to pay him back."

"But you'll give the money back, won't you?"

"In a few days; I need some money, but in a few days, I'll have the funds and I'll settle with him. Of course you understand I'll pay you a commission for helping me obtain this loan."

"All right, let's get the loan," said Bohémier. "Introduce me as soon as possible to this love of a country boy so I can press him to my virginal breast."

"You? Not on your life! You'd scare him off. He needs to meet respectable men like me," said Bagoulard, striking his chest and tossing back his ever-present lock of hair — as usual. "You have the look of a gallows bird about you."

"Not 'bird,' you wretch. But that won't stop me from making the most of your good looks. And now that we've found our fledgling, let's get out of here!"[3]

"Yes, skedaddle! As for me, I'm going with M. Grippard to get acquainted with this paragon from Pingreville."

CHAPTER VII

THE TRAP SNAPS SHUT

A few minutes after the scene we've just described, Grippard was introducing Bagoulard to Léon Duroc in the following terms: "M. Duroc, I have the honor of introducing you to my friend, M. Bagoulard, a lawyer, future member of the legislature, and the most brilliant pleader before the Montréal bar."

"I'm very honored," answered Léon as he bowed and shook the hand Bagoulard held out to him.

The dialogue soon became quite animated. Bagoulard was a very engaging conversationalist, witty and cultured. Bagoulard quickly managed to gain the confidence and respect of Léon, who was an enthusiastic admirer of talent. Grippard, who wasn't much of a talker, left them together, and, after their evening meal, he offered to take the two young men to the club.

"Come with us," Bagoulard had said. "You'll meet a few people who'll try to prevent you from regretting the peaceful life you've been leading up to now."

We needn't describe the various gaming rooms in the Saint Fortunatus Club. Suffice it to say that Duroc, who wasn't a gambler, was so terribly bored that, around ten o'clock, he wanted to take leave of the men who had brought him there.

"Wait a bit, we're going to leave too — unless you want to join us in a game of draw poker — just one."

"I never gamble," said Léon.

"Bah! It won't hurt you to play just once."

In vain did they insist — Léon did not want to play; seeing how things were, Grippard said to him: "Since you don't want to play yourself, why don't you come into this room with us anyway? Messrs. Bagoulard, Bohémier, and I are going to play a hand; it won't take us very long."

If Duroc had known anything about gamblers' habits, he would have realized that a game could last all night if the players were the least bit serious about it. But it did not even strike him how unusual it was to have a three-handed game of draw poker.

Everyone sat down at the table and Grippard's plan was followed to the letter. At a given moment, Bohémier raised the bet to $1,000 and placed a check supposedly drawn on the Bank of Montréal on the table; M. Grippard didn't appear to have any doubts about the check's value.

"You're taking advantage of my not having any money on me," he said. "Well, I'll take the bet. M. Duroc, lend me $1,000 so I can take his check away from him."

Duroc hesitated. It wasn't his money. But he had often heard M. Latour say he would willingly lend M. Grippard $10,000 to $12,000 with just his word as collateral.

"You understand," said Grippard, "I'm going to take his check away from him and give you back your $1,000 immediately. At any rate, even if I lose, I'll pay you back from the money I have in the till. You've nothing to fear; you'll be lending me the money in the presence of witnesses. Besides, my word should be good for $1,000."

"Here's the money," said Duroc, without really understanding what he was doing.

"I'll cover the bet. What do you have?" said Grippard.

"Four aces."

"It's yours; take it away. I fold; I'm broke. Now, M. Duroc, if you want to go back to the hotel, I'll go with you. Unless you want to go with these young men who'll undoubtedly be making a night of it."

"So you're staying with us?" said Bohémier.

"No, thank you. I'm tired and I'm going back to the hotel."

"Then stay with us, M. Grippard. We need you."

"Well then, excuse me, M. Duroc. I'm staying with these gentlemen." And the three scoundrels, wanting to get rid of Duroc in a hurry, left him and went into another room.

And so Léon went back alone to the hotel very unhappy with himself. He tried vainly to tell himself he would get the $1,000 back the very next morning, but something kept telling him that he shouldn't have lent M. Latour's money. He spent a bad night, and the next day rushed to be on the lookout for M. Grippard.

M. Grippard wasn't in a hurry to make an appearance. It was all of ten o'clock before Léon met him and received his assurance that he would see about reimbursing him immediately. The day passed without Léon daring to show his face at Pincemaille and Co. He wanted first to take care of the business with the bank and send the promissory note back to M. Latour. M. Grippard continued to stall him from one hour to the next, from morning to evening, from evening to the next morning. By the evening of the third day after his arrival, Léon had not yet received a cent. So he had resolved to lie in wait for M. Grippard at the Saint Fortunatus Club.

At midnight, M. Grippard arrived, flanked by his two acolytes from two nights before. Duroc asked if he was playing games with him, if M. Grippard intended to ruin him, and what did he mean by delaying restitution from one day to the next?

"I don't owe you anything, Monsieur; I think you must be mad! You never lent me any money," answered Grippard with imperturbable sang-froid.

"But these gentlemen can testify that I gave you $1,000 the other night and that M. Bohémier won it."

"You must be dreaming," said the two others. "We never had any knowledge of such a transaction."

"Thieves, rascals, bandits!" bellowed Léon.

"Calm down," said Grippard. "We are three gentlemen whose integrity is well known. If you dare say a word which could tarnish our spotless reputations, we'll have you thrown in prison."

And the head of the establishment, drawn to the scene by their noisy altercation, came to politely ask Leon to leave the premises immediately. It was then that Leon, feeling dishonored, sensing that he had lost his fiancée's esteem, seeing no way out of the steel trap enclosing him, besides being in an extremely agitated state of mind, had decided to seek peace and oblivion in suicide — that last resort of the unfortunate who lose their faith or their reason. In Léon's case, both faith and reason were clouded for the moment, and he had plunged into the water without really knowing what he was doing. He was the man Joe Vincent and his men fished out of the water near the Bonsecours wharf on that rainy May night in 1864.

CHAPTER VIII

THE RESCUE

t the very moment Joe Vincent grabbed him, Léon was being dragged under-
water by the river current. He hadn't lost consciousness, but his whole body
had turned numb. Feeling the end draw near, he had had the time to think of
God and regret his act of desperation. He realized then the gravity of his transgres-
sion. But it was too late. Even if he had wanted to wrest himself from the watery grave
where he had just buried himself alive, he could not have moved so much as a finger.
Even if he had wanted to fight off the shadow he glimpsed moving toward him
through the rippling waves, he would have been unable to do so. When he saw, rather
than felt, someone grab his clothing, he thought he was in the clutches of some supernatural being, some black demon coming to seize his prey. He wanted to close his
eyes, but his eyelids refused to do his bidding. For a moment, he thought he was dead,
but a gust of fresh air hitting his face as his head was raised from the water made him
realize he had been saved. For a few moments he was unable to breathe in the fresh
air whipping him in the face; but when he had been placed in the lifeboat, his respi-
ratory system gradually began to resume its customary function. He tried to speak so
he could thank his rescuers; his tongue and his lips, still paralyzed, could only produce
a few unintelligible sounds. Finally, he regained his power of speech, and he burst into
tears as he warmly thanked the three men who had brought him to Joe Vincent's
shack, and who rubbed him down after removing his clothes.

The policeman we saw following Léon at a distance had arrived just in time to
witness the rescue. Statements had been taken at the central police station and, just as
Duroc was about to be jailed overnight for attempting suicide, a plainclothes officer
who was a very good friend of Bagoulard's and Bohémier's appeared on the scene. He
had met Léon at the club in the company of Grippard and those other gentlemen on
the evening they had played that infamous poker game. Not knowing about our hero's
quarrel with the trio in question, but aware that the above-mentioned trio had been
at the club that evening, he told the other policemen he would assume responsibility
for Léon and, since Léon was, by then, sufficiently recovered, the detective called a
carriage and told the coachman to go to the club to tell M. Grippard and his two
friends what had happened and take them to the Hotel Canada, where Léon insisted
on going on foot accompanied by the officer.

They had wanted to call a doctor, but Léon wouldn't hear of it, saying that he didn't need one, that he regretted his momentary madness, and he begged those who had witnessed his folly not to mention it to anyone.

When he got back to his room, he changed his clothes, then rang for room service. A bellboy just about Duroc's size, and who even resembled him, soon came to the door.

"Take these clothes away," Léon said to him, "and have them dried for me; don't let anyone see what you're doing. If you don't say a word about what you've seen, I'll see that you get something for your pains."

"You're lucky you're M. Grippard's friend," said the detective when they were alone. "Had it not been for my intervening in your behalf — which you owe to that fortunate circumstance — you'd be in jail now, and you'd have to stand trial for nocturnal vagrancy and attempted suicide. The newspapers would have gotten hold of the story and that would have been quite unpleasant for you."

Grippard and his companions arrived soon afterwards. Léon found it very difficult to hide his feelings of repulsion from the policeman. He realized, however, when he saw those three distinguished gentlemen, that it was in his best interest to avoid a scandal. As for them, our three habitués of the Saint Fortunatus Club had hoped to find Léon unconscious, which would have simplified matters considerably. They were very surprised to find him finishing getting dressed. M. Grippard ran to him, took his hands, and, pretending to be overjoyed to find him safe and sound, declared:

"There, there, my boy," he said, "just because your fiancée is marrying another man — not as good as you are, I admit — that's no reason for you to want to take your life. You're still young; you'll find another who'll make you forget her. Here, have a good drink of cognac, wrap yourself up in some warm blankets, and try to sleep. Tomorrow morning I'll have some good news for you."

Léon didn't deny the story about an unfaithful fiancée. Above all he did not want news about the matter getting out, and he felt he was in the power of these three men. He only asked those around him to keep what had just happened a secret. They all promised him they wouldn't breathe a word. They drank a glass of cognac together and the four men left him after wishing him goodnight.

CHAPTER IX

The Enlistment

The next morning, Léon Duroc woke up refreshed even though he was slightly under the weather. Since he wasn't at all used to strong drink, the glass of brandy he had drunk before going to bed had put him right to sleep. He had sweated profusely and the perspiration had neutralized the effects of the cold bath he had taken the night before. He went down to the lobby where he started reading the newspapers. The dispatches contained detailed accounts of the American war. Grant had just opened the 1864 campaign with the Battle of the Wilderness, a battle where both armies had suffered enormous losses. Determined to win at any price, the Federals were offering substantial bonuses to volunteers. There was even talk of replacements getting up to two thousand dollars for enlisting.

"Two thousand dollars! Why, that would be my salvation!" Léon said to himself. "If they just give me $1,000 in gold, I'll become an American soldier. I'll pay M. Latour's note and my honor would be saved."

He had just gotten this far with his musings when M. Grippard came up to him, saying he wanted to talk privately. They went into an adjoining room where M. Grippard began speaking in these terms: "I told you I'd have good news for you. I do. I've found a way to take care of your business matter."

"Thank goodness," said Léon, who began to have hopes of getting M. Latour's $1,000 back.

"Do you know when M. Latour's note falls due?" Grippard asked.

"I know it's either today or tomorrow. I can find out at the bank."

"Are you familiar with your former employer's signature?"

"Yes, perfectly."

"Can you imitate it if necessary?"

"No! because I'm an honest man."

"There you go again with your convent-schoolgirl principles! I'm not asking you to do anything dishonest; I'm simply suggesting that you renew the note; I'll endorse it and I'll pay it off in a couple of weeks. M. Latour won't ever know a thing about it."

"M. Grippard, I've already told you you're a scoundrel; I'm telling you again, but you'd better get this straight: I'm not a forger."

"Not so loud or I'll have you put in the clink! Nobody knows about yesterday's little escapade thanks to my discretion and that of my friends. If you continue to insult me, I only have to say the word and I'll have you shut up in an insane asylum. The louder you shout, the crazier they'll think you are! You can protest, accuse me, and make a racket; it won't do you any good. You can be sure I'll entrust you to the keeping of people loyal to me and they'll see that you're locked up like a madman as long as necessary. They won't let you out as long as there's the slightest chance of your hurting my reputation."

"You're a scoundrel, I tell you! You're not satisfied with just ruining me by dishonoring me; you want to corrupt me! But I'll have you know that there are still men in this world who value their honor."

"I know there are imbeciles in this world and that you are one of them. After all, if my proposal doesn't suit you, there is another way out — you can try to drown yourself again like you did yesterday. Only if you really want to succeed this time, I suggest you choose another venue. The Bonsecours wharf is too near Joe Vincent's shack — Joe, that hardy rescuer of yours. People might even think you tried to drown yourself there just so someone would fish you out of the water!"

"I'd better go easy," Duroc said to himself. "I'll live, but just to avenge myself." Then, hiding his anger, he said out loud: "I'm in your power. I'll find out today when the note falls due and we'll see what we have to do to settle this business; but at least you'll pay the note as soon as possible so M. Latour will never know anything about it."

"Go on, now. Do you think I'd want to put you on the spot?" said Grippard, as he thought to himself: "If I can manage to get you to falsify a document, I'll have you in my grip and that will teach you to treat me with respect."

An observer looking into the next room would have seen the bellboy to whom who Duroc had entrusted the task of getting his clothes dried. Having noticed the two men talking behind closed doors, he had gone into the room where he had heard the whole conversation. After they had left, he came out of his hiding place, saying, "Another mystery to solve. How I love to study people."

Duroc went to the People's Bank where he found out that the note had come due that very day.

"In the three days grace prescribed by law, I'll send you a bank draft from New York," he told the cashier. "Would you kindly send me a receipt and send the note back to M. Latour?"

Léon went back to his hotel and took advantage of M. Grippard's absence to settle his bill. A train was leaving immediately for New York. He had himself driven to the station where he boarded the train; he was anxious to escape from the excellent M. Grippard's vulture-like clutches. The next day he enlisted for five years as a bounty soldier in the 14th Regular U.S. Infantry. The man he replaced paid him $1,000 in gold; the Federal government gave him $700 in greenbacks. Léon sent a draft for $1,000 to the People's Bank, deposited the rest in a savings bank, and left for his regimental depot at Fort Trumbull, located in New London, Connecticut.[1]

CHAPTER X

THE 14TH REGULAR UNITED STATES INFANTRY

In those days, Fort Trumbull was the supply depot for the 14th Infantry, the 3rd Regular Artillery Regiment, and several volunteer regiments from Connecticut. Here, recruits for these various regiments were trained before being sent off to their respective units. But, at the start of the 1864 campaign, the North was not interested in drilling recruits! Cannon fodder was needed and reinforcements were hurried off to the Army of the Potomac as soon as possible. The 14th Infantry formed part of that army. For three years it had taken part in all the battles fought between Washington and Richmond. It had fought at Bull Run, Williamsburg, Fair Oaks, the Seven Days' Battle (from June 24 to July 1, 1862), the second Battle of Bull Run, Antietam, the siege of Fredericksburg, Chancellorsville, Gettysburg, Wilderness, and Spotsylvania, not counting many lesser skirmishes. Now the regiment, formed in 1861, was badly decimated. From three battalions, each six hundred men strong at the beginning of the war, it now was reduced to one, and the companies were far from having a full complement of men. Constant recruitment was needed to refill the ranks continually depleted by the hazards of war.[1]

Three days after he arrived at Fort Trumbull, young Duroc was leaving for Virginia. In the meantime, he had received a receipt of payment for M. Latour's bill from the People's Bank. When he had sent off the bank draft from New York, he had told the cashier he was going to Fort Trumbull. The letter containing the receipt had reached him there.

His squad consisted of about fifty men: raw recruits, wounded men just released from hospitals, and prisoners of war who, after being exchanged, had spent some time at Camp Parole in Annapolis, Maryland. There, good, wholesome food had restored some of the strength they had lost through privations suffered during stays of various lengths in Southern prisons.

First, they went by sea from New London to New York; there, they crossed over to Jersey City where they joined other detachments waiting to board a special train on the Camden and Amboy line. The train left soon after they boarded. It sped through Newark, Harrisburg, and Philadelphia, made a short stop in Baltimore, where the men ate at the Soldiers' Rest, and it reached Washington that very evening. All along the way, the soldiers were hailed as liberators. Women waved handkerchiefs and blond young misses shamelessly blew kisses at those warriors the convoy was rushing so quickly to the front — a great number of them never to return.

But in Washington, public sentiment had already waned. The Federal capital harbored a number of secessionists of all stripes who would have cheerfully gunned down these blue uniforms if they had dared. The Negro population was quite large, but, used to living in abject subjugation, they did not dare indulge in noisy demonstrations. In fact, the Federal soldiers themselves would not have been unduly flattered by such demonstrations even though they were going to get themselves killed while liberating the black race.

The next morning the troops descended the Potomac by steamboat as far as Belle Plain Landing where they camped for the night. A large number of wounded had just arrived at the landing in ambulance wagons and boarded the ship taking them to Washington where they would swell the ranks of those already overcrowding the military hospitals.[2]

Sad human relics of the murderous battles at the Wilderness and Spotsylvania Courthouse, they were not a very reassuring sight for those who were going to replace them at the front! Some were carried aboard in their comrades' arms or on stretchers. Others, with head or arm wounds, walked slowly aboard, their pace slowed by suffering. Among the walking wounded Duroc noticed a man who had been shot in the mouth. The bullet had exited through the back of his neck — apparently without touching a single vital organ. This poor soldier was forced to keep his mouth open; a kind of bloody, straw-colored fluid was oozing from it. Duroc couldn't help turning his head away in horror and disgust.

The troops camped for the night near Belle Plain, and marched the next morning to Fredericksburg. They crossed the Rappahannock before Fredericksburg over a pontoon whose construction had cost the lives of many brave builders some days earlier. But the city was now occupied by Union forces. Fredericksburg was visibly marked by the two sieges the city had withstood. The stone walls of many of the houses were either in ruins or riddled by bullets. The population had fled as the Federal troops approached.

For several days Duroc had seen many things completely new to him. First he had come to the great city of New York; then, forts Trumbull and Griswold. These forts had been strategically important during the American Revolution. Located near the city of New London, they had been burned down by the traitor Arnold in 1781.

Next, Léon had passed through Jersey City, Harrisburg, Philadelphia, Baltimore, and Washington with its capitol and government buildings. He had noted the almost uniform red-brick color of the soil in New Jersey, Delaware, Maryland, the District of Columbia, and Virginia — all this had struck him even though he was steaming across the region at high speed.

And now he had arrived in Fredericksburg, the city that Burnside's soldiers had so vainly besieged in 1862. Some days before, the pontoon bridge he had just crossed had had to be built under Confederate fire, and the waters of the Rappahannock had carried away more than one corpse that day.

Duroc's squad crossed the bridge following an artillery battery consisting of thirty-two-pounders. The oscillation of the pontoon boats, always a factor even when only a column of infantry was crossing the bridge, had greatly increased with the weight of the horses' hooves and the burden of the cannon. Several horses, frightened by the swaying movement, shied and reared, causing the artillery men in charge of them a great deal of trouble.

There were four artillery men for each cannon and each of them rode one horse while leading another — the rest of the cannoneers rode on the caissons.

At one point, one of the horses hitched to the cannon just ahead of Duroc's squad shied and almost pulled the cannon as well as the seven other horses with him into the river.

The presence of mind of the four horsemen who immediately maneuvered the other horses to pull against him kept him at the edge of the pontoon but they decided it was best to unhitch him. As soon as he was unhitched, the horse plunged into the Rappahannock and swam to the bank about four hundred feet away — the Rappahannock looked to be about six hundred to eight hundred feet wide at that point. The incident had occurred about at the middle of the bridge.[3]

The pontoon bridge had lurched violently and Léon, who clearly remembered all too well his adventure at the Bonsecours wharf, felt a sudden rush of fear that he had gotten under control quickly so he wouldn't be the butt of his comrades' jokes.

The troops passed through the city and struck out in the direction of the Jerusalem Plank Road. They could hear the cannon thundering in the distance. The sounds came from pockets of fighting still going on after the Battle of Spotsylvania. General Lee had fallen back to his second line of retrenchment on the North Anna River. Forced to retreat again following the Battle of Spotsylvania, he had continued, nevertheless, to exchange mortar fire with a Federal artillery battery.

The line of march soon reached a wood showing many signs of the Battle of the Wilderness. The woods had caught fire during the battle and rumor had it that many wounded men, unable to flee, had been trapped and burned alive because there weren't enough ambulance men to carry them off.

Charred tree trunks and smoke-blackened trees, some still standing but shredded by the bullets and grapeshot, others cut down by the bullets; trenches built in haste and breached by cannon bore witness that death had hovered over that sad place.

The wasteland extended as far as the eye could see and this was only a very small part of what had been that killing field. It was May 12 and the armies had fought almost incessantly since the 5th — the day Lee had attacked Grant.

The 5th and 6th of May had cost both armies 30,000 men. On the 8th and the 9th, Grant had gone on the offensive again against Lee, who had retreated to the North Anna. This had led to the Battle of Spotsylvania, begun on the 10th and still going on, as we have seen.[2]

The regiment had left the woods and the line of march advanced with great difficulty down a sandy road. Suddenly they heard a raucous, strident whistle and a shell exploded above Duroc's squad, which was in the lead. All the veterans held their positions, but several recruits, prompted by their instinctive fright, tried to break ranks. They were stopped by the cordon of guards surrounding the detachment. Duroc did not flinch. This first shell hadn't wounded anyone. The ranks closed. Down the road, they could make out some woods a short distance away.

"Double quick march!" roared the commander. The mortars continued to rain down; some landed without exploding; others exploded without hurting anyone. Only one exploded in the ranks, hitting four men, killing one outright and wounding three others. Many of its fragments had flown in all directions with a sinister whistling sound. The man who was killed had been struck in the head and had fallen dead at Duroc's side.

Once they were protected by the woods they resumed an ordinary cadence, even though bullets continued to fly by them for a time without wounding anyone. The Southerners, forced to fire blindly into the woods, soon turned their attention to a new squad. When this squad came to the place where the first had been attacked, they found themselves moving without cover through enemy fire.

At about four o'clock, Duroc and the others reached the general headquarters of the 5th Army Corps to which the Fourteenth was attached. The columns split into several detachments, which all went off to join their respective battalions.

CHAPTER XI

BACK AND FORTH[1]

Duroc soon arrived in the trenches occupied by what was left of the Four-teenth. His squad was split up and sent to several different companies and Léon, who hadn't had the opportunity to speak French since he had donned his uniform, was delighted to find a compatriot — the only French Canadian then in the regiment — in the company to which he was assigned. He was a very young man, almost a child; nevertheless, he had already served for seven months and he seemed to be quite proud of having served longer than more than one heavily-mustached colos-sus. He was bright-eyed, intelligent, alert, and strong, despite his small stature, which just met the minimum requirements — during the war the minimum height had been lowered from five feet seven inches to five feet three inches. Eugène Leduc, more commonly known in the regiment by the nickname Frenchy, was the favorite of the old guard who had gotten to know him the previous winter at Camp Reynolds, near Catlett's Station, where the Fourteenth had been stationed.[2] After Eugène greeted Léon very warmly, the two young men began talking French so volubly that they greatly intrigued their trench comrades.

They soon had to interrupt their conversation, planning to continue it later. Although the firing had stopped, they were well aware of the presence of the enemy entrenched not too far ahead of them through the woods. The soldiers, no longer compelled to keep to the trenches, walked about at some distance from the ramparts, gathering in groups and exchanging stories about the ups and downs of the week of constant fighting they had just been through. They recalled how such and such a dead comrade had fallen under fire from Confederate bullets, cannonballs, and grapeshot.

"Fall in!" the commanding officers of the various companies suddenly cried out.

Like a clutch of chicks gathering under the maternal wing, the soldiers rushed to the trench protected by a breastwork and each one took his place in line. On com-mand, the battalion formed four deep and set off on the double in the direction oppo-site to the one Duroc had taken to get to the regiment. Léon thought at first they were retreating, but Leduc was of the opinion that they were going to reinforce some part of the line.

Indeed, cannon had been firing continually at the battery that had raked Duroc's squad a hour or two earlier as it was on its way up to the front. On first hearing that the battery was decimating the stream of reinforcements as they were arriving, General Warren had first sent another battery forward to answer its fire; he hoped this action would distract the enemy artillerymen. But after a time, seeing that the road in question was still the enemy's principal target, he had determined to dislodge them. However, the Southerners had set the battery up in front of their trenches with a single objective: to regain temporary control of that unprotected section of the road. And, since they did not have any earthworks protecting them, the artillerymen didn't consider it advisable to resist the charge. They cleared off as quickly as possible, abandoning the position to the Federal troops, which occupied it without firing a shot. When the Fourteenth arrived, the fighting had stopped. They had gotten off with a three- or four-mile march on the double. On the other hand, they had the inestimable advantage of working all night digging new trenches, and, the following morning, they set out again to execute a series of flanking movements and forced marches which, for two weeks or so, didn't leave the soldiers a moment to be bored by having nothing to do.

Duroc, though not accustomed to this excessively rough life, didn't show a single sign of discouragement. They marched all day long and into the night; they slept under the stars; most of the time they went without making fires for fear the glow from them, reflected in the sky, would let the enemy guess what move they were planning to make. The exhausted soldiers stretched out on the ground fully dressed with their loaded rifles under their heads; sometimes they slept in the mud despite the pouring rain beating down on their faces.

Rations were distributed for three days at a time. They consisted of coffee, sugar, hardtack, and salt pork.[3] They were given more than enough for three days, but it often happened that the supply train was cut off, and the provisions intended to feed the men for only three days had to last for five or six days. Because they were in enemy territory, foraging was tolerated, albeit not officially authorized. The shrewdest soldiers, pretending to be tired, lagged a little bit behind their regiment so they could get away and "visit" the plantations.[4]

The line of march followed the main road. The men marched four abreast; the supernumerary rank consisting of officers and the noncommissioned officers of the company formed the inner flank. If the head of the column encountered an obstacle, each group of four came to a stop at that point to give the group immediately in front of it the time to cross the ditch or the felled tree meant to block the road. The first ones around the barrier continued marching; those following, since they had been delayed longer, had to hurry to catch up with them. Those who happened to be farther behind had the advantage of resting for a while as they waited their turn — an advantage they paid dearly for because, afterwards, they had to run for quite some time to catch up with the head of the column.

The heat was stifling and the dust, constantly kicked up by these thousands of men marching together, stuck to their sweat, coating the faces of these panting soldiers with a layer of mud.

If it rained, the soil, which was red clay for the most part, became waterlogged and very sticky. Sometimes, for days on end, the ban on lighting fires made it impossible for the men to have hot coffee during the cold, damp nights that followed the oppressively hot days. As they marched along, the soldiers nibbled on hardtack as well as their raw salt pork; some also ate the coffee mixed with the sugar which they usually had in large quantities.

They tramped along in rout step; on the march the musket was carried at will, and, when a soldier couldn't keep up with his companions and gradually fell behind, another less exhausted took his place in rank. When an entire regiment had passed by and the next one had caught up with him, the officers in the new battalion put the soldier in the ranks along with the other laggards. The provost guard at the end of the column, just before the rear guard, rounded up all the stragglers. Those who could march no longer were put in the ambulance wagons, and the others were treated almost like prisoners until they were returned to their respective regiments at the next stop.

Sometimes there would be a long bend in the main road so the grade wouldn't be too steep. From the top of a knoll those in the middle of the line of march could see the column winding and unwinding like a long serpent along the curves of the road; from a bird's-eye view, the head appeared much nearer than the middle section. A straight but steep and narrow path beaten by the hooves of horses and mules but impassable for wagons — a mule path as it was called by the people in that part of the country — led to the plantations and provided a shortcut between the center and the head of the column. Stragglers took advantage of these shortcuts to rejoin their regiments and the officers in the regiments these stragglers had joined momentarily let them take these shortcuts. Since the farms were generally set far back from the road, a good number of soldiers who wanted to forage let their regiments pass them by on purpose so they would have a chance to leave the road.

Almost all the planters served the Confederate cause. The most well-to-do families had fled, taking all their valuables with them and leaving only a few provisions to feed the few Negroes left to care for and protect the plantation. The marauders made off with the fowl and animals. They sometimes managed to eat well and bring something back to treat their comrades. The officers, suffering as much and perhaps even more hardship than their men, were very happy to accept a chicken wing and they were tactful enough not to ask too many questions of the men who had procured this unexpected feast. By following the mule paths, the foragers had time to rest and get back to their regiment before it camped for the night.

When the army had left its winter quarters, the veterans, knowing from experience the miseries which always accompanied a forced march, had discarded everything they could do without, keeping only the bare necessities. For the first few days the new recruits had persisted in carrying overcoats, a change of underclothing, blankets, etc. But all that had been abandoned along the way because of the extreme heat and the fatigue of the march. Each soldier's wardrobe was now reduced to the underwear and uniform he was wearing. Besides this, each man carried a piece of tenting rolled and slung across his chest. Some of them also had a piece of oilcloth. Goodbye dress uniform, shiny belts, and polished brass! Bayonets and rifle barrels had lost their silvery color. This caused Leduc to comment that the white swords had turned into black plowshares.[5]

The shared fatigue, misery, and dangers, while they hadn't exactly relaxed discipline, had at least brought the officers and soldiers closer together — even in the regular army. The men noticed that the officers who had been the most arrogant in the winter camps had become the most accommodating on the march. They were obeying an instinct which might seem childish at first glance, but which will seem quite natural to anyone familiar with the mores of this collection of adventurers from every country in the world — so numerous in the American army. The officers were afraid of being killed by their own soldiers in battle.

The Fourteenth had already lost three commanding officers since the start of the campaign. Major Hudson had been wounded three times at the Battle of the Wilderness, and, refusing to get down from his horse, he had been taken to the hospital despite his protests. Captain Kyse, who had replaced him, had been killed by a straggler from the Twelfth who wanted to get back at this officer for having treated him harshly a few days before. Captain Smedberg had taken command; he had had his right foot blown off by a shell fragment. At one time he had been captain of Duroc's company. That company didn't have a single one of its officers left; it was now commanded by a young second lieutenant just fresh out of West Point whom the men hadn't yet gotten to know.[6] Duroc began to believe he was more than earning his one thousand seven hundred dollars, but he didn't complain; he was energetic and steadfast in enduring all the hardships of the rough career he had embraced more by necessity than by choice.

CHAPTER XII

❧

Eugène Leduc

Duroc and Leduc soon became fast friends. Since none of their companions understood a blessed word of French, they could easily talk as freely as if they had been completely alone while they marched. To kill time, they told each other about their adventures. Leduc had also spent a few years in the United States with his parents. He was still there when the war started. The factories had cut back their hours and salaries by a fourth. Many Canadian families had decided to go back to Canada. Old Leduc had gone back just after the first volunteers who had enlisted for three months returned following the first Battle of Bull Run. Eugène had watched the company from Woonsocket, Rhode Island, go off to war. He had also been there when they received a rousing homecoming. The sight of these brave men with faces tanned by the Virginia sun had excited his young imagination. The few wounded he had seen with arms in slings or dragging themselves along on crutches interested him greatly. Those who had fallen on the battlefield seemed to him like martyrs to the cause of humanity. All the dead, the wounded, and those men who had come back unharmed were heroes in his eyes. He would have left immediately if he had been old enough to enlist, but that was in 1861 and he had just turned fourteen.

His parents, especially his mother, were far from sharing his enthusiasm. Ever since he was twelve, Eugène, who had read and thought about things much more than most children his age, had planned a military career — a career that didn't offer much of a future for the descendant of a conquered people. Our future warrior knew full well that he would never have the chance to defend his national flag since the French Canadians didn't have a flag of their own. He wasn't interested in serving England; but then there was France, that great country which, when all is said and done, the French in Canada will always consider to be their motherland. Therefore, he planned to go to France to enlist in the Foreign Legion as soon as he was eighteen — although he would have been distressed to know that a French Canadian would not be accepted in the French army except as a foreigner.

So as not to dip too much into their meager capital — fruit of each family's hard work and savings — many Canadians had decided to return to their native parishes by wagon. The journey took three to four weeks — but at the end they had the horse and wagon. This mode of travel was far from being as cost-effective as it first seemed;

expenses during the journey came to much more than the price of the trip by train, and, at journey's end, the horse was on his last legs. Nevertheless, that was the way the Leduc family had decided to travel back to their country. The trip had been very long and very difficult, but they had finally arrived safe and sound back at their old home in the parish next to Pingreville.[1]

The following year, Eugène had been placed as a clerk in a country store. The owner didn't know how to read. He was very surly besides. Eugène kept the accounts, measured the molasses, and sawed the firewood. The merchant, who was not lacking in intelligence, received several newspapers. His clerk was given the task of reading the political articles to him. Eugène devoured the serial stories and followed with interest the deeds and actions of Theodore de Cerny and Louis Vermont — two soldiers whose saga entitled *Le Remplaçant et le Remplacé* ran in the *Courrier de St-Hyacinthe*. The exploits of these two heroes interested him much more than the store's business. His master detested him; Eugène gave him back as good as he got. In short, one fine day the merchant threatened to beat him; Eugène, sure he would be battered and bruised, grabbed a four-pound weight and dared his employer to touch him. That escapade caused him to be summarily dismissed.

The following spring he had no sooner celebrated his sixteenth birthday when he entered into service for three years with another merchant who had a store in a parish by the river. Here was another illiterate man who was very interested in politics. He had *Le Pays* read to him. He was rich, owned several farms, and had begun to get rid of his stock without replacing it. When Leduc entered his service, the store was far from being what it had been in its heyday. On the other hand, he was the proprietor of a bakery adjoining the establishment and Eugène's predecessor was charged with teaching the young boy how to make bad bread. The rest of the time he spent doing farm chores.

Eugène got along well enough with his employer, but the latter's wife was terribly shrewish. She often gave Eugène a hard time — especially when she found him reading novels, a literary genre he was perhaps a bit too fond of. During the summer he had left his employer and gone to live with one of his uncles living in the same parish, but the employer made him come back by threatening to have him arrested for running away. For a time, things went a little better, but shortly afterwards the scenes started again and, one day at the beginning of October 1863, Eugène was sent to one of the farms some thirty acres away from the store to look for some cows who had wandered off thanks to the negligent urchin who had been put in charge of tending them.

Along the way, Eugène said to himself that he was now old enough to enlist in the American army. "That will at least be a start," he thought. "In two years I'll be eighteen years old, the American war will be over, and I can enlist in the French army." With Eugène, no time was ever lost between having an idea and carrying it out, and he acted on this one very quickly. He stopped looking for the cows, said a silent farewell to his boss's interesting wife, and started out on foot for Rouse's Point. It was a seventy-two-mile walk and he didn't have a cent in his pocket. He fled across plowed fields and land lying fallow for the rest of the day.

He had left C. . . at three in the afternoon.[2] By midnight he had gone about thirty-six miles. Not having eaten since noon, he was just about worn out.

Seeing a haystack in front of a barn, he climbed on top of it and tried to sleep. The cold kept him awake and, chilled to the bone, he went up to the house and knocked at the kitchen door. When no one answered, he pushed on the latch and the door opened.

Taking his courage in both hands, he entered and lay down beside a large cast-iron stove with a fire still burning in it. Around four o'clock in the morning he was awakened by the master of the house who asked him where he came from and what he was doing there.

"I'd rather not tell you where I come from," he replied, rubbing his eyes, "but I swear I'm not guilty of anything dishonest. I'm going off to war."

"But you're too young. They won't take you."

"I know a young man who went off two years ago. He was only sixteen and he wasn't any bigger than I am."

The farmer tried in vain to dissuade him.

"Please forgive me for coming in uninvited," said Eugène. "I was cold, tired, and I couldn't sleep on your haystack. First I knocked, then I tried the latch. When the door swung open, I didn't feel I should disturb you. Now, I'd like to thank you very much for your hospitality."

"Wait a minute, you must be hungry; you'll at least have breakfast before you leave."

"Thank you. I'm eager to leave, and I can't delay my departure."

"Just stay long enough to have a bite," answered the good man as he put a big piece of bread and a bowl of milk in front of him.

Eugène ate, thanked his host, and started out again.

He passed through Chambly, then St. Jean, and, at about eight o'clock Saturday evening, he was about ten miles from Rouse's Point, but so exhausted and hungry that he couldn't go any farther. He went into a rather shabby-looking house by the railroad, the line he had been following since leaving St. Jean, and asked if they would put him up. The family was eating dinner, but they didn't offer to share it with him. He had to sleep on the floor. When he woke up the next morning, the family was eating breakfast, but they let him go off without offering him anything. His feet were so swollen and bruised from walking that it took him all morning to reach Rouse's Point.

When he got to the train station he began reading the recruitment posters. Soon he saw a man in uniform walking up to him. Eugène told him he wanted to enlist, and the soldier replied that he couldn't do that right away because it was Sunday. Nevertheless, he took Eugène to the hotel, where he saw to it that Eugène got a good meal and a bed to sleep in. Eugène slept all afternoon, ate like a horse at dinner, went to sleep early, and woke up Monday morning fit as a fiddle and ready to go. They gave him his physical, pronounced him fit for service and enrolled him in the 14th Regular U.S. Infantry Regiment.

They had only just started paying bonuses then. Enlistments were for five years and Eugène was to receive a bonus of $400 in installments; the last $50 was not to be paid until his five-year enlistment was up. That mattered very little to Eugène. He hadn't come looking for money; he was after glory.

He was sent to Fort Trumbull where he was stationed for two months; there he wrote his parents about his crazy escapade. He didn't forget his employer, to whom he sent a letter saying that he was looking for the cows, but hadn't found them yet. He added that he would try to find out if they hadn't wandered off toward Virginia. A few days before Christmas he joined his regiment near Culpeper Courthouse. He had taken part in the marches and countermarches that went on before the regiment settled once and for all into its winter quarters. He had spent the season in Camp Reynolds where, being forced to speak English constantly and having read a good many novels in English, purchased from the sutler, he had become thoroughly conversant with the language of the country by winter's end.[3]

CHAPTER XIII

GUERRILLAS

Around the middle of April 1864, Leduc had just finished reading a book the company supply sergeant had lent him. This work, penned by an English officer, contained a very detailed description of the French military system. The author took special pains to emphasize the opportunities for merit promotions. A French soldier could move up through the ranks thanks to his prowess at arms. That was enough for Eugène; he decided to try to join the French army in Mexico.[1]

During the winter, Mosby's guerrillas had been harassing the Federal troops on and off. Mosby and his men operated constantly inside Union lines.[2] For this reason they were considered to be spies and any guerrilla who had the misfortune of falling into Federal hands was hanged from the first available tree. In retaliation, the guerrillas hanged any American prisoners who fell into their hands.

They were fearsome adversaries. Sometimes, disguised as Union soldiers, they wandered unrecognized through the camps, mingling with the men and gathering vital information for the enemy army. Sometimes they fell unexpectedly upon a sentinel and carried him away unceremoniously. They destroyed railroad bridges, attacked supply convoys, and just generally made a damaging nuisance of themselves. It was said that Mosby himself had claimed he would steal the boots belonging to the commanding officer of a volunteer regiment; according to the story, he had won his bet.

Superb horsemen, brave and valiant in combat, at home in a region they knew like the palms of their hands, they traveled swiftly from one point to another using roads through the woods that only they knew. Since all the planters openly sympathized with them, they delighted in thumbing their noses at the Federals. It was reported that Mosby, seeing he had been recognized, shouted his name at an entire contingent of guards and then rode off with all eighteen men firing at him. Slung low on his horse, he had galloped away thumbing his nose at the startled guards.

These were the hard-to-deal-with characters Leduc had resolved to go off looking for, intending to ask them to help him get to Mexico.

American soldiers don't sleep on straw — at least they don't while they're in camp. At that time, they were using red cedar branches, which are just as soft and much cleaner. Eugène left camp under the pretext of replenishing his supply of fresh branches. He walked off without choosing a specific direction since he well knew that he would run into some guerrillas wherever he went. As it turned out, just as he was nearing a rather pretty house about five miles from the camp, the sight of his blue uniform frightened some young ladies with corkscrew curls standing on the doorstep; they rushed into the house when they saw him coming. Eugène advanced into the yard and had just reached the foot of the steps when two men in gray uniforms, revolvers drawn, came out of the house. Eugène, who was unarmed, did not seem alarmed in the least. After greeting them, he crossed his arms and looked them straight in the eye, but his manner was more conciliatory than challenging.

"Are you a deserter?" one of the two men asked him.

"I suppose you might say that," Leduc answered.

"Well, welcome then and come on in," said the planter, a venerable-looking old man who had just appeared in the doorway.

It was dinnertime. Everyone sat down at the table and everyone, including the young ladies, treated their new guest very cordially.

Eugène explained his situation and it was decided that he would accompany the two men who were about to leave for Ritchie's Gap some ten miles distant from the house. These two men were officers in Mosby's corps.

They seemed to be consummate gentlemen. One of them promised to recommend Eugène to his father, a certain Mr. Wyse who lived in Plainville. There Eugène was to take off his American uniform and put on a suit of civilian clothes; then he was to try to get to Richmond while avoiding Federal lines. In Richmond the authorities would probably see about sending him to Mexico.

CHAPTER XIV

From the Frying Pan Into the Fire[1]

fter dinner they set off — the two officers on horseback, Eugène on foot. The two guerrillas weren't wearing swords. On the other hand, each of them had slipped two high-caliber revolvers into their boots. They entered and crossed through the woods by way of one of the many trails, called mule paths, which formed a vast network connecting all parts of the region. These paths allowed the guerrillas to roam freely though the countryside occupied by Federal forces. Ritchie's Gap was just a narrow pass or opening through the Blue Ridge Mountains. Just before the pass stood a small building serving both as home and shop for a blacksmith who was also a gunsmith. Young Wyse tore a page out of his notebook to write a note introducing Eugène to his father.

"Do you have any greenbacks on you?" he asked.

"About twenty dollars."

"Well, in that case I'll exchange them for you. If your people catch you while you're wearing civilian clothes, carrying greenbacks could compromise you."

Eugène obligingly exchanged his greenbacks for Confederate vouchers. He exchanged dollar for dollar although he was quite aware that a greenback was then, even among the Confederates, worth at least twenty Jeff Davis dollars at that time. But these men had helped him and he was at their mercy. Wyse might just as well have said to him in the words of Gustave Nadeau's kindly thief: "Besides, I have two pistols on me."[2]

The two officers pointed out the road he needed to take in order to get to Plainville. Since the sun was about to dip below the horizon, Eugène hurried onward. At about ten o'clock that night he reached the village of Plainville. He went from house to house trying to find out where Mr. Wyse lived. Of course the sight of his uniform frightened the women and children. Thinking that he wasn't alone and that the Yankees were planning to do something bad to Mr. Wyse, no one was eager to tell him anything. He wandered around the outskirts of the village for another hour, having been told that Mr. Wyse lived about a mile away. Finally, he reached the top of a hill where he found a magnificent two-story residence surrounded by some Negro shacks. He went into one of the shacks and asked if this was Mr. Wyse's home. An old Negro answered that the gentleman in question lived a mile farther on. Leduc asked if he could spend the night, but the slave, not understanding how a white could condescend to spend the night with black folks, took him to the plantation house.

The planter, who was about thirty years old, came down to greet him. Wounded while serving the South, he had returned home on sick leave. The Negro had first gone ahead to warn him of the presence of a Yankee deserter. He had stood up on his crutches to come meet his new guest at the door. The servants brought out bacon, milk, butter, and cornbread. The wounded man kept Eugène company while he ate with a hearty appetite.

"We're ten miles from Warrenton Junction," he told him, "and your cavalry often sends scouts out looking for guerrillas who come from time to time to visit their parents. We are always alerted beforehand when the Federals are coming. Since I'm not a member of the independent corps called Mosby's raiders, they won't arrest me. Besides, they won't find me bearing arms. Indeed, if they arrest me just because they suspect me, they might as well arrest the entire male population remaining in the region. As for you, if they find you in uniform, they'll surely take you to Warrenton Junction. Consequently, it would be more prudent for you to sleep in the shed; if any Federals come, they just might take it into their head to search the house from top to bottom hoping to find one of Mosby's supporters."

Eugène was taken to the aforementioned shed. The building was divided in two by a wall with a door connecting the two parts. The second room, used to store agricultural equipment, had a window looking out on the farmyard. Eugène went into this second room where he lay down to sleep fully clothed. He hadn't yet gone to sleep when he heard the sound of galloping horses. The sound was coming nearer. Kneeling near the window, he placed himself so he could see without being seen. Soon, by the light of the moon, he saw four Federal officers who had just dismounted between the house and shed.

"If all four of you will just go into the house, I'll take one of your horses and ride off," Eugène thought to himself.

This was not to be. Three of the horsemen knocked at the door; a Negro came to open it while the fourth remained on guard outside.

Eugène seized a pick handle that happened to be within arm's reach and huddled against the wall by the door.

"Woe to the first man who dares open this door," he murmured. "I'll knock him head over heels before he knows what's happening. I'll dodge the bullets of the three others and, if I don't get hit, and I'm counting on it, I'll let myself tumble down the thicket-covered ravine in back of the shed. They'll have to be pretty quick to collar me."

Eugène began to regret having left the regiment, but he preferred to die fighting to being taken back as a deserter.

The three horsemen left the house, opened the outer door to the shed and looked around quickly.

"There's also that other door," one of them said. Eugène clutched his pick handle convulsively.

"Bah, there isn't anything in there. Let's saddle up and go back to camp."

We can easily understand Leduc's feeling of relief when they rode away. Falling into an uneasy sleep he dreamed all night long of arrests, escapes, pursuits, and fights with the Yankee cavalrymen. The next day, upon getting up, he found his wounded host in his courtyard enjoying the morning air. He pointed out the way to Mr. Wyse's house. Mr. Wyse, who was at home, was a handsome old man with long hair and a full beard — both hair and beard were whitish-gray.[3] He invited Eugène to breakfast and presented him to his daughter, a lovely black-eyed Southern girl. Leduc went into a bedroom where he put on a civilian suit which looked just like a Confederate uniform. Except for the buttons, that's what it was. He inquired about the route he should take to get to Richmond. However, that depended a lot on Union troop movements. As the bird flies, they were seventy miles from Richmond; going around the American lines by way of Staunton, Eugène would have to travel about three hundred miles. Eugène bravely undertook this long route, and for eight days he traveled on foot through the Shenandoah Valley.

He had exchanged his boots which he had bought brand new at the sutler's for $10 in greenbacks for an older pair and $20 in Confederate money. Since he didn't know the country and, because people gave him conflicting directions, he didn't make much headway. One evening, he was annoyed to realize that, after walking all day long, he was right back where he had started from that morning.

Besides, the region was sparsely inhabited; houses were few and far between. Sometimes he would come to a rain-swollen stream with a very swift current. He would find the bridge carried away, no dwellings nearby, and consequently no boats. He had to travel long distances along the riverbank to find a fordable spot.

The inhabitants were very hospitable. They usually refused to accept payment for the meals which were served him.

Several days after leaving Mr. Wyse's he came to a field where Mosby's guerrillas had gathered either to drill or to go on parade. The men were on horseback, but they had fallen out of rank, and Mosby wasn't there. Eugène walked resolutely toward the group of cavalrymen. They surrounded him immediately. These men, who all knew one another, considered each stranger an enemy. They had no difficulty in recognizing that he was an American soldier. Their only mistake was in taking him for a Federal government spy.

In time of war, a spy's fate is quickly decided. He's hanged from the first tree. The guerrillas were in the habit of indiscriminately hanging every American soldier who fell into their hands. To make matters worse, Eugène was in disguise.

The tree was chosen, the rope was ready, two men had seized Eugène by the arms, and, despite his protests, they were getting ready to drag him to the improvised gallows, when young Wyse and his companion rode up. They took Eugène under their wing, much to the great regret of several guerrillas who had a hard time hiding their disappointment at losing the chance to hang a Yankee.

CHAPTER XV

BACK TO THE REGIMENT[1]

ugène resumed his journey after thanking his saviors. The next day, he met two other deserters — an American and an Irishman. These two had not the slightest intention of going to Mexico to do military service. They simply wanted to go wherever they could live without having to serve in the military. They all walked along together for two or three days. The 4th Army Corps, commanded by Siegel, occupied one bank of the Shenandoah. The Army of the Potomac occupied the other. Our three deserters thus found themselves caught between a rock and a hard place. It was terribly hard to get out of Virginia without crossing Federal lines. As for getting to Richmond, Eugène was beginning to realize that this was impossible.

A few days earlier, he had stopped to ask for a bite to eat at a farm. The woman was alone. She had given him supper, and she had kept him company while he ate.

"So it seems that Grant wants to go to Richmond, does he?" she had asked him. Then, without waiting for an answer, she had added: "I hope he does go there. I hope you all go there — as prisoners."

He began to tell himself he couldn't expect much sympathy from the Southerners who, scarcely a few days earlier, had thought they were being very generous by not hanging him from the nearest tree.

One evening, the fugitives came to Front Royal, where they went to a sort of inn on the banks of a river; they were told it was the Rapidan.

The next morning, Eugène's two companions hoped to cross over into the state of Pennsylvania by way of a place called Hot Springs. They needed to get rid of the Confederate currency they were carrying, for that could get them in trouble. That was easily taken care of. They had just enough to pay for their food and lodging. Eugène bought each of his two companions a glass of bad gin which cost him $25 in Confederate money. It seemed to be the going price.

The next day, the Irishman and the American set off for Pennsylvania; Eugène left them, saying that he was going to turn himself in to the Federal authorities. They tried in vain to dissuade him: he had made up his mind. He started off for Winchester and, when he was about three or four miles from that city, he was arrested by a cavalry patrol which took him for a Confederate bushwhacker. He let them take him to the city; there, he let it be known he was an American soldier. An officer came to question him and took down his particulars; that night he was taken by mule wagon to Martinsburg. They put him in jail with the Confederate prisoners, and they treated him like a prisoner of war while they waited to get an answer to the letter they had written to his regiment to find out if he wasn't just another cunning Southerner making up a story so they would let him go.

As it was, he hadn't told the whole truth. Naturally, he hadn't bragged about going off to find the guerrillas. He said they had surprised him in the woods, captured him, taken his uniform, his greenbacks, his watch, and boots before letting him go. He even managed to concoct a daily account of his goings and comings to make them believe he had used due diligence in getting back to the Federal army. His story seemed all the more plausible to his regimental officers because during the previous winter a man had been captured and released by Mosby's raiders under similar circumstances. In short, after a few days, he was sent back via Harpers Ferry and Frederick to Washington; after being kept there for a day at Forest Hall, he was sent back to camp at Catlett's Station.[2]

Camp Reynolds had been abandoned during his absence; the 14th had gone to Catlett's Station, where the men were getting ready to go on the march. The campaign of 1864 was opening on the very day Leduc came back to his regiment. At another time he would perhaps have had trouble making people swallow his improbable story. However, the officers believed it — or pretended to. They were more in need of fighting men than of prisoners, so there was no thought of accusing him of being a deserter. He resumed his place in the ranks and fought in the battles of the Wilderness and Spotsylvania where he distinguished himself by his courage and composure under fire.

CHAPTER XVI

LÉON'S ANGUISH

ugène's account to Léon of his adventures was much more detailed than the one we've just heard and Duroc had found Leduc's story very interesting. With a mixture of astonishment and admiration he watched as this beardless warrior told him about his exploits — as though they were commonplace. His heroic adventures had afforded him the opportunity to play a role well beyond what was expected of a young man his age. A strange kind of adolescent, whom circumstances, trials, and a remarkable precociousness of character had made old before his time, Eugène seemed to have kept childhood's lack of foresight and its capriciousness. He had done so while acquiring the manly virtues which are just the opposite of those flaws and which are ordinarily associated with maturity. This was the first time he had bared his heart; Duroc must have inspired a great deal of confidence for him to reveal the secret of his desertion. Indeed, the least indiscretion on Léon's part could have aroused the suspicions of the military authorities. We need add that he had made a good choice of confidant, for Duroc was not only a man of honor, he was also the soul of discretion.

It was clear, as he was telling his story, that Eugène did not try to embellish the role he had played. On the contrary, he seemed to take pleasure in emphasizing the grotesque and ridiculous aspects of an escapade he appeared to regret sincerely. However, he still hadn't entirely given up hope of serving in the French army. He had simply resolved to stay in the American army until his five years were up.[1] As for his courage, all of his companions at arms who had seen his prowess in battle knew him to be a brave man. Duroc himself would soon see his friend put to the test.

Léon had told Eugène about his suicide attempt; he also liked telling him about his love for Louise. Although he had written to Louise, he was still waiting for her reply, and he was beginning to wonder if he hadn't made a mistake in writing to the woman he loved. His future did not seem to be very promising. It's hard to make your way in the world when you start out as a private soldier in a foreign army. The same scruples which had kept him from first declaring his love now came back to haunt him. How could he ever offer Louise a name and position worthy of her? He had little expectation of doing so. Chances were that he would be killed in combat or come back hideously maimed. He hoped to save a little money, but the five years he would have to spend serving the United States could have been better spent learning about business matters.

He told himself all that, and yet, the thought that perhaps Louise would not deign to answer his letter distressed him. He had told her about being robbed, but he hadn't given her the names of those who had defrauded him. He promised himself he would unmask them if ever the occasion presented itself, but where would he find proof of their guilt? Lacking that proof, he had refrained from revealing who they were. It goes without saying that he hadn't mentioned his plunge into the Saint Lawrence in his letter.

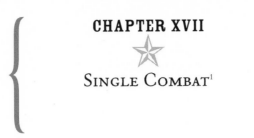

CHAPTER XVII

SINGLE COMBAT[1]

One day, as they were marching, our two Canadians found they were out of provisions. Hunger, which brings wolves forth from woods, made them drop out of the ranks.[2] They allowed the regiment to pass them by. Then they took a shortcut and, about noontime, sighted a superb plantation. Along the way, Eugène and Léon had joined three soldiers from a regiment of Pennsylvania volunteers. Hardly a moment later, two Federal cavalrymen appeared on the scene. They all decided to travel together so they could defend themselves better if they ran into any Confederate scouts. Frequently these scouts lay in ambush in houses along the way. Woe to the solitary marauder who happened to fall into their hands! He couldn't count on escaping with his life.

The plantation house seemed to be abandoned, but several Negro women and many dozens of Negro children could be seen at the doors of the shacks. As the soldiers arrived on the scene, they caught sight of a Negro boy of about fifteen herding some ducks, turkeys, geese, and other fowl which the Pennsylvanians and the two horsemen began to fire upon.

Three or four birds fell to the ground, and the young Negro said to the soldiers: "You mustn't shoot these birds. These are Massa's birds."

By way of an answer one of the cavalrymen shot him in the head. The boy fell dead at his feet.

"You're a mean coward," Eugène said to him.

"What's that, greenhorn?" bellowed the cavalryman. "You don't by any chance want to taste some of my pills too, do you? I've got three of them in my pistol for you." And he spun his pistol cylinder.

While he was doing that, Eugène was charging his rifle and aiming it at him. "We know all about your pills, Mr. Thief. They're only good for killing unarmed children. Go on! Shoot if you want to, you lowdown coward!"

The other soldiers stepped in. Duroc had moved beside Eugène as much to protect him as to calm him. "Come on, relax," he said in French.

"But I'm perfectly calm," replied Leduc.

"We shouldn't be shooting one another," said the other cavalryman. "Daly was wrong to kill the Negro, but the Frenchman insulted Daly; if they want to fight, let them fight with their bare fists. The Frenchman will have a fair chance."

"Wait!" said Duroc. "Eugène is too small for the cavalryman, but since our Mr. Negro-killer insulted him because he's a French Canadian, and since, like him, I too am a Canadian, but older and stronger, I'll stand by my fellow countryman's words and declare myself ready to fight with Daly."

"Since we're talking about national honor here," the cavalryman answered, "you'll fight with me while Daly and your friend settle their score together."

"Why not let me do it my way?" said Eugène. "If we both fight at the same time, if we both put down our weapons, then we'll have all five of them on our hands at once."

Eugène and Daly were still threatening each other with rifle and revolver.

"That's not the way it's going to happen," answered Duroc as he charged his rifle. "We're two against five here. If there's going to be a fight, one of us will have to keep an eye on the others. You insist on having a child-killer fight with a child. So be it. But your three rifles aren't loaded and you're going to stack them. You're going to put the two revolvers on safety and throw them down by the stack of rifles — over there. I'll take care of Eugène's rifle along with my own. I'll blow the head off the first one of you who tries to interfere with the fight or even looks like he wants to touch the weapons. Now, if that's all right with you, throw down your weapons and the two fighters can strip down. If that isn't all right with you, we might as well all start shooting now."

After some discussion, this proposal was accepted.

"Are you at least capable of defending yourself against that animal?" Léon asked Eugène as he was stripping down. "Do you know a little bit about boxing?"

"More than a little. I took some savate lessons from a French fencing-master while I was at Fort Trumbull.³ You'll have a good laugh."

The arms were stacked. A line was drawn on the ground. Daly ran up to it and assumed a fighting stance.

"Well, come on, kid!" he cried.

Eugène moved up calmly and assumed an on-guard position about two feet short of the mark. With his left foot forward he was just about in the classic stance for English boxing.

"Come up to the scratch!" Daly hollered.

He hadn't finished his sentence when Eugène, pirouetting on his left foot, gave the tibia of Daly's left leg a powerful kick with his right foot. Daly cried out in pain; his own punch had gone wide and pulled him forward. Immediately shifting his weight to his right foot, Eugène caught Daly under the chin with the tip of his left foot.

All this had happened in the blink of an eye. Daly had reeled back, bellowing. Keeping his guard up and weaving back and forth, Eugène followed him; with his left foot he kicked Daly in the side. Daly made the mistake of grabbing him by the leg.

He would soon regret it. Eugène spun around, put his hands on the ground, drew Daly toward him all the while pulling his left leg from Daly's grasp — then, Eugène caught him right between the eyes with his heel. With that, the cavalryman took quite a fall. When he got up, his blood was blinding him. Eugène had gone back to the scratch and was waiting there on guard.

"Come up to the scratch," he said to Daly.

But Daly declared he'd had enough.

"That's not the way to fight," he said. "Just you wait. One day I'll catch up with you and I'll box with you again whenever you want…some other time."

"Never put off till tomorrow what you can do today," Eugène answered. "The French boxing lesson that I've just given you is only the first in the series. There are twenty more like it. If you're too crippled to fight today, your friend said a while ago he wanted to fight my friend. While I'm at it, I'd just as soon stand in for my friend. Just a moment ago, he generously offered to replace me. Feel free; there's enough for everybody."

And Eugène, in high spirits because of his success, demonstrated some fancy footwork.

No one took up his challenge.

"Gentlemen," said Léon, "my friend is going to pick up his weapon; you'll pick yours up when we get to the woods three hundred yards from here. Sorry to part company, but, after what has just happened, we really have to split up; and we intend to leave while we're winning. I'm going to back away and I'll fire on the first man who touches a revolver or charges a rifle before we take cover. Just to be sure, we're going to fix our bayonets. I'm warning you ahead of time: I'm a pretty good shot."

"You've got us all wrong," said one of the soldiers. "Granted you're French, but we don't know the two cavalrymen; we're on your side. Stay with us — or if you like, we can follow you."

"We don't know you," said Léon. "Perhaps you mean what you say, but you're a little late in showing your sympathy. You're sturdy fellows, but you'd have let Eugène get the daylights beaten out of him even though he's in the right. I'm sticking to my guns."

"As you please, but you're wrong."

And, with bayonets fixed, our two young men moved away. Duroc walked backwards, as promised, while keeping an eye on the five soldiers who dared not touch their weapons until they saw Eugène and Léon disappear into the woods.

CHAPTER XVIII

MEANWHILE, BACK AT THE PLANTATION

T his kind of foraging won't fill our knapsacks," said Léon. "We came here hoping to find something to sink our teeth into and all we have to show for our efforts are victory laurels and the satisfaction of doing our duty."

"What do you expect? After what happened, I couldn't have stomached sharing the spoils of their chase with those thieves. And I would have felt dishonored hunting for myself in their company."

The two men had stopped under a tree. From that vantage point they could see what was happening back at the plantation house.

"They've picked up their rifles again," Eugène continued, "and now they're heading toward the house. They're tough scoundrels. You were right not to believe a thing that hypocrite of a soldier said. The door is locked. Now they're knocking. If there are any women inside, they're far from being safe. We'd better stay here a little while to keep watch over them."

Inside the house, on the second floor, two women were standing at the window. There, hidden behind the closed shutters, they had seen and heard everything that happened in the scene just described without being seen themselves. One seemed to be about sixty years old; the other, a pretty velvet-eyed Creole, was scarcely more than a child.

"Aunt," the younger one said, "those two men over there are French; I understood everything they were saying to each other. The tall one wants to calm the short one who still wants to fight."[1]

"Those two are gentlemen, Hélène. Did you notice they didn't shoot at the chickens?"

When she had seen Eugène knock his adversary head over heels, Hélène had remarked: "How agile, strong, and brave he is. If I dared, I'd clap my hands."

"Don't be foolish. Let's see what happens. Why haven't the others come? If only those Yankees could just all kill each another before my son and his companions arrive."

"I wouldn't like to see the Frenchmen killed. I'm French on my father's side."

"And American on your mother's. My poor sister whom God has called to him."

"Perhaps Sambo didn't find them at the Curtis place. Perhaps the Yankees captured him on the way over."

"They'll have to break down the door before they get in here. If the Canadians weren't here, three good Southerners would be able to take those five."

"If the Canadians stay and if the Yankees cross our threshold, they won't hurt us; the Canadians will be here to protect us."

"Do you believe that? They quarreled with the others because the cavalryman shot a Negro. They're rabid abolitionists. That's all they are."

"Ah! They're going to go away. There — they are leaving. The tall one is holding the others back with his loaded rifle. They've stopped in the woods. We can see them from here, but the Yankees can't see them from where they are."

"Look, the others have just come knocking at the door. Leave by the back and go to Auntie Nancy's shack. I'll let them knock for a while and then I'll send Suzie to open the door. If they find me they won't harm me. They've already been to Nancy's once and they won't go back there again."

CHAPTER XIX

Two against Five

Indeed, after cursing and swearing at the two Canadians, the three infantrymen and two cavalrymen had picked up their weapons. They had first gone into a Negro shack where they found nothing. They were knocking now at the main entrance to the house.

"Open the door or we'll break it down!" said one of the infantrymen. "If there are women inside, we're going to do a little courting!"

"As a matter of fact," said Daly, "that damned Frenchman mussed me up a bit. I even think that a little bit of soap and water won't do my face as much damage as that barbarian's blasted boots. Come with me," he added, turning to the other cavalryman. "I don't have a mirror so you can tell me when I look dashing enough."

"You're attempting a long and difficult piece of work. You weren't good-looking to start with and the little Canadian didn't make you any handsomer when he blackened your two eyes and bruised your jaw. Besides, you're still all covered with blood."

While they were talking, the two cavalrymen came to Aunt Nancy's shack and went in.

As they crossed the threshold, Hélène, seeing that they had discovered her, rushed between them, trying to get out of the only door in that one-room building.

Daly grabbed her by the arm. "Oh! What luck we came here! The others are wasting their time breaking down a door in the hopes of finding some charming game. And we've caught the timid gazelle. Come on, you pretty little thing, give us a kiss. Don't mind the blood. I spilled it fighting the friends of the black race."

"Let me go, you brute!" answered Hélène, slapping him hard. She tore away from him, leaving him holding a piece of the sleeve from her dress in his hands. Running, she fled toward the woods.

"Let's mount up or we'll lose her," Daly shouted.

Without stopping to think, his companion jumped into the saddle.

From their vantage point at the edge of the woods, the two Canadians had guessed part of what was happening and observed the rest of the scene just described.

"Let's go help her," Eugène said, seeing Hélène fighting to get away from Daly.

"We don't have to. She's coming right toward us," Léon answered immediately.

Indeed, Hélène was running as fast as she could toward the woods. Although she could no longer see the two Canadians, she counted on finding them where she had seen them from the window a few minutes before. The time it had taken the cavalrymen to mount up had given her a slight head start. They caught up with her, however, and passed by her before she could get to the edge of the woods and, stopping their horses, they barred the way.

At that very moment, Eugène and Léon came out of the woods and attacked the two cavalrymen who, with sabers drawn, were defending themselves. But a few bayonet thrusts aimed at the horses' nostrils caused them to rear and the cavalrymen had to leap out of their stirrups to avoid being crushed by their mounts.

"Save me, gentlemen," the pretty Creole said in French, her voice trembling with anguish and fright.

"Run toward the woods and try to get back to the house," Eugène replied in French also as he parried a sword thrust Daly had aimed at his head.

The three infantrymen had come running with their bayonets fixed. The two Canadians, seeing they were forced to fight in hand-to-hand battle two against five, got ready to sell their lives dearly. The cavalrymen, unhorsed, but safe and sound, seeing what they believed to be reinforcements arriving on the scene, had taken out their revolvers. Clashing with swords in their right hands and revolvers in the left, they had fired off several unsuccessful shots.

But the Pennsylvanians weren't exactly rushing away to help out with the fight. While they were trying to break down the door, which resisted all their efforts, they had seen the cavalrymen mount up and ride off at full speed.

Since they didn't see Hélène, who had disappeared behind a dip in the ground, they thought their friends were taking flight. They had scanned the horizon to see what danger was threatening them.

Then they saw what neither Hélène nor the two regulars had seen. Ten or so Confederate cavalrymen were coming at full gallop. Our regulars took to their heels all the while fixing their bayonets.

The Confederates stopped for a moment at the door. From the window, the old woman pointed to what was happening at the edge of the woods.

Hélène had managed to reach the woods, where she stopped upon seeing the Confederates arrive on the scene at the very moment the Pennsylvanians did.

The Federals were promptly surrounded and ordered to surrender.

All of them put down their arms except Duroc and Leduc who adopted a defensive position standing back to back with their bayonets threatening the Confederates' horses.

"You outnumber us," Léon told them, "but if we're taken prisoner here in these circumstances, we'll be considered deserters from our regiment. We'd rather die here!"

"Well, die then!" said a young man aiming his revolver at Léon. He was just about to pull the trigger when a woman threw herself between him and the two Canadians.

"Alfred," she said, "don't touch these men. They're the ones who saved me."

And she told him briefly what had happened.

"You are free, gentlemen," said the officer, for that's what he was. "As for the others, take them away," he said to his men.

"We won't ever be able to thank you enough," said Léon.

"Don't mention it. You conducted yourselves like brave and loyal soldiers. Allow me to shake your hands."

"We leave you in good hands," Eugène said to Hélène. "You'll never know how happy I am that I could be of some service to you."

"Before you leave us," Alfred said, "won't you please come back to the house with us? My mother will want to thank you and I invite you to dine with me."

"You're very kind. We accept your gracious invitation."

The Confederates had already disappeared with their prisoners. The four young people went off toward the house.

"You almost got killed defending me," Hélène said to Eugène. "I saw that cavalryman strike at your head with his sword. When I thought he'd killed you, I closed my eyes. When I opened them, I saw you jabbing at his horse's nostrils with your bayonet. So his sword cut didn't get you after all."

"No, it only nicked my cap. I was a little late parrying his blow but I did sidestep it. Besides, for one glance from your beautiful eyes, I'd be willing to spend my whole life being struck at by a sword like that."

"That wouldn't leave you any time to see that look you paid so dearly for. You're a true Frenchman, as gallant as you are brave," she added, looking at him without even trying to hide her admiration.

"You're as kind as you are beautiful. But aren't you French too?"

"Creole, as they say back home in Louisiana. My father's name is Duchâtel. He's an officer in the Confederate army. I've been here with my Aunt Shelton since last fall."

"And I'm a Canadian of French ancestry. My name is Leduc."

"What's your friend's name?"

"Duroc."

"Cousin Alfred Shelton, allow me to introduce M. Duroc and M. Leduc, two French-Canadian gentlemen worthy of serving the South."

They shook hands all around.

"Now, introduce me to these gentlemen."

"M. Duroc and M. Leduc," Alfred said, "allow me to introduce my cousin and fiancée, Mademoiselle Hélène Duchâtel."

They sat down to eat, and the meal was a merry affair. Despite her deep-rooted hatred for anyone wearing a Federal uniform, Mrs. Shelton took pains to treat her young guests with kindness.

While they were eating, the Negroes had taken the soldiers' knapsacks and filled them with edibles.

When they lit up their cigars, Alfred told his young guests that he and his men were about a mile away when Sambo had come to warn them of the young Negro's murder and the danger the two women were in. At the risk of falling into Federal hands, he had taken ten or so men and, resolved to face any and all dangers to save them, he had rushed to the rescue of his mother and fiancée. Now he was resolved to take them both with him to a place of safety.

So as not to delay the departure of their hosts and so they could themselves make up for lost time, Eugène and Léon quickly took their leave.

By five o'clock that evening they had rejoined their battalion.

Opening his knapsack, Eugène found a letter addressed to M. Leduc.

Unsealing the envelope, he found that it contained a gold ring set with a ruby surrounded by turquoises.

This gift was wrapped in a piece of paper on which a trembling hand had written:

Wear this ring in memory of me. Hélène.

He examined this jewel, precious reminder of a woman he had already fallen in love with, but had no hopes of ever seeing again. Respectfully he kissed the paper bearing Hélène's signature and put the ring on his finger, saying to Léon: "Now I understand what you must feel when you think about your Louise. The thought that perhaps destiny has separated you forever distresses you. Nevertheless, you are engaged, she loves you, and you know where to find her when your enlistment is up. From what you've told me about her I don't have any trouble believing that you'll find she's been faithful to you when your five years are up. I'm much more to be pitied than you are. Hélène is engaged to another; and this ring, which she was kind enough to slip in my knapsack, between two pieces of cold chicken, is nothing more than a gift offered in friendship and gratitude. I'll probably never again have the pleasure of meeting her; nonetheless, I love her. Granted, our respective situations aren't exactly identical, but they're similar enough to strengthen even further the bond of friendship we've felt for each other ever since fate made us comrades in arms."

"Yes, it's one more reason for us to be friends. Unfortunately, I'm afraid that's the only consolation we have left, for, in my estimation, there's no hope for either of us."

CHAPTER XX

THE BATTLE OF THE NORTH ANNA

The day after the incident we just reported, the Fourteenth forded the North Anna River and deployed its men as skirmishers on the opposite bank. Several battalions followed it to serve as its reserves. Thus protected, the engineers quickly finished a pontoon bridge on which the rest of the 5th Corps could cross over.[1]

The contingent crossed a field, reached a road where they wheeled toward the center, advanced in a straight line until they were about four or five miles away from the river, then entered a wood which they crossed through as far as the clearing on the opposite side. There they were protected by a simple rail fence. The rest of the army followed them, stopping at some distance in the woods and began to dig in.

About four o'clock, some Confederate riflemen appeared facing the Fourteenth; they were welcomed by a volley of musket fire. Lying flat on their stomachs, they began a sustained series of volleys at the Federal troops. The firing became very intense. Suddenly, through the smoke, the main Confederate line could be seen charging at them, bayonets fixed, letting out a fearsome yell. The riflemen of the Fourteenth retreated, each man charging his weapon as he ran, stopping some distance away, taking cover behind a tree, and firing at will as rapidly as possible.

And so did the Fourteenth defend the ground foot by foot. Since the rebels were in the open field and their line presented a broad target, they lost a lot of men. Having lost the momentum of their charge and, guessing at their targets, they fired blindly into the woods as they advanced. Alone, as they slowly retreated, the Fourteenth held the enemy off for an hour.

Just as the Confederates, still gaining ground, had reached the edge of the woods, which the skirmishers of the Fourteenth had held an hour earlier, the latter were jumping into the new trenches just finished by the reserves.

At that very moment, the Federal artillery, positioned behind these improvised ramparts, opened fire on the enemy. The rebel batteries, which the men could not see because of the trees and smoke, returned fire; for an hour or two, an earsplitting din prevailed. Artillerymen and infantrymen, each side trying to outdo the other, fired as best they could in the direction of the bullets and shells. Hidden one from another, unable to see what they were firing at, the two armies continued their volleys.[2]

The sun was just about to sink below the horizon when the Confederate firing ceased. The Federals popped off a few more shots. Then the deepest silence replaced the thunder of cannons and the crackling of gunfire.

Léon, who had just been through his first battle, had acquitted himself valiantly. Ten or so men were asked to come forward to reconnoiter and the two Canadians were among those who volunteered and were accepted. A former supply sergeant from Company F — a man Leduc had known very well and who had transferred into the 10th Regulars with the rank of second lieutenant — gave them their orders. They were to deploy so as to cover the whole brigade; then, moving toward where the enemy supposedly was, they were to advance very cautiously. They were to examine every tree trunk, every dip in the terrain capable of concealing an enemy. Insofar as was possible, they were to avoid fighting and were to come back as soon as they had either discovered the enemy's location or verified his departure. Each man was put outside the trenches and set off in the direction indicated. They all disappeared among the trees and were so completely cut off that they couldn't see one another.

Fearing he might be caught unawares, Eugène had charged his rifle. He had just about covered three-quarters of the distance to the edge of the woods when he caught sight of a rebel who, like him, had probably been sent out on reconnaissance. Eugene had spotted him at the very moment that the rebel was looking off in another direction trying to catch sight of a blue uniform. His right thumb was on his trigger; but the trigger was on safety. Sensing the advantage of his position, Eugène, who was only two or three yards away, first got him in his sights, then said in a tone just loud enough for his enemy to hear: "Surrender!"

Startled, the Virginian looked at Eugène, who was threatening him with the barrel of his rifle. Seeing that he was lost if he made a movement to defend himself, the rebel dropped his gun.

"Drop your belt," Eugène continued.

The rebel didn't wait to be asked twice.

"Now walk in front of me. Whatever you do, don't make a sound."

It was dusk when Eugène arrived at the ramparts with his prisoner and handed him over to the officers. After complimenting him on his courage and cool-headedness, they had the prisoner taken to the rear.

A few moments later, the other scouts returned except for one who would not come back alive. All of them had gone as far as the edge of the woods, but none of them had found any trace of the enemy. It was decided that the rebels must have returned to their trenches and, wanting to see if the Yankees had taken off, they had sent out some scouts, just one of whom had been clumsy enough to fall into young Leduc's hands.

The next day they helped the ambulance men gather up the dead left in the woods. Some trees literally had been cut to shreds from top to bottom by bullets; others had been toppled by cannonballs. Not far from the edge of the woods, in a dense thicket that Eugène recognized from having crossed through it the night before, they found the one scout who hadn't returned of the ten who had set out the previous night. His chest had been run right through by a bayonet. The wound had closed and he had hemorrhaged internally.

His face was black — as if he had choked on his own blood. His hands still clenched the barrel of his gun; its stock was broken. He was a well-built fellow, six feet tall. It was obvious that, surrounded by rebel scouts, he had refused to surrender and that after firing his rifle, he had used it as a club. Around him, in a radius of some thirty or so feet, eleven rebels had bitten the dust, and it could be assumed that he had dispatched at least five or six of them. Five literally had had their heads bashed in and the sixth had a bullet in his stomach. No doubt the others had fallen during the afternoon attack. The scout was a Yankee who was identified as belonging to the 12th Regulars.

The previous day's battle had been a very deadly one, but on the Yankee side, the Fourteenth had suffered the most.

Eugène noticed that some soldiers were stripping money and jewels from the dead. He protested, but was told to mind his own business and, remembering his adventure with the cavalryman who had killed the Negro at the Shelton plantation, he didn't insist — not because he was afraid of these grave robbers, but because he was not about to undertake the reform of American army morals, a task he considered to be beyond him. Instead, he looked at his ring and said to Léon in French: "If I happen to be killed one of these days, these thieves might very well take this jewel from me, and since I don't want their dirty mitts to sully it, I'm going to put it in my scapular. No one will ever think of looking for it there. The Blessed Virgin, knowing that it was given to me by a pure angel, won't take offense."

"As a matter of fact, you're right about that. I've already noticed that someone in the company wouldn't think twice about stealing it even while you're alive. You can pretend you've lost it so no one will suspect you have it on you."

CHAPTER XXI

A Few Skirmishes

The same day, rations were distributed and the army set out on the march again. On May 29, it crossed the Pamunkey River. Eugène had thrown away his shoes, which hurt his feet, but he would have been glad to have them back again when the regiment, abandoning the main road, entered the woods where they deployed to provide rifle cover. The three center companies, held in reserve, began to dig trenches and build barricades. It was about one o'clock. Eugène, his tired, throbbing feet bruised by roots, wasn't overjoyed at the prospect of having to spend part of the afternoon going to and fro gathering pieces of wood to serve as a frame for the breastworks. To the left of the line, he could hear the crackling of heavy gunfire punctuated from time to time by the muffled reports of field pieces; it sounded like drum rolls accompanied by the booming of a bass drum. Shells began to rain down on the spot where the Fourteenth's reserves were working on the fortifications.

Suddenly, the commanding officer appeared on horseback in front of the battalion. He was accompanied by a staff officer, also on horseback. The latter seemed composed, but the commanding officer was as drunk as a lord.[1] He was swaying in his saddle. As he began to harangue his troops, he didn't sound quite like Napoléon I who, long ago, fired up his men's courage — those conquerors of the European coalition — with speeches renowned for being brief.[2] A shell landing right by the horse made it shy, almost unhorsing the eloquent officer. Recovering his poise as best he could, the commanding officer addressed his men more or less as follows, hiccoughs frequently interrupting his speech.

"Fellow citizens (hic) — I mean fellow shodiers (hic) — do you believe (hic) that we're going to let ourselves be bo(hic)thered (hic) by that damned mob of Confederate vul(hic)tures (hic)? No, by 500,000 devils! Their pop-guns must be shilenced! I need five good men (hic), five brave men from the Fourteenth (hic) to silence that loud-mouthed Sheshionist battery! (hic) Are you up for it?"

"The commanding officer is a few sheets to the wind," said Eugène, "but devil take me if I don't prefer shooting off a rifle just about anywhere to staying here bruising my feet. I don't have much taste for the kind of architecture they're teaching us here. Are you coming, Léon?"

"But where do you think you're going? The commanding officer doesn't know what he's talking about."

"Don't worry about a thing. We have some sharpshooters posted at the edge of the woods facing the enemy battery. We'll simply go off to find them and watch them shoot."

The two men went up to the commanding officer to offer their services. He congratulated them and shook their hand. Three others volunteered and received their share of congratulations. They all went off to find the sharpshooters and spent the rest of the afternoon with them. They were armed with breechloading rifles fitted out with telescopic sights (at that time the infantry was using muzzleloading Springfield rifles). The sharpshooters were a mile away from the Confederate battery. The rifles could shoot that far even though at that distance they could not fire with any degree of accuracy. However, in the hands of these highly skilled riflemen, one of these breechloaders did as much damage at a mile distance as a Springfield could do in the hands of an ordinary rifleman shooting at a target five hundred yards away.

The battery was protected behind a rampart, but the gun-layer had to come out into the open to aim his gun and the Federal marksmen were taking advantage of that moment to shoot at him. Many shots missed the mark, but in the course of the afternoon, the two friends saw several cannoneers bite the dust. They came back to their post in the evening and found that the trenches had been completed.

The next day they had had to leave these new retrenchments to build others farther forward toward the front. To do that, they had been obliged to push back the enemy riflemen and advance to get within rifle range of the main Confederate line. The makeshift rampart had to be built under enemy fire. The Confederates had one or two batteries facing the Fourteenth which, unable to see the Federals, peppered shots blindly into the woods. The Federals didn't shoot back for fear of drawing to them the various sorts of projectiles which the enemy was raining down on the forest.

Behind the second line of entrenchments was a dwelling now serving as a hospital for the rapidly increasing number of wounded. The troops in the trenches lacking water, several soldiers took their comrades' canteens to fill them at the well by the house. Léon was one of them. When he came back, he looked very sad, saying to Eugène: "You were wise not to come with me. I saw the most heart-rending sight. The house is bursting with wounded, and in the courtyard a great number of them are being hastily bandaged by surgeons and their assistants. I saw one soldier, among others, who had had a bullet pass right through his chest. They've undressed him and have him sitting up. Every time he takes a breath a stream of blood as wide as your finger gushes out through his chest and back. I'm all shaken up."

The line of riflemen was made up of reserve groups taken from the companies in the center, linked to one another by soldiers deployed every five feet. The reserves had begun building on the spot fortifications which, as soon as possible, were to form one continuous line joining together the various scattered sections.

To the left of the Fourteenth there was a road through the woods which intersected the two armies at right angles. The rebels, whose advance line along that road wasn't fortified either, had placed some of their best marksmen in ambush there. They were shooting mercilessly at all the Federals who, when they needed to cross the road, found themselves momentarily exposed to the bushwhackers' murderous lead. A sergeant and several good marksmen from the Fourteenth's reserves were sent to keep them at bay. Eugène and Léon, always ready to volunteer each time there was danger to be faced, were among that number. The Union sharpshooters placed themselves behind some large trees along the road. The 'federates didn't seem to have noticed their arrival.

"Who wants to cross the road?" asked Sergeant Beaston, who had been a soldier in the English army.

"I do," answered Eugène, as he ran off to hide in ambush behind a tree on the opposite side.

Two shots rang out. A bullet whistled by Leduc's ears. The bushwhacker had aimed ahead of his man so he would have hit him if he had continued walking, but since Eugène had taken shelter behind the first tree he came to on the other side of the road, the bullet had passed to his left.

When the rebel poked his head out slightly to take aim, one shot from Beaston and the man fell to the ground.

Two of his companions came out to carry him off.

Three rifle shots rang out from the Federal side.

One of the two Confederates fell, flailed around, grabbed his leg, and dragged himself to cover without getting up; the other staggered as he struggled painfully back to the side of the road.

They could now see three or four other rifle barrels pointed toward the spot occupied by the Union soldiers, but the men holding them were careful not to show themselves.

Taking advantage of the consternation caused by the last shots, Beaston and Duroc had also crossed the road. Eugène, who had put his cap on the tip of his rifle and tilted his weapon so his kepi was in front of the tree, was rewarded by seeing his headgear shot through by an enemy bullet.

"Those fellows are good shots," he said. "In fact they're so good they make me want to try a little experiment."

As he said that, he went around the tree exposing himself to enemy fire. He had noticed that the rebels on the opposite side of the road had only one loaded rifle left, so he carefully watched the tip of that rifle. At the very moment he saw the flash, he made a tremendous leap to the left. Scarcely had he done so when a bullet hit the tree just about chest high where he had been the moment before.

Just as the rebel had raised his shoulder, Duroc had seized that moment to shoot, hoping to hit the marksman before he could fire. The two shots had been fired at the same time, but Léon's bullet reached its mark. The rebel fell backward and lay motionless.

"My calculations were correct," said Eugène as soon as he had resumed his place behind the tree. "Light travels faster than sound; everybody knows that. As for me, I was just about certain that it travels faster than a bullet. I saw the flash and had just enough time to get out of the way."

"That's some experiment," said Léon. "You made me kill a man."

"You're not about to be sorry that rebel died before his time, are you? He wasn't very kindly disposed toward us. You're here to kill men, my boy. You'll have to accept it."

"Well, yes, I do regret that man's death because, if you hadn't been so reckless, I wouldn't have had to kill him to save your life. Whatever made you go out in the open like that?"

"Go on! You know very well I didn't expose myself to danger. That's all right; I thank you for being guilty of a homicide — all the more justifiable because you committed it with the praiseworthy intention of preserving my precious health. I feel like shouting to our dead Mr. Rebel, 'Consider your shot null and void!'"[3]

A few more shots were exchanged with no effect. When evening came, they left that post to return to the battalion reserves.

CHAPTER XXII

THE BATTLE OF COLD HARBOR[1]

It was the 3rd of June. The entrenchments begun by the advanced line had been completed only in certain isolated points. The rebels had intensified their artillery fire. During the afternoon, the fourth division of the 5th Army Corps, under General Bartlett's command, was overwhelmed and driven back behind the second entrenchment line.

The battle, now very fierce, had been going on for two hours; the enemy had been firing blindly at the Fourteenth's reserves, which as yet hadn't fired off a single shot. They hadn't come under attack yet, and were waiting for orders to retreat. On the left, the main line having given way to the rebel attack, orders had been given to retreat. Judging from the sound of the firing, men were now fighting behind the Fourteenth's reserves. In fact, the reserves were just about surrounded by the enemy and cut off from their second entrenchment lines, where they should have withdrawn. The brunt of the attack had been born by Bartlett's division. The Confederates, now right in front of the Fourteenth's center, had probably not gotten the order to advance and continued firing blindly. Captain McGibbon, battalion commander, saw that it was time to clear out and, gathering the men around him, he said: "I need thirty resolute men to guard the flag; the rest of the reserves will deploy and fall back to the second line of entrenchments. Don't shoot till you see the enemy. You men who want to go with the flag, step forward."

Thirty men volunteered immediately.

"Reserves, attention! Front and center, deploy!"

The remaining reserves deployed at double quick march.

The thirty men guarding the flag, our two heroes among them, began to file to the right. Captain McGibbon and a young second lieutenant marched at the head followed immediately by the color sergeant. The commanding officer, addressing the sergeant, said: "I hope we won't be stopped along the way, but if we are, don't worry about me. If I had my horse, I'd risk going through enemy fire to escape. I'm not anxious to go back to the Southern prisons I escaped from, but I'm wounded in the leg and can't run. If the rebels challenge us, don't worry about me. Save the flag."

"Unfortunately, I'm suffering from an old leg wound myself," said the sergeant, "and I can't run fast enough to avoid having the pleasure of their company.

"Don't worry," said Léon, who was walking beside him. "Give me the flag; I'll take care of it."

"I'll give it to you if we're stopped. That way they'll come to me to capture it and I'll pass it to you and you'll take off as fast as you can."

They had covered about half of the half-mile separating the two lines of entrenchment when they heard a less than melodious voice saying: "Surrender, you damn Yankees."

A number of rifle barrels with an equal number of Virginians in gray uniforms behind them were aimed at the little group.

"Lay down your arms, boys; any attempt at resistance is futile," said the Union officer.

Setting the example himself, he threw his sword to the ground. All the Federals had instinctively hit the ground while throwing down their weapons, as if they suspected that the rebels were just about to fire off a volley.

While this was going on, the flag had changed hands without arousing the suspicions of the Southerners.

Battle of Cold Harbor, Virginia, June 1, 1864 — The Eighteenth Corps driving Longstreet's forces from their first line of rifle pits.

However, one of the Confederates, who had left his group, was right in front of Léon as he got up to run off with the flag.

"Give me that rag, Yankee dog," he said, reaching out his hand to grab the staff.

Quick as a flash, Léon extended his arm to move the flag out of reach, while planting a mighty blow on the Virginian's mouth. The Virginian sat down unceremoniously.

"If you're with me, follow me!" shouted Léon as he took to his heels, abandoning his rifle, but carrying off the star-spangled banner.

Lieutenant McGibbon, the commander's brother, Leduc, and about ten others got up carrying their weapons — except for the lieutenant who, in his haste, left his sword on the ground. The furious rebels all fired together at the fleeing men; most of them hit the ground. When that volley went off, Eugène was running as fast as he could as he tried to catch up to Léon. He saw Léon fall flat as a hail of bullets riddled the flag and cut the staff in half. Thirty or so bullets imbedded themselves in a fallen tree at about a man's height.

Thinking for a moment that his friend's body was riddled with bullets, a feeling

of mortal anguish gripped Leduc's heart.

But Léon was soon on his feet, off and running.

He had tripped, and his fall had saved him from certain death.

The fleeing men had taken off away from the rebel position without really knowing whether or not they had run into another hornets' nest. However, after running frantically for five or six minutes, they came to a clearing at the bottom of a ravine.

The New York Zouaves, wearing the French Zouave uniform, commanded a kind of plateau where they had built an improvised rampart. They were shooting into the woods since they thought, and rightly so, that some rebels were in there.

Léon was the first one out of the woods. When the "ZousZous" saw him running toward them with the American flag tattered by rebel bullets, they thought he was being pursued, and, since they couldn't see the colors of the uniforms through the smoke, they fired a volley at Léon's companions as they came out of the woods. Fortunately, no one was hit.

Seeing the red trousers and blue coats of the 5th ZousZous, who had just recently been incorporated into the regular brigade, Léon realized he was saved. He stopped halfway up the hill, planted the half-broken staff in the ground, and cried: "Rally round the flag, boys!"[2]

And the members of the Fourteenth rallied around the precious rag.

There were four of them, including Léon.

Of all those who had braved rebel fire rather than be taken prisoner, Léon, Eugène, the young second lieutenant, and Lieutenant McGibbon were the only ones who had come through safe and sound. All the others had been hit either by the volleys or by the shrapnel from shells, which were still bursting in every direction, making the woods almost uninhabitable. The rebels captured Captain McGibbon and about twenty soldiers.

The rest of the battalion, now reduced to about one hundred men, had rallied in a thicket to the left of the Zouaves. There the color guard, now reduced to the four men mentioned above, went to join them.

There was a rebel battery just in front of them which woods hid from sight; however, suspecting that there was a line of Federals unprotected by entrenchments just ahead, the Confederate artillery began to pepper the spot occupied by the remnants of the Fourteenth.

Lieutenant McGibbon, finding that he was highest ranking officer present, took temporary command of the battalion.

He wept as he thought of his brother, taken prisoner at his side and who would perhaps be recognized as an escapee from the Southern prisons. Enraged as he thought of how the commander might be mistreated, he waved his steel scabbard, bereft of the blade left behind in the woods, and said: "Courage, boys, we're going to pay them back and then some."

Bullets kept hailing down, stripping the trees of their leaves. The men were ordered to lie down and shoot from that position. A battery of thirty-two-pounders came up to support them.[3]

It was night now — as black as pitch; the detonations came one after another, rapidly and at regular intervals, even though it had started to rain. About ten in the evening, the enemy ceased firing and the survivors of the Fourteenth spent the rest of the night fortifying their position.

The next day, Eugène, Léon, and several others were sent out on reconnaissance. They came back after determining the rebels had abandoned the position they had held the previous night.

The troops spent all of the 4th in the trenches. Toward evening, a special contingent was recruited from the various regiments to serve in the outposts. Eugène and Léon were among that number. They were taken three or four miles toward the right where, once again, they had the inestimable advantage of shooting their rifles in the company of soldiers belonging to other regiments in a trench which seemed to them to have been dug at right angles to the main line.

CHAPTER XXIII

INCIDENTS AND ACCIDENTS

The sun was about to set when the rebels attacked the line where our two heroes were entrenched. Since the rampart was not very high, several soldiers "saluted" the enemy bullets — that is, when they heard the bullets whistle by, they moved their heads to avoid them.

Even very brave men can't help making this movement when they hear the whistling of a bullet. "Saluting" a bullet doesn't necessarily prove you're afraid; however, not "saluting" clearly demonstrates that you're not afraid and that you have nerves of steel besides.[1]

Many soldiers in the American army refused to "salute" as one of these messengers of death passed by. Perhaps that's due to the devil-may-care attitude Americans are so famous for. In any case, Eugène and Léon didn't do any "saluting." A man born on American soil, be it in Canada, the United States, or elsewhere, instinctively abhors bowing and scraping. He won't kowtow to anyone without good reason. Unless he has been corrupted, he has no use for men in power; he has to have a good reason to respect them — just the fact that they can harm him isn't enough.

"Lead is a base metal. We shouldn't bow down to it," Eugene stated. "Besides, when someone hears a bullet whistling by, it's already too late to avoid it — even if he knows where it's going."

A young officer had gotten out of the ditch to encourage his men. "No use saluting! No use saluting!" he repeated, each of his words was accompanied by that same involuntary movement with each passing bullet and, as he finished his sentence, he pretended to move his hand to his cap, hoping thus to hide a too obvious movement of his head.

"Then why are you saluting? You lout!" Léon said in French.

The weather was overcast now and the rain started up again.

The fusillade kept up until about nine.

The officers had a hard time bringing it to an end. It was no use shouting to make yourself heard. The officer would say to the soldier next to him: "Pass on the order to cease firing."

And the order went from one soldier to the next. But some smart alecks poked their neighbors after they had passed the order along and added: "Blaze away!"[2]

And the firing would start up again more intensely than ever.

Finally, it was quiet again. The tired soldiers took advantage of this opportunity to go to sleep in the most varied and most uncomfortable possible positions. The men took turns going on watch.

About two o'clock in the morning, whispering, they passed along the order to get ready to retreat quietly; the soldiers had to be careful to keep hold of their canteens so they wouldn't clang against their bayonet scabbards. About five o'clock, they came to a highway where the remainder of the Army of the Potomac already stood in marching order.[3] The detachment dispersed as each group went off to rejoin its respective battalion.

Suddenly, the men began to cheer. General Ulysses S. Grant, commander in chief of the Army of the Potomac, was passing by on horseback with his general staff. He was smoking his irremovable and omnipresent cigar and saluting right and left to acknowledge the cheers.[4]

The army set off on the march again. At noon, they stopped and they were ordered to set up the tents — something which hadn't happened since the beginning of the campaign, a month before. The men rested there for several days. Food, bedding, clothing, etc. were distributed. Eugène, whom Léon had been calling the barefoot boy ever since he had made the stupid mistake of parting with his footwear[5] a few days before the Battle of Cold Harbor, took advantage of this opportunity to shelter his toes from the inclement weather.

On the 9th, they struck camp and set out for Petersburg. For six or seven days they went on a series of forced marches. They scarcely had two out of every twenty-four hours to sleep. On the morning of the 16th they were three or four miles away from Petersburg. The soldiers were asleep on their feet and Eugène asked himself how his legs had managed to get him there without his knowing it. The men had arrived there at night, gone through a few drills, and then stacked their weapons. Eugène had taken part in all this without even being aware of it.

After breakfast they fell into rank again. New reinforcements had come into camp a week before and, because the men were being placed in rank according to their height, the two Canadians had been separated — Léon being much taller than Eugène. Although they weren't next to each other any longer in rank, they still cooked their meals together and found ways of walking next to each other when they were marching easy. But, when they got into ranks for maneuvers, each one had to go back to his own place.

The battalion deployed to provide rifle cover and, bearing obliquely toward the right, it went into some woods. Each man was five paces from his neighbor; the two friends had lost sight of each other as they passed under the trees.

The objective of this maneuver was to occupy the woods so as to command a plain stretching between the forest and the enemy fortifications. It was sweltering: the soldiers, hot, thirsty, covered with sweat and dust, moved forward while attempting to keep their place in rank — all this while skirting the obstacles barring the way.

All sorts of shells and projectiles rained down on the woods. Some of the new recruits were having a bit of difficulty maintaining their distance and their alignment. At one point, Eugène found himself beside a husky Irish fellow. He was a new recruit, a braggart Eugène had seen several times having fun roughing up men who weren't as strong as he. He claimed that Eugène wasn't in his place in line and tried to make him move to the left. Eugène maintained, and with good reason, that the Irishman should move to the right. A fight ensued.

Ahead of them, to the right, men were running to get back to their place in the ranks. Only one of them, a man called Stevens, had noticed the dispute, on the verge of becoming quite ugly, and he had shouted at them as he passed: "If you want to fight, the enemy's in front of you. Save your blows for the rebels."

And he hurried off to join the line of march, thinking that the two others were following him.

The two belligerents advanced slowly as they argued and sized each other up. A tree trunk separated them. The Irishman jumped over it and threatened to break Eugène's head. Eugène, moving back a pace, put himself in the on guard position for bayonet fighting without fixing his bayonet and, standing his ground, he waited for his adversary. The Irishman didn't want to risk fighting him hand-to-hand. After hesitating for a moment, he got Eugène in his rifle sights. Swift as lightning, Eugène ducked; then, gracefully as a tiger cat, he leapt on his redoubtable antagonist. Grabbing the menacing barrel of his adversary's rifle from beneath, he raised it above his head.

The gun went off and the bullet whistled through the air.

At the very same moment, the Canadian, who was holding his rifle by the middle with his right hand, twirled it vigorously. The Irishman had only just enough time to raise his rifle to parry the blow. However, since the Canadian was holding on to his adversary's rifle with his left hand, the Irishman had difficulty parrying it; the butt of Leduc's rifle came down on Pat's head hard enough to knock out an ordinary man.

But our Hibernian's skull was much thicker than that of most mortals. He just fell to his knees — something he hadn't done for a long time. He then made prodigious efforts to force the young man to let go of the discharged gun he was still holding on to with his left hand.

The struggle continued for a few minutes longer. The Irishman, covered with blood, exhausted his repertoire of swearwords. He clutched at the rifle with both his hands, tried to get up again, and fell back to his knees. Counting on his muscular strength, he shook the young Canadian, and lifted him up hoping to dash him to the ground. However, Eugène, showing amazing agility, always landed on his feet and, just as his adversary was attempting to get up, he would trip him, bringing him to his knees again.

"Say your prayers," Eugène would then say to him.

Finally, the Irishman let go of the rifle with one hand and tried to grab the Canadian by the throat. Eugène, who until then had landed only one smashing blow, dodged his adversary's grasp and landed him a telling whack on the forehead.

Blood gushed out. The Canadian struck again. The Irishman fell to the ground where he lay motionless.

Afraid his fallen opponent was bluffing, and not wanting to give him a target, Eugène seized his rifle, took it by the barrel, and hit it against a tree until the butt shattered. Then, satisfied no one was going to shoot him in the back, he ran off to join the line of riflemen who had just about reached the edge of the woods a quarter of a mile ahead.

CHAPTER XXIV

Two Predictions

The line of riflemen had come to the edge of the woods without being seen by the rebels, who were still firing bullets and shells into the forest, killing and wounding a great number of soldiers. To the right, continuing down the line, the 2nd Army Corps had dug in during the previous night outside the woods. Farther to the right, beyond the 2nd Corps, the investment line stretched on as far as the eye could see. As we have seen, the 5th Army Corps had set a line of riflemen to cover it as soon as it arrived. Deployed in the woods, the riflemen were waiting for night to come before building rifle pits, a sort of crescent-shaped breastwork, at some distance in the clearing. The riflemen had been allowed to walk around and gather in groups of four or five. They had been told to be ready to resume their places and distances at the first signal. When Léon and Eugène got together, Eugène described what had happened to him.

"I'm afraid I killed that man," he said. "And I'm very sorry about what happened. I had to defend myself, but God knows I didn't mean to kill him."

"Bah! He'll recover. It'll take more than a few miserable whacks on his thick skull with a rifle barrel to make your Irishman pull some stupid trick on you — like going to join his forefathers."[1]

They talked about their loved ones far away — women as well as men.[2] Léon, remembering that he still hadn't received an answer to his letter to Louise, felt completely discouraged. He had written over a month earlier. Had she already forgotten him? No, of course not! That was impossible! Perhaps she had shown his letter to M. Latour and he might not have believed the story it told. The merchant could have found this account, which was far from being complete, rather unlikely. Wanting to find an excuse for breaking off her engagement to Duroc, M. Latour would be inclined to be suspicious of him.

"In any case," Léon said to Eugène, "my first letter will have to be enough. I can understand that I might have fallen out of favor with M. Latour since I left, but with her? That isn't like her. She wouldn't doubt my word; she knows me too well. And I won't humiliate myself by trying to justify my actions; I've behaved honorably. Even if she's forgotten me already, I feel I'll always love her, but I'll have pride enough not to bother her by reminding her I'm alive."

"Come on, now, how impatient you are! Her letter probably hasn't had time to reach you."

"It's no use trying to placate me. You wrote to your parents at the same time I wrote and you got a reply a week ago at the Charley City Camp. No, it's obvious, she doesn't want to write me. I may have only a few days to live. Things are going to heat up soon. As a matter of fact, the sparks are beginning to fly already. Unfortunately the Southerners are having all the fun. That's all right," he added with a forced smile, "but it would have been a great comfort to receive the assurance that she still loves me — once more, before I die."

"Come on, chase away these gloomy thoughts. Your Louise loves you. You'll live, you'll see her again, and you'll marry her. Trust me."

"Could you be turning into a prophet?"

"I've taken the right road to become one since no one is a prophet in his own country and it seems to me that we are pretty far away from our native soil."

"I must admit if you continue to carry on like this your prophecies will never be called *Lamentations*.[3] Now it's my turn to tell you something that'll make you happy. I'm as much a stranger here as you are. Consequently, I can be a prophet too. Well, then, I predict that you'll never serve in the French army; but on the other hand, I prophesy that you will marry Hélène."

"You're making fun of me."

"Not at all, I'm serious. Although you attempt to deny it, just try saying you have no hope of ever seeing her again, formulating a thousand projects — each more unrealizable than the next — keep on wanting to join the French army; whatever you do, memories of Hélène keep mingling with your plans for the future. Examine your most secret thoughts, your dearest dreams, and tell me if, through the glorious smoke, amid the spoils of battle, the blue uniforms, the crimson-striped trousers, the gold epaulettes, the distinguished cross, the whole kit and caboodle — tell me if you don't still see Hélène's smiling face through it all. And I'm sure she too is thinking of you. Just between us, even though she is engaged, she doesn't seem to love her Alfred. And from what I've seen, she isn't the sort of woman to get married without being in love. You caught her fancy. And she returned the favor, if we can call it that. Between the two of you, there's a law of attraction which will draw you both into the same orbit. This irresistible magnet, this fatal attraction, will draw you to each other, and you'll be under its influence despite the obstacles looming in your path."

"Your theory is wonderful. As far as I'm concerned, I'd like to believe it. I don't have any difficulty in agreeing with it as far as you and Louise are concerned. But how can you see such a rosy future in store for me while you are haunted by such a gloomy future ahead for you and Louise? All the same, you must admit that you're much farther ahead than I am; I don't even know if Hélène loves me."

"I don't know why, but I have a feeling something bad is about to happen."

"Well, get rid of that thought."

"I'll try to, just to please you."

"That's good. Let's change the subject. By the way, why do you say I'll never serve France? You know very well that's what I want to do above all else."

"I'm saying that because your wanting to place your valiant sword in Napoléon III's service has already gotten you into trouble more than once. I'm afraid it will get you into even more trouble. If I have just one piece of advice to give you, it's this: give up this plan. The military life is no career for anyone."

"It is for me, and every French soldier carries his field marshal's baton in his knapsack."[4]

"But you haven't your French soldier's cabbage-chopper in your knapsack yet."

"No, but I will some day."

"God knows when. And besides, it will cost you too dearly. If you'll take my advice, you won't ever try to desert again. You enlisted for five years. Live with it, and, after that, if you aren't completely fed up with military life, there'll be time enough to start over again in France."

"I'll think about it, but I wouldn't have any scruples about taking a French furlough from the service of the United States Army without permission because my enlistment is illegal.[5] They listed me as being eighteen year old. I was sixteen when I enlisted and I told them so. Even at age eighteen they couldn't enlist me in the regular army as long as my parents were alive without getting their consent beforehand. My mother and father are still alive and I told the recruiting officers so. That didn't stop them from putting me down as an orphan and getting the consent of a supposed guardian whom they appointed without consulting me."

"The same thing happened to me. My parents are dead, but I don't have a guardian in New York or any place else. Since you have to be at least twenty-one years old to enlist in the regular army without the consent of your parents or guardian, they found me a makeshift guardian. Nevertheless, I feel I have to serve for five years."

"Perhaps you're right. Now that I've found in you not only a compatriot but a sincere and devoted friend as well, my time remaining in the regiment won't seem so long."

CHAPTER XXV

MORTALLY WOUNDED

To the right, the artillery and infantry of the 2nd Army Corps had been concentrating a heavy barrage on the outer rebel fortifications defending the approach to Petersburg since morning. They stormed the position about four o'clock. Fresh troops moved up behind the 2nd Corps. Swarms of soldiers came out of the trenches, bayonets fixed, and rushed forward, letting out a fearsome yell. Although weakened by the distance, this shout coming from a thousand breasts sounded, to the ears of the men of the Fourteenth, like a woman's piercing cry as it rose above the tumult caused by the detonations. Cannons were vomiting death. The hail of bullets was mowing down the Federal ranks; the men closed ranks as best they could but they made the mistake of answering the rebels with rifle fire. Protected by their ramparts, the rebels easily blasted away at them as they pleased.

Since it didn't seem likely that the Fourteenth would have to go into battle that day, Eugène wanted to enjoy the spectacle of that grandiose combat. He went up to Adjutant McGibbon, saluted him smartly, and asked if he would be so good as to lend him his field glass.[1]

"I'd like to climb up to the top of that tree," he said, "to get an overview of the attack."

"Here it is," said the adjutant, "but try not to let the enemy see you and don't stay up there too long."

Eugène slung the glass over his shoulder and quickly reached the top of a large tree where he could see the enemy without being seen. Three or so miles away in the distance he could see Petersburg. From his treetop, the Appomattox River, cutting through the heart of the city, looked like a long silver ribbon. Some buildings were burning. Eugène kept his glass focused the longest on a spot about a mile away to the right. There, some Federal regiments had leaped into the enemy trenches and were engaged in hand-to-hand combat. These men were whirling around striking, fighting as they passed over the bodies of the dead and wounded; those rifle butts rising in the air and falling on poor unfortunate souls; those bayonet blows given and received — all that carnage was horrible to watch. Yet Eugène couldn't take his eyes away. He closely followed the ebb and flow of that bloody battle until fresh troops came to the rescue of the beaten Confederates, took some of the Federals in the trench prisoner, and forced the others back outside the rampart.

"What a terrible blunder!" Eugène said to himself. "Those men had completely overrun that position, and just because reinforcements weren't sent up to help them out in time, their victory turned into defeat."

As far to the right as he could see, the two sides were exchanging cannon and rifle fire. About half an hour after he had climbed up the tree, Eugène came back down convinced that nothing would come of the battle. After three hours of fighting, the Federals had been thrown back all along the line and were going into their trenches; there they continued to fire as best they could at the rebels who were very proud of having been able to defend their positions.

When night had fallen, the riflemen came cautiously out of the woods, lay flat on the ground, and crawled about fifty yards beyond the edge of the woods. There they gathered in groups of five and dug rifle pits which they placed thirty yards apart; each rifle pit was large enough to hold five men. The officers had had a breastwork built at the edge of the woods; later it was to be extended to form a continuous defense line.

The two Canadians were happy to find themselves in the same rifle pit; there they could be next to each other without worrying about their height difference.

The next day, the rebels greeted the new trenches with a hail of bullets and shells — as if they wanted to test how solidly they had been built. The Federals responded enthusiastically, and for four or five days there was continuous fire. The men kept on firing; they fired just for the sake of firing; they fired to pass the time. If a rebel made the mistake of showing his head above the ramparts, twenty rifle shots were aimed at him right away — mostly they missed their mark.

We'll never know how many projectiles were wasted during the War of Secession. "Waste" is just a figure of speech, because nobody would really dare to state seriously whether the piece of lead hitting a human being was more useful to society than the one that buried itself in the earth without touching anyone.

Needless to say, the rebels weren't any thriftier with their munitions than the Federals. It was a completely useless butchery since, in that part of the line at least, neither side made any pretense of advancing. Thus, after four or five days, a tacit understanding between the belligerents put an end to this system. They decided to hold their fire until one side or the other advanced. If all the shots had hit their targets, the two armies would have annihilated one another within an hour. As it was, even though most of the riflemen were very bad shots, the continual exchange of bullets and shells was rapidly diminishing the number of combatants.

Our two heroes and their three rifle-pit companions had taken it upon themselves to shoot off two hundred cartridges apiece per day. They were fairly successful in doing this. Two of them, Léon and an American, were exceptionally skilled.[2]

And that wasn't all; they distinguished themselves by their coolness and disdain of death. They didn't go in for foolish acts of bravado like their Yankee neighbor in the next rifle pit, who had stood up on the rampart and had been shot stone dead. Léon and the American proved that their bravery could withstand every test. If water was needed or meals had to be prepared, they took turns leaving the rifle pit and crossing the fifty yards to the edge of the woods at a leisurely pace. A hail of bullets accompanied their departure and greeted their return, churning up the earth all around them without ever managing to make the men "salute," a sign of fear. Captain Thatcher,[3] the new commanding officer of the battalion, who was in the officers' trench, seeing them go back and forth, said, loudly enough for anyone who wished to hear: "Those are the five bravest men in the regiment."

On June 20, the fourth day, at about eleven o'clock in the morning, the five men were working conscientiously at reaching their daily quota. It was 102 degrees in the shade. The rifle barrels, heated by the sun on the outside, and by powder on the inside, burned the men's hands. A rebel had just shown his head above the rampart facing the rifle pit at about six hundred yards away. When Léon saw him, he stood up and got him in his sights.

"Watch that man fall!" he said to Eugène.

Suddenly, they heard a bullet whistling by, followed by a dull thud. Hardly had Léon finished his sentence when he fell heavily backwards. Catching him in his arms, Eugène broke his fall somewhat. For perhaps the first time in his life, the poor boy felt his courage fail him. His eyes filled with tears.

Sobbing, he undid Léon's belt, tore off his collar button, opened his shirt to give him some air, and shouted: "Come on now, Léon! Friend, come around! Speak to me! It's me, Eugene. Don't you recognize me?"

He took a canteen and, pouring some water in his hand, he tried to cool Léon's forehead.

"But where has he been hit?"

"Here on the shoulder; the bleeding's started now."

"Below the left shoulder — why, that's very serious! And the stretcher-bearers aren't coming. He's still breathing, though. Stevens, help me. Take one end of this piece of tenting. We'll put him on it and carry him to the rear. The surgeon has to tend to the wound as soon as possible."

Léon had the fixed, glassy stare of a dead man. Blood was now flowing freely. After loading him on their makeshift stretcher, the two men left the rifle pit and made their way to the woods, walking as quickly as the weight they were bearing permitted.

Twenty bullets whistled around them. Stevens cried out, dropped his end of the canvas, and grabbed his left arm.

"I'm wounded," he said as he staggered off.

"George, come over here! Come take Stevens's place. I can't carry him all alone," said Eugène. "I'm afraid I'll hurt him. It's bad enough we let him fall to the ground again."

At that very moment two ambulance corpsmen arrived with a stretcher and lifted Léon on to it. The pain he had felt when he fell back to the ground again had made him cry out and he had regained consciousness.

"Farewell, Eugène," he said in a weak voice.

"Until we met again, dear friend," answered Eugène as he squeezed his hand.

"Let go of him," cried one of the corpsmen. "Do you want to have him killed?"

Indeed, bullets were still tearing up the ground around the group. The stretcher-bearers hurried away with the wounded man and Eugène went off to find the commanding officer to ask permission to accompany Léon to the hospital; he wanted to see that his friend's wound was tended to immediately.

"That's impossible!" answered Captain Thatcher. "Don't worry. Your fellow countryman will be cared for promptly. Your intentions are honorable. I already knew you were brave; I know now that you're a noble-hearted friend. But, if we allowed all friends of the wounded to accompany them to the hospital, there would be no fighting men left. I'll see to it that you get news of your friend just as soon as possible."

"Pardon me," said Eugène. "I was forgetting that my place is in the rifle pit where there are only three of us left now. I'm going to try to avenge Léon. Ah! If I could just get the man who shot that bullet in my sights!"

"Don't worry. Men survive wounds in their left shoulder. Look at me. I took a bullet in just about the same place and, as you can see, I'm fine."

Eugène went back to the rifle pit where he began firing furiously, saying: "If we could just fight hand to hand with knives I think it would make me feel better."

During the following night the Fourteenth was relieved by another regiment and joined the main line in the trenches on the right.

Three days later they heard Duroc had died in the hospital. The bullet, so they said, had remained in the chest lodged near the heart and the surgeons hadn't dared remove it.

"That's strange," one of Eugène's comrades said. "I'm just about certain that it passed on out through his back."

The news had deeply affected poor Eugène. Despite his seemingly devil-may-care personality, many days went by before he recovered some of his normal cheerfulness. During the six weeks he had spent at his friend's side, he had learned to appreciate Léon's openness and loyalty; he had come to consider him a superior man. He had every reason to miss him: if Léon had stayed by his side, his advice would certainly have persuaded him to avoid the many impulsive acts which caused him so many setbacks later on. But let's not get ahead of our story.

CHAPTER XXVI

MEANWHILE,
BACK IN PINGREVILLE

et's get back to Louise, whom we haven't seen since the day poor Léon Duroc left Pingreville. Louise had been painfully affected by her fiancé's departure. She loved him as only a noble-hearted woman can; the absence of her beloved had etched on her pretty face a sadness which she tried in vain to hide. No matter how often she told herself that his absence would be only temporary, that it was even necessary so that Léon could gain M. Latour's confidence, that she might hope to see Léon from time to time as they waited for the happy day when his successes would allow him to come back and ask her father to keep his promises — she could no longer console herself at not seeing him and she pined, knowing how long it would necessarily be before they could be reunited.

Constantly preoccupied with thoughts of him, remembering his elegant manners, the sound of his voice, and the least little thing he used to say, she saw his face constantly before her. With that marvelous intuition with which, to their misfortune, sensitive souls are gifted, she had a premonition. She foresaw some stroke of fate, some misfortune she couldn't quite put a finger on, but which she believed would put obstacles in the path of the beautiful plans for the future which she and Léon had made together.

In this frame of mind, she waited impatiently for news of her dear Duroc who had promised to write her as soon as he arrived in Montréal. Days, weeks, and months had gone by and not one single letter had come to tell her that Léon was still thinking of her. However, in the meantime, she had been told many stories about her loved one which she tried her best not to believe, but they had pained her deeply, nonetheless. This was not her Léon. The Léon she knew was a sensible, virtuous young man with noble ambitions — and now people were telling her that Duroc was a gambler, a debauchee, a libertine. To be sure, everyone admitted that he had always led an exemplary life while he was in Pingreville, but if Lady Rumor were to be believed, Léon had acted hypocritically and all this was just a ruse to gain the confidence of M. Latour whose son-in-law he hoped to become. They told Louise he didn't love her, that he only wanted to marry her so he could use her dowry to give free rein to his baser instincts.

Of course, Mme. Latour wasn't the last to spout this kind of nonsense about poor Léon in his absence. The reader will remember that she had tried, mostly through pique and perhaps with the vain hope of attracting Léon, to prejudice Louise against him. Besides, this gossip did not circulate outside of the Latour home; M. Latour himself had brought it back from Montréal where he had gone three weeks after Léon's departure. Here's how M. Latour had gotten his information — no more true than it was flattering to our hero.[1]

When he had reached Montréal, M. Latour went to stay at the Hotel Canada, where, since it was dinner time, he had sat down at a table in the dining room with his back to the entrance. He had scarcely seated himself when Grippard came in and was placed at the end of another table where he could see M. Latour in profile without being seen by him.

As soon as Grippard saw him, he turned pale and was just about to get up and leave to avoid having to meet him. Grippard did not know that Duroc had paid off the $1,000 note. All he knew was that Duroc had left the hotel after settling his bill; Grippard guessed he had probably risked being thought a thief rather than consent to forging a signature.

Being convinced that M. Latour had had to pay off the note didn't set Grippard's mind at ease, for he figured that Léon, either to get revenge or to exonerate himself, had found a way to let his former employer know what had happened.

Grippard felt he was beyond the reach of the law, since there was nothing to prove him guilty. However, since he wanted to protect his reputation, he was determined to take advantage of the situation by putting matters in the best possible light. He was all the more anxious for M. Latour to have confidence in him because he had already selected the Pingreville tradesman as one of the many victims he intended to dupe. Therefore, he felt a true sense of relief when M. Latour approached him, holding out his hand and smiling.

"Dear M. Grippard! We hardly see you anymore! What's become of you? Are you revolutionizing the grain trade?"

"Just about. I'm very busy these days. But what about you, what are you up to? I haven't seen you in Montréal since the shipping lanes opened."

"As a matter of fact, this is my first trip this spring. I had a few banking matters to settle three weeks ago, but I entrusted Duroc, one of my former clerks — who was coming to work here — with settling them for me."

"Duroc? Wait a minute! A tall dark young man, a debauchee, so it would seem. I met him in a club where they said he had just lost $1,000 gambling."

"Is that possible? No, of course not. You must be mistaken! The Duroc I knew was an honest man of steady habits.[2] Describe the man you ran into at the club."

"He's a bit taller than I am, thin, well built, elegant. He has curly dark hair and a very tiny mustache. He was wearing pearl-gray trousers, a black suit coat, and a light-weight brown overcoat. He spoke to me about you, and, unless you are aware of his having other resources, that was your money he was throwing around."

"Precisely. And yet the bank sent back the $1,000 note I had told him to pay off."

"Perhaps he was lucky enough to win the money back. But what's happened to him? He just took off suddenly from the Hotel Canada and no one has seen him since, so they tell me."

"I took an interest in him; I had recommended him to the firm of Pincemaille and Company; but since he's given himself up to debauchery, I'm withdrawing my friendship from him. I shall go to the bank to find out how he went about redeeming my note. From what you're telling me, he could have forged my signature to renew it. If he did, he'd better watch out; I'll have him thrown in jail." After a moment's silence, he reflected, "And to think that man wants to marry Louise and that he has even managed to make her love him. Ah! The scoundrel!"

"After all is said and done," Grippard said to himself, "even if that damned Duroc had agreed to forge this fellow's signature, I'd have started off by endorsing the note. Today, I'd just have to deny that it was my signature. That way it would look like Duroc forged two signatures." He said aloud to M. Latour, "If you've been robbed and if you need my help settling this matter, my purse is at your disposal."

"I thank you, my generous friend," answered M. Latour. "If you'll be so good as to accompany me to the bank, we'll find out how matters stand."

And the two tradesmen left together. On the way, M. Grippard waxed eloquent on the deplorable morality of the times.

"You see," he said to M. Latour, "the younger generation is rotten to the core. Honesty is a thing of the past. Young men go in for gambling, debauchery, and all sorts of excesses. So here we have a young man who seemed intelligent, but who will come to a bad end."

While they were talking, they came to the bank, where they learned that the note had been paid off with a draft that a certain Léon Duroc had sent from New York.

"He went off to get himself hanged in the United States," said Grippard.

"He's off to a very bad start since he's taken up gambling," answered M. Latour. "That's all right. Some vestige of honesty and perhaps also his gratitude for all I've done for him made him reimburse me. But I can't figure out how he could lose $1,000 in Montréal and send that exact amount of money from New York scarcely a few days later."

"It appears he enlisted in the American army," replied the cashier, "since his letter from New York said we should send a receipt to Fort Trumbull, New London,

Connecticut. Just a minute, here's the address. It includes the name of his regiment: the 14th U.S. Infantry."

"In spite of everything, I can't help feeling sad about poor Léon," said M. Latour. "I had gotten used to thinking of him as a son. I'm going to copy down the address so I can write to him."

"Well," thought Grippard, "Duroc could reveal some things to him of a sort which would hardly recommend me to M. Latour; let's try to persuade him not to write to this young fool."

As soon as they had left the bank, he said to M. Latour: "If I were you, I wouldn't start writing to that fortune hunter who, I'm sure, hasn't had enough decency to send you his regards. However he might have behaved when he was with you, I assure you that the life he led here was too scandalous to warrant your taking any further interest in him. Promise me you won't write him. That would be beneath your dignity."

"I promise, since you insist. But I'm keeping his regimental address so I can find out about his conduct from his commanding officer."

"You're very goodhearted to worry about such a rascal," said Grippard, miffed that he hadn't been completely successful.

"Pardon me, M. Grippard, but I find it hard to believe that a man who has more or less sold his life to the Americans so he could pay me back is a rogue. On the contrary, I conclude that there is still some remnant of honor left in him. I have made up my mind not to consider him my friend any longer, but if I learn that he is conducting himself properly in his regiment, I'll have the pleasure of being able to pardon him for a moment's madness, which, I admit, could have had dire consequences both for him and for me."

"Bah! If the Confederates kill him, it'll be the hangman's loss."

With that, the two friends took their leave, not too happy with each another, but, nevertheless, professing once again their mutual friendship.

CHAPTER XXVII

IT JUST GOES TO SHOW...

H ave you heard anything about Léon?"

That was the first thing Louise asked her father after kissing him when he returned from Montréal.

"Yes, I have — very bad news, unfortunately." Louise turned pale.

"Has something awful happened to him?

"That's a long story. Give me a minute to take off my coat. In the meantime, to reassure you, let me tell that you he's alive and probably in good health. I did not see him in person."

As he said that, M. Latour went into another room and, knowing that Louise was on tenterhooks, he soon returned. Alas, the poor man suspected that his tale would hardly bring his daughter any consolation, but he hastened to bring her up to date on how things stood.

"Forget Léon," he told her. "He's an ungrateful wretch. He spent a few days in Montréal frequenting dens of iniquity. He lost the $1,000 that I had entrusted to him. He didn't even go to Pincemaille and Co. Finally, he slipped away and enlisted in the American army."

When she heard this, Louise cried out, pressed her hands to her forehead, and fell over backwards.

M. and Mme. Latour rushed to her side.

"Daughter! Daughter!" cried M. Latour, his voice choked with anguish. "Come around. I'm a brute. I should have broken the news to you more gently. Speak to me!"

Not as upset as her husband, Mme. Latour had opened the window and was coming back with some cold water to bathe Louise's face and forehead when Louise opened her eyes and got up.

"It's nothing," she said sadly. "Father, tell me everything you know about this unfortunate man whom I still love and who, because of his dissolute behavior, has no doubt gone off to get himself killed because he couldn't bear to live with the shame of what he had done."

M. Latour told her what he had learned about Léon and, when he said that undoubtedly Léon had used his bonus to pay the note, Louise interrupted him.

"That's my own dear Léon, always noble and forever honest! Despite appear ances, after that magnificent gesture I find it hard to believe he strayed from the straight and narrow path. But tell me, Father, besides M. Grippard, whom I detest cordially, did someone else tell you Léon behaved badly in Montréal?"

"No, but I have every confidence in M. Grippard's word. He's a very respectable man — besides, why would he want to slander him? What's more, Léon's flight is proof of his guilt. My $1,000 was completely spent. He had lost the money in one fell swoop gambling and he went to New York to avoid going to prison."

"To prison?"

"Most likely he would not have been able to replace the money he had embezzled and…"

"And you would have had him arrested?"

"I'm not saying that, but he might have believed I would."

"Well, I think he went there with only one purpose in mind: to pay you back. If he weren't honest, what would have prevented him from keeping for himself the money he received from the American government? Even though he runs the risk of getting killed while he's in the American army, he's safe from any legal measures you might take. He was robbed in Montréal, and perhaps those who are accusing him of misconduct have something to do with the theft."

"You're raving, my girl. Your grief is causing you to make unjust accusations. What? Question worthy M. Grippard's honesty? That's madness."

"And what about Léon's honesty, questioned by the same M. Grippard; doesn't that mean anything to you?"

"Léon's honesty! We know all about that," Mme. Latour interrupted. "I never wanted to accuse him while he was staying with us because I was afraid of bringing M. Latour's wrath down upon him. I still wouldn't be saying anything if that were possible. But, seeing that Louise persists in believing he's a little saint, it's my duty to speak up. Well, then, you should know he tried twenty times over to make me forget my wedding vows."

"You're lying, Madame!" said Louise, beside herself.

Then, thinking better of it, Louise said, "Pardon me. I don't know what I'm saying any more."

And she left the room to go off to cry in her own bedroom.

Mme. Latour, as we have said before, was better at being coquettish than she was at being intelligent. In making the supposed revelation, she had several goals in mind. She thought she'd get revenge for Léon's disdain, hurt Louise whom she considered a rival, make M. Latour believe he had an ever-faithful wife, and boast of having made a conquest without meaning to.

All these possibilities had rushed confusedly through her obtuse mind. She had spoken impulsively without realizing that she risked overshooting the mark by stating that she had repulsed Léon's alleged advances twenty times.

Louise had understood perfectly the absurdity of her stepmother's accusation and, shut away in her room, she asked herself as she sobbed how it could be that everyone seemed to have ganged up to slander Duroc. Since her stepmother had no compunction about accusing him so brazenly, was it not possible that Grippard had acted likewise? Little by little she persuaded herself that a plot had been hatched against her fiancé, and she almost believed that Mme. Latour and M. Grippard had conspired to blacken the reputation of her absent beloved.

As she thought about Léon's being a victim of those two conspirators' machinations, she felt her love for him growing even stronger.

She knew that her stepmother was a coquette and she had suffered from this in silence, trembling for fear that her father would notice and be upset. She had observed how Mme. Latour had made advances to Léon and how coldly he had repulsed them. And now, this very same woman was claiming that Léon had tried to seduce her — not just once, but twenty times.

If Louise had not been certain Léon had never felt anything but antipathy for Mme. Latour, the declaration which Mme. Latour had just made might have made her believe Léon was her accomplice — more so than her seducer. After all, it was hardly natural for a respectable woman to force herself to be constantly showering with kindness a man who had made twenty improper advances.

And Louise was quite sure that neither Mme. Latour's flirtations nor Léon's coldness were staged. She had seen them together when neither one suspected they were being observed. She had recalled those circumstances, which she had never told to a soul, when she heard Mme. Latour unjustly accuse the man she had vainly tried to inflame. At that moment, enraged by her stepmother's effrontery, Louise had thrown caution to the winds; she had called her stepmother an outright liar.

Then, Louise, realizing that to defend Léon to her father she would have to tell him the truth about his wife, had preferred to apologize to the very person she secretly despised, rather than make him miserable.

As for M. Latour, when his wife had made her supposed revelation, he had cried out, "What? The wretch! Twenty times! And you didn't say a word to me about it? I'd have wrung his neck. And that vile seducer wanted to marry my daughter! What am I saying? He bewitched her so completely she'll be forlorn her whole life long because of him. She was just disrespectful to you. Please forgive her. She's ill, poor child. She's deranged and can't see things clearly. But I pray you, Rosalie, in the future if anyone tries to flirt with you, be so good as to tell me the very first time it happens. I assure you, I'll straighten things out."

"You have too much of a temper; you'd make a scene."

"But, you, you poor soul! Do you wish to expose yourself to the obsessive behavior of boors like Duroc?"

"Have confidence in me; I'm virtuous enough and strong enough to fend off and discourage them without making a fuss. As a matter of fact, Duroc had completely stopped bothering me when he left."

"But tell me. Has anyone else ever dared to force his attentions on you?"

"Never. The others are not as tenacious. A look, a reproach suffices. They don't try again."

"What sort of times are we living in? Good heavens!" cried M. Latour. "Are all men libertines these days?"

And he went into his store.

Mme. Latour's boasting had backfired. Louise hadn't believed her and, for the first time, M. Latour felt that green serpent, jealousy, gnawing at his heart.

CHAPTER XXVIII

A Letter from Léon

M. Latour, torn between wanting to hear about Duroc and the resentment he felt toward him, based on his wife's testimony, wondered whether or not he should write to Fort Trumbull. He had difficulty believing Duroc would have made advances to Mme. Latour twenty times over if she hadn't given him some encouragement. Either his wife was lying or she had behaved quite improperly by indulging Léon. Léon had always struck him as too sensible and prudent to risk angering over and over a woman who could have ruined him with just one word.

The reason Mme. Latour put forward to explain why she had thought it best to remain silent while the alleged guilty party was in residence didn't seem plausible to him. And the admission she had let slip regarding her less enterprising admirers didn't say much either about the strength of her moral character or her intelligence. M. Latour told himself that a woman who, by her own admission, let men showing her disrespect off with just a word, a reproach, and allowed all that to happen without alerting her husband, was scarcely worthy of his confidence.

Mme. Latour admitted having deceived him by neglecting to tell him about threats to his honor; how could he not believe that she might have failed in her wifely duty, if, among the many admirers whose advances she boasted of having tolerated, there had been one capable of inspiring one of those whims that flirtatious women are prone to? And how could he believe a woman who would risk besmirching her honor? Yes, he would write Léon; he would heap reproaches on him, and he knew he would be quite capable of sorting out the truth in the reply the soldier sent him.

He had reached this point in his musings when his mail was brought to him. Sorting through it, one letter caught his attention. It was addressed to Louise; one of the postmarks on it was from Washington, D.C.

M. Latour had no difficulty recognizing Léon's writing. He was already starting to tear the envelope open when he stopped himself. Should he open this letter? Bah! His daughter should have nothing to hide from him, and besides, wasn't it his duty to protect her from the criminal intrigues of the man who had tried to seduce his wife? He broke the seal telling himself that he'd be able to read this Don Juan's villainous intentions between the lines. The letter read as follows:

My dear Louise,

Please allow the man who no longer dares call you his fiancée to send you his regards. Alas, why was I allowed to glimpse so much happiness? You'll remember the reasons sealing my lips and preventing me from revealing my tender secret — the secret I would never have dared to confess if you hadn't had the kindness to make me do so. After the somewhat heated scene between M. Latour and me that followed, your worthy father was good enough to promise that he would smooth away the difficulties along the road I had to travel to reach the highest goal, the object of my dearest wishes. May heaven reward him for his great goodness. Whatever happens, I'll be eternally grateful to him.

I went to Montréal with high hopes for the future. Your father had entrusted me with the sum of $1,000 to pay off a note. Since the director of Pincemaille and Co. was absent, I came back to the hotel, where, to my misfortune, I ran into a rich merchant who shall remain nameless. Suffice it to say that he is a friend of your father's, who has held him up to me more than once as a role model. For once, I regret to say, M. Latour's usual insight failed him completely. The tradesman in question is a thief — nothing more, nothing less. I know what I'm talking about because he's the one who, with the help of two accomplices, swindled me out of your father's $1,000. I won't go into details about the plan he hatched and carried out to rob me. I'm ashamed to tell you how naive I was. Would to God I could have seen then how he was manipulating me as clearly as I see it now. I'll only tell you this much: supposedly I was to lend him the money for just a few hours; he gave me his word in the presence of two witnesses, his accomplices. I thought I had every reason to believe they were respectable; but, when I came get the money back the next day, they had the gall to deny, as he did, having any knowledge of the transaction.

What could I do? I saw myself dishonored, sullied in your eyes and your father's. Suicide seemed the only way for me to escape my shame. I chose a compromise by enlisting in the American army which gave me enough money to pay off the note. I am in possession of a receipt from the People's Bank. My honor is saved, but I find it impossible to carry through with the plans we had made for our future happiness.

I've already been under fire, but until now, enemy bullets haven't touched me. Fate has so cruelly thwarted our plans; I have so completely lost all hope of marrying the only person in the world I could ever love that I would consider death to be a blessing. I've enlisted for five years. If I survive all the battles we have yet to fight, I'll leave the army as poor as I am now, and much less expert in commercial affairs.

Under these circumstances, as a man of honor, I must free you from your promises. I no longer have a future, and I don't want to chain you to my sorry fate. Forget me and find happiness with another. I will have no right to complain and I won't do so. However, if truth be told, I'll go to my grave loving you. Perhaps I should not have written you, but I owed you an explanation. I value your esteem too much to let appearances make you think the less of me. I swear before God that I've remained worthy of you.

I am convinced that a man honored by your love is even more obligated than other men to lead a life free of all reproach. So, I'll strive to live always as if you knew my innermost thoughts. Though I can no longer dream of marrying you, I'll be faithful to my memories of you. I will never marry and you will always be my guardian angel preventing me from straying from the path of duty. I'd like very much to hear from you, but if you find it too painful to tell me that you are putting me out of your mind, don't write. I'll understand your silence and won't love you any the less for it. I've discovered that love without hope, with all its hardships, also has its charms. Don't try to justify my actions to your father. You won't succeed. Appearances are against me.

Your adoring,
Léon Duroc

CHAPTER XXIX

LOUISE IN DESPAIR

As he read that letter, M. Latour was moved to tears. He had no difficulty recognizing Grippard as the merchant Duroc was writing about. He remembered how quick M. Grippard had been to accuse Duroc. He also recalled how Grippard had insisted that he shouldn't write to Léon. On the other hand, although Duroc's letter had the ring of truth that convinces even the most incredulous of souls, it didn't contain enough details to shake M. Latour's faith in M. Grippard. It would have been enough to convince Louise, but, as for M. Latour, it only caused him to say: "One of two things has to be true: either Duroc is a consummate hypocrite or Grippard is an out-and-out scoundrel."

Then he came to the conclusion that Léon had probably lost the $1,000 gambling as M. Grippard had told him, but that Grippard was probably the one who had won the sum of money. If this were so, both would have had reason to hide the truth. Duroc, after losing the money, would have tried to get it back by saying that the money belonged to his employer and Grippard had probably refused! Thinking back their conversation, M. Latour remembered also that M. Grippard had seemed troubled when he had shaken hands with him at the Hotel Canada.

Then he wondered if he should give the letter to Louise, but he told himself: "That boy is right. Even if he has done nothing to violate the laws of decency and honor, his present circumstances make it impossible for him ever to marry Louise. I find it very generous of him to release her from her promise of his own accord, but Louise would never take it that way. She would answer him and everything would start all over again. We'll keep the letter.

"I'm going to write his regimental commanding officer to find out about him. If he behaved dishonorably in Montréal, he must have continued to behave the same way in the army. I'll keep this letter, and I won't show it either to Louise or my wife. When I have received news of Duroc, and if I find out that he is behaving honorably, I'll write him personally and ask him to explain himself. Until then, nobody must know I've received this letter."

When the family had gathered for dinner, M. Latour said to Louise, whose eyes were red with tears, "Dry your tears, child. If Duroc were still at Fort Trumbull, I would write to him and you could write to him also. But Fort Trumbull is just a depot. I'm going to write to the commanding officer there to get the address of Duroc's regiment and we'll soon have some firsthand news about him."

"You're very kind, Father, and I thank you for this new proof of your goodness."

However, two weeks went by before M. Latour did as he promised, for it pained him greatly to doubt M. Grippard's integrity. On the first of July, he received a letter from Major Thatcher, the commanding officer, written from the siege lines before Petersburg, informing him that Duroc had distinguished himself by his bravery and good conduct since he had known him, that he had been mortally wounded during the siege of Petersburg on June 20, and that he had died in the hospital on the 23rd.

Louise was thunderstruck when she heard this. Her parents vainly tried to break the news to her gently. She had feared such a calamity since she had first heard that Léon had gone off to war and it left her grief-stricken. She refused to be comforted. Since Léon's letter was still being kept from her, she wondered why he hadn't written her. She felt he should have trusted her enough to confide in her about his troubles.

She had pardoned him, however, and she intended to love him always, in spite of everything. She had feared for the life of her beloved, and perhaps exaggerated, if that were possible, the dangers surrounding him; nevertheless, she clung tenaciously to the faint remaining hope that she might see him safe and sound one day.

And now this letter was removing her last shred of hope. She remained for some time dry-eyed, staring straight ahead of her, heavy-hearted, crushed by the weight of her grief. Then tears flooded from her eyes, assuaging her grief just in time and saving her from death or madness. Swearing that she would never marry, that she would remain faithful to Léon's memory, she went off to cry her eyes out freely.

Then, to console her, her father gave her Léon's letter. She no doubt felt a bittersweet joy as she thought that at least Léon had loved her right up to his very last breath, but she felt growing in her heart the regret that she had not been able to answer him.

"Father," she said to him sweetly, "you should have given me this letter. Perhaps, driven to despair by my silence, and thinking that it meant I'd forgotten him, he took greater risks than he might have if he had been sure I still loved him. What noble feelings he expresses! What refinement! Ah, that's my dear Léon. How right I was to persist in believing you were honorable — even if I was the only one to do so."

She refused to eat a thing, cried all night long, and the next day the poor child came down with a brain fever which kept her hovering between life and death for a month. Her mind wandered; she no longer recognized anyone; and she reproached her father bitterly, saying that he was responsible for Léon's death. Finally, her robust constitution, helped by medical care, triumphed over her illness. She regained consciousness and was soon up and about. Her cries of intense grief gave away to a gentle melancholy. Not daring to put on mourning for fear of causing gossip, she resolved, nevertheless, to dress only in black. That is to say, she put on mourning dress, except for the black armband. Smiling sadly, she said that that black, better than any other color, "seemed to suit her sad thoughts."[1]

Her family tried in vain to take her mind off her sorrows. She avoided the gatherings, dances, and parties that young women her age are so fond of, saying that the sight of those worldly pleasures, far from taking her mind off her sorrows, saddened her even more.

CHAPTER XXX

THAT WORTHY M. GRIPPARD

Dear reader, you already know that M. Grippard was one of those "respectable" con men whose reputation as rich men shield from censure. Charlatans have existed in every country since the beginning of time, but there has never been a land of golden opportunity so full of so many plums ripe for the picking as the American continent. The Yankee himself, despite his apparent skepticism, loves to be taken in; he'll always get even by taking someone else in another day. Anyone who doubts this has only to look at the long list of huge fortunes amassed in the United States from the sale of some universal panacea widely touted in newspapers all over the country.[1]

In America, more than anywhere else, the quack carries his head high. He is as respected and admired as he is successful. And that cynical P.T. Barnum, that prototypical American pitchman, knew his audience well when he published a book where he modestly proposed himself as a model to be imitated by all those wishing to be rich and famous.

We would be wrong, however, to cast stones at our neighbors. We here [in Canada] do on a small scale what they bring off there on a large one. They would not have been the last ones to notice that playing jokes on people is very popular here. For a long time now, they've been sending us their drugs and their quack medicines.[2] Like them, we have our political charlatans here — our religion peddlers, our conscience dealers, our overrated reputations, and our idols with feet of clay. We bow down before the golden calf as much as they do, and, if we can't surpass their servile admiration for gilded vice, the honest man convicted of the crime of chronic and inveterate poverty is much more deeply despised here than he is in the United States.

Let's talk about men like M. Grippard. Here's a man who didn't let a little thing like scruples stop him! He always had money in his pocket. He was, therefore, a very respectable man. Admittedly, there were some who claimed that his conduct while he was in Montréal wasn't beyond reproach. They were but envious nobodies. How can you believe in a nonentity without two pennies to rub together? Isn't virtue always being persecuted?

Five or six years earlier, M. Grippard, who was at the time without a blessed cent, and therefore not yet respectable, had formed a partnership with an honest man of independent means to build a steamboat.

The rich man supplied the money and M. Grippard furnished the experience. Three years later, M. Grippard was the one who had the money and his associate had the experience. Consequently, his partner had become a man without standing in the community while M. Grippard had earned the reputation of being a respectable man. Virtue is always rewarded.

Nothing is handier than a maxim if you have money. If people dare to blame you, they are persecuting your virtue. Have your guilty efforts been crowned with success? There will be plenty of flatterers proclaiming that heaven is rewarding your virtue. M. Grippard had set up business in Montréal where he had opened an agency. In his capacity as broker he had managed to fleece a lot of men. Shortly thereafter, he rented an estate, built a mechanized sawmill, and opened a store in a parish very close to Pingreville. He formed a corporation with several backers and founded a new navigation company. He had acquired a taste for that type of business dealing. For his associates, it was just as good a way as any of throwing their money down the drain.

Always using other people's money, Grippard, who had never had any his own, founded the Picourdy Sawmill Company with a subscribed capital investment of $300,000. Being founder and manager of that company with a salary of $1,000 per year did not prevent him from borrowing heavily against it. When we first met him, he had five or six stores in various parishes, and bakeries just about everywhere. He had set out to corner the flour monopoly between Picourdy and Montréal. He was manager of the two companies we have just mentioned and was thought to be in possession of an immense fortune.

He spent money freely, threw around other people's money as if it were his own, and lived like a lord. He frequented the Saint Fortunatus Club for the purpose of recruiting dupes or investors — who were one and the same to him — rather than to gamble. He was a hard drinker, but knew how to feign sobriety when necessary. He spread his money around, dazzled gullible men, and knew from experience that, in this country, a man who does not pay his debts but spends a lot commands far more confidence than the honest man who manages to settle his accounts by dint of economizing.

"It's not my fault," he was wont to say, "if people are so stupid. You have to live in grand style to have unlimited credit. If some poor devil has the misfortune to find himself short of money, all his creditors join forces to crush him. So long as you dazzle them, they'll jostle to be first in line to mark you down for credit in their ledgers."

He had known poverty. He had been despised by the very people who now groveled at his feet and hung on his every word. He had told himself that honesty doesn't get you anywhere. So he had thrown himself into a life of speculation and shady dealings. Handling a lot of gold intoxicated him. What did the rest matter?

He preferred being praised by imbeciles to having the satisfaction which comes from doing one's duty. In that respect, he was hardly any different from other hypocrites who, unfortunately, are only too numerous. What distinguished him most from the others was his unbridled audacity. In business, M. Grippard was a dyed-in-the-wool Yankee businessman. He was a hard bargainer. His lavish spending quite often left him broke, and then, no matter what, he managed to get the money he needed, caring very little about what he had to do to get it.

Bagoulard and Bohémier were just his drinking companions. He knew they had no more money than they had principles. So he didn't seek them out to exploit them. They were both witty and talented, but Grippard wasn't so naive as to admire them just for these meager attributes. He had become their friend quite simply because they had introduced him to a world men who lead well-ordered lives are not in the habit of frequenting.

Bagoulard was a lawyer famous for his eloquence, but he was still too young to inspire much confidence as a legal expert. Besides, it was well known that he did not spend much time studying the legal code. Since he devoted more time to carousing than he did preparing his briefs, his practice didn't bring in much money.

As for Bohémier, despite his undeniable talent, he seemed irrevocably destined to lead the life of a student from here to eternity. He wrote poetry with quite a bit of success and his naughty verse delighted the demimonde he traveled in. He was a bohemian in every sense of the word. He had no scruples about exploiting his most intimate friends, and, without their indulgence, and the frequent intervention of a rich uncle who protected him, he would have been imprisoned twenty times over.

CHAPTER XXXI

PHANTASMAGORIA
WITHIN REACH
OF THE WORKING POOR

Y ou'll remember that, after his suicide attempt, Léon had handed all his wringing wet clothes to the bellboy at the Hotel Canada to have them dried. Besides
his undergarments, his outfit included a brown overcoat, pearl-gray trousers,
and the black dress jacket mentioned by Grippard when he described Duroc to M.
Latour. Because our hero had left the very next day, firmly resolved to join the American army, he had not bothered to reclaim his clothes which, in any case, were still
damp. As a result, the bellboy had inherited the outfit in question.

We have said that the boy looked a lot like Duroc. He was the same height and
had the same features and expression. He was exactly like Duroc except for his hair.
The bellboy had straight blond hair while our hero's hair was dark and curly. This
double of Louise's lover was called Brindamour. He was mischievous and intelligent,
but he had the deplorable habit of listening at doors and he took pleasure in playing
tricks — some of which were pretty rotten. He was a friend of Bohémier's, who met
him often at the home of a hussy more remarkable for her beauty than her virtue.
Needless to say, that while Brindamour physically resembled Duroc, he didn't act like
our hero in the least. We would have preferred him to be perfect, but rascal we found
him and thus do we present him. We'll add, however, that he wasn't really an evil person. He was a flighty rake as so many are in large cities. He didn't have the same social
standing as Bohémier, but vice is a leveler that brings together men which social dif-
ferences seem to keep apart. It goes without saying that they pretended not to know
each other when they met in public and, when Bohémier went to the hotel, they
chatted with each other only if they were quite sure they wouldn't be seen.

Several days after Grippard and M. Latour had run into each other at the Hotel
Canada, Brindamour put on the suit which he had come by easily thanks to his dou-
ble's unexpected departure, and went off to see his Dulcinea. There he ran into
Bohémier.

"Say there, you're certainly all dressed up!" Bohémier remarked. "My, my, it looks
like you inherited that suit from a certain country boy I know."

"I'm probably not the only heir," retorted Brindamour, stung to the quick. "And
if I wanted to, I could say something about people who haven't taken the old man to
the cleaners yet but have done a better job than I have on the young one."

"What do you mean by that?"

"I know what I'm saying. I overheard a certain conversation which told me all I need to know about the people who drove that young man to suicide."

"But what, exactly, did you hear?"

"The day after the incident that brought you, Bagoulard, and Grippard to the hotel — you know, the night when this suit of clothes was placed in my keeping — Grippard suggested that the young man forge his employer's signature. He refused and they exchanged heated words. I didn't feel like putting my hands over my ears so I know enough to harm you if I wanted to tell what I know. But I'm a good-natured sort, and, since I'm basically a curious fellow, I'd rather not tell anyone provided you tell me the rest of the story."

"As for me, I don't mind telling you what I know. You've confided in me; I'll confide in you. Does that suit you?"

"Perfectly. Let's go."

The two cronies went to a nearby restaurant where they sat down at a table and told each other what they knew about the Duroc affair.

"Do you know," said Bohémier, "that sometimes I suspect you're a secret service agent?"

"And you're not far from the truth. Since we're friends, I can tell you that much. The detective at the hotel on the night in question could tell you a few things."

"Oh, him. You can tell him what you like about me. He's one of us."

"Damn you! I'm not in the habit of ratting on my friends."

"Speaking of Grippard, he told me the day before yesterday that Duroc had enlisted in the American army and that he had paid off his employer's note. He claims that he is going to write Duroc to give him back the $1,000, but I don't believe a word of it. He is telling me that so I won't ask to split the take. He's not stupid. The Americans are really going at it right now, and Grippard is hoping to inherit that $1,000 — besides, he's never had the slightest intention of repaying it. Just between us, he has been very stingy with Bagoulard and me. He only gave us $25 apiece and what we did was worth a ten percent commission at least."

"Would you like me to really scare him out of his wits? I think I look like Duroc. If I had a curly black wig, some makeup to darken my mustache, and this outfit, he would think I was Duroc."

"That's a wonderful idea, but it would be even better if Duroc were dead, as he probably will be before long; then Grippard will think you are his victim's ghost. In the meantime, don't let anyone see you in that outfit. Keep it for our experiments. As for the wig, I'll get you one. I know a wig-maker who'll let me have one on credit because I have an honest face and who won't ever get paid a cent for it. Have you ever heard anything about phantasmagoria?"[1]

"Don't know him."[2]

"Well, it's the art of making ghosts appear. You've seen magic lanterns, haven't you?"

"Certainly, but I don't see what that has to do with our conversation."

"Hold on a minute, blabbermouth, and let me explain. With the magic lantern, you make life-sized portraits and other figures appear on a screen. Light simply passes through the drawings which are enlarged and reproduced on the screen placed at the back of a darkened room. Now suppose the screen is placed between the lantern and the viewer. That way the person would see forms in space seeming to rush toward him only to vanish immediately. There's nothing to stop you from making yourself up to look like Duroc. You could put on those clothes and your image could be sent through the keyhole of our worthy M. Grippard's bedroom door. You're a ventriloquist and you could give him a short lecture — but to do that, we have to wait till Duroc is dead. That won't be long."

"That 'fantastic gorilla' must be a wonderful science and I intend to learn all about it."

"Start by learning the right name," Bohémier replied, laughing. "I said 'phantasmagoria.'"

"Phantas...?"

" — magoria."

"Phantasmagoria. The devil you say! If the science is as difficult as the name, I'll need to spend some time learning how to do it."

"It's not that difficult. Besides, we'll study it together. We'll set up a few experiments."

"Yes, but while we're waiting for Duroc to die, couldn't we send a few little devils through M. Grippard's keyhole?"

"Nothing easier, if we're only talking about sending some simple luminous shapes glowing in the dark without precise outlines — simple shapes like paper cutouts. I'll take care of that."

"And what about M. Grippard, what if he knows about that — the phantasmagoria?"

"Him? Go on, now. Not even very many educated people know about this art, and M. Grippard barely knows how to read and write."

"When shall we try our first experiment?"

"Tomorrow evening. I'll go to the hotel, and, if I run into M. Grippard, I'll come up with some sort of excuse to leave him. We'll go to work practicing in his room while he's out. Above all, don't say anything to anyone about this."

"Calm down. And don't tell anyone I've inherited Duroc's clothes either."

And the two conspirators took leave of each other to go back to their respective lodgings.

CHAPTER XXXII

PHANTASMAGORIA PUT TO THE TEST

Do you have any ice?" Bohémier asked the next evening as soon as he saw that he was alone with Brindamour.

"We can get some. Do we need a lot?"

"Two or three pieces as large as your fist."

Brindamour soon came back with the ice Bohémier had asked for.

"Here's some potassium," said Bohémier, displaying some bits of a silvery white metallic substance he had in a piece of paper. "I'm going to set the ice on fire."

"Are you crazy?"

"Not at all, and I'll prove it."

He had placed one of the pieces of ice — on which he dropped a bit of potassium — on the floor; as it began to burn, reddish flames burst forth.

The metal burned a hole through the ice, then went out as it turned to potash.

"That's the trick," said Bohémier. "What we have left is a piece of ice with a hole in it and a bit of potassium oxide — potash, if you will. Old Grippard will have a fit when he sees it."

"That's all well and good, but I don't see how we're going to manage to put your potash on the ice without Grippard noticing it."

"First of all, it isn't potash; it doesn't become potash until after it burns."

"Well then, its crude potash."

"Crude yourself. And you always will be. You'll never change.[1] But I've already foreseen the difficulty you're pointing out. I'll carve a piece of ice so it slopes gradually down to a ridge on one side. I'll cover this slope with a piece of paper and I'll leave the ridge exposed. The potassium will slide slowly down the slope so some time will elapse before it ignites, since it has to reach the ridge first. I just happen to have a piece of ice which seems to have the right shape. Let's try it out."

They wrapped the piece of ice, taking care to cover the ridge so as not to waste the potassium needlessly. The substance took only five minutes to slide from the top to the ridge.

"Now I'll go down to keep M. Grippard company and I'll tell him ghost stories. When he's ready to go to bed, I'll call for a round. That will be the signal. You'll serve us. Then you'll go right up to his room to get everything ready. Be sure you wrap the potassium well. Do you have a spot we can watch him from without being seen?"

"In winter, a stovepipe goes through the wall of the next room into his. It's unoc-cupied now. There's a hole in the wall about seven to eight feet above the floor; at the moment there's a tinplate covering it. I'm going to remove it and bring over a steplad-der so we can easily climb on top of it to see what effect our trick is having."

"That's the idea, but we mustn't have any light in that room or he'll get suspi-cious."

This plan was put into effect down to the last detail. Toward midnight, Grippard went up to his room after drinking one last glass with Bohémier and some other com-panions. He quickly got undressed, kneeled by the side of his bed for a few minutes — more out of habit than devotion — then put out his lamp and got into bed.

He was just about to go to sleep when he caught sight of a sort of smoldering object on the carpet in the middle of his room. It shot forth little reddish sparks and partially lit the room which had been pitch black only a moment before. His first thought was to shout "fire." He sat bolt upright, rubbed his eyes, and realized some-thing which scared him half to death: it wasn't the floor of his room that was burn-ing.

Through the eerie glimmer of the sparks, he could make out a glowing body reflecting the flames like a mirror. His imagination, overheated by the stories he had heard before going to bed, and even more so by the unexpected spectacle greeting his alarmed gaze, made him believe he was witnessing a manifestation of the supernatu-ral in this phenomenon.

A shiver of horror passed through his body. He would have liked to convince himself that he was having a bad dream, but he felt wide awake and the glowing ember was still there — as if to taunt him. He made an especially large sign of the cross. The fire burned on. He then jumped out of bed and let out a cry. At that very instant a loud noise like the sound of a heavy object falling from the ceiling came from the next room and the light went out. Grippard lit his lamp. He looked at the spot where he had seen the fire, and found a piece of ice which he didn't dare touch, imagining that only the devil himself could have transformed a burning ember into ice.

Grippard's shout caught Brindamour and Bohémier off-guard. But Brindamour had the presence of mind to jump down off the ladder, making a lot of noise, so as to frighten Grippard all the more. He got right back on the ladder, handed Bohémier the tinplate cover, and whispered: "Take that and block the hole. Stay here and don't make a sound. I'm going to his room to ask him what's the matter."

He then went out and resolutely knocked at Grippard's door.

"Come in," said Grippard.

"Was that you crying out, M. Grippard? Are you ill? What can I do for you?"

"It's nothing," said Grippard. "I was dreaming. Did you hear something else besides me crying out? I thought I heard something falling."

"I heard you cry out. That's all I heard."

"What's that?" Grippard said, pretending to be surprised as he looked at the piece of ice."

"A piece of ice," said Brindamour. "The maid must have dropped it instead of putting it in your water. I'm going to throw it out and bring you another piece."

"Good. Throw it out, but don't bring me any more. If you don't mind, come back here; you'll sleep with me. I'm not well. Bring up two glasses of cognac for us."

"I'll be right back," said Brindamour, as he went out taking the redoutable piece of ice with him. Although it had a hole in it, it could still be put to use another time.

Once he was out of the room, he walked heavily pretending to go away; he then tiptoed back to join Bohémier.

"Now you're stuck spending the night with Grippard," said Bohémier, "but you don't give a damn. You're going to do some drinking, both of you. By the way, could you bring a third glass? Grippard doesn't usually check the bill when he pays."

"I'll see that you get your thirst quenched. Stay here and behave yourself. I've got the piece of ice. It's still usable. Do you still have some potassium?"

"Here's the paper with the metal in it. Since you're going to spend the night with him in his room, it'll be easy to begin the experiment all over again. As for me, I'm going to stay here and enjoy the show. When you get through with the potassium, I'll send a series of little devils through the keyhole. I have everything I need here to do that."

"Why, that's wonderful! We'll have great fun. I'll hurry off to get something to wet dear M. Grippard's whistle."

Brindamour went downstairs, then returned a few minutes later, carrying the tray with three glasses. Bohémier took his glass and went to his hiding place after saying: "If he asks you what you see, answer that you don't see a thing."

Grippard and Brindamour lifted a few together. Then the bellboy began to get undressed.

"If you follow my advice," Grippard said, "we won't go to bed now. I'm going to get dressed again; we'll talk. I'm not sleepy."

"But I have to get up early," answered Brindamour. "Besides, you're indisposed, I think; your pallor proves it. A little sleep will do you good. After all, if you want to talk, we'll talk after we're in bed."

Brindamour could have added that the ice was melting in his pants pocket and that it was making him uncomfortable, but for some reason or other, he didn't feel it was appropriate to tell Grippard that.

"As you wish," said Grippard who got back into bed and pulled the covers over his head.

Brindamour got undressed, put out the lamp, unwrapped the piece of ice, put it exactly where it had been before, threw the rest of the potassium on it, and went to bed.

When he saw that his companion was getting into bed, Grippard stuck his head out from under the covers and placed himself so that Brindamour could make himself comfortable. Instinctively his gaze turned toward the spot where he had seen the apparition and, horrors! The fire was still there, burning with newfound fury. Grippard crossed himself again, but this time it didn't work. His hair stood straight up on his head.

"Boy," he said, trying vainly to stop his voice from quivering, "do you think this hotel is haunted?"

"No, I've never heard tell that it was; besides, I don't believe in all those fantastic apparitions people keep harping about."

"Well, then how do you explain what we see over there, right in the middle of the room?"

"Me? I don't see a thing. Do you?"

"I beg your pardon. I see fire and if you don't see it, you must be blind."

"Fire? Come on, now. Excuse me for saying so, but you must be dreaming."

"You're the one who's dreaming. You mean you don't see those flames that look like they're coming out of the floor?"

"Why, no. It's as dark as pitch and I don't see a blessed thing."

"Then I must be seeing things. There, it's going out. I bet you we'll find ice on the carpet if we light the lamp."

When he heard this, Brindamour couldn't help himself — he burst out laughing. Grippard, who didn't see anything funny about the whole matter, cried out, "You're laughing and you think this is all very amusing. Well, I'll bet you a hundred bucks against the bill for the drinks that there's ice over there."

"I'll take that bet," said Brindamour, who started to get up to light the lamp.

"Wait a minute," said Grippard. "You might just remove the ice to win the bet. I'm going to light the lamp myself."

"And you're going to put ice on the carpet before you light the lamp."

"So you think I've got some ice? I'm going to light the lamp without getting up. I can reach my matches from here."

"If you find any ice, it's because you put some out there before you went to bed, but since I've placed my bet I won't back out now."

Grippard lit the lamp. The two men got up and examined the carpet.

There wasn't any ice.

Shrunken and melted by the first experiment, and by its stay in Brindamour's pants pocket, and then subjected to the simultaneous workings of several pieces of potassium, the piece of ice had melted away completely.

"You owe me $100," Brindamour said, "but I don't want to take advantage..."

"What do you mean, 'take advantage'? Do you think I'm going to welsh on a bet? I've got your $100 on me and here it is," he added, taking his wallet out of his coat pocket and giving Brindamour his winnings in ten-dollar bills.

"All the same, there's some water here," Grippard commented as he examined the carpet again.

"A minute ago you said there was a fire, then you said there was some ice, now you say there's some water. This time you're right. Of course there's water; you had me pick up a piece of ice when you asked me to come sleep with you."

"You think this is all very strange and you must think I'm drunk. However, I'm not the least bit under the influence of alcohol. I saw fire here and I saw it twice. The first time I found some ice and now I'm finding water. This is all very odd."

"Since I've won the bet, the least I can do is buy us a drink," said Brindamour. "What'll you have?"

"A glass of cognac. But come right back. I'm afraid."

Brindamour brought three more glasses, left one with Bohémier, and came back into the room with the other two.

"Watch out for the little devils now," Bohémier had said to him as he took his glass.

"You didn't see anything while I was away, did you?" Brindamour asked Grippard.

"No, but I was afraid of seeing something. If you don't mind, we'll leave the lamp lit."

He went back to bed and pulled the covers over his eyes.

"What do you say, M. Grippard," said Brindamour, "why don't I get a bottle of brandy? I should have thought about that, but I forgot. You're in a bad way and you might need to have a drop."

As he was speaking, he took the matches and put them in his pocket without Grippard noticing.

"I don't need anything, but if you want to, go ahead, get a bottle," Grippard answered.

As he left, Brindamour said to Bohémier, "Just imagine! That lout wants to leave the lamp lit all night long. But I took away his matches. When I come back, I'll blow out the lamp and pretend I've forgotten what he wanted me to do. Be ready to get to work with your little devils."

When Brindamour returned, he offered Grippard a drink; Grippard drank it right down. Then Brindamour undressed and blew out the lamp.

"What are you doing?" Grippard said. "I told you to leave the lamp lit."

"So you did! But I forgot!"

"Scatterbrain! Light it again!"

Brindamour pretended to fumble around on the table.

"I can't find any matches," he said.

While Brindamour was undressing, Bohémier introduced through the keyhole an apparatus which would project light from a dark lantern into the room. First he projected the light through some devilish shapes which filed past one another between the light source and the lens and were reflected as specters glowing in the dark.

Brindamour had hardly finished speaking when a devil armed with a pitchfork appeared on the wall.

"Do you see that?" Grippard asked, scared to death.

"What do you see now? Fire?"

"What? You don't see that ghost on the wall?"

"My word, if I didn't know you, M. Grippard, I'd think you had a case of *delirium tremens.*"

"There, it's disappearing. Now it's a dragon."

"You're making fun of me."

"Not at all. Light the lamp again, I tell you."

"I told you I didn't have any matches."

"Go get some."

"And leave you alone with the devils?"

"No, stay with me. Now it's a snake!"

"Admit it: as a bedfellow, you're not much fun."

"Here's another devil in profile. He's got snakes entwined around his arms and body."

"Try as hard as you like, you won't manage to scare me."

"But don't you see anything? Here's a whole group of little devils holding hands; they look like they're dancing. Light the lamp or I'm going to yell."

"Do you want me to get a doctor?"

"No, go and get some matches."

Then Brindamour heard a scraping sound as Bohémier pulled his apparatus out of the keyhole.

"Did you hear that sound?" Grippard asked.

"I didn't hear anything. I'm going to look for some matches."

"Come back up as soon as you can. If you see someone downstairs, don't tell them what I saw."

Brindamour went out and rejoined Bohémier.

"That's enough for tonight," Bohémier said. "You won $100; you should give me some of it. Otherwise I might talk. I'll go back to the room with you. I'll tell him I ran into you downstairs, that you told me he wasn't well, and that I followed you back upstairs. He doesn't look like he wants to go to sleep. We're going to help him drink the bottle of brandy you brought back."

"I'm not very sick," Grippard said when Bohémier inquired about his health, "but I do feel like staying up and getting drunk. How does that sound to you?"

"That suits me just fine," Bohémier answered.

They emptied the bottle and Grippard went to bed with his head spinning.

CHAPTER XXXIII

AMONG FRIENDS

The next day, Brindamour and Bohémier split the $100. They agreed not to bother M. Grippard for a while. The experiment performed the night before had sufficed to show him that supernatural phenomena really did exist; he was now all set to be duped by the new tests the two meant to submit him to. At that time, the details involved in starting a new business venture kept Grippard almost constantly in Montréal and he had decided to make the Hotel Canada his home for the time being. The free but mandatory spectacle the two young men had treated him to had impressed him deeply. The very next day, he had consulted a doctor whom he knew to find out if, by chance, he might not have suffered an attack of delirium tremens.

This disciple of Aesculapius[1] who, unlike many of his colleagues, was a studious and observant man, assured Grippard he must have been the victim of a hallucination. Reassured that alcohol had not yet damaged his nervous system, Master Grippard told himself that he could get drunk in his room each night before going to bed with no ill aftereffects. He didn't think this would ward off the ghosts, but he hoped alcohol would give him the courage to stand the sight of them without crying out if they did appear.

"We won't tell anybody about this lugubrious adventure," he told himself. "If it happens again, it's because the room is haunted; if it doesn't, I'll believe, as the doctor does, I was just having a waking nightmare."

Grippard had given some money to Brindamour and made him promise to tell no one about the terrors he had suffered in his presence.

Days and weeks passed without M. Grippard's seeing the ghosts who had frightened him so. He was beginning to forget this adventure when one day, as he was passing through Pingreville, he learned about Duroc's death from M. Latour.

"That's one less scoundrel," said he.

"I beg your pardon," said M. Latour. "I always found him to be an honest young man and I'm saddened by his death."

"Oh! Well, then, please excuse me. I thought that after what had happened to him in Montréal you would have realized you were wrong about him, but I could have been mistaken."

"Lots of things happened to him in Montréal; I should never have let him go there," replied M. Latour. "I don't know why, but sometimes I think that he was victimized by someone seeking to entrap him."

"Well, that's possible; you know him better than I do."

M. Grippard had just noticed he was taking the wrong tack in trying to make M. Latour think less of Duroc. He had started out by slandering Léon to lull the Pingreville tradesman's suspicions, but now he told himself he should have done just the opposite. He suddenly changed tactics and began to sing Léon's praises.

"That beggar has perhaps written a letter denouncing me," he thought. "In that case, the more I praise him the less people will believe him." Then he began again, aloud, "I didn't know that young man very well. I only saw him once or twice. He seemed quite intelligent and very well brought up. I offered to buy him a drink and he refused. I only told you what I'd heard from others who may perhaps have had some reason for wanting to ruin his reputation, and since you are interested in him, I thought I should warn you as a friend."

"You are very kind; I very much appreciate this proof of your friendship."

"Did M. Duroc write you before he died?"

"No. I wrote to the regiment to find out what had happened to him; they wrote back saying he was dead and that he had always conducted himself properly. Here's the letter. You read English, no doubt?"

"Yes, fairly easily."

The letter told in detail how Duroc had been wounded; it ended by saying that he had died of his wound.

"Poor young man!" exclaimed Grippard, trying to sound sad. "If he had stayed here, perhaps he would have had a fine future to look forward to."

M. Latour was touched by the excellent M. Grippard's compassion for poor Léon. He had already forgotten that he had had to defend Léon's reputation a moment earlier.

People who think as we do are always right; all M. Grippard had needed to do to regain M. Latour's full confidence was to agree with his opinion.

M. Grippard, who acted only out of self-interest, had a reason for flattering M. Latour's somewhat changeable moods. As it happened, he had come to see M. Latour to offer him a good investment…one that would be advantageous for himself as the founder and future manager of a new company, and, by the time he left Louise's father, he had "interested" him in investing a considerable amount in the aforesaid company.

On the evening of that very same day, Grippard, back in Montréal, told Bagoulard and Bohémier down to the last detail what was in the letter announcing Duroc's death. He had the effrontery to add that he had sent the $1,000 back to Léon. Unfortunately, Léon had died without acknowledging that he had received payment, or so he said.

"We've caused that poor young man's death," Bagoulard said pensively. "As for me, I've always regretted the part I played in the transaction which led him first to try attempt suicide here and later pushed him to enlist in the American army."

"I feel the same way, said Bohémier. "I know that ill-gotten gains do no one any good — especially the one being fleeced."

"If it's money you need," Grippard answered sharply, "just come right out and say so; I'm sick of hearing your recriminations over and over again. I've had enough of your whining. I paid each of you a large commission and I paid Duroc back the money I had borrowed from him. I don't want to hear any more about it."

Bagoulard frowned. His pale face came to life and his gray eyes flashed. "M. Grippard," he said, "we are not beholden to you, thank God. As for me, I can do without your money. We've condescended to honor you with our friendship — for, let me tell you, you're nothing but a cad, a well-dressed beggar, and you will never again drag me away from the straight and narrow path which I never strayed from except in the company of you and your kind. I'm not asking for money. I'm going to give you back the commission you gave me. It's blood money. I don't want it anymore. From now on, we're finished."

"As for me," said Bohémier, "I'll give you back my commission just like you gave back the money to Duroc. Perhaps I'm not any more honorable than you are. But, while you may have money, I have my intellect. We can't all have everything. I'm going to do like my friend Bagoulard; we're through. I'm not interested in being treated like a slave."

"Wash your hands of me if you like, my little lambs. I won't be any the worse for it and my wallet will be the fatter."

The two friends left, leaving M. Grippard fairly unhappy about the way their conversation had turned out.

In the course of the evening, Bohémier met Brindamour and brought him up to date on what had happened. "Duroc is dead," said Bohémier, "and we've broken off with Grippard. Now's the time, if ever, to try the effect of our concave mirror on him."

Some of our readers have, no doubt, seen those mirrors that some restaurants put in their establishments for publicity and to amuse their patrons. These concave or convex mirrors are attached to the wall on a swivel which allows the mirror to be turned so that the surface can be presented either vertically or horizontally. If they are arranged lengthwise on the vertical, the faces they reflect appear extremely long and gaunt. These are the faces of men who do not eat in the restaurant. If the mirrors are turned on the horizontal, then these same faces appear extremely wide and chubby. These are the faces of the men eating in the establishment. At that time the Hotel Canada had a concave mirror; it was just what was needed for Bohémier's and Brindamour's experiment.

These two interesting characters had acquired an instrument very much like a magic lantern. It had a funnel for trapping the light and a conducting lens which could be inserted into a keyhole so as to project the faces reflected by the concave mirror after reducing them to their natural shape.

Taking advantage of Grippard's absence, they had rehearsed in his room. It was equipped with a wardrobe pushed right up against the wall to the neighboring bedroom described earlier. Brindamour and Bohémier had made a hole in the wall behind an engraving. This hole was in line with a hole through the back of the wardrobe and one through its door, which made it possible to introduce the end of the conducting tube through them.

In the room, a piece of ice, reacting to some sodium or potassium, or just a few drops of warm water scattered over the carpet, could create a column of humid air on which to project the images.

Sure of not being disturbed, the two conspirators could shut themselves up in the room and work at their leisure. Bohémier was to put on a devil mask and place his face right up to the stovepipe hole — partly to intercept the light and also to observe the "patient's" movements.

They had agreed on certain signals to let Brindamour know what Grippard was doing. Brindamour, dressed in Duroc's clothes, placed himself in front of the mirror gesturing and prancing about while his ghost-like reflection executed the same pantomime in Grippard's room.

A curly black wig and some makeup on his mustache and eyebrows made him look like Duroc. Brindamour was a good ventriloquist, so, as he talked, the ghost seemed to be speaking. Both of them had learned their roles so well that they played them to perfection.

On the evening in question, everything was prepared for an extraordinary séance. They had thought of everything. Bohémier had reserved the adjoining room. A piece of ice had been carefully arranged with some potassium on top of it so it would catch fire at just the right moment. It had been placed in Grippard's room a few minutes before he was ready to go to bed. The room next to his was brightly lit. The funnel, mirror, and tube were in place and Brindamour, made up, wearing a costume and wig, was at his post. He was waiting for Bohémier, standing on the stepladder, to give him the signal.

CHAPTER XXXIV

PHANTASMAGORIA REVIEWED, CORRECTED, AND CONSIDERABLY AUGMENTED

M. Grippard had just put out his light and gone to bed. His back was turned away from the spot where the fire had appeared to him a few weeks before. However, since his bed was in the middle of the room, there was a fair amount of space between him and the wall. That space was aligned with the door to the wardrobe which the two operators had chosen as the stage for their experiments. Because Grippard hadn't had any reason to go on that side of the bed, he hadn't noticed the piece of ice that had just been placed on the carpet. He had scarcely gone to bed, as we were saying, when the potassium burst into flame.

Frightened, he was about to get up to light the lamp when a sudden apparition sent shivers up and down his spine. Duroc was there, right in front of him, surrounded by light, pale and eyes flashing.

"What do you want from me?" Grippard asked, his voice trembling.

"What do I want?" answered the ghost. "You dare ask me that? You weren't satisfied with robbing me and causing my death; you sullied my reputation in the eyes of those whose good opinion I valued the most when I was alive. Why, even today, you insulted me by calling me a crook. You have to give me back the $1,000 you extorted from me."

"I don't have the money with me, but I'll give you a check."

As he was saying this, Grippard jumped to the floor, seized a nearby chair with both hands, raised it over his head, and, with all his might, struck a mighty blow at the phantom's head.

Naturally, instead of hitting a solid body, the chair passed completely through the specter from head to toe and crashed on the carpet. Breaking apart, it collided with the piece of ice which shot off like a bullet, then broke into pieces after hitting a vase and shattering it. M. Grippard was still holding the back of the chair in his hands. Since he had swung the chair as if it were going to come into contact with a solid object, the chair-back had recoiled, hitting him in the thigh and making him cry out in pain.

The ghost broke out into gales of laughter.

"If I were still alive," he said, "I'd pull your ears for your lack of respect toward me. You can't do a thing to me; as for me, I've a thousand and one ways of getting my revenge. I'll have no trouble getting $1,000 worth of vengeance out of you."

When he heard the specter asked for reimbursement of the $1,000 he owed Duroc, Grippard decided that such behavior was a bit too worldly and he told himself he was dealing with some sort of flesh and blood scoundrel. He was only half wrong. But instead of wasting his time striking at a shadow, he would have been better off paying a visit to the next room. However, he was miles away from suspecting that mortals could produce phenomena like the one he had just witnessed. Aghast, he stared numbly at the ghost.

"In my world, I've no need of your check," the ghost continued. "I don't have any direct heirs either. My only relative left on earth is my father's natural son. I did not know him when I was alive, but I declare him to be my heir. I'm not asking you to give him the $1,000. He's inexperienced and wouldn't know what to do with it. I want you to take him under your wing and help him out with services worth least one thousand dollars. Set him up in business and I won't ask anything more of you."

"Where is this bastard?" Grippard asked, somewhat reassured.

"In this very hotel. His name is Brindamour and you know him."

"I'll protect him, since you require it."

"Yes, and I demand that you do so immediately. If you don't obey me, you'll hear from me, I warn you."

And the specter vanished, leaving Grippard to his thoughts.

Grippard had told Bohémier and Bagoulard about his conversation with old Latour. Bohémier had, of course, reported everything to Brindamour, which explains why the specter reproached Grippard as he did.

"Not bad," Bohémier whispered to his companion as the latter was removing his makeup in the room where they had set up operations. "The phantasmagoria will make you rich. You showed great presence of mind."

"Grippard's got to protect me," Brindamour replied in the same tone of voice. "Take it from me, we'll keep putting him to the test until he agrees to take me under his wing."

"He's had enough for tonight. And if we return to the attack too often, we could ruin ourselves at this game."

"If he doesn't start protecting me by tomorrow, Léon Duroc's ghost will just have to visit him again tomorrow night."

"I bet he has already lit his lamp again and you know that tomorrow he'll leave it lit all night long."

"Don't worry. I'll fill his lamp three-quarters full with water. I'll put a little oil on top of it, and it will go out as soon as he goes to sleep. Once it's out, we'll make some noise so he'll wake up and we can start our experiment. We'll do without the potassium. I'll put a bit of warm water in his spittoon; that'll give us our column of damp air. We need to vary our show a bit."

"That suits me. Tomorrow, I'll try to get hold of an American uniform; we'll put some red paint on it to look like blood coming out of a wound on the left shoulder. I'll also have a rifle and the whole outfit."

"Fortunately we've thought about what might happen if he changed rooms — and that could very well be the case. We don't have many guests in the hotel right now, so I think we can always manage to find an empty room next to his. However, in case he does decide he wants to move, we'll have to have the ghost go through the keyhole in the corridor door. If need be we could set up operations in the corridor, but that would be risky. Another difficulty: we won't be able to see him, but we'll try to hear him if he decides to answer the ghost. If he grabs the ghost, the specter doesn't have to seem aware of it."

"I'll try to come tomorrow so we can have an evening rehearsal. Don't forget to see to the lamp and the spittoon. Just to be safe, perhaps I'll bring along some sodium or potassium. I'll go get it at the McGill College laboratory."

"As for me, I'll hurry up, change clothes and go down to put the mirror back. Grippard could very well ring for something to drink. You know that fear makes him thirsty. I'll come up to see what he wants and I'll get a drink for myself."

"What a pity we've had a falling out! I wouldn't mind tying one on at his expense tonight."

"I'm not supposed to know you've quarreled. I'll tell him I saw you downstairs. Perhaps he'll be sorry for the row you two had today and he'll invite you up."

With that, Brindamour took off his wig, cast off Duroc's suit, and removed the makeup from his mustache and eyebrows; then he went downstairs with Bohémier, carrying the concave mirror under his arm. He put the mirror back into place while pretending to show it to Bohémier. In this way, he made his actions seem plausible to the boozers still lingering in the bar.

He was just finishing putting it back up when the bell to M. Grippard's room rang furiously. Brindamour went back up.

"What can I do for you?" he asked Grippard as he entered the room.

"Ah! It's you, Brindamour. Bring us two glasses of cognac, will you, or rather bring me up a bottle. If you see anyone I know downstairs, tell him to come up."

"I saw M. Bohémier. He's alone and he gave me the impression of being extremely bored."

"The devil take Bohémier!" Grippard said testily. Then, thinking the better of what he'd just said: "Tell him I'd like to see him."

Brindamour went back down, then quickly came up again followed by Bohémier and bringing back a bottle as requested.

"I was a bit hasty a while back," said Grippard, extending his hand to Bohémier. "You mustn't hold a grudge against me. I was really angry with Bagoulard — not you. His butter-wouldn't-melt-in-my-mouth airs get on my nerves."

"For goodness sake! I don't hold it against you and as to that matter concerning Du…"

"Shush!" said Grippard, glancing at the bellboy.

"Do you need anything else?" said Brindamour, pretending he was about to leave.

"No, but stay with us. You're welcome to. We've gotten drunk together before, if memory serves me right. I like intelligent young men like you who don't presume to take advantage of kindness shown to them in private by being too familiar in public. Please sit down, gentlemen. As a matter of fact, I have only two chairs. The other is broken. That vase is too. I don't know how in the devil that could have happened but somebody seems to be fighting in my room when I'm out. If I don't get better service here, I'll change hotels. Brindamour, go and get another chair and try to replace this broken vase. I don't want people to say I'm the one making all the ruckus in my room."

Brindamour picked up the pieces of the broken vase, which he carried off with the chair, and got replacements for those two items in another room. They uncorked the bottle and this second gathering ended, like the first one, in a right old drunken orgy.

CHAPTER XXXV

THE SO-CALLED
GHOST'S ULTIMATUM

Grippard, who had gotten royally drunk the night before, rolled out of bed rather late on the day after the experiment just described. Taking care of his business affairs having required his complete attention that day, he had hardly had time to see about keeping the promise the ghost had wrung out of him the previous night. Nevertheless, hoping to avoid the apparitions haunting his old room, he had had his belongings carried into another one. Brindamour had been placed in charge of this move, which allowed him to make preparations for the following evening.

Needless to say, the story about Duroc's illegitimate brother was a complete fabrication. The only true part about it was that Brindamour was an illegitimate child. He was counting a lot on the phantasmagoria, if not to extort money from Grippard, at least to get him to be his patron. He was resolved, whatever the cost, to put his future protector to the test by showing him Duroc's apparition — wounded and dressed in an American uniform.

As for Bohémier, he had managed to get the uniform, the rifle, and the equipment. When evening came, Brindamour went to get the concave mirror for the rehearsal. As he was climbing up the first stairs with the mirror under his arm, he unexpectedly came face to face with the owner of the establishment, who asked him curtly, "Where are you going with that mirror?"

Completely taken by surprise, Brindamour stammered: "I'm going to shave."

He wanted to keep on going, but the owner grabbed him by the arm and applied his foot to Brindamour's backside.

"Take that mirror back where you got it. And don't let me catch you again wasting your time on nonsense instead of doing your work."

Brindamour didn't have to be told twice. He put the mirror back in its place and, as soon as he was free, he went to tell Bohémier about his mishap. Bohémier was waiting for him to begin the rehearsal.

"This isn't the 'vexed' mirror," said Bohémier.

"It's the concave mirror," Brindamour answered, not getting the play on words.

"No, you're the one that's being 'vexed,' you idiot."[1]

"You are also since our experiment has failed."

"As far as I'm concerned, I'm not. I know where I can borrow a concave mirror. I'll have it put in a trunk so we can get it up here without arousing suspicion."

"Why didn't you say so sooner? You could have saved me a lot of trouble — not to mention the kick I just got."

"You still feel sore about that kick, don't you?"

"Not exactly. But if you can get the mirror you're talking about we'll keep it here."

"I can borrow it for the night, but I'll have to put it back."

"Idiot! Take it without asking the owner."

"I don't think that'll be easy, but I'll try."

Bohémier went out and came back a little while later. He was accompanied by two young men carrying a trunk which they put in the apartment across from Grippard's new room. When he was alone with Brindamour, Bohémier said to him as he took the mirror out of the trunk, "I bought it cheap. I put a dollar down on it. It belonged to a former barkeep. He went out of business because he drank up all his profits. Right now he's probably tying…"

"Tying what?"

"'Tying one on,' for goodness sake!"[2]

"Grippard was doing a good job of tying one on last night. As for you, your tongue was getting thick. Do you recall him asking me if I remembered Léon Duroc?"

"I certainly do. I can even tell you word for word what he said on that subject. Here are his very words: 'Do you remember seeing a tall dark young man with curly hair here at the beginning of May last year? He was about your height and looked a lot like you. He stayed in this room for two or three days.' When he said that, you put on your dumbest look. And no one can look as stupid as you do when you want to."

"Flatterer!"

"And you said to him, 'Is that so? I don't remember. We see so many people….' 'He looked a lot like you,' he repeated. Then I interrupted and told him I remembered the young man he was referring to and that he really didn't look all that much like you. First of all, I said, he was dark and Brindamour has blond hair. Secondly, no offense to Brindamour, but he was much more distinguished looking."

"That's it exactly. I asked myself if that sly old Grippard suspected something. At any rate, I think my stupid look (and I can't say whether or not it's inherited because I'm a foundling) — as I was saying, I think my idiotic look threw him completely off the track."

"I hope so. But let's get on with our rehearsal."

We won't tire our readers by giving them a blow-by-blow account of the scene which followed this conversation. Let's just say that the rehearsal succeeded perfectly.

Bohémier had rented the room in which they were rehearsing for the night. And so the young men didn't need to worry about being disturbed. They waited patiently until Grippard was asleep. As they had predicted, Grippard had left his lamp lit and, convinced that no specter would dare visit him if the light was on, he had gone to sleep, a sleep which had nothing in common with the sleep of the just.

From time to time, the two young men went to peek through the keyhole. As soon as they saw that the lamp had gone out for lack of oil, they positioned their apparatus, and, when everything was ready, Bohémier kicked the door hard enough to wake Grippard. They heard him ask in a surly voice: "What do you want?"

Hardly had he finished speaking when he saw Duroc's ghost two feet away from him — this time wearing an American uniform. The phantom had a rifle in his hands which he put it to his shoulder as if he were aiming at someone; next, staggering as if he were about to fall over backwards, he disappeared, then reappeared immediately. His left hand pressed the tip of the rifle barrel whose butt was resting on the floor. His right hand was pointing to a wound beneath his left shoulder from which blood was spurting out. The specter repeated this routine two or three times, then he said in a sepulchral voice: "You ask me what I want? I want to warn you once again that, if you fail to keep the promise you made me yesterday evening, I'll make you regret it. I won't wreak my vengeance on your vile carcass, but your business affairs will suffer."

Grippard had gotten up, struck a match, and was trying vainly to relight his lamp. He would have liked to grab the cord to ring for help, but the ghost was still there, seeming to bar the way and repeating its routine. Grippard didn't dare cry out for fear of waking people in the neighboring rooms. He had the reputation of being a skeptic and he wasn't eager to have everyone in the house know how frightened he was. He finally worked up the courage to charge head first through the ghost to get to the lifesaving bell cord. As in the case of the preceding night, Grippard encountered no resistance from the ghost. Unfortunately, he caught his feet on the spittoon and knocked it over. He had passed right through the specter, which still stood there striking the same pose. Now he had gotten hold of the cord and was yanking on it furiously.

Bohémier, who was standing at the door, had guessed from the noise what Grippard was doing. Hastily withdrawing the apparatus, he went back into the room across the hall and shut the door without worrying about the noise he was making.

A bellboy ran into Grippard's room.

"And the lamp was no longer burning," as the song goes.

"Bring me a lamp," Grippard said to him. "This one isn't working."

The boy hurried off to do as he was told.

"Is young Brindamour here?" Grippard asked him when he returned.

"He's out, but he should be back soon."

"Send him to me as soon as he returns."

"Yes, sir."

Bohémier, who had been listening with his ear to the wall, informed Brindamour, who was just finishing getting washed up. Brindamour had indeed asked for some time off so as not to be disturbed and he had pretended to go out. Once he looked like himself again, he went out to the street through a back door and soon came back in again through the front door. He was told M. Grippard was looking for him, and he went up to the merchant's room.

"Would you spend the night with me?" M. Grippard said. "I saw a ghost again tonight. This is the last time I'm going to sleep in this hotel. I'm sure it's haunted, but don't say a thing to anybody. I'm going to settle my bill with the proprietor without telling him why I'm leaving."

Brindamour accepted the invitation and he and Grippard spent the rest of the night — free of apparitions.

"And the lamp burned on," as the French song continues.[3]

This time they went to sleep without drinking anything. Grippard offered to take Brindamour into his service. The phantasmagoria had produced the desired effect.

CHAPTER XXXVI

OUR OLD ACQUAINTANCES FROM MONTRÉAL AND PINGREVILLE

The next day, Grippard and Brindamour left the Hotel Canada: Grippard to try to get some rest in a hotel where he hoped there were no imps and ghosts in residence; Brindamour to the country to be a clerk in one of Grippard's stores. The previous night, Grippard had questioned Brindamour about his abilities. The bellboy's answers had convinced him that Brindamour would be a competent clerk. The hotel proprietor, remembering the scene with the mirror and having noticed for some time that Brindamour was almost never there when he was needed, didn't mind at all getting rid of that scatterbrain. Brindamour, who resolved to use the phantasmagoria on his new boss whenever the time was right, had not forgotten to take his apparatus along with him.

At M. Latour's, no one was satisfied with his or her fate. Louise was still inconsolable as she thought about the untimely death of the fiancé she had so loved and loved still — for the yearnings of a loving heart follow the loved one beyond the tomb. She had yet another cause for sadness. She sensed that her father was unhappy.

As a matter of fact, Mme. Latour's allegation about Duroc had opened M. Latour's eyes to the character of the woman he adored but didn't really know. He had become jealous and had begun keeping an eye on his interesting other half. That was all he needed to do to become absolutely certain of something that was clear to everyone but himself whose blind confidence in her had prevented him from discovering: that Mme. Latour was as coquettish as she was stupid — and that was saying a lot.

M. Latour mourned his vanished illusions. Waking up from a lovely dream is always painful even when you are still of an age where the future always seems to be so very bright, when we have so many illusions that between the fading dream and the new one on the horizon there is scarcely any time to grieve. But M. Latour had lived past that time of life when new hope always comes to banish old disappointments. His unhappiness was irreparable. He thought he had loved a noble-hearted woman, an intelligent woman, a woman of character. Instead, he had fallen madly in love with a woman completely devoid of all those qualities. To have made such a mistake at his age! He, a man who prided himself on knowing what was in people's hearts! What good was all his experience if he hadn't realized in time that the second Mme. Latour had married him for his money?

He was angry with himself for not having seen through her. His pride was wounded. To think that he had been duped by a woman — his inferior in intelligence, talent, and experience. He knew, of course, that until now, she had only been flirting, but he told himself that her eagerness to seek out other men's attentions didn't bode well for the honor of his name. Continually obsessed by this thought, he became morose, taciturn, and surly without being aware of it.

Mme. Latour, who had never loved him, but who had been willing to tolerate him as a husband as long as he fussed over her, now found she heartily detested him and, consequently, she felt unhappy. Instead of doing everything she could to regain her husband's confidence, a confidence she had lost through her own fault, she resolved to look for consolation elsewhere. Unfortunate lady, little did she know that a dutiful love, the affection of a goodhearted man who had adored her for many long years and who asked nothing more than to stay by her side, was highly preferable to the passing fancy she might inspire in a libertine who would only see her as a fallen woman and couldn't help but despise her after sullying and dishonoring her.

Being completely devoid of all the qualities of heart and mind, she had no idea what sway those qualities can hold, she could never have understood that these virtues alone can inspire a deep and lasting love. She wanted to be adored for her beauty alone. But, however beautiful the woman, if the charming wrappings don't enclose a beautiful soul, a noble heart, she'll inspire only a temporary passion which is not love, but only a kind of intoxication.

M. Latour had loved her passionately as long as he had believed her endowed with those qualities of heart and mind that she utterly lacked. Or rather she wasn't the one he had loved but the imaginary being he took her for. The spell was broken! The illusion had vanished! His eyes were wide open, and the merchant now saw before him a fallen woman when for years he had thought her the most perfect of all possible beings.

With her usual perspicacity, Louise guessed at what was going on in the hearts of the two spouses. She suffered in silence, knowing full well that it would be impossible for her to mend her father's shattered illusions. She pretended to believe he was happy, so as not to add to his woes the sorrows of a daughter unhappy on his account. And so, this house, where peace, contentment, and happiness had reigned, was now inhabited by three beings who, each for quite different reasons, regretted the past and had no hope for the future.

Thanks to his oratorical talent, Bagoulard was already considered a distinguished criminal lawyer. He worked to improve his eloquence, wrote out his speeches, and learned them by heart so while he was giving them he could extemporize at a given moment, then pick up the thread of his written text after having delivered his impromptu digression. If he had to defend an important case, he would entrust Bohémier and some of his other friends with the task of leafing through the law books to provide him with arguments he knew how to develop, given his extraordinary talent.[1]

Bagoulard was truly a genius. He felt born to command. He was convinced of his own superiority and he counted on it to succeed. This was not a bad thing — quite the contrary. As a matter of fact, he should have counted on it even more — counted only on it and honesty. Instead, he mistakenly believed his talents alone would get him nowhere and that duplicity was the key to success. He had everything he needed to fight prejudice; he preferred instead to reinforce it. A first-rate orator, his success on the hustings[2] went to his head. He promised himself he would accede to power and accomplice great things. Only he forgot that if he rose to power in the usual corrupt way, once he had made it, he would be dragged down and have to wade through the mud of the beaten path. Anyone wanting to govern should, it seems, intend to do a better job than those who have gone before him.

"Others have succeeded by scheming. So will I," Bagoulard said to himself. Perhaps he was unaware that this was just like saying: "Others have kept their positions by plotting; I'll keep mine the same way when I get there." He didn't realize that the straight and narrow path[3] is the best one to follow on the way to success when you are blessed as he was with superior ability. An honest man — as everyone aspiring to govern should be — shouldn't want power just for power's sake. He should seek it to bring about necessary reforms which he deems necessary and should abandon it rather than compromise his duty.

In our country [Canada], the legal profession runs everything. And the word lawyer is synonymous with "exploiter of miseries, injustices, and prejudices." If it weren't for these three things, there would be no lawyers. Members of the profession, who are far too numerous for their own good and ours, find it to their advantage to have all these woes increase in direct proportion to their numbers. They are so used to fleecing the unfortunate plaintiff that they don't have any compunction about fleecing the public. Accustomed to conniving, plotting, and oratorical jousting, it's not surprising that they all have a pronounced taste for politics, which thrives on all of that. Almost all of them aspire to become members of Parliament at least; too many of them succeed, and the biggest rascals become ministers, then judges. That's the supreme ambition. Consequently, our laws, forever being modified, amended, and re-amended, have become a veritable hodgepodge, a legal grab-bag. And, while the public loses, the legal profession profits.

During his apprenticeship as a clerk, the lawyer studies the art of deception — either using his words to make bad causes appear good or by interpreting the laws or drawing up documents. Thus prepared, he ends up by believing only in trickery and skill. Anyone without a hidden agenda is, in his eyes, an innocent of the first order.

His character has been molded so that, if he enters politics, nine times out of ten, even if he has all the qualities needed to be a statesman, he'll never be more than a clever politician whose skill will be more detrimental than useful to his constituents.

As is the case with all the other law students, Bagoulard had promised himself that, when he finished his studies, he would give his country some new laws before he died. With his fiery temperament, he soon became one of Montréal's most cynical libertines — which is saying a lot. It was a strange way of recommending himself to a fairly straitlaced constituency. His first oratorical successes were won in the dives he frequented where he loved to go impress the sirens of the demimonde with the charms of his eloquence. He had become their spoiled darling. And, since he didn't try to hide his escapades, his fame as an libertine was just as dazzling as his reputation as an orator was brilliant.

When he had a criminal to defend, he would rise and toss back a rebellious lock of hair (which persisted in hanging down from his forehead in the direction of his nose) from his forehead with a movement of his head, then begin in a calm, measured tone of voice, gradually become more and more animated, gesticulate, and shake his head, making the irrepressible lock of hair do a jig.[4] He wooed the jurors one by one, fixing on one of them with his hypnotic gaze and seeming to be addressing him alone. He would not look away from his "victim" until he had made him cry. He would then go on to the next one, mesmerizing him in the same manner.

About the time the events we have undertaken to describe were happening, Pingreville was the scene of a trial which created quite a stir. Bagoulard was put in charge of defending the accused — a murderer who was, nonetheless, condemned and executed. But he had been defended in such an eloquent fashion that the judge, fearing that the crowd packing the courthouse might riot, ordered the silver-tongued defender to stop speaking. Confident of his rights, Bagoulard continued talking. Those who witnessed this spectacle maintain that they had never heard anything which could be compared to the eloquence Bagoulard displayed on that occasion.

Twilight was beginning to creep into the courtroom; still Bagoulard kept right on talking. The crowd was almost delirious with excitement; and, in spite of the bailiffs, they applauded wildly. The judge ordered the courtroom evacuated and a fight would have broken out had it not been for the presence of mind of several in the audience who lifted the lawyer up on their shoulders, shouting to him to continue talking. They carried him out followed by the enthusiastic crowd. The speech continued uninterrupted outside the courthouse for an hour and a half longer.

After Brindamour left, Bohémier devoted himself exclusively to taking advantage of his goodhearted uncle who cursed him a bit, but, in the end, always paid for the havoc wreaked by that incorrigible bohemian that Heaven had given him for a nephew.

CHAPTER XXXVII

BEFORE PETERSBURG

L et us go back to the lines before Petersburg where we left Eugène Leduc grief-stricken since hearing that Duroc was dead. After spending some time in the trenches, the brigade of regulars, decimated by a month and a half of almost continuous combat, had been relieved and sent a quarter of a mile to the rear to join the reserves. A brigade camp had been set up outside of artillery range. Straight, wide streets 150 feet long were laid out, the ground cleared, and each regiment set up its tents two to three rows deep along these avenues. The brigade general headquarters with the brigadier general and his staff was set up some distance away. Huge tents with awnings, called marquees, had been set up for the officers' use crosswise to the ends of the streets nearest the enemy.[1]

Young trees cut down in a neighboring wood surrounded and covered the tents with a sort of green framework, protecting them somewhat from the burning rays of the sun. They were replenished as soon as the leaves dried out too much. Camp life would have been pleasant enough for the soldiers if they hadn't been kept constantly busy and given hardly any time to sleep. They had begun to furbish their weapons and polish their gear as if they were back at the garrison. Guard duty, work details, and battalion maneuvers followed one after the other without interruption. Often, being on duty two hours out of every six and having stood guard the night before, a soldier relieved of guard duty at nine o'clock in the morning would have to go out at noon to work in the trenches under enemy fire.

No one who hasn't seen the siege fortifications built up before Petersburg and Richmond can possibly have an accurate idea of how enormously extensive they were. The Army of the James, commanded by the famous Ben Butler, had just come up on the right of the Army of the Potomac, thus completing the siege line. In the form of a large crescent, it half surrounded the towns of Petersburg and Richmond. This semicircle of iron and firepower was gradually closing in; the following spring, with the help of Sherman's army which had came from the west to cut off all of Lee's escape routes, it would finally crush the valiant Southern army.

Now, if we consider that Petersburg is twenty-two miles away from Richmond, we can understand how many men it took for a line that long. Taking the curve into account, the line must have been at least thirty miles long. Now, to form a continuous line of ramparts over this distance, about 150,000 men were needed — not counting the officers — if they were placed two ranks deep, as is always the case with such lines. But there were also the advanced lines, the mounted sentries, the reserves, and the munitions and supply trains, all of which must have brought the numbers in the two armies of the James and the Potomac to just about 300,000 men including the noncombatants.

These are not the official figures — all the more reason to believe they are accurate. Lee had scarcely more than 40,000 men.[2] The Union newspapers tried to muddy the figures so as not to admit that with an army seven times larger, Grant either did not dare or did not want to take the two cities by force. The main line was composed of a series of earthen forts, solidly built and joined together by a line of ramparts. Large siege cannons had been positioned in the fort loopholes. Every day new ones arrived to be placed in the newly constructed parapets. Heavy wagons covered with canvas and pulled by eight mules brought munitions. Many trenches had been dug so they could reach the ramparts without drawing rebel fire. The wagon trains would vanish from sight as they descended into them. Behind the forts, caves had also been dug to serve as powder magazines.

Burnside, commanding the 9th Army Corps stationed immediately to the right of the Fifth, had started excavating a long tunnel. A rumor was running through the ranks that this tunnel was to be used to mine and blow up one of the forts in the Southern line. But with the exception of a few who were in on the secret, no one knew for sure.

Duty details recruited from the reserves were used especially for these various kinds of work. Ten or so men were taken from each company and placed in groups of two to three hundred. Each man was given a pick and shovel, and they were taken to the work site, where they stacked their weapons. Available men who managed to escape the first work detail were just about certain that, once night fell, they would be part of a new detachment of workers which would inevitably be called for. As a result, the reservist rarely spent a night in his tent.

Although they weren't as deadly as pitched battles, these expeditions were, nonetheless, quite dangerous. By mutual agreement, the two sides had stopped shooting at each other for the simple pleasure of using up cartridges. At certain places in the line, some soldiers from the Federal and Confederate pickets talked with one another by shouting from one rampart to the other. In other parts of the line, distance would have made this impossible. The sentinels from the two armies were separated by distances varying from five hundred yards to three-quarters of a mile. Opposite the forts, no one even considered fraternizing, for it seemed as if combat would then have degenerated into an artillery duel between the two armies. When the enemy sighted a work party, he fired his guns at them — which explains why night was the preferred time to have work done on the most exposed parts of the defenses.

The artillery on both sides had very high caliber weapons for the times. In addition to the rifled cannon used in attempts to breach the enemy fortifications, there were mortars which, though not elegant, were extremely deadly. Some of them could shoot hollow round projectiles weighing up to six hundred pounds, which is impressive for projectiles.[3] They didn't follow a direct trajectory. They were shot at an oblique angle into the air so they would land inside the fortifications. There they exploded, providing the gunner had rightly calculated the distance when he set the fuse which produced the explosion.

When it was sighted at night traveling through the sky, that glowing fuse allowed onlookers to follow the bomb's path. It was like a ball of fire jerkily making its way up into the firmament. The whistling noise made by the six-hundred-pounder sounded more like a locomotive than a shell. Eugène had had the opportunity to see and hear them at close range. One evening when he was on work detail, as he was making his coffee before sunset, knowing full well that he wouldn't be allowed to make a fire after nightfall, a bomb had suddenly burst over his head. One of the fragments had killed a man right beside him; another blew away coffee, kettle, fire, and fuel. It had buried itself in the earth after covering two or three of his campfire mates with sand. The men ran to take shelter behind the rampart. They had just reached it when a horrible detonation rang out. A powder magazine about fifty feet away had just exploded, covering them with yet another layer of earth.

When they had all finished rubbing their eyes, they began to argue about what had just happened. Some claimed that the powder had been set off by a fragment of the bomb that had just killed a man and blown away Leduc's coffee. Others maintained that it was another bomb which, as it fell back to earth, had cut through the eight feet of earth and timbers which covered the cave. No one ever found out who was right.

The regiment had received reinforcements. Some were the wounded who had been declared fit and released from the hospitals, others were exchanged prisoners from Camp Parole, still others were new recruits. The Irish colossus whom Eugène had been afraid he had killed in the woods on June 16 had also came back with a scar on his forehead and another on his arm. He only talked about the latter, which a Confederate bullet had made on his arm. When he was asked about his head wound, he would say that it was probably from a shell fragment. Thus the quarrel earning him that scar remained a secret between him and Eugène with whom he had pretended to make his peace.

Battle of Petersburg, Virginia, June 16, 1864 — Eighteenth Corps carrying a portion of Beauregard's line.

CHAPTER XXXVIII

A Mine Explosion[1]

At that time the 2nd Army Corps had in its reserves a brigade composed entirely of Pennsylvanians of German origin. Eugène had had the chance to see them on maneuvers and had noticed that they were being given their commands in German. It should be noted that German is not an official language in the United States. A few years before, when Eugène was in Canada, he had asked why militia battalions composed entirely of French Canadians weren't given their orders in French. He had been told that English was the language used in the British army. Therefore it would be impossible to maneuver in time of war if the army decided to use the only language understood by the men from Lower Canada, even if they comprised the vast majority of the militiamen from that territory. Now he had the proof that this was only one of many pretexts used to relegate the French language to second place in a province where it is officially recognized and when plain good sense demands that it occupy first place.[2]

General Burnside, commander of the 9th Army Corps, had in his command a brigade of Negroes, most of whom were slaves who had fled the Confederate states to escape slavery. In the slave states, no Negro was even permitted to carry a gun. ("To tote a gun," as the Southerners said. The word "tote" is the same as "carry" in the Southern dialect.) The slave owner considered the Negro a piece of property — not a human being. In practice, he had the power of life and death over his slave.

A Negro deserter, even if he had never borne arms against the Southerners, knew they would kill him if he fell into their hands. All the more reason for him not to expect mercy if he were captured bearing arms. And, in fact, all Negroes taken alive by the Confederates were brutally massacred by them. Thus, in retaliation, Burnside's black brigade had adopted as its motto these terrible words: "No Quarter."

On July 30, 1864, around three o'clock in the morning, the regular brigade was ordered to support the left of the 9th Corps. As the sun rose, the Fourteenth was in columns, waiting with their rifles upright at their sides, some distance back from the ramparts. A very deep silence still reigned all up and down the line. It was the quiet before the storm.

Suddenly a great cloud of smoke rose above the enemy line a little to the right of the position held by the Fourteenth. A moment afterwards, a terrible detonation rang out. Burnside's much-talked-about mine had just blown up an enemy fort, destroying two Southern regiments.

The pen refuses to describe that horrible sight. Artillerymen and infantrymen, trenches and ramparts, munitions baskets and brushwood, siege cannons and gun carriages had all been blown into the air and fallen back to the ground in an indescribable chaos. The artillery from the besieging army opened up fire along the whole line. The besieged replied with equal vigor. For an hour or two it sounded as if all hell had broken loose.

Taking advantage of the confusion caused by the explosion, the Negro brigade plunged forward at double quick march with bayonets fixed to their rifles. The air resounded with their frenzied hurrah. The sight offered by that mass of black devils rushing at their former masters and resolved to wreak a terrible vengeance for the centuries of oppression which their race had suffered was most impressive. Here and there, in the middle of each regiment, a black flag could be seen floating beside the star-spangled banner. Against the black background could be seen a skull and crossbones, signifying quite clearly that they didn't expect to escape alive if they were defeated and that they had no intention of giving the rebels quarter. A battle to the death was about to be joined.

The Negroes were commanded by white officers. But such were the racial prejudices, even among the Federals, who were nevertheless fighting for the emancipation of the blacks, that many men preferred to serve as common soldiers in white regiments than command a black company.

The assailants headed for the breach created by the mine explosion. The time it took for them to get there allowed Southern regiments to move up to bar the way. After fierce hand-to-hand combat, the Southerners were pushed back. The Negroes rushed after them, but soon they were caught in heavy crossfire between two enemy batteries not of a mind to ration their ammunition. The rebels had regrouped behind their second line of defense from which they blasted away at the brave blacks. These men made valiant attempts to break through the second line; but, seeing that they couldn't, they beat a hasty retreat. As they rushed to the rear, withdrawing to the line of white reserves who had moved forward, they were met with the bayonets of an entire Federal regiment. Whether they wanted to or not, they had to resume their assault. Their hearts full of rage, they returned to the attack and performed incredible acts of valor, but they were repulsed once more. This time the white Unionists allowed them to take shelter behind the ramparts because they too wanted to do so. Besides, there were so few left that it wasn't worth making a fuss. From their vantage point, the soldiers of the Fourteenth had been able to see the blowing up of the fort and the Negroes' attack. The regiment had had several men killed and wounded by enemy shells and the men returned to camp without firing a single shot.

The respective position of the two armies had remained the same as it had been before the assault; the Federal troops hadn't judged the time to be right to occupy the

Explosion of the mine before Petersburg.

site of the destroyed fort. The rebels were so furious that they refused to parley for three days. Each time the Federals, who wanted to bury the dead lying on the field of battle between enemy lines, showed a white flag, the rebels fired on the truce party, which is absolutely contrary to the rules of war.

Between the two lines lay thousands of Negroes, poor devils who had never smelled too sweet while alive and whose decay, hastened by the blistering heat, had not helped in that respect. A poor soldier from the Fourteenth had had a son killed in that battle. His body lay between the two lines. The day after the assault, the unfortunate father went to the ramparts looking out on the scene of the carnage. And, having persisted in looking over the breastwork in the hopes of recognizing his son's body, he was shot in the head and fell backwards stone dead into the trench.

Three days later, the rebel themselves couldn't stand it any longer. Afraid of sickness breaking out in the ranks, they agreed to a few hours' truce so that the victims of that murderous battle could be buried.

Constantly busy, thanks to frequent guard duty, exercises, and work details which scarcely gave them any time to sleep, the reserve soldiers were exhausted. One night when Eugène was on guard duty, he was found asleep at his post. Under the military code, such dereliction in the presence of the enemy is punishable by death, but the corporal of the guard, a good sort of man, who knew how to take circumstances into account, had not reported the guilty party.

CHAPTER XXXIX

The Sutler

The sutler, the American army's traveling salesman, who hadn't been seen since the beginning of the spring campaign, had just set up shop again in the camps where the reserves were stationed to give the military men a chance to spend their pay. In the garrisons, the sutler runs the canteen — nothing more, nothing less. In the field, however, he is much more: bookseller, clothes merchant and tailor, restaurateur, liquor salesman, etc., etc. Thousands of tradesmen had obtained licenses to profiteer from the soldiers fighting in enemy territory. Each battalion had its own sutler who, protected by one or two guards, displayed his wares in a huge canvas pavilion. At one end of the tent stood a wooden counter where soldiers stopped to make their purchases. At the other end there was a kind of apartment separated from the goods by a canvas partition. This was the sutler's inner sanctum, open to officers only.

When they presented their money to the sutler, the soldiers received a number of tokens in varying denominations equal to the total. These tokens then served as legal tender to purchase the goods they needed. On payday, which came every two months while the army was in winter quarters, the sutler stood by the paymaster, presented his bills as the names of the soldiers who owed him money were called, and made sure he was paid before they got a single cent of their pay. Since the ordinary American soldier got $16 a month in addition to his food and clothing, and practically all of that money was spent at the sutler's, the merchant did very well indeed.

You could find just about everything in his establishment, from the works of Alexander Dumas, translated into English, to butter at $1 a pound and eggs at $1 a dozen. A good many soldiers threw away their rations and ate like kings while their money lasted. Others threw away their issue caps and bought fine ones for $2.50. Sky-blue jackets with brass buttons like the officers wore cost from $10 to $20. Napoleon-style boots sold for $10 to $12. In short, soldiers were afforded every possible opportunity to squander their money.

The sutler's return reminded Leduc of an adventure he had had the previous spring a few days before leaving Catlett's Station. In their winter quarters the soldiers had built themselves cabins from split oak logs caulked with the red clay found in abundance in Virginia. Pieces of tent buttoned together were used for the roof and gables. In the back, a brick fireplace faced down a narrowed aisle lined with wooden planks which served as bunks at night and benches during the day. An opening cut in the wall facing the fireplace served as a door, which was covered by a length of canvas. Outside, streets ran the length of the rows of huts. Each row housed a company.

Leduc had spent the whole winter at Camp Reynolds lodged with three soldiers who had served in the outfit since the battalion was formed three years before.

These men had enlisted for only three years. During the winter, the army had offered very generous re-enlistment terms to all the veterans whose enlistment was going to be up in the spring. The army promised to cancel the time remaining on their current three-year term, offered them bonuses which, when added up, came to $1,500, and threw in a thirty-day leave to visit their families. Leduc's three companions leapt at the offer, got their money, and went home. Only two came back. The other, choosing to extend his leave with what the Yankees called a "French furlough,"[1] had taken his bonus and left for Canada. The two who returned had done what most of those who re-enlisted did at that time. They had spent a good portion of their money during their absence and had come back with a phenomenal thirst. And yet, this wasn't for want of having drunk a great deal during their absence — quite the contrary. Both had brought back officers' uniforms which had cost them $150 apiece and which they had been allowed to strut around in while they were on leave.

At the beginning of winter, soldiers had been able to buy whiskey at the brigade canteen by presenting an order signed by an officer. Those who were known to be drunks, well aware that they couldn't possibly get such an order themselves, approached men with a reputation for sobriety. More than once, Leduc had obtained vouchers or certificates at some tippler's request after making him promise that he wouldn't get sloshed. Toward the end of the winter, the authorities realized that sober men were getting vouchers signed so that the drunks could continue to get soused, so they closed the canteen. The sutler still sold whiskey by the bottle, but only to officers in uniform.

One of the two veterans mentioned above was named Downer. He was just about Leduc's size. One day when he felt like having a drink, he said to Eugène: "Frenchy, here's my lieutenant's uniform; it hasn't been getting much wear lately. Let's put it to good use. I don't dare put it on myself; I'm too well known. Why don't you get into it and go get a bottle of whiskey for me at the sutler's?"

"Sure," answered Leduc. "I'm going to risk getting caught just so you can have the satisfaction of wetting your whistle."

"If you'll go, I'll give you a $1 commission for each bottle of whiskey you bring back to me."

"It's a deal," said Eugène, who tucked the uniform under his arm, and went off into the woods to put it on. He made his way to the sutler's in the neighboring camp, marched imperiously into the tent, and, after chatting for a few minutes with the sutler himself, came back triumphantly with the rotgut requested.

He made several such successful trips, but one fine day Captain Smedberg entered the sutler's tent unexpectedly. Caught by surprise, Eugène was just about to leave when the sutler detained him.

"Captain Smedberg," he said, "allow me to introduce Lieutenant Morton of the Twelfth."

Smedberg was wearing his sash, indicating that he was on duty as officer of the day. As he looked Leduc over, he could hardly keep from laughing and said to him: "My word, you are a funny-looking lieutenant! Guard!" he added as he stuck his head out of the tent, "Call the corporal of the guard!"

When the corporal arrived, the captain said to him: "Arrest this man; take him to the guardhouse and have him walk guard duty with the sentry, carrying a stick over his shoulder instead of a rifle."

About a quarter of an hour later, Smedberg sent Leduc back to his quarters, after having made him promise never to return. Leduc had got off cheap thanks to Smedberg's lenience, for he was fond of him.

Recalling that incident, Leduc was reminded of the fact that poor old Downer had been killed in the Battle of the Wilderness; that the other veteran, his pal, had been wounded in the leg; and that Smedberg lost a foot in the same battle.[2]

Soldiers in camp visiting the sutler's store.

CHAPTER XL

Jeff Davis's Promises

Leduc had seen everyone he liked disappear one by one. And now he felt isolated in the midst of the crowd — the worst possible kind of loneliness. When he lost Duroc, he had lost a true friend, a wise advisor. Henceforth, left to his own resources, and to his hotheaded, vivid imagination, he felt once again an overwhelming desire to serve France.

In the midst of all this, a copy of the *Richmond Enquirer* fell into his hands. A truce party had received it along with other secessionist papers in exchange for Union newspapers. The *Enquirer* in question contained a proclamation by Jeff Davis, president of the Confederation of Southern states, offering to protect and repatriate the many foreigners in the Northern army if they wanted to desert to the enemy.

"That's just what I need," Eugène said to himself. "Jeff Davis can do what Mosby's guerrillas could not. I'll get myself shipped off to Mexico on board one of the Confederate blockade runners." And he resolved to defect to the enemy at the first available opportunity.

The Fourteenth was still under the command of Captain Thatcher, who was five feet ten inches tall, had broad shoulders, a lanky frame, and prominent cheekbones. He was dark-skinned with black piercing eyes, a beaked eagle-like nose, and a thick black mustache which divided his face in half. When he took off his uniform and donned a sort of Mexican outfit, which suited him perfectly, this eccentric personality looked exactly like a buccaneer or desperado on vacation. The following incident proves there was something to that.[1]

One day the commanding officer of the Twelfth and Captain Thatcher began quarreling in the latter's tent. They had been drinking heavily and playing cards. Any other two officers would have blackened each other's eyes or engaged in a duel. These two preferred to settle matters by having a very unusual battle. Each regiment was charged with defending its respective commander. Accustomed to obeying orders and not quite understanding what was expected of them, the two regiments lined up facing each other, separated only by a street's width.

First the two commanding officers ordered their men to charge at will, and, finally understanding what was what, the men began sizing one another up. Up to that point, the soldiers of both regiments had always been on very good terms. They bore each other no ill will — in fact, they felt no rancor toward the other regiment at all. And yet they were about engage in a lethal battle.

Company pride and an instinct for self-preservation would of necessity have turned this fight into an uncommonly fierce and relentless struggle.

In such a combat there would be no question of taking prisoners; the men would be shooting at one another almost point-blank.

After a moment's hesitation, Captain Thatcher had his men fix their bayonets and the commanding officer of the Twelfth then gave same order, which his men immediately executed. A moment more, and the two regiments would have begun to fight, but at the crucial moment, just as Captain Thatcher was opening his mouth to order his men to charge, the provost guard arrived from the brigade's general headquarters and put the two regiments under arrest — by order of General Hays.

Warned in time by the officer of the day, the brigade general had quickly taken measures to prevent the fratricidal fight which, had he not intervened, would have resulted from the thoughtless rage of the commanding officers.

Weapons were stacked and placed under the guard of an infantry picket who was ordered to keep the soldiers from reclaiming their rifles. This happened around noon. The soldiers from both regiments, knowing that they were freed from any sort of duty as long as they were kept under arrest, rejoiced at this turn of events. As for Eugène, he resolved to take advantage of the situation to carry out his plan for deserting to the enemy.

A few weeks earlier he had acquired a small Smith and Wesson pocket revolver. This little seven-shot pistol, a real little silver-plated jewel, took a bullet which was, in the words of Mark Twain, the size of a homeopathic pill. It took seven of them to make up a dose strong enough for an adult. Eugène loaded his weapon and put it in his pocket.

The officers were all under arrest. There was no point in asking them for a pass, since they had no right to grant one — even if they had been so inclined. Ordinarily, if a soldier deserves to be punished, he is slapped in the guardroom. Only commissioned and noncommissioned officers are entitled to be released on parole. In this instance, the soldiers weren't guilty of any wrongdoing — they had simply been following orders as required by military discipline. The provost guards on sentry duty were posted in the street along the rows of stacked weapons and their orders were only to prevent the soldiers from touching their rifles. Consequently, Leduc was able to leave camp without even arousing suspicion.

He headed for the entrenchments, then moved along them toward the Weldon railroad, where he spent part of the afternoon passing the time of day with the soldiers manning the ramparts; all the while looking for a place suitable for acting on the plan he was pondering. About five o'clock, he was three or four miles away from camp. He had managed to get as far as the line of vedettes placed outside the picket line and spread out about thirty yards apart. There the forward posts of the two enemy lines were three-quarters of a mile apart in a wooded area. To avoid being surprised by an enemy sortie, since the raiding party could have used the woods for cover and caught them unawares, the Federals had built an abatis extending fifty yards beyond the mounted sentries' position.

These sentries had built cabins or shelters of sorts for themselves from young trees whose leaves protected them from the burning sun. Eugène came upon one of these cabins just as a violent storm, which had been threatening for some minutes, began raging furiously. The sentries huddled under their thin leafy shelter were more pre-occupied with trying to protect themselves from the rain than with paying attention to what was going on around them. Leduc boldly entered a cabin where a tall bean-pole of a Yankee was standing with his hands crossed on his rifle butt whose stock was resting on the ground.

The two men soon began talking about the rain and the thunder which at times rumbled dully and then came crashing down around them. The clouds were so thick that it was almost dark as night. Eugene, who had sized up his man while they were talking, put his hand in his pocket and cocked his pistol; then, pointing the gun at the man's temple, he said in a low voice, but with a very unreassuring air: "Drop that rifle or I'll blow your brains out."

The rifle dropped to the ground.

"Now, don't make any noise! You're going to go under the abatis and crawl toward the woods on your hands and knees. If you make a single sound or try to dis-obey me, I'll kill you! Go on! Move! I'm coming with you!"

Half dead with fear, the poor soldier plunged under the protective cover of the felled trees with Eugène following — still menacing him with his revolver. After hav-ing alternately crawled and walked in a crouching position for five minutes, the deserter and his prisoner reached the spot where the shelter ended and the forest began. As soon as he saw he was out of the reach of the other sentries, Eugene said to the Yankee: "Now, you, if you aren't going to desert, return to your post; as for me I'm going off to find the rebels. I don't need to tell you that if you say that you were forced to leave your post without sounding the alarm, you will be shot on the spot. You can go. By the time you get to your rifle, I'll be safely away."

The Yankee didn't have to be told twice. He hurried back to his post. Since he was taking great pains not to be seen, he had to go back under the abatis the same way he had come. As for Eugène, he plunged into the forest toward the enemy position.

CHAPTER XLI

MAKING A PROMISE IS ONE THING; KEEPING IT IS QUITE A DIFFERENT MATTER

The thought of capturing the sentinel had only just popped into Leduc's mind when he found himself alone with the Yankee. He had said to himself: "If I go off alone into the storm, that will seem so strange that he'll naturally feel like watching me. If I wait for the storm to pass, I won't have as good a chance of getting to the woods without being caught. Right now, the other lookouts are doing their best to take shelter from the rain. The noise of the storm will prevent them from hearing a fight if there is one. Let's carry off this beanpole. He doesn't look like much of a hero." And Leduc had done just that.

After letting his prisoner go back to his post, Eugène moved forward a bit in the direction he felt should take him to the rebel lines. But he stopped after a few moments thinking that he could be mistaken, and that he could be going back to the Federal lines without realizing it. The rain was still falling; it was quite dark under the tall trees whose thick foliage nevertheless blocked a goodly part of the downpour, which didn't stop until after the sun had set. Not daring to venture any farther in the half-light, Eugène resolved to wait until the next morning when he could more easily get his bearings. He spent the night sleeping on the damp ground between the two enemy lines. The next morning he moved forward cautiously until he recognized a Confederate uniform.

He raised his hands above his head to let the rebel sentry know he wasn't armed. The sentinel motioned for him to advance and alerted his comrades who were a short distance behind him. A group of them had already gathered at the edge of the woods when Leduc got there.

"Hello, Yank!" (diminutive of Yankee) they yelled out to him. "Do you have any greenbacks?"

And four or five starving Virginians seized and searched him without further ceremony. His revolver, his greenbacks, and his shoes were confiscated as quick as a wink. Eugène found that way of doing things quite cavalier, but they told him he was a prisoner and that those trinkets belonged by right to the soldiers who had seized them. He referred to Jeff Davis's proclamation and they told him he that he would be treated as a deserter, not as a prisoner of war, which would give him the right to spend a few weeks in a Richmond prison while he waited for the government to be ready to arrange for him to leave the Confederate states.

This wasn't a very joyful prospect. But the authorities informed Leduc that such a precaution was taken to prevent the riffraff deserting from the American army from plundering the countryside, left unprotected since all able-bodied males were in the army; they feared for their women and children left at home.

The authorities were right. A crowd of new recruits, real cutthroats from the slums of New York City, Boston, and other large cities, had enlisted fully intending to receive their bonuses and then desert at the first possible opportunity. Jeff Davis's proclamation was bound to attract the scum of society to the Confederate cause. Allowing such bandits to move about freely throughout the Confederate states would have been tantamount to encouraging pillage, rape, and murder. Eugène understood why he was a prisoner, which was some consolation, but he would have preferred not to understand and be spared a taste of Southern prison life. He had heard enough about that regimen to have no desire to sample it.

He spent part of the day with the provost guard and, in the afternoon, he was incarcerated in the Petersburg prison where he found himself in the company of other deserters. Since the beginning of the campaign, he thought he had learned what it was like to go without food, but the future held in store for him trials that would have made Tanner flinch.[1] In the American army, soldiers went without rations when the supply train was accidentally cut off. In Southern prisons, going without food was the order of the day. To get your standard ration was an event and it was unheard of to eat your fill.

Eugène, who hadn't eaten the night before, didn't get a thing to eat until the day after his imprisonment. They gave him just enough wheat bread to whet his appetite and as much muddy Appomattox water as he wanted to drink. In short, having spent two interminable days in the Petersburg prison, during which time their only distraction was thinking about their hunger pangs — if you call that amusing yourself — the deserters were sent by train to Richmond, where they were housed in a former tobacco factory converted into a prison for American deserters.

This building was just across from Castle Thunder, the Richmond Bastille, where criminals, spies, and suspected Union sympathizers were indiscriminately imprisoned. Horrible stories were told about this prison. It was said that, if the walls of these dark cells could talk, they would have hideous tales to tell. Since the prison where the deserters were held was the counterpart to Castle Thunder, it had been called Castle Lightning. This name didn't mean much of anything unless someone wanted to suggest that the little bit of food brought there disappeared with the speed of lightning; in that case, it wouldn't have been too much of an exaggeration.

During the first days of their incarceration, each of the deserters received about a pint of boiled rice a day. Later on, the rice was cut out, and the deserters were placed on a regimen of cornbread — the ordinary Southern prison fare. Each man was given about a half a pound a day; when they complained, they were told that they were getting about double what the prisoners of war were receiving. That argument, while consoling, was hardly nourishing.

The deserters slept on the floor of a huge room. Their Federal uniforms had been taken away, but they had been given Confederate uniforms to replace them. They hadn't gained anything by the exchange, since the gray uniform was just as apt to attract the attention of the American "bloodhounds" as the blue. And we'll see later that the protection promised by Jeff Davis to deserters only amounted to imprisoning them for a time before sending them off to states under Federal control.

Perhaps the Confederate government had done everything it could. In any case, Eugène later became convinced that Jeff Davis had acted in bad faith and that he had persuaded soldiers to desert so they could then be handed over to the vindictiveness of the Federal authorities.

At the time we're talking about, the rebels didn't wear a uniform. Any gray outfit was a uniform, and it would have been difficult to find anything but a gray outfit because all the men were under arms. The task of guarding the prisoners in Richmond was entrusted in part to children aged fourteen to sixteen, to old men over sixty, and to invalids. Then, because the South wasn't importing any more merchandise, all the clothing was made from a locally produced cloth called Kentucky Jean. That fabric only came in gray. No one had ever seen it in any other color.

To ask the Southerners to give the deserters civilian suits would have been as senseless as asking them to feed their prisoners of war. People don't get feed prisoners of war when the only food available is bad cornbread — and just an infinitesimal amount of that. They don't dress thousands of deserters in black wool suits when all they have are some old discarded uniforms made from Kentucky Jean material.

There were men from all over the world in Castle Lightning: French, Italians, Germans, Spanish, Portuguese, Yankees, English, Scotch, Irish, Danish, Swedish, Hungarian, and Montenegrans. This cosmopolitan gathering was composed in part of sailors. "Blacklegs" from New York were there in large numbers.[2] In the space of two weeks, the detainees numbered about two hundred, so the authorities decided it was time to send them to the Kentucky lines.

The deserters were searched once again and all the valuables still in their possession were taken from them. Each individual appeared before the provost marshal, who took down his particulars, asked him as a mere formality where he wanted to go, and told him that he would be sent to the border separating West Virginia from Kentucky. In vain did Eugène insist that they send him by sea to the Lucayes Islands where the blockade runners usually made port, for he hoped to go to Mexico from there. But his prayers were wasted on them. They simply told him they needed those ships for carrying merchandise and that they couldn't be used for transporting passengers.

CHAPTER XLII

Serving the Confederacy

Eugène was utterly discouraged. They were sending the deserters to Kentucky! They might just as well have handed the men over to Federal authorities! At that time there was a substantial bounty offered for capturing deserters from the American army, and in that state bordering the Confederacy, public sentiment was running so high that a goodly number of the planters would have considered it their duty to denounce the guilty or to make life hard for them. From the very first days of his captivity, he had been sorry he deserted. Now he would have given a great deal to be back in the regiment.

The squad of deserters left Richmond by train under heavy guard. It was the beginning of September and, at each station, Negro men and women came to sell peaches, apples, and the ubiquitous johnnycake (or cornbread). The prisoners, who weren't fed any better during their journey than they had been in prison, would have been willing enough to eat the fruits, the cornbread, and even the Negroes selling them, but they didn't have a cent, and the sight of the guards' bayonets instilled notions of obligatory honesty in men who would otherwise have been inclined to appropriate other people's property — if Negroes can be thought of as other people. In these circumstances, the poor starving prisoners had to be satisfied with devouring with their eyes food they could neither buy nor steal. They would have had to eat a lot of those imaginary meals to assuage the hunger gnawing at their entrails.

The train went toward the southwest crossing, first through Danville, then Lynchburg. During the war, the railroads in the Confederate states weren't what you would call the best means of transportation. At the time we're talking about, the country was unspeakably impoverished.

Most of the slaves had run off. The white men were fighting in the ranks of the Confederate army. The women, accustomed to living a life of ease and indolence, found themselves obliged not only to work as overseers but often to work the plantations themselves. These courageous women were only too happy when the government — which didn't know how it was going to feed its army, and as matter of fact did a poor job of it — didn't requisition the fruits of their hard labor. In spite of everything, these valiant secessionist women stated that they did not regret their hardships. They would even have willingly gone on suffering for a long time more if their sacrifices were the price to be paid for the ultimate success of the Confederate army. Courage worthy of heroic times, worthy of a better cause, worthy especially of a better fate!

Meanwhile, the country's production couldn't supply the railroads which, since they were used almost exclusively by the government, had to be maintained by it. Suffice it to say that they were poorly maintained, when the poverty of the government was taken into account, for it was probably the poorest institution in that country where three years of out and out war had heaped ruin upon ruin. From time to time, a Federal cavalry raiding party would make a foray into the interior, tear up some rails, demolish a bridge, and go back behind Federal lines. Given those conditions, a derailment was always to be feared. There were thus many excellent reasons for the locomotive to proceed slowly and cautiously.

After two or three days travel by rail, that mode of transportation was abandoned and the prisoners proceeded on foot. That evening they camped at Abingdon, Virginia. After a two or three days' march, they came to Glade's Springs on the Tennessee border. It was an abandoned village serving as a depot for the Virginia 7th Cavalry Regiment, which was part of the Confederate brigade commanded by the famous Morgan. The soldiers belonging to that brigade were nicknamed Morgan's horse thieves.

The 7th Virginia Cavalry was a strange regiment. It had no doubt seen better days. At this time, its real complement had been reduced to fifty or so fully armed horsemen. In addition, it also had a hundred or so men who were without horse and just waiting for the opportunity to mount up at the expense of the Federal cavalry or planters suspected of Unionism.

Of this number, about fifty were more or less armed. Some had revolvers, others had Spencer repeating rifles, some had Mississippis, others had Springfields, some had hunting rifles, and others were armed only with simple jackknives.[1] The remaining fifty had this in common with the fourth officer in the Marlborough cortège: they weren't armed with anything.[2] On the other hand, some didn't have hats, most didn't have shoes, but they all had fleas, the only creatures who managed to live well in that interesting town called Gladesville.

Colonel Prentice,[3] who commanded this model regiment, hearing deserters of French origin speaking together in their mother tongue, addressed them in that language, which he spoke flawlessly. A personable man, he had traveled in France and was so successful in gaining the confidence of both the French and the Canadians that five or six of them, worn out by trials, tribulations, and sickness, agreed to join his regiment.

Eugène was among that number. The other deserters were escorted to the Kentucky border where they were released after being given rations for five days. Life in Gladesville was fairly monotonous, the rations weren't too plentiful, but the duties were easy enough — especially for the unarmed soldiers. Eugène stayed there for about ten days, and during that interval the whole regiment went on parade. The mounted and armed cavalrymen, who were almost always off fighting with the rest of the army, had come back to Gladesville for the occasion. This was the first time that Eugène had ever drilled barefooted and without a weapon.

But that is not quite right, for he had slipped a sharpened table knife through his belt.

Each morning the Gladesville soldiers received a small quantity of cornmeal. And near Gladesville there were huge orchards filled with half-ripened apples and peaches, but the soldiers weren't very particular. They ate most of them as is, but one of the Frenchmen, who fancied himself a cook, took it into his head to mix green apples in with the cornmeal mush to give the daily ration more consistency. That resulted in a stew that even the dogs wouldn't eat. In short, after ten days or so, Eugène had had enough of the menu, the Gladesville fleas in general, and the Gladesville duties in particular. One fine morning he was absent at roll call. They had never even had a chance to have him swear allegiance to the Confederate government; the Confederates had neglected to have the Federal deserters who had joined the 7th Virginia Cavalry Regiment go through this formality.

CHAPTER XLIII

A Wandering Canadian[1]

Eugène was in a fine mess! A fugitive from two warring armies, he was in the heart of disputed territory, occupied first by one side, then the other. Although he wasn't yet seventeen and a half, according to the military code he had already earned the death penalty under two different governments. Any man he met would feel it his duty to turn Eugène over to the authorities.

The Confederates didn't waste any time with deserters. They shot them without showing any mercy. As for the Federals, he was even more guilty in their eyes. If he fell back into their hands, he would inevitably be convicted of desertion to the enemy, a crime punishable by being shot before a firing squad. He was also guilty of treason for having enlisted in the enemy army, a crime punishable by hanging.

In the region he was attempting to cross, he could expect to run into men serving either one government or the other. All able-bodied men had been conscripted. The inhabitants all served the Confederacy. The intruders were all Union soldiers. This being the case, he thought up two diametrically opposed stories: one meant for Federal ears; the other, for the benefit of the Confederates.

But there was one drawback. Scouts traveling in enemy country usually borrow the uniform of those they want to spy on. How could he avoid getting into trouble with these men traveling in disguise? Eugène had to rely on his instincts, which failed him on two occasions in three weeks' time. Twice he told the wrong story, and twice he was captured, then released, thanks to the Christian charity of those men into whose hands he had been clumsy enough to fall. Praised be those generous souls who placed humanity above what the customs of war made them consider a sacred duty! The first time, he ran into two Confederate soldiers belonging to Morgan's brigade. They let him go after promising each other they wouldn't say anything about the incident. The second time four Union scouts took pity on him after listening to the story he had made up for the Confederates. On behalf of the man who owes them his life, we express our gratitude to both groups — a gratitude as deeply felt now as twenty years ago when the poor boy, half dead from fatigue and hunger, thanked them with tears in his eyes!

Three weeks of suffering, hardships, danger, and despair had managed to make Eugène almost indifferent to his fate. He was fully aware that it would be impossible to serve in France. He only hoped he could manage to get out of the predicament he found himself in without holding out much hope of seeing this dream come true. First of all, he had to avoid falling into the hands of the Confederates occupying West Virginia. Then he had to avoid the Federal troops wanting to dislodge the rebels and who were maneuvering all along the boundaries separating Kentucky and Tennessee from Virginia.

He calculated that, as the crow flies, approximately four hundred fifty miles separated the Kentucky border from Sandusky, Ohio, on the banks of Lake Erie, which he would then have to cross to reach Upper Canada. Rumor had it that Kentuckians had lynched sixty of the deserters he had left behind at Gladesville. They had tried to cross the states of Kentucky and Ohio to get to Lake Erie. This was not very reassuring.

Mountainous, covered with woods, almost entirely without viable roads — which, in any case, were in Eugène's best interest to avoid — such was the region our fugitive had to travel over. The creeks, nearly dry ordinarily, and which were the only routes of communication, became raging torrents in the rainy season when it poured. Eugène followed them walking barefoot on their gravel beds. When he happened to get lost in the mountains, he followed the ravines, which almost always led to one of the creeks. People in the sparse dwellings along them had shown themselves to be very hospitable.

There were wild apples and peaches growing there, but that insubstantial fare was hardly of the sort to give much strength to a man already exhausted by hardships. Inhabited houses were few and far between; Eugène had gone as long as three days without running into a single one; but despite the terror the sight of a stranger always inspired in those troubled times, the natural hospitality of the inhabitants overcame all other feelings. They shared their last bit of bread with him. When they didn't have any flour, they scraped an ear of corn and managed to send him on his way with his hunger somewhat satisfied. This was offered spontaneously so that the traveler could avoid the humiliation of begging.

One night, Eugène stayed in the house of a man who had also served in both armies. He had decided to come home without asking anyone's permission. Unlike Eugène, however, the Kentuckian had no taste for the military adventures which had turned him into a soldier serving under two enemy flags. He had been conscripted into the Confederate army. As soon as he learned that the Federals had occupied the land where his house was situated, he had returned home only to be conscripted again — this time by the Federal government. So, the poor devil went off to serve the Union. Finally, the two armies had moved their theater of operations a little farther off. And, hoping no one would come looking for him in his house hidden away in the Cumberland mountain gorges, he had decided come home, but he was always on the alert lest he be surprised by a reconnaissance party from either side.

This worthy Kentuckian, who knew from experience what hardships are endured by soldiers in battle, also knew that those suffered by men on the run are equally grueling. He insisted Eugène sleep on a feather bed. There was only one in the house. In vain Eugène protested that he preferred a harder bed, that he was used to sleeping on the hard ground. The Kentuckian insisted.

The next morning after breakfast, he told his guest, "You're six miles away from Piketon! Go to the village. There you'll cross the Pike River. The Federal cavalry general Burbridge is in Williamsburg twenty-five miles farther down the river. He'll come through Piketon in a few days. He's going on to Saltville to fight Morgan. Once you've passed over the river, you're almost certain not to run into his men. They'll only cross at Piketon. You can come over the river again at Paintsville. Burbridge and his 13,000 cavalrymen will be here and you can go on your way."

Eugène thanked him and went off in the direction of Piketon.

CHAPTER XLIV

{ WHERE A CERTAIN INFANTRYMAN
BECOMES A CAVALRYMAN }

E ugène's bare feet were bloody after three weeks of walking on the pebbles in
the creek beds. He had crossed the Allegheny, Clinch, and Cumberland mountains and was very pleased to feel the smooth dirt of the main road leading to
Piketon under his feet. Used to fearing encounters, he proceeded with caution, paying attention to every little noise and scanning the horizon. The sound of a wagon
crossing a bridge at the bottom of a ravine startled him, and he hurried to huddle
behind a stone wall separating the road from a nearby field. The wagon had just gone
by and he was about to start off again when he saw five or six Federal cavalrymen
chatting among themselves as they trotted along. He let them pass by and then proceeded on his way again, wondering where those cavalrymen could have come from
and if others might not be nearby.

Several miles away from the house where he had spent the night, the road became
a narrow pass hemmed in between two mountains. Eugène entered this pass, which
he crossed without incident, but, as he emerged from it, he found himself unexpectedly in a Federal cavalry camp. It was Burbridge's army which, according to his host
of the night before, was supposed to be in Williamsburg.

The army had traveled twenty-five miles during the previous night and was resting while awaiting its departure, scheduled for noontime. Escape was out of the question. One of the camp sentries arrested Eugene, who asked to speak to an officer. The
men surrounded him and bombarded him with questions.

"Hello, Bushwhack!" (diminutive of "bushwhacker," a sniper in the rebel army).
"Where do you come from?"

As Leduc was unfortunately wearing the Confederate artillery uniform that he
been given in Richmond and that he had always worn ever since — even when he
was in the 7th Virginia Cavalry — everyone thought he was a rebel soldier. They took
him to a man in his forties wearing a captain's epaulettes. The captain questioned him
according to military regulations.

"Where do you come from?" he asked him.

"North Carolina."

"What county?"

"Ashe County."

"Whereabouts?"

"We didn't have any neighbors."

"On which creek?"

"Folks call it Kelly's Creek, after my father. It isn't an important creek. Our house is the only one built on it."

Eugène had chosen his information carefully. He knew Ashe County was sparsely inhabited and that it was in rebel hands. Not wanting to say where he had came from, he had tried to seem as ignorant as possible, pretending to come from a thinly populated country so he could avoid having to answer a lot of questions.

"When did you leave?" the captain asked.

"About a month ago."

"What road did you take?"

"I don't know. I just took a road and followed it."

"Did you go through any towns?"

"I didn't go through any. I went around them. I was afraid of being arrested if I crossed them."

"Why?"

"I'm seventeen years old and I was avoiding conscription. I don't want to go to war."

"Where are you going now?"

"To Kentucky."

"But you're in Kentucky now."

"I want to go even farther away where there'll be no danger of the rebels coming to look for me, somewhere I can find work."

"Do you know the names of the towns you went around?"

"No, I didn't dare ask because I didn't want to arouse suspicion."

"What kind of work can you do?"

"Plantation work of any kind."

"You say your name is Kelly? You must be of Irish stock."

"Yes, but I was born in North Carolina."

Eugène lied with such ease that you wouldd have thought he had done nothing else all his life. He spoke English well enough so he could imitate various accents. He could speak like a Yankee, a German, a Negro, a Cockney, or like an Irishman. He had practiced accents the winter before. He had delighted his comrades with his comic songs which he sang while imitating these various accents. In answering the captain's questions, he had thought it best to mix a bit of Irish brogue with "right smart I reckon," "tote," and "thar" that he scattered here and there in his speech so he would sound like a Southerner.

"Well, Kelly," the captain said to him. "You're going off to war with us...."

At that, Eugène felt a lot like laughing, but he restrained himself. He started — pretending to be terrified.

"Don't worry. You won't be fighting."

Eugène's face lit up as if that pleased him, but the reader knows him well enough to realize he would have preferred combat simply for the pleasure of fighting.

"You'll be my servant. You'll ride with us. I have a horse here we've been resting for several days by using him as a packhorse. You won't be armed. In five or six days we'll come back and I'll take you with me to Bourbon County, Kentucky, where I'll put you to work on my plantation. Our regiment, the 40th Mounted Kentucky Riflemen, has served out its time, but it has volunteered to serve in the present campaign. We're going to Saltville to fight Morgan and destroy the saltworks. That won't take very long. Does that suit you?"

"Perfectly."

"Then you're going to put on an American cavalry uniform, put your bruised feet in large boots with spurs, and ride with us. Meanwhile, take good care of this chestnut. It's yours. I'm not asking you to do anything else. I'll take good care of my own horse."

They set about finding a uniform for Eugene. In a few minutes he was wearing the American cavalryman's dark blue jacket with gold braid and sky-blue trousers. Most of these Kentuckians were veritable giants so it wasn't easy to find a uniform short enough and narrow enough so Eugène wouldn't look like a dressed-up broomstick in it. He slipped his feet into a pair of huge boots fit for a certain former Montréal alderman and at noon he leaped into the saddle, happy as a prince. Just across from Piketon there was a ford across the Pike River, but the water was quite high; the horses lost their footing and swam across without seeming to be bothered by the weight of their riders. Then the mighty cavalcade surged forward toward Saltville, Virginia.

CHAPTER XLV

HIS FIRST RIDING LESSON

The army commanded by General Burbridge was composed of excellent horsemen recruited from Ohio, Indiana, and Illinois — but mostly from Kentucky. They were all sturdy farm boys accustomed to life in the fields. There were no foreigners among them. Eugène never met a single one of them born outside these western states. When they joined the army, these men, who had never taken a riding lesson, but who had been riding since they were very young, held themselves in the saddle much better than three-fourths of those little fops who prance around with their beasts, the one carrying the other, along the streets of our cities.

Under the dubious pretext that they're riding English style, how many of our dandies suffer from the mania of flaunting their awkwardness in public. Just look at them, monocle in one eye, riding crop in hand, riding horses with bobbed tails, trotting along as they raise themselves up so they can show everyone the color of the seat of their pants. This useless and ungainly bouncing tires both horse and rider. Looking down on the world from the height of importance which his mount gives him, the rider seems to be telling the pedestrians watching him, "Admire me. As you see, I have a horse and I can make him trot along for a quarter of an hour without having him throw me. Very few of you can ride like me. I've taken riding lessons. I can ride English style."[1]

He's right. A man has to take lessons to learn to ride in a way radically opposed to the most elementary principles of good sense and reason. The Apaches, Comanches, and other Indians spend their lives on horseback. They guide their mounts without stirrups, bridle, or spurs, but with a movement of the knee or heel, rather than with the simple rope which for them replaces the bit and the double reins. They gallop fifty or sixty miles without seeming to tire.

Try asking your horseman riding English style to do as much! First, he would lose his monocle before he succeeded in getting his horse to gallop. He would probably be unhorsed before he got to his destination, but, if by some miracle, he gets there, you'll see before you a man who'll be too polite to sit down for three months. All because his . . . pride . . . has been too deeply wounded.

The Apache, the Comanche and all who, without having taken riding lessons, ride better bareback than the little fop does with saddle, double reins, spurs, riding crop, a monocle, and all the other folderol, do exactly the opposite of what the English-style equestrian does. That's the secret of their success. The horseman who does it for show keeps his heels in and points his toes out, which gives him opportunity to tickle his horse with his spurs without meaning to. If the horse has mettle, he'll throw his rider three times in the space of an hour.

According to the rules of French horseback riding, which are based on simple common sense — rules adopted by the American cavalry — the heels should be held out with the foot perfectly parallel to the horse's body rather than being at an angle to it. Instead of rising and falling in the saddle each time the horse moves, the rider must stick to him, as if horse and rider constituted one and the same being; he must direct the horse's movements or follow them with slight flexing of the knees and reins. He mustn't let his full weight fall on the saddle, whose sole function should be limited to serving as a means of support.

For six whole days in a row, they were in the saddle for twenty-two hours out of twenty-four, and Eugène had these rules explained to him on more than one occasion. In the end, he was able to put them into practice in a fairly acceptable fashion. Riding right beside him was a huge devil of a Kentuckian, a sergeant-major. In a French cavalry regiment, he would have the title of *maréchal-des-logis-chefs* or *marchet*. This particular giant didn't joke around when it came to horsemanship. He didn't hesitate to correct Eugène in very blunt terms, but the discipline, the strangeness of his situation, the need to treat his new friends with great care, his weakened state — all this provided more than enough reasons to inspire caution in the former infantry soldier, now a riding student, whose first lesson had been a three-hundred-mile journey across the mountains.

Despite everything, his condition had improved so much that when he thought about the misery he had endured during the six weeks which had elapsed since his departure from the 14th Regular Infantry Regiment of the United States, he was inclined to put up with the noncommissioned officer's brusque manner without complaining. He was filled with the deepest gratitude for these men who had welcomed him without abusing their right to question him and who treated him as if he belonged in the regiment. After having taken him in, half-dead from exhaustion and hunger, they had put him on a horse and had undertaken the Herculean task of letting him eat his fill.

They had succeeded in doing so after stuffing him for three days with hardtack, bacon, and coffee. His first, very plentiful meal had seemed to appease his hunger, but his stomach very quickly remembered its long imposed fast and the second meal had to be as copious as the first. In short, his appetite returned to normal only after he had eaten ten or so Pantagruelian meals, and that happened just when he had to begin enduring a long series of privations once again.

The army was crossing through a very picturesque region. Sometimes, when the road led the cavalrymen on to a high plateau, the surrounding countryside presented the spectacular view of an immense range of mountains, their peaks turned blue by the distance, which seemed like the waves of a storm-tossed sea. There were quite a few plantations along this road. There were very few plots of land suitable for cultivation that weren't at least partially tilled.

The presence of Federal troops didn't seem to please the inhabitants very much, for they detested the Unionists. Needless to say, these feelings were mutual. Burbridge's army, partially recruited from the states bordering the Confederacy, was made up of men who brought into combat a soldier's courage as well as the partisan's hatred. Such hatred is always stronger in those living in the immediate environs of a war zone than in those who don't.

One day, as they were crossing through a village, a rather funny incident occurred which greatly amused those who witnessed it. The company in which the young Canadian found himself had just stopped to water its horses and an officer asked some women standing in a doorway if they had some papers from Richmond. Everyone knows that among English-speaking populations the word "papers" means "newspapers." One of the women disappeared and came back a few minutes later carrying a rumpled piece of grayish yellow paper used to wrap merchandise. She gave it to the officer saying in a very pronounced Virginia accent, "I don't know if this comes from Richmond, but I reckon it must. I got it from the grocer who buys his goods in Richmond."

Everyone let out a laugh and an officer shouted to the man who had just received this odd present, "I calculate you're going to find heaps of very interesting bits of information on this Richmond paper and I presume you'll share it with us."

The reader will remember that the army commanded by Burbridge had been recruited primarily from the states neighboring Virginia, so almost everyone in the regiment spoke almost like the people they were going to fight.

The New England Yankee always "guesses" and he guesses with a nasal drawl. Seldom does he say more than ten words in his nasal twang without adding, "I guess." The Southerner doesn't guess, he reckons, calculates, or presumes. Sometime he supposes, but mostly he reckons. If you ask him the distance from one place to another, he invariably answers, "It's a right smart of a distance, I reckon."

You're not much better off for his advice. "A right smart of a distance" can mean anything. It can mean twenty miles or half a mile. The Southerner doesn't have to "reckon" to give you such a vague answer, but he "reckons" just the same or at least he pretends to from force of habit.

Did the woman with the wrapping paper want to play a joke on the Yank or was she in earnest? No one was ever able to find out. What is certain is that, despite what was said about the circulation of newspapers among the rural population of the United States, three-quarters of the white population in that part of Virginia knew about the existence of periodical publications by hearsay only.

A kindly old woman was surprised to see that the Yankees, as the Southerners called all the Federals, were, without exception, built like other men. She couldn't get over it. "What? Are you Yanks?" she asked them. She didn't find their faces frightening enough, for they did not correspond to the idea of ugliness which she had imagined. Yet, it seemed to Eugène that if she had tried a bit harder, she could have been satisfied on that score with the grotesque face of the Kentuckian who had become his riding instructor.

CHAPTER XLVI

Where a Certain Cavalryman Becomes an Infantryman Once Again

Saltville[1] gets its name from the rock-salt mines located nearby. These had become a precious resource for the Confederate states where salt was extremely rare. The secessionist newspapers tried their very best to produce salty humor but succeeded not at all, given the ill-humored state of mind Confederate reverses had plunged them into, for that sort of salt had never managed to replace cooking salt for seasoning food. It is true that the Southerners had scarcely any food to season, but this sort of poverty made them all the more alarmed about going without a seasoning considered absolutely necessary by all civilized peoples.

Not wanting to miss any chance to be disagreeable toward the Southerners, the Federals had sent Burbridge to destroy the Saltville factories and close down the mines. Morgan, warned in time, had gathered all his forces and holed up in the endangered little town. It was rumored that he had only 2,000 men to hold off Burbridge's 13,000, but he had cannon and he would be fighting from a protected position, which gave him a marked advantage. Besides, to attack him, the whole cavalry had to dismount. Every fourth man had to hold four horses while his three comrades joined ranks with the others to fight like infantrymen. Thus the number of Federal combatants was reduced by one fourth.

Eugène was thus going, at least to be present at, if not take part in, a fight against the Confederate brigade which the 7th Virginia Cavalry Regiment belonged to. That was the very regiment he had left without permission three or four weeks before. Since he wasn't armed, they arranged for him to hold four horses during the battle. He was just as exposed as the men who were fighting and a bullet killed one of the horses he was holding.

The battle sounds intoxicated him; the old warrior instinct took hold of him. He would have liked to be in the thick of battle. When the Federals charged, letting out their traditional yell, he forgot himself to the point that he said out loud, "That's a charge if ever I saw one!"

"Do you hear that damned bushwhacker?" said one of the horsemen who had stayed behind to hold the horses, pointing to Eugène. "It seems he knows what a charge is even though he's always claimed he's never borne arms."

Eugène bit his tongue.

"I know what it is because I've heard about it," he said.

The combat was very bloody, especially for the Federals. From where Eugène was standing, he saw several wounded pass by as they were carried to the rear. Among them he saw the brigadier general, who had been shot in the groin and was dying.

When night fell, the Federals had been beaten up and down the line. To use a Confederate expression, they had come for salt and had been thoroughly peppered. They had to mount up and gallop off as fast as they could ride. Whenever the fleeing vanguard entered a pass, they were just about sure to find the road in front of them blocked. An invisible and elusive enemy lay in ambush on the mountainside, from which large rocks were sent crashing down or shots were fired mercilessly on the Federal horsemen. The Federals then had to take the time to clear the road or go over the obstacles. They would then set off at a gallop abandoning the dead and wounded to the tender mercy of the detachment in hot pursuit of Burbridge's men.

It was no longer a retreat; it was a complete rout. The rebels, who were from that part of the country and knew all the shortcuts, had sent out numerous parties and, by using the back roads, were lying in wait for the fleeing Federals — striking them down without warning before they had a chance to defend themselves.

The horses, tired by the long march, could go no farther. For long distances, the infantry is preferable to the cavalry. Difficult as it may be to believe, when it comes to enduring fatigue and privations, a man can outlive ten horses. For a quick two- or three-day expedition, the cavalry is quite useful, but a forced march of five or six days wears the horses out.

Two days after the Battle of Saltville, a large number of American cavalrymen, whose horses hadn't been able to keep up with the others, had fallen into rebel hands. Others, seeing that their horses were unable to continue, had abandoned them and struck out on foot. Eugène was among them. He was very afraid of falling again into rebel hands, for if they recognized him, they would surely shoot him as a deserter.

A large number of horses and mules, for there were mules in Burbridge's cavalry, had been abandoned along the way. All of them were saddled and were cropping grass along the roadside. Eugène spied a mule who seemed to him to be in good enough shape and jumped into the saddle. He was soon obliged to abandon it because of the smell it gave off. Its entire back, covered by the saddle, was an open, maggot-filled wound. He set off again on foot in the company of many other cavalrymen who were trying vainly to make their mounts move along faster than at a walk. Toward evening, he took possession of a white horse that had just been abandoned. As the sun was setting, his group was joined by several cavalrymen who had succeeded in making their horses gallop and, as they passed by them, they shouted, "You're going to be captured. Morgan's advance guard is barely two miles behind. All of our men farther back there have been taken."

Each man dug his spurs into the flanks of his horse, which groaned with pain and moved forward as fast as his tired legs would carry him. Eugène's horse even broke into a trot which lasted him about thirty yards.[2] Then he went back to his usual pace which was about as fast as the English infantryman's slow march. In vain did Eugène use his spurs; he soon found himself completely cut off from his comrades. The horse was all used up.

Eugène got down from his horse, rid himself of his large boots, and ran off. Far ahead in the distance he could see the light of campfires dimly reflected on the sky. He continued to march, moving swiftly along for two hours, slowing down when he was too tired, then rushing off again after resting a bit. When he reached the camp, he found that it was deserted.

The fires were still burning, having been built to glow all night long. A very large number had been lit and Eugène understood that it was a trick to keep the enemy at a respectful distance as well as to allow what was left of the army to use the rest of the night to try to get to safety. Judging rightly that he wouldn't be bothered here by the rebels, he roasted several ears of corn left over from the meal of some horse or mule, then lay down near one of the campfires. He slept all night long. The next day, he set out again, realizing that it would be impossible to go very far without being arrested. Indeed, as he was about to pass the first house, three Virginians came out armed with those long rifles which mountain men in that region used so skillfully to kill all sorts of large game from deer to Yankees.

"You're my prisoner," said one of the three men.

"I won't argue with you," replied Eugène, "but notice that I am not armed. Please say that to the men you hand me over to."

CHAPTER XLVII

THE WANDERINGS
OF A PRISONER OF WAR[1]

Poor Eugène! His prospects were far from being good. He seemed to be forever doomed to go from Charybdis back to Scylla. His most immediate danger was the possibility, the likelihood even, of running into someone who had known him in the 7th Regiment of Morgan's horse thieves, since he had been taken prisoner by men from that very brigade. If he managed to escape that danger, he would be sent to Richmond where he also ran the risk of being recognized. Another hitch: even if they were content to treat him merely as a prisoner of war, sooner or later he would be exchanged and probably sent back to the Fourteenth, where he would have to face charges of deserting to the enemy. He could see no way out. No matter which way he turned, he foresaw death as the inevitable outcome preceded by a more or less lengthy period of misery and suffering.

The three Virginians took off immediately across the fields with their prisoner. Two or three miles farther on they turned him over to several cavalrymen. These men already had custody of five prisoners: two whites and three Negroes. The Negroes were former slaves who had been captured bearing arms. The two white men were a Federal officer in disguise and a planter-cobbler who had given him sanctuary.

The guards made no bones about saying that these five characters would pay with their lives for their crimes against the Confederacy. The Federal officer, having been found in disguise behind Confederate lines, was to be treated like a spy. The planter was to be shot as a traitor, but the guards contented themselves with turning both prisoners over to the authorities, giving them a chance to defend themselves before a court-martial. As for the Negroes, there was no need to go to such bother; the guards took it upon themselves to shoot them without a trial of any kind.

They began marching along back roads, the guards on horseback, the prisoners on foot. The prisoners knew when they were passing near Federal troops because they were forced to run.

Around noontime, the escort, judging that they had covered enough ground to be beyond the reach of a Federal surprise attack, they stopped briefly to decide what to do with the Negroes. One of them was a colossus — six feet three inches tall and built like Hercules. How ridiculous to let a slave like this go to waste. The guards agreed to split the price he would bring and spared his life.

The two others begged for their lives in vain; their pleas went unheeded. One of the cavalrymen ordered them to stay behind with him while the escort and the other prisoners set off again. They had hardly marched more than a few yards when they heard five shots ring out in succession followed by the cries of the dying. The cavalryman reappeared, reloaded his smoking gun, and began talking casually as if he had done a good deed. Oh, what prejudice can lead to! This soldier didn't seem to be such a bad man, but the way he had been raised allowed him to feel no more remorse at killing those two Negroes than he would have felt about killing two mad dogs.

That evening they were billeted in the home of a Confederate brigadier general. It was decided that the tall Negro would become his slave. The general, about sixty years of age, seemed to be a fine gentleman. He belonged to Lee's army and had just spent a few days' leave with his family. "I wonder," he said to Eugène, "what the Confederacy could possibly have done to Canada, Ireland, Germany, France, and all the other countries in the world to make their people want to fight her."

When Eugène told him that he had not been caught bearing arms and that all he asked was to go back to Canada, he replied: "You seem a likable enough young man, but you're like old dog Tray. You've been caught in very bad company."

Eugène hadn't eaten since the previous night and even before then. He hadn't had a good meal since the evening of the battle. His miseries had begun with Burbridge's retreat. Now they dined and breakfasted with the general. These were the only two meals Eugène was to have for the next two days, with the exception of some chestnuts the guards allowed the prisoners to gather in a wood along the way.

The next evening they came to a place called Lebanon, just in time to miss getting something to eat. Other prisoners were waiting for the departure of a freight train which was to take them to Liberty.

Eugène and his companions were put into a cattle car already full of prisoners, including about thirty wounded. They had to wait for another hour while the locomotive maneuvered back and forth, either to drop off a car on a siding, or to add another to the long line of cars making up the train. As it moved back and forth, it tossed the prisoners one on top of the other, wrenching cries of pain from the unfortunate wounded.

Cold nights are the general rule and not the exception in Virginia, even during the summertime. And on that particular night it was even much colder than usual. Two inches of snow fell. This was considered an unprecedented event for that time of year, even by the oldest inhabitants of the region. It was the night of the 7th to the 8th of October 1864, and Eugène would forever afterwards remember it as a night of unspeakable suffering. Even so, he saw beside him wretched wounded soldiers who were far more to be pitied than he was. The car was open to the elements, for it was made up only of open slats as is the case with all cattle-cars. The soldiers were bunched so closely together that they couldn't move and it was pointlessly barbaric to shut the prisoners in there an hour before the train left. Finally, the train started out and about midnight the prisoners were unloaded at Liberty, where they had to wait two hours for another train to arrive. The prisoners had to get off in the snow and Eugène, whose bare feet had been bruised by two days' forced march, found the two-hour wait for the convoy train very long indeed. He tried to keep warm by jumping up and down. The train finally arrived and the prisoners took their places in a car intended for passengers, but on the inside it didn't look in the least like a first-class car. The day passed by without anyone offering the prisoners anything to eat. The first rays of the sun had melted the snow and the day was even rather warm.

About seven in the evening, they arrived in Lynchburg, where the prisoners were taken to the prison to spend the night. Naturally, they arrived too late to receive any rations. They had to sleep on the stone paving in the prison yard. The next morning, each man was given a pound of wheat bread which he hastily devoured while washing it down with water from a pump in the middle of the yard. The bread was supposed to last them until the next morning, but an hour after it was distributed not a single crumb could be found among all those starving men.

During the afternoon, they took their places in a supply train which deposited them toward evening in Danville. They were taken to the prison where they had the privilege of yawning as much as they wanted to replace the lunch that hadn't come and the dinner they wouldn't have. However, they weren't at all unhappy to be able to sleep with a roof over their heads and the next morning they received rations similar to what had been distributed to them in Lynchburg. "After having done justice to the delicious meal, etc., etc.," as newspaper articles are wont to say much more appropriately about champagne dinners, the prisoners took the convoy train to Richmond where they arrived about nine in the evening.

Part Five: Prison Life

CHAPTER XLVIII

CASTLE THUNDER

I n the train convoy, Eugène had approached the sergeant of the guard to tell him
that, since he hadn't been captured bearing arms, he didn't want to be considered
a prisoner of war.

"I'm a deserter from the Union army," he added, "and as such the government
sent me to the Kentucky border. Later on some of Burbridge's men picked me up.
They took me with them to Saltville as the servant of one of their officers. But I
haven't taken up arms again against the Confederacy and I would like to have new
measures taken to have me repatriated."

Naturally, Eugène was quite careful not to add that, once he had arrived in
Gladesville, he had enlisted in the Confederate army which he had left a few days
afterwards without authorization.

"It's not up to me to decide that matter," the noncommissioned officer answered,
"but when we get to Richmond I'll see that the proper authorities are notified."

When the prisoners got off the train in the Confederate capital, they were taken
to a place opposite the infamous Libby prison, where the sergeant called the roll. Having found all present and accounted for, he said: "If there are any deserters among you,
let them step forward."

Eugène didn't have to be asked twice. An American followed his example. It would
be hard to describe the chorus of imprecations and curses that poured forth from the
group of prisoners. And to repeat the rather harsh words said on that occasion would
hardly be polite. The deserters were booed, threatened, insulted, sworn at, sent to the
devil, and the others promised to hang them high if ever they should meet them.

The sergeant handed the prisoners over to the Libby prison warden and led the
two deserters to the provost marshal, who thought he recognized Eugène.

"What's your name?" he asked.

"Washington C. Joslin," Eugène answered without blinking an eye. That was the name he had given to the sergeant of the guard. The name belonged to a deserter who had been sent with him to Gladesville. Instead of enlisting in Colonel Prentice's regiment like Eugène did, he had taken off. He looked somewhat like Eugène; he was Eugène's height, but he was of a much darker-skinned complexion.[1]

"You've already been here?" the provost marshal continued.

"Yes, I left here four weeks ago with a squad you sent to the Kentucky border." Then Eugène repeated the story he had told the sergeant and, when the provost marshal had heard it, he had him taken to Castle Thunder.

Needless to say, Eugène wasn't given anything to eat that night. It was the rule in all Southern prisons that new arrivals weren't to be fed. The stay in these prisons was so pleasant that to be worthy of partaking of that pleasure you needed to prepare yourself by fasting and to continue fasting thereafter out of gratitude to a solicitous government which had found you such wonderful lodgings.

The castle was five or six stories high, and Eugène was billeted in the attic where he found himself in the company of seven or eight suspects from all walks of society. There were no bars on the windows. It had been decided, and rightly so, that those being detained there couldn't escape from such a height. At the very most they could commit suicide, but that didn't matter. During his stay there, Eugène had the opportunity to see a poor devil, desperate with hunger, plunge from the window down to the courtyard pavement below, where he died instantly of a broken neck.

The food was even less plentiful and the menu even less varied than it had been at Castle Lightning. The bread ration was the same as at Libby prison — two pieces of cornbread a day. These pieces were about two inches wide, two inches long, and two inches thick. Put on a diet like this, a man in robust health could die of hunger within five or six months. It would have been more humane to kill him outright than to make him suffer so long.

Eugène had been in Castle Thunder for about two weeks when a man wearing a Federal cavalry uniform was brought up to the attic. He was in serious trouble. A former Confederate soldier, he had been taken prisoner by the Union army and had taken the oath of allegiance. The Confederates had caught him bearing arms. He and Eugène had confided in each other and had plotted to escape as soon as they could under cover of a dark night. It was quite a daring plan. The cavalryman, who probably belonged to a secret society of some sort, had managed to get a rope long enough for him to slide down to the court below and strong enough to hold the weight of two men. There were two sentries in the courtyard and another on a third-floor parapet. They would have to come under fire from these three men, then climb a palisade of vertical planks about eight feet high, and, finally, run the risk of being arrested in the street. This bold escape attempt was never executed. The day after they had laid their escape plans, the cavalryman was put under lock and key and Eugène was called before the provost marshal. The provost marshal made him swear that he had never taken up arms again since his departure from Richmond at the beginning of the preceding September. They then sent him to Libby prison, where he was listed in the register under the name of Washington C. Joslin.

CHAPTER XLIX

An Unfortunate Encounter

L ibby prison, like Castle Lightning and Pemberton prison, had once been a tobacco factory. It was a large brick building with a ground floor and two additional stories. The interior consisted of three vast rooms, one above the other. Open stairways with trapdoors cut through the floors connected the three rooms. Light and cold entered the rooms through barred, paneless windows, which on one side looked out on the main street and on the other on the James River.

The Richmond prisons served primarily as warehouses and schools of fasting for the prisoners. During the summer months, there was a continual population turnover. Some prisoners were sent to die of hunger at Andersonville and Salisbury. But in winter, with only minor skirmishes being fought, Libby and Pemberton had enough room to house just about all those who had been captured in the vicinity.

The prisoners were ahead of the game since, although they died of hunger just as easily in Richmond as elsewhere, at least Libby offered them the advantage of having a roof over their heads while the prisoners at Andersonville or Salisbury were exposed to all the inclemencies of the weather.[1] As a result, the average mortality rate among the prisoners of war in those prisons was much higher than in Richmond.

To give some idea regarding the numbers of victims of the privations that the Southerners made their prisoners endure, we need only say that the infamous Wirz, former camp warden at Andersonville, who was hanged after the war by Federal authorities, was accused of having starved 30,000 men to death during the four years he was in command. That was, perhaps, an exaggeration. However, if even 45,000 men fell into his hands during that time, it is quite possibly true.

Upon arriving at Libby prison, Eugène was first billeted on the ground floor with about one hundred Negroes and about twenty whites. It certainly wasn't their humanitarian spirit that had led the rebels to spare the lives of these prisoners of the black persuasion. At first they had been put to work on fortifications under enemy fire. But then General Butler noticed those workers wearing Federal uniforms. Realizing, as he glued the larger of his two eyes against the lens of a field glass, that these new embankment workers had been tanned more than could be expected by the Virginia sun alone, he had hurriedly rounded up all the Confederate officers who had recently fallen into Union hands and made them work on the fortifications under fire from their own side. The result: the rebels had finally brought the Negroes back to Libby prison where they hoped these dark-skinned prisoners would make themselves very useful by driving mad the few whites it pleased the warden to throw their way.

As long as the Negroes had been working outside, they had been given a dinner substantial enough to allow some of them, at the end of the day, to bring a piece of bread or a slice of bacon back with them to the prison where they spent the night. Among the whites imprisoned there were some who treated the Negroes with supreme disdain. This did not prevent them, when they believed that no one was watching, from picking up and putting in their mouths either a bone or a piece of bacon rind that a Negro had thrown away after having chewed on it for an hour or so without managing to swallow it.

Eugène could not understand such illogical behavior. He knew these men weren't faking their repugnance for Negroes. He could not imagine that their hunger could be excruciating enough to make them overcome this disgust. He didn't yet know to what extent hunger can triumph over all aversions.

It should be said to the credit of the Negroes that blacks and whites would have gotten along beautifully if all the representatives of the white race had known and practiced the most basic rules of politeness. The descendant of the British races, be he English, Scotch, Irish, or American, is always of the opinion that the mold he was cast from was broken after he was made.[2] He heartily detests all other races. For him, the Anglo-Saxon race is absolute perfection. Those who, although they aren't Anglo-Saxon, belong to the Caucasian race, can still find favor in his eyes, provided they acknowledge the alleged superiority of his race over that of other people's. But he finds the Negro hardly fit to live. When he is well mannered, the Anglo-Saxon succeeds more or less in dissimulating the profound contempt that foreigners inspire in him, but if not properly brought up, he doesn't miss a single chance to display his arrogance.

There was among the whites a cavalryman who was an outstanding boxer. He began a friendly sparring match with a young Negro. The object of the match was to see who could knock the other's cap off first. The white got the upper hand. He took on another Negro, then another, then yet another until he had defeated five or six of the most dexterous. Finally, a Negro stepped up and knocked his cap off to great applause from the swarthy Africans. The white went back on guard, but, after a few feints, his cap flew off again. In short, after losing his cap seven or eight times, he was blind with rage and began hitting back like a madman, with fists clenched tightly shut, insulting all Negroes in general and his adversary in particular. The Negro parried almost all his blows and gave him a thrashing the likes of which he had never felt. A few whites tried to break up the fight. For their pains they were showered with blows which made their eyes look as black as those of any black African.

From that time on the twenty whites became virtual slaves to the one hundred Negroes.[3] The world had turned topsy-turvy. At that time, besides the minuscule bread ration, each prisoner received about a tablespoon of soup made with little black beans. This was brought to them in a sort of small vat made from a barrel sawed in half. The Negroes positioned themselves so the whites couldn't get to the pot. The situation had become intolerable. The whites complained to the guard who told them: "These Negroes are your protégés, your favorites, your equals. You have fought to win the privilege of making them your masters. What are you complaining about? You should bless the black hands that strike you."

Fortunately, a few days later the Negroes were taken from Libby prison to be sent heaven knows where.[4] Other white prisoners came in great numbers. They were billeted on the ground floor and the Negroes' former companions were moved to the second floor, where there were already about two to three hundred men. Eugène was struck with terror when he recognized among them some of the men from the squad he had come with to Richmond on his return from Gladesville.

Five weeks of deprivation had quite disfigured them and Eugène wouldn't have recognized them if he hadn't had very good reasons for doing so. When these men had last seen him two months earlier, he had been suffering almost constantly from hunger. He had already lost so much weight that the last five weeks of suffering hadn't changed him as much as it had these men who had entered Libby prison well fed. So they didn't have much trouble recognizing him. One of them, a young man of about twenty, said to him: "So there you are, you damned deserter, you traitor to the flag. I recognize you; you're one of the two cowards who stepped forward from the ranks in front of this prison five weeks ago."

"That's right! That's right! Let's hang the wretch!" cried two or three voices.

Eugène sensed he had to act boldly.

"I don't know you," he said to the young man. "I don't know what you want …"

He interrupted himself to land a blow to the pit of the other's stomach, which made him double over. Continuing to hit his accuser he went on: "And that will teach you to insult your betters. Ah! So you're calling me a coward? Wait a minute; I'll show you who's the coward."

Eugène was the smaller of the two and he had the upper hand. If the others had known he was a Canadian, their sympathies would have been with his adversary, but they believed him to be an American and, since he showed pluck, everyone cheered him on, with the exception of two or three of the Kentuckian's friends who didn't dare intervene, however. Finally, Eugène forced his adversary to admit he had been mistaken and he emerged from the fight safe and sound.

He told himself that the man he had just given a good hiding might very well manage, with the help of his friends, to convince the others he was telling the truth about Eugène in order to get his revenge. In that case, they would probably hang Eugène from the prison rafters. This action would not have been without precedent since in another prison, Salisbury, if we are not mistaken,[5] Federal prisoners had taken justice into their own hands and hanged six of their comrades during the night.

{

CHAPTER L

The Horrors Of Libby Prison

}

E ugène waited feverishly for the jailer to return; he came twice a day accompanied by his aides to distribute the rations. He was a big, muscular, surly fellow with the looks and manners of an overseer;[1] Leduc had already seen him rush down the stairs and, with his revolver and knife, threaten the crowd of black and white prisoners who were fighting over their meager pittance. He came at the usual hour and, as he was climbing the stairs leading to the top floor, Eugène tried to follow him. The guard yelled at him to go back down, and when Eugène tried to explain that he would consider it a great favor if he granted him permission to visit a friend upstairs, the jailer turned and punched him so hard right in the face that Eugène was thrown back down the two or three steps he had just climbed. As the Canadian got up, he noticed that the jailer was pointing the barrel of his cocked pistol right at him.

"Well, go ahead and shoot, you coward! And be damned!" yelled Eugène as he wiped away the blood flowing from his nose.

"Try to go up those stairs and you'll see if I don't shoot."

"Who says I was trying to go upstairs without your permission? I asked you politely if I could go up to see a friend and for that you hit me."

Seeing Eugène was no longer trying to go upstairs, the guard jailer continued on up to the top floor. He most likely regretted his brutality, because when he came down again he spotted Eugène, who was still standing not far from the staircase, and said: "You can go up, but if you do, you'll stay there. I hit you because I thought you wanted to attack me when my back was turned. If I allowed prisoners to follow me on the stairs, my life wouldn't be worth a plugged nickel. I'm letting you go up because I think I had the wrong idea about your intentions."

So Eugène was able to go to the top floor and thus escape impending danger. When the Kentuckians moved up to the last floor two months later, Leduc had gotten so thin they no longer recognized him.

The three or four hundred prisoners held in each room were divided into squads of sixteen men. Each squad leader divided the four loaves of cornbread, each one weighing about one pound, into sixteen exactly equal parts. When the loaves had been divided in this way, he asked the assembled men if they were satisfied with the allotments. As long as there wasn't unanimous agreement that all the portions were of equal size, he had to take a crumb from one portion to add to another until everyone was satisfied. Then one of the men took the booklet containing the names of all the men in the squad and turned his back to the sixteen rations laid out on the floor. Another man put his hand at random on one of the rations and asked: "Whose is this?"

"John Smith's," said the man with the booklet as he made a mark by the aforesaid John Smith's name.

"Whose is this?" repeated the first man as he pointed out another ration.

"Washington C. Joslin's," said the man with the book, without looking, always keeping his back turned to the rations and checking off the names as each man got his share.

And so it went until the last name on the list had been called out. To further insure that the guarantee of impartiality was even more complete, the two distributors were chosen on the spot to make it practically impossible for them to have an understanding beforehand.

It needs to be kept in mind that in Libby prison the smallest crumb of cornbread was considered worth its weight in gold. The prisoners looked like veritable walking skeletons. Some, though they could no longer stand up, found the courage to crawl on their hands and knees to squabble over a crumb of cornbread no bigger than a plum pit — a crumb that a prisoner who wasn't as hungry had let fall into the spit and tobacco juice on the floor. These struggles usually degenerated into fights. Then you would see three or four of these living specters, with every bone showing through the skin of their gaunt faces, jumping on one another, rolling on the floor, hitting each other without having the strength to do any damage, trying unsuccessfully to strangle one another, and finally, each in turn, falling back on the floor exhausted.

They all had scurvy, and, when someone grabbed hold of them, the tip of his finger seemed to sink into the little bit of flesh remaining, leaving a hole that disappeared after a few minutes.

For a time they were given bones which passed for meat. All the meat which hadn't been removed from the carcasses before sending them to the prison was divided into microscopic portions for the prisoners. As for the bones, they were distributed by lot. You were lucky if you got a bone. The happy mortal whom fortune favored by making him owner of such a treasure began by breaking it open with a stone to extract the marrow. Then he pulverized it so he could munch on the crumbly parts.

When the inner parts of the bone had been gnawed so nothing was left but the hardest surface, he boiled what was left to make a delicious soup as fatty as if he had boiled a stone. The poor devils who only had the bones poking through their own skins would give a half-ration of cornbread for a pint of that so-called soup. Each time the bone was cooked, it was beaten once more and gnawed at again. When it had provided ten soups or so, the little bit that was left had become tender enough for the prisoner to crush with his teeth.

A bone went for a good price. In fact, there was a lot of bartering going on in Libby prison. The prisoners smoked and chewed tobacco. Instead of giving up their pipes, some smokers had taken up the tobacco-chewing habit in prison in spite of the fact that each pound of tobacco consumed in prison meant foregoing one day's ration for the average prisoner.

Some prisoners had smuggled greenbacks into the prison. How had they managed to elude the vigilance of those whose mission it was to search newcomers when they entered prison and to confiscate all valuables found in their possession? There's a mystery that has never been explained satisfactorily.

At the beginning of the winter of 1864-65, flour went for eight hundred dollars a barrel in Confederate currency and promised to go even higher.[2] The inmates of Libby prison who happened to have some capital contemplated making it last by speculating on the misery of their comrades in captivity. Human nature is the same everywhere. By bribing the guard, they had wheat bread brought in, which they displayed before the others' starving eyes, and which they traded for cornbread rations, always managing to make a certain profit.

They also sold tobacco. Starvation had so weakened the minds as it had weakened the bodies of the poor prisoners that they didn't hesitate to exchange half a day's ration for a plug of tobacco. These goods were hoisted up at night by means of a rope let down from a window looking out over the James River. They remained displayed in broad daylight without the guard saying anything about it. It is quite likely that he took his cut from this trafficking.

As the others became weaker, the speculators, who kept themselves fat and sleek, became more arrogant. The disproportion in physical strength between them and their unfortunate victims became greater and greater. They took advantage of this situation, never letting pass an opportunity to bully men too feeble to defend themselves. They were heartily detested and it was rumored that it was men like these who had been hanged by the Salisbury prisoners in revenge for the bad treatment they had made them endure.

There were two stoves in each room, in which three armloads of softwood were burned in each twenty-four-hour period. The winter was very cold and air entered through the paneless windows. When there was wood, the stoves burned red, but the supply was quickly used up. When there was a fire, the strongest gathered around it and drove the others away with their fists.

As long as the authorities continued to give bones to the prisoners, those who couldn't get near the stoves consoled themselves by pledging half of their next ration for a pint of that famous soup that at least had the virtue of warming them. When they no longer got any more of this carrion, they were content to pay the same price for hot water that had been salted and peppered. It should be noted that all these transactions were done on credit. A prisoner would never have agreed to barter his ration when he had it in hand.

Interior of Libby prison, Richmond, Virginia, with prisoners from General Lee's army confined after the surrender.

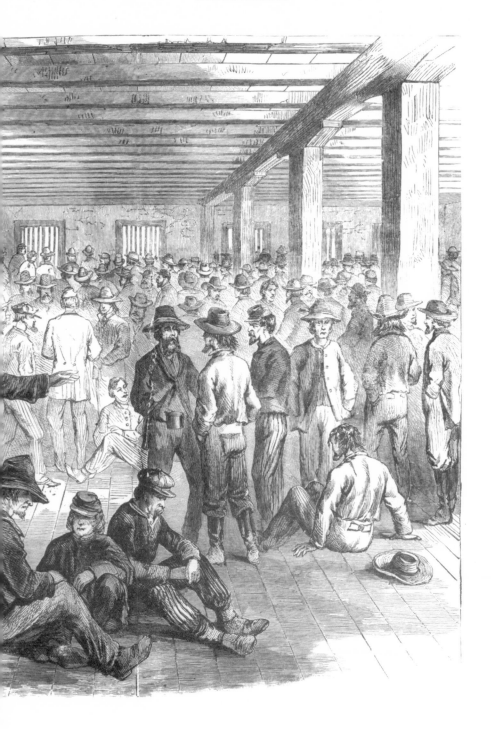

The creditor was always there to get his share when the provisions were distributed. And, since he was usually a well-fed man while the debtor couldn't stand up or found it difficult to remain standing, he never experienced the slightest difficulty in getting paid.

A few days before Christmas, the prisoners were served a kind of small cod, which they ate raw and found to be excellent. Hunger is the best seasoning for any dish. After two or three days, the cod disappeared and was never seen again. From that time on, the prisoners had to be content with the infinitesimal ration of cornbread. Despite their misfortune, or perhaps because of it, the prisoners often sang. Was this due to the soldiers' naturally carefree nature or the weakening of their mental faculties? No one can say. But one thing is sure: these fits of gaiety didn't last long and those who sang the most weren't necessarily those who cried the least.

CHAPTER LI

You Can't Get Enough
Of a Good Thing

On New Year's Day, each of the prisoners received a blanket, which the United States Sanitary Commission had had delivered to them under a flag of truce. The folks back home hadn't forgotten them. People knew they were suffering and made every effort to help.

Up to that time, the prisoners had bedded down on the floor with no covers at all. They huddled together to keep warm and they slept "spoon style," all lying on the same side. They would stay one hour in the same position; then, since they heard the sentinel calling out the hour as was the custom in the Confederate army, the row leader called out: "Left spoon!" or "Right spoon!" as the case might be, and everyone turned to that side. The arrival of the blankets put a temporary end to that nightly exercise. They went back to it later when most of the blankets had been converted into edibles, as we will see later. Meanwhile, the prisoners grouped themselves in threes. They placed two blankets under them to make a mattress and covered themselves with the third.

This change brought great relief to those poor wretches whose bodies, wasted by privations, had become so emaciated that sleeping on the floor had rubbed their skin raw and they all had sores on their sides.

They were also literally eaten up by vermin. Each man was a millionaire as far as that went — he had millions of insects on him of the most disgusting type. There wasn't any remedy for that. How can you ask men dying of hunger and shivering with cold to strip themselves naked so they can wash in ice-cold water the tattered rags covering their emaciated bodies? All of them or almost all had recurring fevers. The prison doctor gave them quinine and made them drink castor oil right out of a one and a half pint bottle. Privation had so corrupted their taste that that oily substance seemed delicious to them and they drank long draughts of it.

The story goes that the insects we've been talking about were so huge that the prisoners could jump on their backs, grab hold of one of their ears, and gallop around the room at sixty miles an hour. That, of course, is an exaggeration. It's like the story told by the soldier who said he woke up one night in camp thinking that he saw a stranger seated in his cabin. After rubbing his eyes, he had realized it was a huge flea that had eaten all his hardtack and was picking his teeth with a bayonet.[1]

Although this story seems hardly believable, it is true that the guests in Libby prison were so covered with vermin that they killed them while sleeping and that, a few days after the blanket delivery we have related, while the prisoners were walking around with the aforesaid blankets on their shoulders you could not have stuck a pin through those improvised shawls without being guilty of "insecticide."

The prisoners had no amusements of any sort. They were forbidden to go near the windows on pain of death. If the sentry saw a head leaning on the window bars he would shoot first and shout afterwards: "Get away from there, damned Yankee."

One poor devil, far from suspecting what he was risking, had the audacity to want to take a look at the street, and his skull had been shattered by a bullet.

As winter went by, deaths occurred more and more frequently. When it was obvious that a man was dying, he was sent to the hospital where, more often than not, he passed away, even though conditions there were much better than in Libby prison. Ordinarily, when a man was sent to the hospital, he was too weak ever to leave it again. It's true that if every man whose weakened condition demanded immediate care had been sent to the hospital, the prison would have been emptied on the spot and the hospital would have been much too small to hold them all. A great number of men died in each of the three rooms and Eugène himself had lost all hope of leaving that earthly hell alive.

Leduc had formed a corporation with a Philadelphian and a German. Their capital consisted of the three partners' blankets. However, the Canadian, who seemed to be the weakest of the three, outlived the two others, who died of starvation some two weeks after having helped squander the association's capital. One night of extravagance was all it took to ruin them, for it's true that the best-established companies cannot maintain their success when the owners take to spending the profits.

Eugène was fast asleep, all the while chasing insects and dreaming that he was attending a magnificent banquet; that was the habitual dream of these poor wretches who, during the day, couldn't stop talking about delicious sauces, exquisite dishes, and how to prepare them. This kind of talk and the dreams that followed never failed to whet appetites which were already fierce enough.

All of a sudden, Leduc felt someone shake him by the arm and, opening his eyes, he noticed the Philadelphian, who kept tugging at him.

"Why don't you leave me alone?" he said. "I was enjoying a splendid meal."

"Don't waste your time dreaming now! We're finally going to eat. The guard is buying the blankets. We're going to sacrifice one of the three and get a loaf of wheat bread in exchange. A one-pound loaf to split among the three of us! It's a godsend! Are we going to eat our fill or not?"

"Let's sell one blanket....You don't object, do you, Dutchy?"

"Ja, I haf no injection."

"Then let's be quick about it. I like to have things move along when I'm doing business."

The Philadelphian went to the end of the room, handed over the blanket, which was lowered by rope, and soon came back with a pound loaf. With what meticulous care they divided the bread into three precisely equal parts and how each one relished his share! It was so good that they couldn't resist the temptation of eating another, and so a second blanket was sacrificed on the spot. Then the Philadelphian, taking advantage of the Prussian's absence, stole his blanket and sold it.

Despite his honesty, Eugène hadn't had the courage to refuse his share of the profit from this illegal sale. May those who have behaved better in similar circumstances cast the first stone!

Thus they sold their last blanket, which the Prussian tried in vain to claim was his. It belonged to Eugène and bore his mark. The next day the company didn't have a single blanket left, but each of its the members had eaten a pound and a third of wheat bread — a feast without precedent in the annals of Libby prison.

CHAPTER LII

Hunger Is a Bad Advisor

Toward the beginning of February 1865, Eugène, sole survivor of the corporation founded for the express purpose of dealing in Uncle Sam's blankets, had become so weak that his row neighbors were obliged to bring him his ration. When he had eaten his frugal meal — the word frugal[1] isn't an exaggeration — he regained enough strength to drag himself with difficulty as far as the faucet that supplied water to the prison. After having a drink of water, he came back to his place exhausted and remained lying on the floor until another meal allowed him to get up again and undertake his twice daily journey once again. He sensed that another two weeks on this regimen would certainly be the death of him and he was resigned to his fate. He resolved to eat his fill one more time before dying.

The speculators had become unbearably arrogant. They had found a way to get applejack, which is apple whiskey, in spite of prison regulations. The regulations! What a joke! No laws or regulations can withstand the almighty power of money, that god worshiped in every country in the world and especially in the United States!

The speculators in question — we are using the word "speculator" because that was the term used in prison to describe these bloodsuckers — were always slightly intoxicated. They policed the room, and good God, what police! More than once Eugène had seen three or four of these big brutes get together and beat a poor half-starved devil black and blue. Their display of wheat bread naturally aroused the envy of these poor starving wretches, and the least honest or perhaps the most desperate of them tried to help themselves surreptitiously during the night.

Woe to the guilty man caught in the act or whose guilt was discovered. Two or three burly fellows seized him while another struck him repeatedly with all his might using a board two inches wide.[2] The battered and bloody body would be left lying there. One of Eugène's neighbors, who had been ordered to go wash his face and who had refused because he didn't have the strength to move, had been hit with a cane on his forehead, resulting in the loss of a lot of blood. He had to be taken to the hospital and probably never left there alive.

In Eugène's weakened state, defying the wrath of those brutes with human faces was like risking death. Nonetheless, he didn't think twice about it; he wanted to eat — that was all he knew and that was all he wanted. The consequences mattered little to him.

During his stay in the room on the top floor, he had swapped many of his rations and half-rations either for tobacco, or for bones, or for the famous watery soup, or for portions of wheat bread. Like all the others, he had always made his deal on credit and, not having been able to do otherwise, he had always paid with great regularity; therefore, his credit was good with the Dun & Bradstreets of the institution.

He resolved to take advantage of that circumstance to gorge himself, and there he was buying portions of wheat bread from five or six different speculators and promising his next ration to each one in turn. He did so well that when the time came to distribute the food, he was no longer hungry. If he had been able to multiply his ration so as to satisfy all his creditors, he would have been the happiest of men.

Now he saw that the fatal hour of retribution had come, and he expected to face a quarter of an hour of reckoning that would make the famous Rabelaisian quarter of an hour seem like a St. Jean Baptiste picnic.[3] To remain lying down and pretending to be sick wouldn't get him anywhere; so he decided to face up to the danger and be present when the rations were distributed.

"Whose is this?" the distributor asked.

"Washington C. Joslin's."

"His ration's mine!" cried out a chorus of five or six voices.

"Gentlemen," said Eugène, "I admit my guilt. I wanted to eat before I died and I've eaten. I know you're going to beat me and that I won't long survive the beating you're about to give me with your board. Get on with it and try to put an end to this long agony I've been enduring for the almost six months now."

"Well, so be it. We're going to take what's coming to us out of your miserable hide," said one of the speculators as he grabbed him by the throat.

One of the creditors intervened. "No violence," he said. "Let's overlook this first offense of his. I'll be responsible for reimbursing the others. If he lives, he'll pay me back in time." Eugène was moved to tears. He seized his protector's hand. "Be assured that my gratitude ..."

"The devil take you and your gratitude," interrupted the other. "You can prove it by repaying me."

Eugène never was to have the opportunity to pay him back. The very same day one thousand of the weakest prisoners were released on parole from Libby and Pemberton prisons.

The reason for this choice is easy to demonstrate. It was in the Southerners' interest to exchange men who were likely to die in their hands — and who, for the most part, would take a long time to regain their strength before being able to take up arms once again — for Confederate prisoners getting fat in Northern prisons. They kept the strongest, that is to say, those who hadn't been reduced to skeletons for want of food. That group was made up of the speculators — who were to expiate their sins by staying in prison longer than the others — and the new arrivals.

Eugène's feast almost cost him dearly. The ample repast he had just eaten had restored his strength so well that he wasn't considered weak enough. He saw the others lining up to leave while he was condemned to stay. That sight threw him into such despondency that he felt the blood draining from his thin cheeks, which had taken on a healthy color after his abundant meal. He was shaking with fever and was seized with a spasm at just the right moment. He took advantage of this to slip into the ranks of those who were supposed to leave; he got there just in time to give his name to the doctor who didn't seem to remember that he had examined and rejected him. The prisoners were brought down to the ground floor where they were given a double ration and where they spent the night.

The next day, the doors of the prison opened and the prisoners staggered out like drunken men. Their lungs were no longer used to the open air and their spindly legs could barely hold up their emaciated bodies. Dirty, disgusting, covered with body lice, they were gaunt to the point that just by looking at them you could have studied anatomy without using a scalpel. They looked like repulsive rags covering walking bundles of bones.

Many had to walk barefoot on the frozen cobblestones. Others, whose shoes were worn out, had ingeniously managed to re-attach the soles to the uppers with rags. When these flapping soles caught on some crack in the pavement, the poor devil thus shod fell full length, dragging a half a dozen or so of his companions in misery down with him.

Nevertheless, despite these many falls, despite the fatigue brought on by the journey, all those angular faces were smiling. They boarded the steamer *William Allison,* but it was impossible to leave that day because of the ice blocking the shores of the James River. They had to return to Libby prison, where all the prisoners who were to be released on parole were locked up on the ground floor. The usual ration was doubled and the authorities even had the good grace to bring them a container of sorghum molasses. However, the prisoners, who had neither plates nor bowls, had to receive their portion of molasses in their upturned caps. Eight days later they left again — this time, never to come back.

Part Six: Desertion

CHAPTER LIII

PAROLED[1]

The prisoners paroled from Southern prisons weren't to take up arms again until they had been duly exchanged for an equal number of Confederate prisoners. The thousand men released from Libby and Pemberton prisons were to travel under a flag of truce down the James River on board the *William Allison*. Two or three miles upstream from Wilcox Landing, they were to board the steamboat *City of New York* and proceed to Annapolis, Maryland, where Camp Parole was located.

Eight days earlier, ice had prevented the steamboat from leaving port.[2] The captains in that part of the country aren't at all accustomed to obstacles of this sort. Their ships aren't built to contend with such a rare inconvenience. The winter of 1864-1865 had been extremely harsh; quite understandably the trip was postponed for eight days because of ice.

The *William Allison* traveled down the James River. The banks were bristling with high-caliber cannon. Moreover, it was a known fact that the river bottom was well lined with torpedoes; only the pilots that the Richmond authorities had entrusted with the secrets of their locations could navigate around them. The famous General Mosby was on board and the prisoners could examine him at their leisure.[3]

Along the banks of the river the Federals had positioned their forces as follows: the Army of the Potomac had its right on the right bank of the James; the Army of the James had its left close to the opposite bank, and Union gunboats held the area in between. Naturally the *William Allison* couldn't go beyond that line. It came to a stop at a respectful distance and, having disembarked, the prisoners went on foot to Wilcox Landing.

As they came aboard the *City of New York,* each soldier received a large hunk of wheat bread, a huge slice of ham, and a tin cup containing a full pint of steaming coffee. Then they went to the saloon where they could munch away at their leisure. Toward evening, they passed City Point, where Grant had set up his general headquarters.

The next morning, the prisoners came down to get their ration of bread, ham, and coffee. To prevent disorderliness and crowding, a cordon of guards with fixed bayonets had been placed right in the middle of the steerage quarters. The prisoners went down one of the stairways, filed to the starboard side, entered a room at the front of the boat, received their ration, went out by another door, returned by passing to the port side, and went up the other stairway.

Army surgeons had been ordered to see that these poor devils didn't get any more food than their ruined stomachs could digest. But the memory of hardships they had endured made the prisoners worry about what the future might bring. They felt they were having one of those fantastic dreams with which their imaginations had so often comforted them during their captivity, and were afraid that they would wake up to find themselves suffering hunger pangs again.

Haunted by this childish fear, all they thought about was getting food so they would have it when they needed it. When they had gulped down their first meal or put away what they hadn't been able to eat, most of them returned for more. They slipped by, or rather we should say, bypassed the sentries, for this must be said in praise of the guards: not a single one of them would have had the sad courage to use his weapons to push back that mob of ragged skeletons.

They had been feeding the prisoners breakfast for three hours — at least 1,500 rations instead of a thousand had been handed out. The crowd was still at the door shoving and clamoring to get food. Naturally the men yelling the loudest were those who had come back for more, and had already derived some strength from their hearty breakfasts; it is likely that there were still some poor devils who had not yet received a thing. The surgeon-major lost his patience. The guard was removed and two cases, each containing 150 pounds of hardtack, were tossed out like fodder to the prisoners.

Never had a charge against Confederate positions been executed with more gusto than the stampede on those two boxes. The *furia francese* pales by comparison with the ensuing attack.[4] The thin boards covering the hardtack were smashed; then there was a free-for-all with fists flying. Leduc was right in the middle of the mêlée, filling a large oilcloth bag to the brim with hardtack while the others exchanged blows.

Only one man was wounded — a poor devil who fell under the others' feet and got his arm broken — but several unfortunate wretches died in the aftermath of that brawl, not from mortal blows, but from eating too many of the biscuits they had so desperately coveted.

A hardtack biscuit measures about five inches long by four inches wide and is hardly a quarter of an inch thick, but it's as hard as a brick. If you put it in hot water or in coffee it swells up and thickens to amazing proportions. Ten of these biscuits weigh a pound. A poor Zouave who had eaten forty-two of them in a six-hour period choked to death while eating the forty-third. By the time the ship put into port at Fort Monroe, three men had died from overeating. Ten or so others were in not much better shape. Everyone was very ill. It was ascribed to seasickness, but it was really hardtack sickness, because the sea was quite calm the entire time they were steaming along on Chesapeake Bay.

The *City of New York* was a magnificent ship. The velvet-covered saloon furnishings must have kept living souvenirs of the prisoners who were aboard. Eugène hadn't seen a mirror for six months. When he had last seen himself, he had thought he was handsome enough, but as he passed by one of the mirrors in the saloon, he saw what he had become. At first he thought he was looking at a stranger; then he moved and he realized that that horrible face was really his own, and he burst into tears.

He had become frightfully thin; his eyes were sunk in their sockets. His features had lost their natural roundness and had become quite angular. He had been a handsome blond-haired boy with rosy cheeks — he was now as pale as a corpse. His face was covered with a thick layer of filth which looked like it had been there since the discovery of America. His hair, now down to his shoulders, sheltered countless parasites. A clump of yellowish hairs growing on the side of his chin also housed a very tightly packed and very active population. His old threadbare uniform, dirty and covered with vermin, hung in tatters on his shrunken chest. He turned away in disgust and moved on deeply convinced that, decidedly, his stay in prison hadn't improved his looks.

When they arrived at Camp Parole, the prisoners — we continue to accord them that title because they hadn't yet been exchanged — were first taken to bathhouses of a sort, where they had to wash thoroughly before entering the barracks. After throwing off all his old rags in the anteroom, each man stretched out in a bathtub full of warmish water, where they let him soak for a while. Then he was soaped and scrubbed vigorously. When he had been cleaned thoroughly, he went into another room, where he received new linen and a new uniform. He was then released after being told to get a shave and haircut.

These bathhouses were some distance away from the camp itself, so the new arrivals were taken by wagon to the barracks. Then, they were placed in the care of doctors who put them on strict diets and gave them the medicine they needed, since almost all of them came back with scurvy and ague.[5]

Each soldier released from the Southern prisons could claim two months' pay plus a pension of $7.00 per month for each month spent in captivity. He was also granted a thirty-day leave as soon as he was fit to travel without endangering his health. Upon arrival, Eugène had given his real name and had counted on getting his leave and using it to return to Canada before anyone could check his record. Two weeks after his arrival, he was strong enough to move about without getting tired too easily. He was gaining weight, but he was still pale. Three weeks later, he was granted his leave, drew a six-month pension, and two months' pay. He left for the Northeast, fully intending to go back to Canada.

He took the troop train at Annapolis in the company of another soldier from Camp Parole who was going on leave. This man was a thirty-five-year-old Scotsman, a former sailor who had traveled the world over. They soon struck up a friendship and the Scotsman suggested that Eugène join the navy with him. In New York, he knew a former sailor who would not hesitate, so he believed, to help them both get some civilian clothes and join the navy. They arrived in New York at night and they went to stay with the man the Scotsman had told them about who owned a boarding house for sailors on Hamilton Street. By the next day both soldiers had donned civilian clothes.

CHAPTER LIV

Adventures and Misadventures

t that time, a $900 bonus in addition to the regular sailor's pay was being offered to anyone signing up for nine months in the U.S. Navy. Eugène said to himself: "I suffered miserably in the army and I never got a bonus. Instead of returning to Canada penniless, wouldn't it be better to do nine months' sea duty? I'll either put the $900 dollars in the bank or send it to my parents; that way I'll have a nest egg at my disposal when I go back to Canada."

Besides the bonus, a commission was also being paid in those days to anyone bringing in a recruit. Leduc had been in New York for a week when the landlord of the house where he was staying offered to accompany him to Brooklyn where he hoped to have Eugène join the navy. After visiting several frigates, Eugène's guide took him to a recruitment office. If Eugène had only taken the pains to read the posters by the door, he would have noticed that this was a recruitment office for the army's regular infantry, and not for the navy. This was bound to happen since, if there was a hornets' nest somewhere, Eugène would always manage to stumble blindly right into it.

No sooner had he walked through the door than he found himself face to face with the ex-supply sergeant of his old company, Company F of the 14th Regular Infantry Regiment of the U.S. Army.

This individual had been promoted to second lieutenant in the Tenth. He was the very officer who had sent Eugène out on reconnaissance at the Battle of the North Anna.

Eugène hadn't said a word, but his agitation gave him away. He had changed a great deal since last seeing the former sergeant from Company F. He wasn't as emaciated as when he had first got out of Libby prison, but he was still thin and very pale. He was no longer the round-faced rosy-cheeked young man they had known back in the Fourteenth and the second lieutenant probably wouldn't have recognized him, but Eugène's inability to hide his emotions put him on the right track.

"What's your name?" asked the second lieutenant.

"James Randall," Eugène answered.

"That's a lie. You're Eugène Leduc and you belong to the 14th Regular Infantry Regiment of the United States Army."

"You seem to be better informed than I am about myself; but since you already

In the trenches before Petersburg.

know my name better than I do, why do you ask?"

"Apparently, I have my reasons," answered the officer. Then, turning to two young soldiers, he said to them, "Take care of this man. He is your prisoner. Take him to Tammany Hall and hand him over to Major Smedberg."

The landlord had taken off as soon as he realized what was going on.

Eugène had the thirty-day leave pass from Camp Parole in his pocket, which showed he still had more than half of his leave left. If he had kept his head, he could easily have given a plausible explanation for his visit to the recruitment office which would have been considered satisfactory. The officer didn't know how and when he had left the regiment. Eugène could have convinced him that he had been taken prisoner at the Battle of Weldon Railroad — a battle that the Fourteenth had fought in. He could have told him he was just passing by to pay his respects. Instead of thinking of all this, while doing his utmost to deny he was Leduc, he had his hand deep in one of his coat pockets and was tearing up the pass that could have saved him, saying to himself that this document could get him in trouble if it was found on him.[1]

The two soldiers who took hold of him were two greenhorns[2] who had obviously never been under fire. That was quite evident from the way they threw their weight around. They placed Eugène between them and, with revolvers drawn, they escorted him to the New York ferry. With their posturing, these rookies seemed to be announcing to the public at large: "Admire us. We have a prisoner. Not every soldier has a prisoner."

Every time they were about to turn a corner, they waved their guns menacingly at Eugène and shouted directions at him so everyone on the street could hear them. They acted as if they were afraid their prisoner might take off at any moment.

Eugène thought about how much he would like to wring both their necks. He told himself that if only he had been in good health, he would have knocked one head over heels with a single punch and would have been shot at by the other whose bullet would very likely have hit some innocent bystander. He would then have slipped away in the crowd, perhaps to be arrested another day.

On board the ferry, he took the fragments of his pass out of his pocket and threw them overboard right under the noses of his guards. They asked him what those papers were and since he had already had just about enough of them, he answered sharply: "Mind your own business. You've been ordered to take me to Tammany Hall. You have no right to question me."

At Tammany Hall, Eugène found himself in the presence of Major Smedberg, Colonel Ilges, and some other officers on the general staff who had been just captains when he was in the Fourteenth.

"Major Smedberg, Lieutenant Morehead of the Tenth presents his respects and asks if you know this man," said one of the guards.

"Well, yes, I seem to recognize him," said Smedberg. "At any rate, I'll take charge of him. My compliments to Lieutenant Morehead."

The guards saluted and left. "Yes," continued Major Smedberg, "it seems to me I used to have a Frenchman who very closely resembled this man in my company. He was perhaps a bit heavier and not so pale. He was an excellent little soldier, always neat as a pin. Attention! Right about face!"[3]

Eugène executed the move awkwardly.

"You don't look so good, now. What's your name?"

"James Randall."

"Ever since my leg was amputated, my memory isn't as good as it used to be, but it seems to me you had another name back in the regiment."

"Ah! You lost a leg?" Eugène answered, trying to change the subject. "No one would know by looking at you."

"They gave me an artificial foot. My foot was blown off by a shell fragment at the Battle of the Wilderness. I think you must remember that incident."

"Memory is a strange thing. Some people get confused after being wounded; others forget everything when they are unjustly arrested."

"Let's see if everyone has lost his memory," interrupted Smedberg. "Sirault, do you recognize this man?"

The individual so addressed was a Canadian who had just come in. Eugène had known him as a cook in F Company to which he had returned the previous spring after spending the winter in the hospital. The cook, one of the regiment's veterans, was now a corporal doing his service in the recruitment office.

"I know him," Sirault answered without hesitating. "His name is Leduc and he belongs to F Company in the 14th Infantry Regiment."

"I'll leave him in your custody, Sirault. See to it that he's sent to Fort Trumbull this very afternoon."

Sirault took Eugène to the Hotel Lovejoy where he bought him dinner. He spoke to him in French. Eugène didn't answer, for his ill-conceived plan required him to be a man named Randall who didn't know any French.

"Do you remember writing letters to my parents for me?" said Sirault.

No answer.

Sirault repeated the question in English.

"I wrote letters for you in the regiment you're talking about?" Eugène answered in the same language. "Then you must admit you have a strange way of thanking me for that service."

"Listen," Sirault said in French. "I'm only doing my duty. I'm sorry I've done you wrong, but you shouldn't have tried to say you were someone else. Major Smedberg had recognized you."

Eugène was taken to a steamboat headed for New London; he was put far down in the hold in a room measuring about ten feet square, where he found himself in the company of ten or so soldiers from the Fourteenth. Many of them were former acquaintances of his. These soldiers were armed. They were returning from Governor's

Island, where they had taken a squad of soldiers condemned to forced labor. They were all in varying stages of drunkenness. Furious at being given such quarters, they were making a hell of a racket.

Some had even fired their rifles out to sea through a porthole.

They were especially annoyed at the sergeant who had put them there and who was now strolling about the upper deck. Attracted by the noise, this sergeant, a man named Brady, appeared at the hatch. Eugène recognized him as another ex-cook, an old braggart with quite a bad record in the regiment; he now wore a sergeant-major's chevrons. Eugène was telling himself that the kitchen was the surest route to advancement in the American army, when his attention was drawn to an altercation between the sergeant and his subordinates.

The grossest insults were being hurled from both sides. Suddenly, Brady pointed his revolver at one of the mutineers. Immediately there were ten rifles aimed at him. At that point, Brady jumped into the hold, squared his chest, and cried out in stentorian tones: "Shoot, damn you all!"

The rifles were lowered. Both sides had it out and, as a result of that run-in, the soldiers were allowed to leave their hole after promising to behave themselves. Eugène was placed on a wooden platform about two feet high covering part of the steam engine. He lay down with the intention of going to sleep under the powerful protection of a sentry who stood guard with fixed bayonet beside this new kind of bed.

CHAPTER LV

UNDER GUARD

A sentry entrusted with a prisoner must not only prevent his charge from escaping, but also keep him from talking to others. He must not allow anyone to insult the prisoner in his keeping; what's more, he should defend his prisoner if someone dares to attack him. Eugène was stretched out on the platform, trying without much luck to fall asleep, when Brady arrived, accompanied by another sergeant and a soldier Leduc had never seen before. Seeing that the prisoner was not asleep, Brady said to him, "Hey, Frenchy, how's about sitting up and talking with an old buddy for a while?"

Eugène sat up and the three soldiers sat down beside him — the two sergeants were on his left and the private on his right. They all faced the sentry, who stood three or four feet away in front of the group.

"My, aren't you well dressed!" Brady went on. "It seems like the bounty jumper business must be very profitable. You must have done quite well for yourself since you left the regiment."

In those days, someone who enlisted in one regiment, pocketed the bonus, deserted, enlisted elsewhere, and deserted again was called a bounty jumper. Eugène had not done that, but, his having been caught dressed in the latest fashion, after a seven-month absence from his regiment, gave a certain degree of plausibility to the sergeant-major's remarks.

"I'm not a bounty jumper and I don't know you."

Eugène had not yet finished his sentence when the soldier seated on his right grabbed him by the throat and threw him back on the platform while Brady tried to grab his legs and the other sergeant turned his pants pockets inside out.

Eugène shouted as loudly as he could.

Instead of coming to his defense, the sentry said, as he pressed the tip of his bayonet against Eugène's chest: "If you yell like that again, I'll run you through."

Eugène shouted again and, at the same time, with his right leg, still free despite all of Brady's efforts to grab it, he managed to land a kick with his heel between Brady's eyes, which made him let go. Hearing the shouts, the ship's police rushed in at that very instant; the three scoundrels ran off as they saw them coming.

The guard, who had been their accomplice, shouldered his weapon when he saw the police.

The police had arrived too late to intervene, but they had seen enough not to reproach Eugène for crying out. They confined themselves to asking him what had happened.

"Two thieves wearing stripes, accompanied by another in uniform who wanted to earn his own stripes, came over here. They tried to rob me while the guard there threatened to kill me if I cried out; I shouted anyway because I knew he was too much of a coward to do anything."

"Did they take your money?"

"No. They didn't have the time. They just went through all the pockets of my pants but there was nothing there. I denounce this guard as their accomplice."

"Liar!" the guard interrupted.

Beside himself, Eugène rushed at the guard and tried to hit him, but he was restrained by one of the policemen.

"Calm down. You can see that this man is armed and on duty."

"That's true. But isn't there some way to see that justice is done? If you can't arrest this man because he's on duty, you can no doubt still arrest the three others. You will be able to recognize one of them easily enough. I blackened his eye with the heel of my boot."

"We can't arrest them because they're in the military. But their officers are on board and we will report them."

"Could one of you please stay with me while the other brings back an officer so I can talk with him? If you leave me alone with this lout, he certainly won't protect me from the others, who may well feel the need to come back to settle their score."

One of the policemen went off and returned accompanied by Major Brady, the new commanding officer at Fort Trumbull. This Brady was a gentleman and no relation to Sergeant-Major Brady. Eugène had first known him when he was just a lieutenant. When he had last seen him, Brady had been aide-de-camp to the brigadier general of the first brigade of the second division of the 5th Army Corps.[1] Major Brady listened rather coolly to Eugène's recriminations. The latter complained bitterly about the way he had been treated and he concluded by saying: "Up to now, I thought that in a free country like this, prisoners should at least be fed and protected against insults and ill-treatment. I seem to have been mistaken. It is now nine o'clock and I haven't had my supper yet; what's more, when the two sergeants and a private tried to rob me, this guard lent a hand."

"We'll see about that," said the major as he went off to give some orders.

The prisoner was fed. The guard was relieved and replaced by another. As for the other guilty parties, Eugène never knew if they had been punished. He did learn that, on the same voyage, Brady and some other soldiers of his ilk had opened cases of merchandise, stolen shoes which they had sold, and made away with a hunting rifle belonging to a passenger, which they were forced to give back to its rightful owner.

The voyage ended without further incident. The boat arrived in New London about midnight; Eugène and the others proceeded on foot to Fort Trumbull, where Eugène was placed in the guardroom. Eugène knew the place quite well, having often been on guard duty there, but it was the first time that he had been in the compartment reserved for prisoners. Before putting him in there, the sergeant of the guard had said to him: "If you have any money or valuables, you'd better give them to me, since the respectable fellows locked up in this cell will certainly take them off your hands."

What had just happened to him aboard the boat had not left Eugène with much faith in the honesty of recently promoted noncommissioned officers, but he told himself: "If this one's a thief, at least he's a polite one. I'd rather have him rob me than the others."

And he gave the sergeant his wallet, which contained very little — a cigar holder[2] worth about a dollar and a pocketknife worth about a dollar and a half. Then he entered his new lodgings.

"Fresh fish!" ten or so voices shouted, and just as many soldiers surrounded the newcomer.

They bombarded him with questions and he was starting to answer when a man standing behind him pulled a blanket over his head. He was thrown to the floor, and they held his arms and legs as they turned all his pockets inside out.

"We've been robbed!" said one of the gang[3] as he kicked Eugène. "That'll teach you to come in here without a cent."

All of them let go and went off to sit down here and there around the room, leaving the blanket over Eugène's head. He got up sheepishly.

"Any fresh fish coming in here needs to be salted," said the leader, who was called Black Jack. "This is our initiation. Now that you've been 'salted,' you're one of us."

"I'm flattered," answered Eugène. "You all seem to me to be eminently respectable men, but the initiation you're talking about seems a little crude. That part of the ceremony which we'd call an attempted robbery in the civilized world is bad enough, but you didn't have to hit me. Even though I'm weak, sick, and exhausted after six months of privations, I still feel I'm capable of fighting the coward who hit me, whoever he is, provided that the others don't join in."

"Well then, I'm the one!" said a short brown-haired man as he stood up. "And I take full responsibility for what I did."

"Ah, you're the one who shows such a talent for savate. Wait just a minute, I'll teach you a lesson."

Eugène's opponent had squared off. [4]

"All right, you others. He kicked me, so I'm going to kick him. Do you promise not to intervene?"

"Go ahead, we won't interfere; Bob doesn't give a darn about your kicks."

"Well, then, he'd better watch out for this one . . . and that one. . . and that one! What do you think about that, Bob? How does this one feel on your jaw?"

A few well-placed kicks had put the Yankee out of commission and he asked for mercy.

"Now," said Eugène, "since we have to stay together, I'll try never to offend anyone, but I swear that if I don't kill the first person who even thinks about hitting me, it will be because I'm not able to."

He didn't dare sleep that night for fear that someone might take advantage of his sleeping to beat him up, and he resolved to cry out like one possessed if two or three of them ganged up to attack him.

The next day, Bob left the guardroom and that reassured Eugène somewhat, but even though the others protested that they had no intention of avenging him, Eugène still kept up his guard.

Of course, the sergeant of the guard, who was relieved by another the next day, forgot to give him back his money. Leduc kissed it goodbye with good enough grace. It wasn't a lot and he would have had difficulty holding on to it in his present surroundings.

Each time a new prisoner arrived, he had to undergo the salting test; Eugène soon became convinced that some of the sergeants of the guard were in cahoots with the prisoners to strip the new arrivals of their possessions. One fact caused him some astonishment: Black Jack and some of his friends had found a way to get out at night and return to prison before daylight. Another infraction of the rules: Black Jack had a revolver in his pocket, even though it was the duty of the sergeant of the guard to remove all lethal weapons which a man might have in his possession before putting him in the clink.

CHAPTER LVI

Back to Annapolis

Eugène had given his name as James Randall[1] and refused to answer roll call when his real name was called. As a result, after a week or so, the authorities finally accepted his assumed name — at least for calling the roll. Some time after his arrival at Fort Trumbull, he had been transferred to an old storehouse made into a prison for the accused who were scheduled to appear before a court-martial.

If the guardroom occupants weren't the most reputable in the world as far as honesty and standards of behavior are concerned, what can be said about most of the storehouse inmates? Some twenty-odd men had been locked up there, and among them were at least ten real bounty jumpers. These men were hardened criminals. One of them boasted that he had enlisted nineteen times. They all wore leg irons and dragged behind them, at the end of six-foot chains, iron balls weighing thirty pounds. The others were either ordinary deserters or soldiers accused of major infractions of the military code.

The storehouse, which had been built for munitions storage, was lit only by a single very narrow grate which let a thin shaft of light filter through during the day. A stay in that jail was a sad enough business, but it was much better than staying in Libby prison. There was a little less light, but it was well heated and the prisoners ate well. Eugène was visibly gaining weight despite the awkwardness of his situation, which should have made him quite uneasy.

One day, an escort came to take the prisoners to the parade grounds where the whole garrison was already mustered. Sentences passed by the court-martial in session at Fort Trumbull were to be read.

Eugène had already attended such a ceremony at Catlett's Station where he had heard one of his comrades condemned to death for having had been found sleeping at his post, the year before, while in the presence of the enemy. The sentence hadn't been carried out and Cooley, the condemned man, had been pardoned, but that didn't prevent him from deserting shortly afterwards. No one had seen him ever again.

So much had happened since that day, almost a year before, when Eugène, well brushed and polished, had stood at attention at that Virginia camp parade. Now a prisoner, he was not only about to hear the reading of the sentence but witness the actual carrying out of a series of the most horrible punishments.

Eleven of Eugène's companions were condemned to the following punishment to be carried out forthwith: a red-hot iron would brand the letter D on the cheek, signifying they were deserters. The D was to measure an inch and a half by three-quarters of an inch and be burned deeply enough in the skin to leave an indelible scar. After the sentence was carried out, the condemned were to be taken back to prison. There they would be put in irons. Thus fettered, they were given two months time at hard labor in a military prison. At the end of the two months, their heads would be shaved, they would receive dishonorable discharges, and would be formally drummed out of the service.

The garrison troops were arranged to form three sides of a square. The open side was occupied by the company battery and the general staff; the prisoners and their escort stood facing them. As each condemned man was called, he marched forward a few steps, took off his cap, stood at attention while his sentence was read, and then, having put his cap back on, returned to his place in the ranks. Besides the eleven deserters we've just mentioned, many others had been condemned to various other punishments ranging from six months of hard labor wearing the ball and chain and confiscation of salary to five years of hard labor, confiscation of salary during that time, and dishonorable discharge.

The last sentence was pronounced against a very young man, newly enlisted for five years; while on guard duty he had let himself be bribed by a deserter from whom he had gotten $500 for letting the man escape from prison, but the money had been taken away from him.

Once these sentences had been read, the punishments began. The prisoner was stretched on his back over one of the cannons; his arms and legs were firmly tied around the barrel of the artillery piece; the executioner took the heated iron out of a brazier and pressed it against the condemned man's cheek. The smoking flesh could be seen, the moans could be heard as the red-hot iron was applied; then it was over. The poor wretch would be untied; the surgeon would examine his cheek, to which he applied some ointment, and then it was the next man's turn. This spectacle was excruciating to watch. Eugène was very painfully upset when he was taken back to the storehouse in the company of those poor disfigured souls; some swore by all the gods that they would rather have been shot.

The night before the sentence was to be carried out, the condemned, who probably knew what fate held in store for them, had concocted a plot: they would call the corporal of the guard on some pretext or other. When he opened the door a little, they would fell him with one of the balls, then rush the sentry and reach the Thames River, where a boat would be waiting, thanks to the measures taken by the man who had enlisted nineteen times. But the corporal of the guard refused to open the door; he merely talked to them through the bars, saying he rather suspected what they intended to do to him.

Leduc had been a prisoner at Fort Trumbull for three weeks. He had begun to tell himself that they could very well keep him prisoner until he proved he wasn't Leduc. He understood that the way to make it impossible for the authorities to court-martial him was to claim his rights as a Confederate prisoner out on parole. It was a fact that he couldn't be put on trial until he had been officially exchanged. He hadn't thought of that before because he didn't know about this particular regulation. Having obtained this information from a man he judged to be well informed, Eugène asked to be taken to the fort's commanding officer, Major Brady, to whom he made roughly the following statement: "You're right, I am Leduc; I said my name was Randall because I was afraid of what would happen if I was arrested, but they were wrong in calling me a deserter. I belong at Camp Parole, where I was given a thirty-day pass which hasn't expired yet, but which I was clumsy enough to lose."

"What were you going to do at the recruitment office in Brooklyn?" asked the officer.

"I certainly wasn't going there to enlist in the Tenth. I'd gone in with a friend who ran away as soon as he saw that I was being arrested. Nobody can say I asked to enlist; I'd lost my pass and, when I saw I was suspected of being a deserter, I thought they would let me go if I kept on denying my real identity. If you don't believe me, write to Camp Parole and you'll see I've been given a pass that will expire a few days from now."

"All this seems very fishy to me. You seem to be too intelligent to have made the blunder you blame yourself for. At any rate, I'm going to write to Camp Parole; if everything is in order, you'll be sent back to Annapolis."

A few days later, Eugène left for Annapolis guarded by a German corporal. They had made him take off his civilian clothes and replaced them with a new uniform. A pair of steel bracelets, also new, completed his getup, but, since these bracelets were held together by a small chain which prevented him from being in the at-ease position, Eugène considered that ornament to be superfluous. The corporal was armed with a revolver and a noncommissioned garrison officer's sword.

They had stopped in Baltimore where they had dined at the Soldier's Rest. They had just boarded the train to travel the eighteen or twenty miles separating Baltimore from Annapolis when Eugène, pretending to be indisposed, took off in the direction of the toilet;[2] the German, who had found Eugène to be very well behaved up to this point, didn't feel obliged to accompany him.

Once he was alone, Eugène, who had very small hands, began working to get rid of the cumbersome handcuffs. He managed to do so in two minutes, though it seemed like two centuries. The car he was in was the last in the troop train. The door to the platform was next to the compartment he had entered. Fast as lightning, he raced through those two doors. He estimated that the train was traveling at only about ten miles per hour. He jumped and landed on all fours alongside the track.

His calculations were off. The train was traveling faster than he thought; he felt as if his fall had rattled every bone in his body;[3] but, finding he was safe and sound, he took off across the fields in the direction of Baltimore. Arriving in town all out of breath, he ran into a patrol which demanded that he show his pass.

That was a blow. Martial law was in effect in Baltimore; soldiers not on duty could not move about freely unless they had passes. He was in uniform and hadn't thought about that. As always, he had no sooner gotten out of one hornets' nest than he fell into another. They arrested him and, seeing that his escape attempt had failed, he wanted to spare the German corporal any embarrassment, for he had always treated him decently. Eugène said to those who arrested him that he had just escaped and that his guard, seeing him gone, would no doubt be out looking for him.

And, indeed, the corporal arrived soon afterwards. He hadn't seen Eugène jump, but, noticing that his prisoner was taking a long time to return, he had gone into the toilet where he had found the empty handcuffs. Then he had had the train stopped and one of the employees had told him he had seen a soldier jump off the train a few minutes before and run off toward town. Rightly suspecting that his prisoner would be arrested in Baltimore, he had had no trouble finding him when he had spoken to the authorities.

The two travelers boarded the next troop train and this time the German managed to hand over his prisoner safely at Camp Parole where Eugène was placed in solitary confinement.

CHAPTER LVII

The Knights
Of the Guardroom

The sumptuous apartment at Leduc's disposal measured about five feet square. The light, or, to be more precise, the half-light came in through a diamond-shaped opening in the door which opened onto a long corridor lit by a window. Like all the camp buildings, the prison was constructed of wood and the prisoners in solitary confinement weren't allowed to smoke. Their pipes, matches, and tobacco were taken away from them. Their only activity was receiving their ration three times a day; it was at least plentiful and of good quality.

From all appearances, the establishment must have run out of space in its seven or eight cells because the day after he arrived, Eugène was given a companion, a young German who only spoke a few words of English. On the other hand, he laughed a lot, sang even more, and seemed to be very witty…in German. They were separated two days later to their mutual relief since the cell, already too cramped for one person, was practically unlivable for two.

Eugène spent a week in this garden of delights. He was removed to undertake a journey whose destination has remained an impenetrable mystery to this day. He was attached to another prisoner with a single pair of handcuffs — leaving each man with one free hand. Some ten or so other prisoners, similarly manacled, journeyed with them escorted by an infantry squad.

Guards and prisoners took a troop train to Washington, where they crossed the city on to Georgetown. There they boarded a steamboat which took them down the Potomac to Alexandria; on the way they caught a glimpse of Mount Vernon, site of the illustrious Washington's old residence and his tomb. At Alexandria, on their way to the prison there, the prisoners passed by the house where Colonel Ellsworth had been assassinated at the beginning of the war.[1]

Eugène remembered that, in 1861, when he was living in New England with his parents, he had heard more than once a popular song about that tragedy. Now as he found himself in front of the house where the event had taken place, the refrain came back to him:

> *Strike, freemen for the Union!*
> *Shield your swords no more,*
> *Whilst remains a band of traitors*
> *On Columbia's Shore.*[2]

In his mind's eye, he saw the hand-painted engravings he had so often examined with interest in the display windows of music stores. They showed Colonel Ellsworth coming down the stairs holding the Confederate flag, trampling it under his feet, and being shot right in the chest, almost point-blank, by a hunting rifle fired by the proprietor. To the left of the group, a Federal soldier is taking aim at the assassin.[3]

For the sake of those readers who haven't read the newspapers from those times or who have forgotten the event, we feel it necessary to recount briefly the circumstances surrounding that drama.

A detachment of Federal troops had just occupied Alexandria. The residents, almost all of them rabid secessionists, were exasperated. One of them had decided to raise the rebel flag on a staff which rose above a sort of pavilion on top of his house. If memory serves us right, the house in question was then being used as an inn. Colonel Ellsworth, enraged by this challenge flung in the face of the Federal authorities, went to the house, accompanied by some soldiers, climbed the stairs leading to the pavilion, lowered the flag, and came back down. Just as he arrived on the ground floor, the owner, who had gone to get a hunting rifle, fired the weapon point-blank, hitting Ellsworth in the chest.

The secessionist had just enough time to see his victim fall before dropping to the floor himself, his head shattered by a bullet and his body run through by bayonet thrusts. He probably knew what fate had in store, but in him, hate had proved stronger than the instinct for self-preservation.

Having arrived at the prison, the captives were relieved of their handcuffs and placed in a large room with fifty or so other soldiers guilty of violating the military code. A few days later, Eugène and some other prisoners were taken to the Soldier's Rest, a shelter where they were relatively free and could move about the vast walkways of the establishment just like the soldiers who were not prisoners. However, those who were not prisoners had an immense advantage over those who were, because they could obtain passes to go walking in the city, while the suspects could never get beyond the cordon of sentries surrounding the institution.

Eugène enjoyed himself thoroughly here. He took advantage of this semblance of liberty which had been granted him to write to his parents, who had received no news of him since he had left the Fourteenth before Petersburg. Fearing, however, that his letter would be opened and that a way would be found to translate it into English, he composed it in such a way as not to compromise himself vis-à-vis the authorities. He would willingly have prolonged his stay at the Soldier's Rest indefinitely, since he expected that nothing good could come of his being sent back to his regiment. Nobody bothered to consult him about his preferences. Several days later, he was taken back to Annapolis via Washington.

At Camp Parole, he wasn't put back in a solitary confinement cell possibly because the men bringing him back from Alexandria hadn't found it necessary to handcuff him.

That's how it always goes. The more miserable the man, the more miserable everybody wants to make him. The better off he is, the better he is treated. Because Eugène had been well treated on the way back, he was therefore imprisoned in the large guardroom with about forty other prisoners.

As had been the case in the Fort Trumbull guardroom, the cry "fresh fish" greeted his arrival. He expected someone would throw a blanket over his head, but that didn't happen. All they did was arrest him, as if he weren't already under arrest, and brought him before a sort of tribunal, more or less properly organized. The judge, seated on a block of wood, addressed him more or less as follows:

"You've been summoned to take part in our august gathering. We will not ask what has brought you here. It doesn't matter to us a bit whether you were insubordinate to your officers or whether you courted a Negro woman without first having a revenue stamp glued to your backside.[4] We're above all the miseries, the ambitions, and the common prejudices which drive the vile plebeians in the outside world. We belong to the very exalted and distinguished 'Order of the Knights of the Guardroom.' Before conferring this illustrious title upon you, we will submit you to our initiation. You will have to make a contribution of fifty cents to the common fund for buying cigars, tobacco, and novels for the knights. If you can't pay up, you are condemned to be blanket-tossed forty times. What do you have to say in your own defense?"

"I plead guilty. I haven't a cent. Bring your blanket and let's get on with it."

The guardroom was a single large room. The flat roof, which was about twelve feet from the floor, also served as the ceiling. Toward the middle, there was a large trap door which was opened to air out the room when the weather was nice. The trap door happened to be open. The forty men seized a blanket, stretched it out, and, holding it waist high with both hands, they invited Eugène to lie down on it and assured him he wasn't in any danger as long as he didn't try to hang on to the blanket. He answered that he was quite familiar with this sport because he had already taken part in it in the camps. He then positioned himself.

"One, two, three!"

On the first two counts, the men let the blanket sag a little bit and then pulled it tight again. On the count of three, they pulled with all their might. Eugène flew into the air, out through the trap door to a height of ten feet or so beyond, and fell back on the blanket without hurting himself in the least.

"One, two, three!" the men repeated as they tossed him into the air once more. And so it went until they had sent him sailing out of the room forty times. Each time he flew out, he regretted having to go back down and was amazed that the great law of gravitation was powerful enough to bring him back down to prison against his will. When the ceremony was over, the mock-judge said: "Now you've been initiated. You are a Knight of the Guardroom entitled to all the rights and privileges of our society."

CHAPTER LVIII

BACK TO NEW LONDON

In the Camp Parole guardroom, Eugène spent as happy a month as could be expected, given the fact that he was a prisoner burdened with such grave accusations. The guardroom occupants changed as time went on. Many prisoners left, but there were always others coming in, all of them hail-fellows-well-met. The association's income was plentiful enough to allow all the knights to buy cigars, tobacco, and books. What more could they want! Good weather was back again and the prisoners had the advantage of taking turns doing fatigue duty on the outside. In other words, they went out from time to time and went through the motions of working under the supervision of the sergeant in charge of their escort and this gave them a chance to breathe the fresh air. They were well fed and Eugène had become quite portly.

He was still in Camp Parole when the news came that Petersburg and Richmond had been captured; that announcement was followed almost immediately by news of General Lee's surrender. There was great rejoicing everywhere, but the joy felt by the friends of the Union cause was soon dampened by the news of President Lincoln's death; he was assassinated by Booth at Ford's Theater in Washington on April 14, 1865, just eight days after Lee's surrender.[1]

Vice President Andrew Johnson took the presidential oath of office and one of the first acts of his administration was to disband the army. At that time there were more than one and a half million men at arms in the Northern armies. Naturally, the small nucleus of men in the regular army needed to be preserved; since he was a deserter from the regular army, these events in no way affected Eugène's situation. At best, he hoped he wouldn't be shot by a firing squad after the war; but it was likely that he wouldn't get off with less than twenty to twenty-five years at hard labor on the Dry Tortugas, sandy islands to the southwest of Florida where the American government uses condemned military prisoners to build fortifications that disappear at the first sign of wind. Since that wasn't a very encouraging prospect, Eugène promised himself he would do everything possible to make his escape.

Pursuant to the executive decree, the military authorities at Camp Parole received the order to disband the volunteers and to send the regulars back to the headquarters of their respective regiments. Naturally the prisoners needed to be sent back under escort.

A cavalry sergeant, in charge of the guardroom and cells while he was at Camp Parole, was entrusted with taking Eugène to Fort Trumbull.

A great many prisoners had quite a few bad things to say about the sergeant, but Eugene himself had never had reason to complain about his actions. Prior to leaving, the guard took Eugène to the camp sutler's establishment and bought him some oyster soup, a glass of beer, and a cigar. While they were both smoking their cigars as they waited for the train, the sergeant said: "Colonel Chamberlin,[2] our camp commanding officer, said I should handcuff you. I told him that wasn't necessary; with my revolver and sword I'd dare the devil himself to get away from me."

"You were right and I thank you for sparing me that indignity. I'll try not to give you a reason to use your weapons."

They took the train at about four in the afternoon, traveled all night without stopping, and, at about nine the next day, they crossed over from Jersey City to New York.

Eugène and the sergeant were, of course, traveling at government expense. So they had to go to the shipping company office where the sergeant presented his papers and asked for a pass for two. Since they gave him only steerage quarters, he paid the difference, and got two cabin-class tickets, which gave each man the right to a bed and two meals on board.

The ship wasn't going to leave until four-thirty and the sergeant, whose pockets were well lined, decided to lift a few with Eugène while waiting for the boat to leave. Leduc pretended to hesitate, telling the sergeant he preferred not to drink since, having no money, he couldn't return the courtesy, but his keeper insisted: "What does that matter? I've enough money for both of us. Drink, eat, smoke, and don't worry about a thing. I haven't had a drink of hard liquor for a year and here's one I'm going to toss back to your health. So go ahead, get yourself something."

Eugène, who was secretly delighted to see him so disposed, resisted no longer and began to smoke furiously and drink as little as possible. By noon the sergeant was in his cups and Eugène had his pockets full of cigars. They dined in a restaurant and, around three o'clock, the sergeant had washed the meal down so well that his legs were refusing to function.

"Frenchy," he stammered, "I believe, God damn me, that I'm listing slightly. I am, so to speak, three sheets to the wind, and I'm bound and determined to go on a binge. I'm drunk, by God! to put it poetically."

The sergeant had been a sailor once upon a time and the alcohol fumes were inspiring him to launch into nautical tirades.

"Frenchy," he began again, "you old sea dog, when are we going to set sail?"[3]

"I don't know," Eugène answered, "but I intend to set sail as soon as the wind is right."

"Wait a minute. Do you think I'm going to let you sail off without me? You know very well that your old hull belongs to me. When you've taken a prize you don't let it go. I've got my grappling hooks on you and I'm going to tow you into New London and don't you forget it!"[4]

"I'm not going to argue with that. You don't seem to be afraid of the elements. Tossed by the stormy waves, the man-of-war will tow the helpless ship."[5]

"What have I done to make you treat me this way? We've been traveling together for just about twenty-four hours and have I allowed myself to make even the slightest pun? I'm armed and beware of the pun-ishment if you keep on. Call me a thief, a murderer, an idiot, but don't make puns."

"Bah! It was such a bad one that all it did was sober you up."

"That's already quite enough. And what if I want to be drunk? Let's have another drink and then go on board. It's 3:30, but it's better to arrive too early than too late."

The sergeant settled the bill, got himself a bottle of gin, and left with Eugène. They took a carriage to the ship and went on board. As soon as they arrived, the sergeant stretched out in an easy chair and promptly fell asleep. Since Eugène wasn't handcuffed, nobody suspected he was a prisoner. He could have gotten off the ship without incident, but he remembered his adventures in Baltimore only too well to risk getting arrested in New York because he didn't have a pass. Colonel Ilges, the former captain of the German company in the Fourteenth, was on board, but he didn't recognize Eugène and Eugène felt no desire to renew old acquaintances.

The steamship had been under way for an hour; its paddles were vigorously churning up the waters of Long Island Sound. Eugène had gone down to the steerage deck where, mingling with the crowd, he was admiring the large island's scenery when the sergeant woke up. Not seeing his prisoner, the sergeant thought that he had perhaps disembarked in New York before the boat's departure. Being a prudent man, he resolved, however, to search the boat before sharing his fears with the passengers. When he found Eugène on the steerage deck, he said to him: "I thought you'd gotten off while I was sleeping. I'm very pleased to find you here."

"Me? Get off the boat? Do you think I'm afraid of going on trial at Fort Trumbull? Something tells me I won't be convicted."

"I don't know if you're guilty; I don't even know what you're charged with, but I do know that things will go much easier for you now that the war is over. But to change the subject, let's have a drink. I don't know what to make of it, but my throat is as dry as dust today."[6]

CHAPTER LIX

To Each His Own

They had a drink, then another, and then a third. In short, they soon had polished off the whole bottle. However, Eugène only pretended to be drinking. They went to bed around ten o'clock. The sergeant, who was drunk as a lord, took the lower bunk for the very good reason that he would never have been able to climb into the upper one.

At midnight, the passengers were awakened with the news that the boat had arrived in New London and that those disembarking there could, nonetheless, sleep until morning and have their breakfast on board, since the boat wasn't going to leave for Boston until nine o'clock in the morning. A crew member had tried in vain to wake the sergeant. A few muffled grunts were all he had been able to get out of him.

"Leave him alone," said Eugène. "He's with me. We're having breakfast on board."

At five o'clock, Eugène jumped out of bed and noticed that his companion had thrown up part of the liquid he had gulped down the previous day. Leduc hadn't dared get off the boat alone during the night for several reasons. First of all, he didn't want to run the risk of running into Colonel Ilges, who might perhaps have had him arrested if he had seen him alone; second, except for having seen it on the map, he wasn't at all familiar with the first leg of the journey he was about to set off on. Besides, he had told himself that since the sergeant was in his cups, he wasn't very likely to be able to wake up early the next morning.

Eugène was just finishing dressing and was about to take off when the sergeant said: "Is that you, Frenchy? If you only knew how sick I am. My head's splitting."

"You know our tickets include breakfast. Come on and eat something; that will put you right."

"I couldn't possibly eat. Go eat alone. When you've finished, come back and get me. I'll try to get up and debark."

Eugène went toward the dining room, entered by the starboard door, and exited by the port door nearest the wharf, reached the gangplank, and rushed down to set foot on solid ground as fast as he could. A few unarmed soldiers were strolling along the wharf. They had the 14th Regiment number on their caps, but they were new recruits whom Eugène didn't know. He passed them by without seeming to notice them, and started walking along the railroad tracks in the direction of Norwich. He knew that Baltic, a manufacturing town where there were French Canadians, was some twenty miles farther on. He didn't know anyone in Baltic, but he knew that by asking his fellow Canadians for help he would find a way to replace his uniform with less compromising clothes. He turned his back on Fort Trumbull, only a half mile away in a straight line from the pier where the boat was docked.

The previous evening he had promised the sergeant he would set sail on the first favorable wind, and he was keeping his promise. However, he didn't breathe easily until he was about three miles from New London. Finding himself out in the country where no one could see him, he quickened his pace, happy to feel free and so absorbed in joyous excitement that he almost got crushed by a train which bore down on him just as he was nearing the end of a railroad bridge. He had barely enough time to get out of the way.

Before reaching Norwich, the tracks coming from New London go down a rather steep grade. From that vantage point, Eugène could see part of the city located below and, spotting some uniforms on one of the streets, he felt it would be imprudent to run the risk of coming face to face with the men wearing them. He left the tracks and took a long detour through the countryside to avoid Norwich.

Seeing a soldier pass by, the good country folk, who just about all had relatives in the army, came out to ask him for news of the war. Eugène answered his questioners as briefly as possible, assuring them that the army had been disbanded and that they would soon see their relatives and friends.

He arrived in Baltic around four o'clock in the afternoon. All the able-bodied inhabitants were at the factory. Only the old, the women, and children were at home. The sight of a uniform naturally excited the children's curiosity. Eugène caught sight of a handsome old man talking in French with some children. Eugène spoke to him and, in a few words, apprised him of the situation and what he needed.

"Come into the house," said the patriarch. "We'll try to save you."

They put their heads together and it was decided that Eugène would stay hidden for a few days in old Labonne's house to put the authorities off the trail. They would undoubtedly be telegraphing and looking for him in the big cities. M. Labonne was the head of a large family. Eugène slipped on clothes belonging to one of his sons and the uniform was carefully hidden. That evening, a meeting of the Canadians of the town was held; they took up a collection to give the deserter the money he needed to return to Canada.

Eugène refused to accept it, saying that he didn't like to take charity. He thanked them profusely, adding that he would rather walk the whole distance to the Canadian border. They overcame his scruples by saying the money was being given as a loan. Handing him a list of their dead relatives, his benefactors asked him to have masses sung for the deceased when he could — as many as the loan would pay for.

Praised be those honest workers who not only risked having legal proceedings brought against them by the authorities, but also sacrificed part of their hard-earned wages to aid a countryman! Brave hearts! The masses have long since been said, but the soldier they returned to his family feels that he can never repay the debt; on his behalf, we can assure them that he will be eternally grateful.

Eugène was deliriously happy. Since he couldn't go out, he entertained himself by singing in spite of *Père* Labonne's admonitions not to. The old man pointed out the danger of attracting the neighbors' attention. Eugène would stop for a moment only to start up again. He had sung in Martinsburg prison, where he had learned "The Bonnie Blue Flag" and other secessionist songs; he had sung in Castle Lightning, Castle Thunder, in Libby prison, in the Fort Trumbull magazine, in the Alexandria prison, and the Camp Parole guardhouse; now that he felt he was almost safe, he couldn't stop singing.

At midnight one Sunday evening, after shaking hands with his benefactors, who had gathered to say goodbye to him, Eugène set off on foot for Wauregan, fourteen miles away, where he took the train to Worcester, Massachusetts. In Worcester, he took the night train to Montréal, arriving there the next morning at 9 a.m. That afternoon, he boarded the *Chambly* — where he came face to face with his former employer, the same man he had run away from in October, 1863, when he had gone off to enlist in the American army. Recognizing each other, the two men stood somewhat dumbfounded; then the old merchant held out his hand and said, "Well, did you find the cows?"

"Unfortunately not, in spite of all the rounds I made! I saw cows of all sizes and colors, but not a one that had a family resemblance…to yours."

"Anyway, to each his own; the cows are well looked after."

The next day Eugène arrived at his parents' home, where it goes without saying that he was welcomed with a joy heightened by the fact that they had just about given up all hope of seeing him again alive.

Part Seven: One Soldier Comes Back from the War

CHAPTER LX

A Visit to Pingreville

S oon after his return to Canada, Eugène had the opportunity to go to Pingre-ville and took advantage of this to stop at M. Latour's house. He knew M. Latour by reputation only, but he wasn't the one Eugene wanted to see; it was that Louise Léon had talked about with such enthusiasm. It had been almost a year since poor Léon had fallen by his side in battle — with a bullet in his left shoulder. In the midst of all the harsh trials and tribulations which had beset him since, Eugene had never forgotten his late lamented friend.

More than once he had told himself that if he had followed his friend's advice, he would never have deserted and would have avoided the innumerable misfortunes he had endured since his departure from the regiment. For the sake of the friendship which had united them, Eugène felt duty-bound to go see the woman Léon had loved so much. He wanted to tell her how he had come to admire his friend's noble char-acter and to assure her that Léon had died a death worthy of her and had always been faithful to the memory of the Louise he adored.

Before going to the Latour house, Eugène made some discreet inquiries about Louise. If he had learned she was engaged to someone new, on no account would he have paid that visit. He would have told himself that "Louise is a coquette not wor-thy of the love of a man like Léon. Let's not flatter her vanity by telling her how much she was loved by this man she was too heartless to regret. Besides, I'm not sure I could refrain from reproaching her, and that would hardly be the right thing to do."

But everyone agreed that the Louise they had known, always laughing and play-ful before Duroc's departure, was now in the depths of despair and that she had firm-ly resolved never to marry. In a small town, everyone knows his neighbor's business much better than his own and, even though neither Louise nor her parents had ever revealed the causes which had led the young girl to make reach a strange decision, everyone had guessed that Duroc's sudden departure and his premature death had broken Mlle. Latour's heart.

Given these circumstances, Eugène thought she would be grateful if he told her what he knew about his dead friend. He went to M. Latour's and asked for Louise. He was ushered into a parlor where, after he had waited a few moments, a charming blonde wearing a black dress appeared.

"Do I have the honor of addressing Mademoiselle Latour?" he said as he stood up and bowed.

"Yes, sir."

"Pardon me, Mademoiselle, for taking the liberty of coming here since I don't have the honor of knowing you personally. My name is Leduc. When I was serving in the American army, I was close friends with someone who was quite interested in you."

Hearing these words, Louise began to tremble. It seemed to her that this the stranger was tactfully trying to prepare her for the possibility of seeing Léon alive. Perhaps Léon himself had sent him to announce the news of his return! Hope, fear, anxiety, grief, and joy — all of those contradictory feelings were doing battle in her heart. She felt she was being tortured. She wanted to cry out and she was afraid she was about to faint. However, she managed to get her emotions under control, but her inner turmoil had not escaped Eugène's careful scrutiny. Yet, she was sufficiently composed to be able to ask in a voice which she tried in vain to give some semblance of calm, "Do you mean M. Duroc? When did you see him last?"

"Yes, I was referring to Duroc. Alas, our last time together ended quite tragically. The memory of that fatal day will remain deeply etched in my mind forever. It has been almost a year now, yet I can still see him just as he was the instant when he fell into my arms — struck down by the bullet which caused his death three days later."

"Good heavens! It's true then," Louise cried out as she collapsed in a chair, no longer trying to hold back the tears choking her.

"Can you ever forgive me, Mademoiselle?" said Eugène. "I came to console you and by my blundering I've shattered an illusion you must have been holding on to since you seem shocked by the news of my friend Léon's death. If I had thought you were still hoping to see him alive, I would not have been cruel enough to shatter your illusions — but what am I saying? The hope you were clinging to is a complete revelation to me. If only he were still alive! Now it is I, his friend, asking to be consoled. Might you have heard anything about him?"

"Not since last July 15. My father had written to the 14th Regiment and he received a letter from the commanding officer informing him that M. Duroc had died in the hospital on June 23. Don't blame yourself. That hope you are talking about — you gave it substance. When you spoke to me about Léon Duroc, I foolishly imagined that you were coming to tell me he wasn't dead, but I now understand you only wanted to talk to me about a dead friend whom you miss and who had talked to you about me. I thank you for your kindness. Talk to me about him. Tell me about the last moments of his life. You see that I'm calm now, and I promise I won't interrupt you again."

"On July 15, I was still with the regiment. I left it for the last time on August 15, and at that time all the only news that we had heard was that he died three days after he was wounded. Obviously the officer who wrote didn't know anything more than I did.

"But, now that I think back on it," Eugène continued as if he were talking to himself, "the hospital sent word that the bullet, after passing completely through the left arm, had entered his side where it lodged; however, I'm certain Duroc was wounded in the shoulder, not the arm. Eastman even alleged that the bullet had come out through his back. I've not returned to the regiment since August 15. What if Duroc came back to the regiment after six months in the hospital? But that's impossible — if that were so, he would have written you!"

"As a matter of fact, he had already written me one letter. Since I received the letter and the news of his death at the same time, I didn't answer it; but I have the regimental address and I'm going to write again — even though I don't dare hope anymore."

"Write anyway; he'll answer you if he's alive. As for me, I may not stay in the country long enough to receive an answer from him, and, since I've deserted from the regiment, it would be inadvisable for him to write me if I return to the United States."

"Alas! I'm very much afraid that the sad news is only too true. But you still haven't told me a thing about what you came here to say. You were his friend; this entitles you to my trust and I'm eager to know everything that happened to him during his short military career. Don't worry about boring me; you can be sure I'll follow every little detail of your story with the greatest interest."

Eugene then told her all he knew about Léon, and he made it a point to stress his bravery, his valor, and noble character. Louise thus learned how Grippard and two others, whose names Eugène didn't know, had conspired to rob Duroc of M. Latour's $1,000. Satisfied that she had guessed right, she promised herself not to say anything about the matter unless Léon's honor was questioned again. The conversation lasted a long time and Eugène went away convinced that Louise was exactly as Léon had described her.

CHAPTER LXI

AH, THE GOOD OLD DAYS WHEN I WAS A DESERTER

E ugène had worked at several trades but he had mastered only one: being a deserter. He had learned that one well enough to be a bounty jumper — if he had been a dishonest man and if the war had lasted. But he had become a deserter in the same way he had become a soldier — partly because he didn't think about the consequences and very much for the love of glory. He had wanted to be French soldier for four or five years and had agreed to a five-year enlistment in the American army, believing that this was just a roundabout way of achieving his goal. This was not a logical way to go about it; but twice deserting his regiment and hoping that the Confederates would provide him with the wherewithal to reach Mexico was not any more rational.

Even so, Léon was far from lacking judgment. But he was a hot-blooded character, a happy-go-lucky fellow who acted on the spur of the moment without thinking about the consequences. His overpowering thirst for adventures had prompted him to enlist; then he told himself he had made a mistake and that he belonged in Mexico. Like a child, he acted on impulse, but he had a man's energy.

His trek with the guerrillas should have taught him a lesson; as a matter of fact, he perhaps would never have thought of deserting again if the Fourteenth hadn't received the order to retreat with the reserves behind the lines, and especially if his friend Duroc had remained at his side. Curiously enough, this boy who dreamed of devoting his life to a military career had no liking for either camp or garrison life. He had gladly borne the hardships, the fatigue, and the privations of the campaigns; the danger of being in combat seemed to intoxicate him; but he felt disgusted with regimental life each time he was forced to be inactive.

Twice he had deserted merely on a whim, but the reader has seen that Eugène deserted the next time from necessity to escape the punishment he had earned by deserting to the enemy before Petersburg. A man gets used to everything. He would have been very astonished if anyone had told him that he had acquired a taste for the deserter's trade — thankless and unproductive as it was — for, without suspecting it in the least, nostalgia for the deserter's life now filled his mind. At least that seems to be what the new whim that he acted upon during the summer suggests and that truth requires us to record here.

Eugène had nothing to do; he had done his utmost to find work and hadn't been able to get a permanent job. All the merchants in the countryside had all the help they needed. To find work in the city, you had to start well in advance and be strongly recommended. In the American army, he had learned how to endure fatigue and handle a rifle very well, but when it came to handling a plow, a harrow, or a scythe, his training was very fragmentary. He succeeded, nonetheless, in earning some money during the harvest season by taking manual laborer jobs which didn't bring in much and had the drawback of not lasting long enough.

His parents, overjoyed at having him with them, either did not notice or didn't want to acknowledge that he was old enough to be earning his own living; but he noticed, and told himself that instead of increasing his family's financial difficulties, he should be making every effort to help them out. Eugène could pretty well guess what people were saying about him behind his back. Some remarks passed along to him by obliging friends filled in the missing pieces. Here's the sum and substance of the opinion given the most credence among the worthy *habitants*[1] who wanted everyone to be cast from the same mold from which they had come.

Eugène had been away for more than two years and he had come back without a cent. Therefore, he was a spendthrift, a good-for-nothing, a ne'er-do-well. He would always be a bum. He had wasted his entire childhood going to school and didn't know what it was like to work for a living. He was heartless because, instead of bringing back money to his parents, he was living at their expense while he should have been out earning his keep.

That last accusation cut Eugène to the quick. It was undoubtedly unjust and premature, but there was some truth in that brutal reasoning. Any impartial observer would have considered it unjust and understand that, far from being able to save money while he was in the American army, Eugène had experienced every possible difficulty in just saving his skin. It was premature in the sense that Leduc hadn't yet had the time to wear out his welcome at his father's, and that he had never said he intended to stay with his parents indefinitely. It was also irrelevant because old man Leduc didn't owe anyone a cent and his honest labor had always brought in enough to feed his children and clothe them appropriately, as well as provide them all with an elementary education. He had accomplished all this without ever going into debt or asking for help from anyone, which was a lot more than could be said about Eugène's detractors.

Eugène didn't worry much about the people who were surprised that he hadn't come back a millionaire at age eighteen. He didn't much care whether they had a very flattering opinion about him, but he was bound and determined to take away the pleasure they would get if their predictions came true. In spite of his exuberance and impulsiveness he was still worth more than they were. He was quite willing to pardon them for being unquestionably superior to him in their aptitude for manual labor. Why then would they not forgive him his superiority over them in schooling and general knowledge?

Spurred on by his desire to provide for himself, Eugène resolved to make one last effort to become something more than a gentleman of leisure — as the *Gazette Officielle* defines the term. He took leave of his parents, saying that he was going to visit some villages along the Richelieu River, hoping to get some sort of job. That much was true, but little did they suspect what he was thinking. He had decided that if he wasn't successful, he would turn himself in to the American authorities at Rouse's Point.

After having taken every possible step and exhausted every single possibility, he turned toward the border with the intention of putting his disastrous project into effect. Without stopping in the village of Rouse's Point, he reached Fort Montgomery, a half mile away on Lake Champlain, where he hoped to find a garrison.

"Since I'm no longer fit for being anything but a military prisoner, I might as well take up my old trade and set sail for the Dry Tortugas," he said to himself.

Contrary to what he had expected, there were no men garrisoned in the fort, but he went up to an old soldier in uniform who had been left there to guard the war supplies and told him what had brought him there.

"Are you crazy?" the old veteran said to him. "Do you think an old soldier like me is going to get mixed up in anything like this? Go talk to somebody else." Then in more kindly tones he said, "Young man, it is wrong to listen to the voice of despair. You might get yourself shot."

"I deserve it and life isn't so good."

"It's all very well for you to talk like that; you're just a boy and you don't know anything yet about life, despite the sufferings you endured in the South. But, you poor soul! They might not shoot you. They might send you to the Dry Tortugas for twenty to twenty-five years; that would be even worse. Believe me, take an old man's advice and give up this damnable plan. Do you have parents?"

"Yes, parents who are sincerely devoted to me," said Eugène, trying to hold back his tears.

"And you want to plunge them into the most horrible grief? I don't know you; I've just laid eyes on you for the first time, but I've got to tell you what I think of you: you're heartless!"

"At least you're telling me this to my face. I prefer that. In my parish, some people said I was heartless because I had came back home penniless and stayed there for three months. You're calling me heartless just because I'm taking the only way left to me to provide for my own needs."

"Your way is too extreme. If there isn't any work on the other side of the border, there should be some on this side. Try looking and you'll probably find something. No one will give you any trouble provided you keep your secret. They're not looking for deserters like they used to. Go on, promise me you'll give up your deplorable plan."

"I promise," answered Eugène, convinced by the old soldier's reasoning, "and I thank you for your sound advice."

Covering part of the eastern shore of Lake Champlain looking for work to no avail, Eugène went home convinced that work was as hard to find in the United States as in his native province. He came back to his parents' home after a three-week absence which had been replete with difficulties and privations of all sorts. When autumn came, he was finally able to find work as a delivery boy in a Montréal grocery that paid him $5 a month plus room and board, besides providing him the prized advantage of taking care of a horse and making deliveries to customers.

This all happened at the time of the famous Laprairie Camp.[2] In Eugène's presence, a cadet friend of the grocer's family detailed in glowing fashion the enormous advantages he expected to obtain from being the bearer of a certificate from a military school. According to him, military officers would soon be in great demand. The military life was finally going to become a career in Canada. A permanent army was about to be organized and every cadet would have a commission in that army.

That was all Eugène needed to hear to make up his mind. The account he had just heard wasn't meant for him. Oh, no! The cadet in question would have thought it beneath his dignity to speak to a civilian of such a humble social condition as Eugène. The former American soldier said nothing about his plan, but he quit his job and immediately took steps to get himself admitted to the military school, which he entered several weeks later.

CHAPTER LXII

GHOSTS IN DIFFICULTY

After leaving the grocer's employ and before entering military school, Eugène went to M. Latour's to find out if they had heard anything about Léon. Louise had written a letter addressed to Léon while M. Latour had asked the commanding officer of the Fourteenth for new information. Louise's letter had gone unanswered; as for M. Latour, he had received a letter from commanding officer Thatcher that went as follows: "We've already told you that Duroc is dead. You cannot expect us to bring him back to life to please you. A year ago he was as dead as dead could be; don't expect him to be any more alive today than he was when we buried him."

Everyone agreed that the letter was quite rude and inappropriate. M. Latour, a man everyone in Pingreville respected, was especially furious to be treated that way. The truth, however, was that M. Latour had found a way to intercept his daughter's letter to Duroc, and he hadn't written to Thatcher either; the latter's reply was a complete fabrication. The merchant had convinced himself that Léon, if he were alive, would never be a suitable match for his daughter and that it would be better to let the passage of time console Louise.

Given his frame of mind, Latour hadn't dared write the regiment for fear of learning that Léon was alive. Louise became convinced of her loss and she fell once more into a deep depression. After his first meeting with Louise, Eugène had harbored the hope that his friend had survived the wound he had received. Now, not suspecting M. Latour's deception, he was left with the impression that Duroc was dead.

Brindamour was still working for M. Grippard.

Thanks to the phantasmagoria, Grippard had, in the end, made him his secretary. He had brought Brindamour to Montréal where he had put him in charge of his agency. M. Grippard, who traveled frequently to the United States and elsewhere, continued to make Montréal his base of operations. Brindamour, who never went anywhere without his phantasmagoria equipment, had fun with Bohémier from time to time, frightening completely harmless people, just to keep in practice. He hadn't put Grippard through the ordeal of witnessing an apparition for quite a while; but he was getting ready for a command performance to constrain his employer to set him up in business.

The military school cadets had for the most part been recruited among students. Each certificate was worth $50 to the owner, and, since both certificates could be obtained in three months, the time spent studying the military arts was handsomely rewarded. Many of Bohémier's friends were cadets and he often visited them either at the Bonsecours market hall where they drilled or at their various boarding houses. One day, Bohémier was present when Eugène who, like all military men, enjoyed talking about the campaigns he had fought, was telling some of the other cadets how Duroc had fallen mortally wounded at his side. He had mentioned Léon by name, had described him in laudatory terms, and, with tears in his eyes,[1] he had said how acutely the news of his beloved friend's death had affected him.

Bohémier was careful not to tell Eugène that he knew Duroc, cleverly steering the conversation around to the subject of ghosts. Most of the cadets in the group sitting around chatting maintained that no one should give credence to old wives' tales about alleged apparitions from the dead. As for Eugène, he declared that he didn't believe in such superstitions.

"If the dead could come back," he added, "I'd be delighted. For poor Duroc — the man I was talking to you about a moment ago — would have visited me already and I'd be so happy to see him!"

At that moment, the bugle's sonorous notes sounded the call to form ranks and Bohémier left the room. He rushed to Grippard's office where he knew he would find Brindamour alone, M. Grippard having gone to New York.

"I've got some good news for you," he said, wiping his brow. "I've found an excellent subject for our phantasmagoria experiments. I know where he's boarding. He's at the Laprairie Hotel. The proprietor's son is one of my friends and he's very discreet. I want to see our prospective test subject's room and we can start setting up this very afternoon."

"And who's the happy mortal about to be honored with a visit from beyond the grave?"

"He's a cadet from the military school, a former soldier in the American army, a hard nut to crack and an adventurous sort. He knew Duroc in the army and we have to make him see Duroc. No more of those phantoms wrapped in shrouds like we've shown our last subjects. We have to replay Duroc's death scene."

"All right, but that's dangerous. I hope you didn't do anything foolish like telling him he was going to see his friend. He knows that scene, and it's possible that we won't play it just right."

"Don't worry. He doesn't suspect a thing. He doesn't know I met Duroc. As for the scene, he just described it in my presence. We'll just have to modify our program a little bit to make it look like what he described. I'll run over to the Laprairie Hotel and come back immediately."

Bohémier left and returned a half hour later. "Success on all fronts!" he said upon entering. "There's only a thin wall separating the room I've rented from Leduc's room —

Leduc is the cadet I was talking to you about. The wall has a stovepipe opening and another small one just large enough to insert my apparatus tube. After thinking things through, I don't think we should try to show Duroc falling as he is being struck by a bullet. He'll appear in uniform — wounded, but standing, leaning on his rifle. I'll be wearing my devil mask and watching Leduc through the stovepipe hole and mimicking his movements so you'll know what he's doing; if he says anything, you'll be able to hear him easily for the wall is very thin."

In the afternoon, the two pals went to the Laprairie Hotel, where they set up their apparatus, and, when evening came, while the owner's son looked on, they practiced some experiments that succeeded perfectly. All agreed that, if the apparatus worked as well when Eugène was in his room, the cadet would certainly be scared stiff. They laughed a lot in advance at his expense; that was at least something.

Around eleven o'clock, Leduc returned from visiting a friend. He said his prayers, got undressed, blew out the lamp, and got into bed. They had miscalculated the time it would take for the lump of potassium to come in contact with the ice and Eugène fell asleep before they could enjoy the show they had prepared for him. Just as the potassium began to burn, the sound of someone kicking the door of his room woke him up with a start. He grabbed his blankets and was about to throw them on the fire to put it out when he saw an American soldier looking very much like Duroc hovering above the flames.

His first thought was that the ghost, since that's what it seemed to be, was not Duroc. First of all, Léon had been struck in the shoulder, but higher up than where blood seemed to be flowing from the ghost's wound. The ghost, standing with his hands resting on his rifle barrel, wore a dress jacket and an issue cap, and was freshly shaved; however, when Duroc was wounded, he was wearing his field jacket, his head was covered with a hat, and his face was framed with a six weeks' growth of black beard. It seemed to Eugène that if Duroc had wanted to visit him he wouldn't have bothered to shave and put on his dress uniform.

Believing that someone had come into his room to frighten him, Leduc resolved to seize the weapon and send his nocturnal visitor packing after disarming him. To do so, he needed to attack quickly. He sat up calmly, pretended to rub his eyes, and with a bound lunged forward to seize the rifle.

His hands closed on thin air.

Since the ghost hadn't budged, Eugène got the idea of turning his back on it and looking in the opposite direction to see if the ghost would follow his gaze. Having determined that nothing of the sort was happening, he looked around the room and noticed, through the stovepipe hole, the back of a head with mask ties around it. It was Bohémier who, to signal Brindamour that Leduc had turned his back on the phantom, had turned around himself. A second later he turned his face with its cardboard mask, surmounted by two horns and covered with phosphorescent paint, back to the opening.

Eugène told himself that this masked devil must have something to do with the ethereal but slightly lethargic apparition.

Without saying a word, he slid under the bed, crawled to the other side, spied a chair by the wall under the stovepipe hole, got up against the wall where Bohémier couldn't see him, jumped on the chair, and struck the mask with his fist. Bohémier cried out as he fell off the stepladder where he had been perched.

Taking advantage of the confusion, Eugène pulled himself up to the opening and, glancing quickly around the adjoining room, he saw Bohémier getting up sheepishly as the ghost's double and the proprietor's son went over to help him. The three began talking to one another in hushed voices in front of the concave mirror and Eugène, having come down from his chair to the floor, could see the group reflected quite well by the apparatus in his own room.

"Hey, my friends," he shouted when he was back in his bed, "I can't hear you, but I can see you quite clearly. If you don't want yourselves on show, take away that machine you've put through the hole in the wall. On second thought, leave it there; I'll come join you. I'd like to see how it works if you don't object. Besides, you won't have very much to explain. I saw everything through the stovepipe hole."

"You're welcome to come join us," said the hotel owner's son, wishing to appear friendly so Eugène would forget that he had wanted to have a good laugh at his expense.

CHAPTER LXIII

AN IMPORTANT DEPOSITION

Without taking time to dress, Eugène went into the next room.

"M. Leduc," said the hotel owner's son, "allow me to present M. Bohémier, a law student, and M. Brindamour, M. Grippard's secretary."

"Pleased to meet you, gentlemen," Eugène said, bowing.

"We've already met," said Bohémier.

"Yes," answered Eugène. "And, if I'm not mistaken, we were in quite close contact through the opening in this wall not too long ago."

"You hit hard; and that is not meant as a compliment. If you had hit my eye instead of getting me on the forehead, you would have disfigured me and that would have been quite regrettable: as it is, I now have a bump which I could have done without. It seems you don't like phantasmagoria, but your way of showing your disapproval isn't very pleasant for those of us who love this type of amusement."

"Ah! So you were the devil. I beg your Satanic Majesty's pardon. I hit you as hard as if I were dealing with Beelzebub in person; I should have known I was simply making an amateur devil come tumbling down. Besides, why didn't you warn me? I would have pulled my punch according to the degree of resistance I was about to encounter."

"What are you drinking, gentlemen? I'm paying a round," said the hotel owner's son to change the conversation.

When everyone had ordered drinks, the hotel owner's son went down to serve his guests. As soon as he had left, Bohémier said to Eugène: "I hope you won't hold it against us for wanting to frighten you, especially since you acquitted yourself so honorably when we put your courage to the test. I'll just ask one favor of you: please don't tell anyone what happened here this evening."

"Why?"

"I don't see any reason to hide the truth since you already know that M. Brindamour is M. Grippard's employee. If his employer heard about this business, he would have the key to a puzzle he's been trying in vain to figure out for more than a year. It is in our interest for him to remain forever in the dark on this matter."

"I'll keep the secret provided you tell me all about the mystery puzzling M. Grippard, although I think I've guessed part of it. I know this M. Grippard by reputation, for the man Brindamour was impersonating this evening talked to me about him. I regret to inform M. Brindamour that I consider his employer to be an out-and-out scoundrel. As for you, M. Bohémier, your name came back to me this evening and I know you were an accomplice in working a scam on poor Duroc. You see that I already know quite enough to make it difficult for you to sink further in my esteem. You need me to be discreet and I need your confession and your help in wringing a confession from M. Grippard. Don't protest! Take it or leave it. Nothing obliges me to keep quiet. These are my conditions: a secret for a secret; a confidence for a confidence; I'll help you and you'll help me."

At that moment, the hotel owner's son came in with the four glasses. Bohémier signaled Eugène not to talk while he was there and began explaining how the apparatus worked. Then, as Leduc was getting ready to return to his room, he said to him: "Stay; we need to talk. Louis, why don't you go get us some cigars, then you'll have to excuse us; we have business with M. Leduc and we want to be alone with him."

When the hotel owner's son had left the room, Bohémier said to Leduc: "Personally, I've nothing to fear. Denounce me if you like, but I can't say the same for Brindamour. If I understand your proposition correctly, you want me to confess my role in the Duroc affair?"

"I want a written confession from you and one from M. Grippard."

"What will you do with them?"

"I could just say that's my business; however, I'm willing to agree never to use these documents unless I need them to clear my departed friend's memory or reputation."

"You're asking the impossible. I'm perfectly willing to make the confession you're talking about, but how will we ever get M. Grippard to consent to such an admission?"

"If it's impossible, we'll have to leave it at that and I'll tell M. Grippard about what I have seen. Do you think I haven't guessed that you must have used your phantasmagoria to put M. Brindamour's employer to the test? That's the only plausible explanation for your being afraid that he could find out about your secret. I suspect that Léon's ghost has made him do lots of things he would never have dreamed of doing if it hadn't been for the nocturnal apparitions which must have haunted him — thanks to you.

"In my position as an old friend of the unfortunate Duroc, I find the funereal farce I've seen you act out this evening to be completely tasteless. But, since you've used Duroc's name up to now to blackmail Grippard, the least you can do is to use the same means to extract from him a confession that can restore his victim's reputation. In any case, I leave it up to you to decide how you'll do it, but I need this confession in writing; that's the price of my silence."

Realizing that they were at Leduc's mercy, Bohémier and Brindamour brought him up to date about what they had done so far and what they proposed to do. It was agreed that, at the first available opportunity, they would put Grippard through a new ordeal to make him sign a confession admitting that he had wronged Duroc.

Leduc, Bohémier, and Brindamour would work together. Eugène, dressed in an imp's costume, was to get into Grippard's room, hide under the bed and reveal himself just in time to carry off the signed confession; as soon as Grippard signed it, the two others would set to work from the room across the hall.

They took advantage of the few days remaining before Grippard's return to rehearse their roles and make sure this risky undertaking would be a success.

M. Grippard returned somewhat tired but completely delighted with his trip. He retired early without in the least suspecting that a man disguised in a formfitting black batiste costume with phosphorescent stripes had come into the room before him and was hidden under his bed. Exhausted, he got into bed and went to sleep immediately.

As soon as he heard M. Grippard snoring, Eugène crept cautiously from his hiding place, put out the lamp Grippard had left burning, unbolted the door, and set on the carpet a chunk of ice that he had brought with him, threw some sodium on it, and then got back under the bed with his head at the foot of the bed. Next he reached out his arm, grabbed the blanket, and pulled it violently off the bed, making a loud guttural sound as he did so.

It was the signal Bohémier was waiting for. He had placed one of the instruments in the keyhole and started to make a whole series of little devils and other glowing figures parade across the room.

The sodium was blazing on the ice and Grippard, waking up with a start, watched aghast at this spectacle he recalled having already seen at the Hotel Canada.

His bed gave a jolt as if it had been lifted up by an invisible force and, at that very moment, Duroc, dressed in the same clothes he was wearing when he jumped into the river, appeared hovering over the flames.

"I'm summoned to come back to see you," said the ghost in a cavernous voice, "but this time I'm coming back for a very special reason. Over a year ago, I ordered you to set young Brindamour up in business and you haven't done so. I know that, as your employee, it would be wrong of Brindamour to complain about the way you treat him, but Brindamour is no ordinary employee and, if he knew what you owe him, he might perhaps be less satisfied than he is. You excel at fooling mortals who are more naive or more honest than you are, but you can't fool me. You're already planning to declare an enormous bankruptcy. When you are ruined or when people consider you to be ruined, what will you do for this young man you've promised to protect? I order you to set him up and right away! It won't cost you any more, seeing you haven't the slightest intention of paying your debts. Are you prepared to obey me, or must I use against you the supernatural means I have at my disposal?"

"I'll do as you say. I'll open up a store in the country for him," said Grippard, terrified in the extreme.

"That's all well and good, but I need some guarantees that you are acting in good faith. Therefore, right this very minute, as I dictate, you're going to write out a confession to the crime you committed against me; you'll sign it and I shall keep it in my possession and use it if the need arises."

"I'm too frightened to write and I have no light."

"I have not come here to wait on you and I'm not obliged to furnish you with a lamp. Light your lamp. I'll disappear, but you'll hear me talking, and I'll have someone here to receive the document from your hand. I advise you to do as you're told in the presence of the being who will be supervising you, and I'm warning you in advance that he shouldn't be crossed. Go on, light your lamp, and let's get this over with."

While Grippard was striking a match, Eugène crept out of his hiding place without making a sound, and tiptoed over to where the tradesman was. When Grippard had lighted his lamp, he happened to glance at the spot where the phantom had been a moment earlier. Duroc's ghost was no longer there, but Grippard recoiled in horror as he saw before him a black devil with a pair of horns and the traditional tail.

The black batiste costume was covered with phosphorescent stripes which glowed in the dark, and, since Eugène, who was smaller than Grippard, was careful to stay between Grippard and the light, some of these stripes were visible even by the light of the lamp. Leduc didn't say a single word. He just motioned to Grippard to start writing and moved closer so he could watch over his shoulder. When Grippard was ready to write, a voice seeming to come from the ceiling uttered these words: "Write what I dictate."

> *I, the undersigned Charles Auguste Grippard, merchant, declare that on May 4, 1864, in the presence of Messrs. Alphonse Bagoulard, lawyer, and Elzéar Bohémier, law student, I borrowed the sum of $1,000 from M. Léon Duroc which he placed in my hands and which I promised then and there to return it to him the next day; that I never returned that sum of money even though he asked me for it several times; that on the seventh of the same month, when he insisted that I pay him, I denied ever having received that sum of money or any other from him; that I did so again in the presence of the aforesaid Bagoulard and Bohémier who backed my denials; that, on the eighth of that same month, I proposed that M. Duroc forge the signature of his ex-employer, M. Latour, a Pingreville merchant, to renew the note owed by the aforesaid M. Latour, which had fallen due, and which the $1,000 I had extorted from Duroc was intended to pay, and that the aforesaid Duroc indignantly refused to forge M. Latour's signature.*
>
> *In witness whereof, I have signed the above deposition on this nineteenth day of October 1865.*

M. Grippard had had to force himself to keep on writing to the very end, but the presence of the black devil looking over his shoulder had overcome his hesitation. He signed with a bold hand and breathed a sigh of relief. He had hardly finished writing when Eugène grabbed the document, blew out the lamp, and rushed toward the door, which he opened and closed noisily as he left the room.

Grippard hesitated for a moment, then, suspecting he had been tricked, he ran to the door and tried to open it; but as he put his hand to the latch, he cried out in pain. The latch was burning hot. Quite convinced that he was dealing with supernatural beings, he went back to his bed and buried himself under the covers. The mysterious voice forced him to look again. Léon's ghost had just reappeared, telling him: "I'm pleased with you and if you keep your promise, you have nothing to fear."

Eugène's escape had been arranged in advance. His accomplices had removed the apparatus momentarily and then replaced it immediately. Heat had been transmitted to the latch by a brass wire put there ahead of time. As soon as Leduc got past the door, an electric battery connected to the latch had heated it until it was red hot.

Grippard relighted his lamp and went back to bed.

As for Eugène, he had Bohémier add the following declaration to the document Grippard had signed:

> *I, the undersigned Elzéar Bohémier, certify that the above document in which M. Grippard states that certain events happened in my presence and in that of M. Alphonse Bagoulard's is true and accurate.*
>
> *Elzéar Bohémier*

Armed with this precious document, Leduc took leave of his two companions, resolved never to have anything more to do with them.

CHAPTER LXIV

An Eventful Life

On February 6, 1866, just a year after getting out of Libby prison, Eugène got his first certificate from the military school. He went back to live with his family. The following spring, he left with five hundred other young men, recruited from the surrounding parishes, who were all going off to work in the New Jersey brickyards.[1] They went by steamboat up the Richelieu River as far as Chambly, then on foot to St. Jean. These farmers' sons who spent each summer in the American brickyards were sturdy fellows. They could, perhaps, have been criticized for being a bit rowdy, but, all in all, they were as peaceable as young men of any other nationality from the same class would have been. Everyone who had seen them arrive agreed they were fine representatives of their strong and manly race, but everyone seemed astonished to see Eugène in their company. The cadet's refinement in dress and manner made him stand out in the crowd. One of his companions noticed this and said: "My goodness, Eugène, you're a handsome fellow, but your good looks alone don't explain why all these strangers are interested in you. Nobody knows you here, and yet, I've heard people say, 'What's he doing with all those fellows?' You see, you're used to living with gentlemen and that shows in your manners."

"They probably think I look like more of a rascal than you do," Eugène answered, laughing.

This was at the time of the Fenian invasion.[2] Besides the Royal Canadian Rifles garrisoned at Fort St. Jean, four companies of volunteers were stationed in the city and billeted with families. Eugène believed he had found the opportunity he had been looking for to put his military school certificate to good use. He informed an officer he met in town about his plan and was told: "You could always join my company as a noncommissioned officer while you're waiting for the opportunity to receive a commission; you won't have to wait long because one of the battalion captains is thinking of resigning."

So Eugène became a sergeant in Major Marchand's battalion, but two or three days later the soldiers were sent back home. Their services were required for only two days of maneuvers each week at the company's general headquarters. Eugène, who was in one of the companies attached to the municipality, had to look for a job to cover his expenses while he waited for another call to arms for the volunteers.

He recalled that he had started learning the baker's trade once upon a time and finally found a job at a nominal salary in a bakery in St. Athanase, now known as Iberville. He stayed there for three weeks, but since he didn't know enough about the trade to satisfy his new employer, who let him know it, Eugène offered to quit — a proposal accepted with such enthusiasm that Leduc found it rather unseemly.

He went to Montréal and found work in another bakery where he stayed for a while. Since he had made it clear that he didn't know anything about the trade, his new employer didn't expect as much from him as the one he had just left. He could have stayed on indefinitely if he had wanted to, but there was a new call to arms. Volunteers were flocking to the border and Eugène couldn't resist the urge to rush to his country's defense.

Many of his former comrades from the military school were now officers in the volunteer militia battalions. One of these, a lieutenant in the *Chasseurs Canadiens,* offered to resign his commission so Eugène could replace him, and also sell him his officer's uniform on credit, but his unfortunate experience at St. Jean had made Leduc cautious. He didn't want to incur a $100 debt when he wasn't sure if the battalion might not be disbanded after a few days. He enlisted as a private and was made a sergeant the very next day at Laprairie, where the *Chasseurs Canadiens* battalion, which he belonged to, was stationed for a few days. From Laprairie, the *Chasseurs Canadiens* were sent to St. Jean. After camping for a few days on the common there, they received their marching orders.

The left wing was sent to Philipsburg and the right wing was sent to Hemmingford. Eugène was with the battalion's right wing. After a couple of weeks, the Hemmingford troops broke camp and the volunteers were taken back to Montréal, where they were dismissed and where they had all sorts of trouble getting paid. The companies sent to Philipsburg hadn't come back and they needed reinforcements; Eugène went off to join them and served for two weeks more as a sergeant. When the Fenian War was over, he returned to Montréal, where he waited in vain for another two weeks to be paid for his services. He did everything he could to find a job, but none of his efforts paid off. Tired of trying, despairing of ever being paid what was owed him, he took the boat for Québec where he hoped he could find a way to work his passage to France. The urge to enlist in the French army had come back to him stronger than ever.

A job contractor gave him a place to stay in a tavern on Champlain Street while he was waiting to get a job for Eugène as a cook aboard the *Tarifa.* Without telling Eugène, he had recommended him as one of the best cordon-bleu chefs in the two Americas. Eugène wasn't too frightened by the prospect of cooking for sailors. During his stay in the American army he had learned a bit about cooking. But the captain's wife was going to be on board, and that complicated things immensely. Try asking a man who only knows how to cook a steak and make coffee to bake pastries!

The *Tarifa* was a new brigantine on her maiden voyage. Moored at the Commissaires' wharf, she was scheduled to set sail the next day.[3] Eugène, who had had the good sense to sign on under an assumed name, began his duties immediately. The crew had not yet embarked; only the officers and the captain's wife were on board. Not used to cooking on a coal stove, Eugène had no end of trouble preparing dinner.

By two o'clock no one had yet had a bite to eat. The captain, the second officer, the boatswain and the ship's steward came one after another to heap reproaches on him, and Eugène told himself he would never succeed in pleasing these people. Ashamed of himself for having signed on to do a job beyond his abilities, he decided to slip away quietly. Leaving his coat on board, he took a bucket and left the ship, pretending he was going to fetch some water in the next street. As soon as he saw that he was far enough away from the ship, he dropped his bucket in the street and went off toward Charlesbourg.

Yet one more desertion to chalk up to his craving to serve in the French army. It would be the last stupid mess of this sort he got himself into because of that silly impulse.

He retraced his steps, went through Lorette, then St. Augustin, and, three days later, he was arrested in the church at Pointe-aux-Trembles in the lower city where he had stopped to say his morning prayers.

A rifleman from the regular army, who happened to be stationed in the secret service at Pointe-aux-Trembles, had seen Eugène go into the church. Struck by his military bearing, he assumed that Eugène must be a deserter from the regular army and, since he was under orders to arrest deserters, he got another man to accompany him and found Eugène kneeling in the pew. Leduc knew that they would never manage to convict him of deserting from the English army — that wasn't what bothered him. But he didn't want to be taken back to Québec where he could be in a lot of trouble for deserting from the *Tarifa*.

Luckily for him, he carried in his pocket a picture of himself wearing the uniform of a sergeant in the *Chasseurs Canadiens,* which he showed to the police officer. It was clear from the facings[4] on the uniform that Leduc had really belonged to a volunteer battalion. That being the case, it wasn't very likely he could have been in the regular army at the same time.

"You can take me back to Québec if you like," Leduc said to him, "but that won't do you any good and you would be doing me a disservice, because I've just deserted from a merchant ship the day after signing on."

The soldier was quite pleased to meet someone he could talk to. He didn't speak a single word of French and no one spoke English at Pointe-aux-Trembles. He invited Eugène to lunch and kept him for the rest of the day.

Eugène had been well dressed when he left his parents and he didn't want to go back home in shirtsleeves, so he went to the Eastern Townships looking for work. He finally found seasonal work with a Scots farmer near Richmond where he spent two months helping with the harvest.

Decked out in new clothes, he went back to his parents and, shortly afterwards, he found work as a clerk in a country store. He didn't stay there very long, for the owner's wife was a shrew who meddled too much in the store's business and Eugène wasn't the sort to let himself be treated like a slave.

The following spring, he left for New England. After spending the summer working hard at unpleasant jobs and making bricks for three months, he became a clerk in a dry goods store in a small city near Boston.

He had been there for just a short time when he learned from the Canadian newspapers that a detachment of *Zouaves Pontificaux Canadiens* was being organized. He wrote right away to the pastor of the parish where his parents lived, imploring him to do everything possible to get him admitted to the ranks of these new crusaders. He received a very flattering letter from the priest, who was his friend, and who promised to do everything he could to get him admitted, but soon afterwards another letter from the *curé* informed him that the contingent had all the men it needed, that the request had come too late, and that a great many candidates had been turned away. Eugène promised himself he would apply right away if another detachment was formed, when something quite unexpected came up to make him abandon his dreams of military glory once and for all and caused him to put all his efforts into doing something more tangible.

CHAPTER LXV

An Unexpected Encounter

hrough all the vicissitudes of his stormy life, in all his wanderings, there were two objects Leduc had carefully preserved: Hélène's ring and the admission of guilt he had wrung out of Grippard. His scapular had been the ring's jewel case, protecting it from all searches.

Whenever he found himself in a civilized setting and his clothes were in keeping with the ring's rich appearance, it had reappeared on his finger. When times weren't so good, when he was threatened with some sort of danger, the ring disappeared from sight. His finger had become a veritable barometer. Embellished by the ring, it proclaimed that times were good; devoid of that ornament, the finger portended stormy weather. Ever since he had been "in the world," as he put it to express the fact that he had managed to pull himself out of grinding poverty, the ruby in its turquoise setting sparkled between the two knuckles of the ring finger on his left hand, the same side as his heart. Eugène hadn't forgotten Hélène, but he thought she had long since married and he remembered her as we recall those angelic visions our childish imaginations conjure up at an age when sweet illusions come to gild our carefree existence. Marriage must have changed her, but he was still as much in love with Hélène as she was when he had seen her at fifteen. He felt that, if she had been free, he would have loved the woman just as he loved that ideal face imprinted in his imagination — the same way the sun's light fixes images on a daguerreotype.

He had vowed to worship that ethereal form which reminded him of the time when his innocent heart had first opened to love's sunny rays. The woman belonged to another — he didn't love her any longer, or at least he thought he didn't, but the angel whose face she had borrowed had remained with him; it was that angel he loved and he surrendered himself completely to that emotion which was both sweet and pure, tender and passionate, without feeling the least remorse.

One evening the store was filled with customers and, being very busy, Eugène rushed around doing his best to serve the numerous clientele.

"Over here, please, M. Leduc," the owner entreated.

Hearing this name, a beautiful very well dressed young woman raised her eyes. Upon seeing Eugène, she paled and glanced immediately at Eugène's hand, which still bore Hélène's ring. Barely suppressing the cry which was about to escape her lips, she leaned on the counter. At that very moment, Eugène, who had just come face to face with his customer, turned pale himself. Hélène Duchâtel was standing before him — Hélène, three years older, but even more beautiful at eighteen than she had been when Eugène had seen her last in Virginia.

Completely taken aback, Eugène couldn't find a word to say and it was Hélène who finally managed to regain her composure first. Holding out her hand, she said to him in French: "This is a very happy though unexpected pleasure for, thanks to that ring you're wearing on your finger, I'm absolutely sure that I must be talking to M. Eugène Leduc."

"I have kept this ring with me always. This is the first chance I have had to thank you for this treasured gift. It's all the more precious to me now since you recognized me because of it; as for me, I would have recognized you anywhere."

"I remember very well how you looked when last I saw you. You were blond then, but you must admit that your black mustache" — Eugène was having the mustache he was just starting to grow dyed black — "could have thrown me off somewhat if I hadn't heard someone call your name and, even more so, if I hadn't seen the ring on your finger which put me back on the right track. But we are being watched; please show me this lace. You must have a lot to tell me. I know I have a great deal to tell you. I'm going to give you my address and I hope you'll do me the honor of coming to visit an old acquaintance and that we'll be able to have a nice long chat without being disturbed."

She handed Eugène a perfumed card bearing the following address:

> Mlle. Hélène Duchâtel
> Teacher of French
> Ladies' College

Glancing at the address, Eugène could scarcely hide his joy. Not only had he found Hélène again, she wasn't married to someone else, as he had feared up to that time.

Recovering his composure somewhat, he said: "Has it been a while since you saw M. Alfred Shelton and Madame his mother?"

"They are both dead. Poor Alfred was killed at Cold Harbor and his mother didn't survive him for long. That terrible war also took my poor father from me; he died fighting for the South. I thought that death had taken away everyone I loved. Imagine how happy I felt this evening to realize that you at least came away safe and sound from that time of suffering and danger. And M. Duroc, what has become of him?"

"He's dead also. He fell mortally wounded by my side before Petersburg. I left the regiment shortly thereafter. By the way, nobody knows I was in the service, and I have reasons for not wanting anybody to know, for I must admit that I am a deserter."

"I mustn't keep you any longer. If you are free tomorrow, come see me and we'll chat. I won't tell anyone where we first met."

This entire conversation having taken place in French, no one in the store had understood a single word. Hélène made some purchases, then went off, leaving Eugène even more smitten than before. As you might imagine, Leduc took care not to miss the next day's rendezvous. These two young people who had loved each other since they had first met had many things to say to each other. They confessed their inner feelings to each other and Hélène declared to Eugène that after seeing him for the first time, she had resolved not to marry Shelton because she had realized that her heart no longer belonged to him. The cousin she believed she loved when they became engaged had died in battle without ever suspecting that one of the young Federal soldiers, in whose company he had dined at his mother's, had replaced him in the young girl's affections.

Orphaned and penniless, she thought she might put her knowledge of French to use by becoming a teacher in a boarding school for girls, so she had come to settle in New England where Yankees have the good sense to remunerate dedicated teachers adequately. She thanked heaven for having made that decision, since it had allowed her to be reunited with the only man who had inspired in her that deep and abiding love that a noble-hearted woman feels for the man she consents to marry.

When the young couple parted that evening, they had become engaged in the eyes of God and set their wedding day. They were married six months later and Eugène, now the happiest of men, set to work with renewed energy. Hélène continued to teach French at the Ladies' College and the couple saved as much as best they could so they could go back to live in Canada.

Eugène had his eye on the Eastern Townships, where he was considering opening a store.

He was one of the principal founders of a *Société Saint-Jean-Baptiste* and a literary circle in the little American city where they lived. Several U.S. and Canadian newspapers welcomed his submissions and, from time to time, Eugène published noteworthy articles supporting repatriation and colonization. Possessed of an eloquent pen and a vivid imagination, his polished style and ardent patriotism were the qualities distinguishing him as a writer. He contributed to a great extent to the awakening of that national sentiment which produced such happy results among the Canadian French who emigrated to the United States. By 1870, the young couple, having saved a fairly respectable sum, came back to Canada, but before going to settle in the Eastern Townships, Eugène wanted to visit his parents, accompanied by his wife, whom the Leduc family did not yet know. We'll leave them there for the moment enjoying the private happiness of the family home. We'll soon rejoin them in Pingreville once we have brought the reader up to date on what's been happening to our old acquaintances since their lucky star had risen on the henceforth cloudless horizon as Eugène and Hélène gazed toward the future.

CHAPTER LXVI

The Dead Man's Fiancée

Thanks to M. Grippard's protection, Brindamour had been able to open his own store in one of the parishes along the majestic St. Lawrence. He had given up the phantasmagoria, since that occupation had outlived its usefulness, and devoted himself actively to his business.

M. Grippard was thought to be very rich. As a matter of fact, the show he made of throwing other men's money around dazzled idle onlookers. He was a daring, unscrupulous entrepreneur. Whenever he needed money, and God knows he needed money to live as he did, he always managed to get some.

He took off once with two barges of construction lumber from the Picourdy sawmills, went to the United States where he sold the ships and their cargo, pocketed the money, and kept it. Another time he bought large amounts of grain which he sold immediately, paid himself, and neglected to pay the *habitants*.

Such honest behavior could not go unrewarded. In the general elections of 1867, he presented his candidacy in two different counties. At that time, the double mandate was in effect and so he was elected both as a member of the House of Commons and to the Legislative Assembly.

Naturally his adversaries in this dual battle could not measure up to him. Put quite simply, they were honest men. Gullible fools! Cartouche and Mandrin, had they been alive, would perhaps have been as popular as Grippard. But, since the death of Entaya called Baptiste Pierre, not a single man was left in Canada to compare with M. Grippard.[1]

Shortly after his election, the new deputy declared bankruptcy in the most spectacular fashion. This collapse brought about the ruin of several well-established businesses. A grain merchant, thought to be a millionaire, was reduced to abject poverty because he had backed M. Grippard's notes.

Before the news of his business failure got out, Grippard resolved to make the most of the credit he still retained with some country merchants. He nearly killed a good many horses racing between Montréal and Trois-Rivières on both sides of the St. Lawrence. He would arrive at a store or a farm belonging to a man who looked upon him as his benefactor, exchange his exhausted horse for another, promising to pay the difference in value between the two animals, borrow $50 or $100 from the *habitant,* and gallop off again at full speed.

The individual who had just been fleeced would rub his hands with satisfaction. Loan money to M. Grippard! What an honor! And it was such a sure thing! Everyone had so much confidence in him that when they learned he was bankrupt they couldn't believe it. Many of the people he had defrauded insisted that he would pay one hundred cents on the dollar — with interest.

As soon as Grippard had finished his rounds exploiting human gullibility, he gathered his creditors together and offered to settle with them at fifty cents on the dollar. All of them flatly refused to consider his offer. Later on, he offered them twenty-five cents, which they still rejected. A third meeting took place at which Grippard deigned to treat his creditors to champagne.

"Drink up, you damned fools," he said. "You stole from me at retail, but I'm robbing you wholesale." (This, dear reader, is quoted verbatim). "First I offered you fifty cents on the dollar, then twenty-five cents, and you passed it up. Now I'm offering you ten cents on the dollar. Take it or leave it."

Such an advantageous offer couched in such polite terms was bound to be accepted and so it was immediately.

European readers will perhaps tell themselves that this account is quite implausible. We insist it's completely true in every detail. However, it would be wrong of them to conclude that our citizenry is dishonest. Here, the common man considers the fraudulent bankrupt to be a thief and he's right. Our domestic mores are pure and if our sense of morality is a bit tarnished in our business circles, it is the fault of the Europeans who created our commerce and who set the tone in business matters.

Here as elsewhere, wealth excuses many crimes, but if you want to have an idea of how deeply the bankrupt man is despised, just notice how people avoid the man whom bankruptcy has left penniless. It doesn't matter that he has stripped himself of his possessions, and sacrificed everything to pay his debts; people will perhaps admire his honesty, but they'll never forgive him his poverty.

As for the bankrupt man who has enriched himself by stealing from his creditors, he is criticized very harshly for his dishonesty when it's so blatant that his detractors can't be faulted for seeming envious; but the admiration that is felt for the rich man soon makes people forget their scorn for the thief. Alas! We aren't any better than other nations when it comes to this, but those whose countrymen have done everything they could to corrupt our political and business mores shouldn't be the first to throw stones at the Canadian people when they see one of us do cynically in the light of day what the Europeans have taught us to do secretly.

Thanks to the compromise he had reached with his creditors, Grippard was able to retain his two mandates: one in the local and one in the federal parliament. This much should be said in his favor: Grippard's speeches never caused the legislative sessions to be unduly prolonged. Would to God that as much could be said of certain gasbags with their long and pointless speeches. He confined himself to plotting behind the scene, occasionally serving on committees, and voting with the opposition when he wasn't away from his seat whenever a vote was taken.

Still living like a lord, if he had a trip to take, he chartered a steamboat, telegraphing ahead to reserve a hotel room. He told everyone who would listen to him that he wasn't really interested in politics — that what he really wanted was money.

He had formed a railway company for which he was the highest bidder and principal contractor — having been one of its sponsors in the legislature.[2]

In the provincial parliament, he found his old acquaintance Alphonse Bagoulard, who had been elected by acclamation in a county which need not be identified here; but the two old friends found themselves in opposite camps. Grippard was as silent as Bagoulard was loquacious. Needless to say, Bagoulard scored some brilliant successes in that arena, where his reputation for eloquence preceded him long before; all his colleagues agreed that he had a brilliant future ahead of him.

Bohémier, more besotted than ever, was dealing the final blow to his health, impaired by filthy orgies and debauchery of all kinds. The most widely held opinion among his acquaintances was that he didn't have much longer to live.

Bagoulard's friends, seeing him destined to play an important role in politics, thought of marrying him off in the hope of getting him to settle down. Since he didn't have a cent to his name and that his title of deputy obliged him to live in a style he could ill afford, they had decided to find him an heiress, and Louise Latour was one of those they recommended to him.

"That one," they had told him, "won't be an easy conquest. She has refused several excellent matches and you'll have a dead man for a rival."

"Hell," he answered, "I'd rather do battle with a living one. I'd attempt to have him do something stupid in her presence, or I'd strive to be more kind and attentive than he was, but how can you fight a dead man? Since her love has survived the death of her beloved, to the point of making her sacrifice everything to worship his memory, that proves she is a noble-hearted woman. A living man would have to be pretty perfect to take the place of an idealized being in the shape of a man and who is no longer here to disillusion the woman who adores him. No matter, such an example of constancy is so rare that it piques my curiosity. What's this interesting beauty worth?"

"Somewhere in the neighborhood of $30,000, not including what she'll inherit. She's an only child. And Old Latour is worth at least $150,000."

"That's a pretty sum. And her looks, she's passable, at least?"

"She is as beautiful as a band of angels; she's quite witty and looks very distinguished."

"Then I accept the challenge. I'll see if this pearl of great price can resist me, for in certain circles I'm considered quite the Don Juan."

A few days after that conversation, Alphonse Bagoulard had himself invited to M. Latour's. He found Mme. Latour very affected, M. Latour very pleasant, and Louise beautiful but very reserved. He took advantage of their invitation to return and, soon afterwards, he proposed to Louise. He didn't succeed any better than Duroc's other rivals. The vexation he felt at this turn of events was all the more violent because, without meaning to, he had become enamored of Louise.

He was handsome, elegant, well proportioned, and brimming with wit, eloquence, and talent. That was more than enough to turn the heads of most of the young girls thereabouts. His reputation for being a brilliant orator and his being a member of Parliament added to his seductive powers, and yet all of this was for naught where Louise was concerned. He had, however, succeeded in inflaming Mme. Latour, but he didn't seem to be aware of it. If he had been, it would have deeply humiliated him, for he would have considered this facile conquest a bitter mockery of fate.

"I'm not asking you to forget the fortunate man you love so deeply," he said to Louise. "I'd willingly die for the pleasure of being regretted by you as you mourn him, but I assure you that you would find in me someone who would love you as much as M. Duroc ever could."

"If I could love another," Louise answered, "I don't see why you couldn't be the one. You seem to be possessed of all the qualities a woman could want in the one she loves, but if I told you that what I feel for you can be compared with what I feel for M. Duroc, I would be lying. Let's be friends if you like, as we would be if Léon were alive, for I believe he would like you, but I beg you not to place me in the painful position of having to refuse a love that I may not deserve, but that I could never agree to accept."

"At least leave me some hope so that later on, when time has better healed your wounded heart, I would be allowed to renew my proposal of marriage."

"Do not hope for anything of the sort and I pray you not to insist."

"Then forgive me if I've been importunate. Blame it on my passionate love for you — a profound and abiding love."

M. Latour was very vexed when he heard that Bagoulard's proposal had been rejected. For Latour, having Bagoulard for a son-in-law seemed the epitome of happiness. This man, who had been so scandalized when M. Grippard had told him about Léon Duroc's supposed misconduct, considered Bagoulard's excesses to be mere peccadilloes, youthful follies, even though the young member of Parliament flaunted these escapades with such cynicism that, in the city of Montréal, proper young men didn't speak Bagoulard's name in the presence of young ladies for fear of offending their modesty. When need be, M. Latour knew how to use a double standard. How many unjust preferences have been based on nothing more than this absurd rule!

CHAPTER LXVII

A FAMILY PUT TO THE TEST

A series of misfortunes befell the Latour family barely a few days after the scene just described. M. Grippard's bankruptcy had claimed many victims and M. Latour was one of them. His business was completely ruined. To re-establish himself, he would have had to risk using Louise's dowry, and he was so crushed by the blow which had just struck him that he didn't feel he had the energy necessary to begin the struggle again under those conditions. Louise insisted that he use what he needed from the money that was coming to her to pay off all his creditors. He let her persuade him to do this much, but he never consented to risk the rest on new commercial ventures.

The meager income from his greatly diminished fortune was just enough to support the three members of the Latour household in extremely reduced circumstances. The luxury of bygone days had to be given up. Louise did not complain. She was happy to see her father rest from his business worries and she had advised him to go back into business only because she believed he was attached to the feverish pace of the life he had led ever since she had known him.

As for the incomparable Mme. Latour, she was more surly, cantankerous, and sullen toward her husband than ever. She reproached him bitterly for having been taken in by M. Grippard and she cited the example of other businessmen that M. Grippard hadn't been able to ruin for the excellent reason that they had nothing to lose. More than ever she tried to please the few dandies attracted by her simpering ways. She pleased them so much that one of them resolved to seduce her. That would prove to be easy, since that was just what she was looking for.

Their first rendezvous took place away from the Latour residence but, as is always the case in such situations, the guilty couple were soon emboldened by the fact that Louise had gone to spend two weeks visiting a friend living in one of the nearby parishes. Each time M. Latour was away for a few hours, Mme. Latour's lover, warned in some mysterious way, would go to see his Dulcinea.

M. Latour's dishonor had become the talk of the town and he was the only one left who didn't know what was going on. Then a kind friend — such as can always be found in similar circumstances — told him what was going on. M. Latour pretended not to believe a bit of it, but, as soon as he could decently get rid of the person who had just poured poison into his heart, he strode somberly toward the home that his wife's conduct had sullied. On his threshold he came face to face with the man rumored to be his wife's seducer, and, hiding the rage wrenching his heart, he could not help noticing the agitation of the man he had nearly caught in *flagrante delicto*.

"What a pleasant surprise!" said M. Latour. "If I had arrived two minutes later, I would have been deprived of the pleasure of seeing you. Come on in, have a glass of wine, and talk with me for a bit."

"I thought I'd find you at home," the other answered. "I came to propose that we go into business together. Mme. Latour told me you weren't supposed to return before noon and I was leaving, but since I've run into you, I'm happy to accept your gracious invitation."

When they had entered the house, M. Latour called out to his wife. "Rosalie," he said cheerfully, "so you're showing my friends the door when I'm away! You could have been more hospitable and kept dear M. Faraud a bit longer. To punish you for this neglect, you're going to give us a glass of wine and you're going to drink with us."

"It's not my fault," Rosalie answered. "I did everything I could to persuade M. Faraud to stay, but you men are always in such a hurry."

"As for your business proposition," answered M. Latour after finishing his drink, "I can't possibly give you an immediate answer. I have another venture in mind and at ten o'clock tomorrow evening I have to take the boat for Montréal where I'm awaiting an answer to my proposal. Upon my return, I'll see if we can come to an agreement."

Needless to say, dear reader, that the proposed voyage was just a ruse. Observing the guilty pair without seeming to, M. Latour noticed they had exchanged meaningful glances when they heard about his imminent departure.

The next evening, he pretended to board the boat, debarked, hid among the cords of wood piled along the wharf, armed himself with a thick club, and came back to his home just an hour after he had left and caught the couple in the act.

Thanks to duplicate keys he had obtained unbeknownst to his wife, he had been able to get back into the house surreptitiously and enter the room where he found the guilty pair.

Without saying a word, he fell on the man who had robbed him of his honor, striking him over and over again as hard as he could with his heavy club. And, when he saw him lying senseless at his feet, he spoke to his half-dressed wife, who was running panic-stricken about the house trying vainly to get out, for M. Latour had locked the doors and pocketed the keys. "No use trying to escape unless you want to leave me now that you've dishonored me. I won't strike you. You are as guilty as this cur is, but one murder is enough."

Then, bending down to look at his victim, he said, "He's still breathing, and I hope he'll recover. I'm not angry anymore. Now I must answer for my act before the law. I'll have him taken back to his wife. Unfortunately, this scoundrel has a wife and three children."

Rosalie had thrown herself at his feet and was asking him to forgive her.

"Never!" he answered somberly. "You can go on living here, but I no longer know you. It is all over between us!"

He left the room, called a carriage, and had the still-unconscious M. Faraud taken to his home. Then he went to the police station to give himself up; there he was immediately released on bail.

What a terrible awakening for Rosalie! She now realized what an outrageous error she had committed. Ever since she had seen M. Latour avenge himself so forcefully for the affront he had received, her husband had risen very high in her estimation. She was beginning to love him when it was too late and her deplorable behavior had raised an insurmountable barrier between them. She had hated him as long as she had believed him to be too naive, too credulous, and too good-natured to defend the honor she had betrayed so shamefully, and now she loved him because he had killed the lover she had preferred over him.

And, in fact, peace-loving M. Latour did have a murder on his conscience. The unfortunate Faraud survived the blows administered by the betrayed husband for only three days. Before dying, he confessed to the error of his ways, declaring that M. Latour was justified in having treated him as he did, and asked to be pardoned for the scandal he had caused and the wrong he had done to his neighbor. He died after receiving the last rites.

Following this scene, Mme. Latour came down with a brain fever which soon led her to her grave. M. Latour wasn't prosecuted. A verdict of justifiable homicide was handed down at the inquest, but the remorse and the pain he suffered also brought him to death's door.

Louise, called back home because of these harrowing events, found the house transformed into a hospital. She was everywhere at once, lavishing the two invalids with attention and attempting to console her father. This was not an easy task, for the shock the poor man had received had brought him to the brink of madness.

The doctors had strongly advised Louise to avoid anything that might upset him — and everything upset him.

While all this was happening, M. Bagoulard reappeared on the horizon. Louise had hoped that the news of her father's ruin would have rid her of his pressing solicitations. That was not to be the case. Bagoulard had sought Louise out for her dowry, but, in the end, he found that he loved her with all the ardor of his fiery nature. Unfortunately for Louise, he spoke to M. Latour who, happy once again to caress a dream he had abandoned, urged Louise so strongly to accept that she found herself torn between the desire to spare her father a displeasure which could be fatal to him and the revulsion which the idea of offering another the place that only Léon could occupy in her heart. As a result she was in the throes of the most poignant anguish and terrible perplexity imaginable.

One day when Bagoulard was pressing her to give him at least a glimmer of hope,

Louise, beside herself, said to him: "What you are doing is despicable. You are taking advantage of my father's weakened condition and you're counting on my filial devotion to force me to consent to something I would never agree to otherwise. You know the doctors are telling me not to cross my father and you've got him thinking he should insist that this marriage take place. However, understand this once and for all: if you can be satisfied with a wife whose heart belongs to another, then take advantage of the sorry position I find myself in. I'll marry you for love of my father, but will never love you. Quite the contrary, the memory of how little you respect my feelings will only make me despise you deeply. You might have won my esteem, admiration, even my friendship, but my love? Never!"

"Louise, you misjudge me greatly! If I had known what a delicate position you are in vis-à-vis your father, I would never have made the mistake of speaking to him about our plans. I want to be loved for myself alone. I value your love and I want so much to have you love me that, hoping to deserve your love in time, I would be resigned to occupying second place in your heart, since the first place is taken by a man who is no longer alive. But I don't want to force you into marriage under such circumstances. Nevertheless, the damage is done. Your father has his heart set on this marriage and..."

"You can make him give up the idea by saying you are no longer interested."

"I could never do that, and besides, it wouldn't be any use. That would upset him as much as if you refused to go through with it yourself. But I can tell him that circumstances beyond my control oblige me to put off our marriage. In the meantime, I'll try to forget you, if you'll promise to try to love me. I pray that you will succeed! As for me, I am certain I will not."

"It will be easier for you to forget me than for me to...to forget the one I'm mourning, but in return for the few months' reprieve you are giving me, and as proof that I believe you when you say you didn't know how things were between my father and me, I'm willing to promise that I'll try to get used to the idea of marrying someone other than Léon. I cannot promise you anything more."

CHAPTER LXVIII

SOMEONE REALLY DOES COME BACK[1]

éon Duroc had been dead for six years, or rather he had been thought dead. However, he was very much alive and no longer had the desire to die since we now find him in Santa Fe, New Mexico, buying his ticket for Montréal. In the hospital tent where Léon had been transported after being wounded in the shoulder, there was another man with a bullet in his left side. That man had been wounded in the left arm, a little below the shoulder, and the bullet, after missing the bone in his arm, had lodged in his left side near his heart, and, naturally, the surgeons hadn't dared to remove it. Three days later this soldier, who belonged to the 12th Regulars, had died of his wound.

Someone had gotten the two regiments mixed up, with the result that the comrades of the soldier from the Twelfth had learned that their friend had been sent to one of the hospitals in Washington while the men of the Fourteenth were told Duroc had died. Errors of this sort were only too frequent during this period of battles which kept the surgeons and their aides so busy.

Duroc's bullet had struck him under his front left shoulder, passed through his thorax, and then had come out the back after breaking his shoulder blade.

After two months of dreadful suffering and four months spent convalescing in the hospitals and barracks at Fort Trumbull, Léon had rejoined his regiment before Petersburg, where he was told that Eugène Leduc had probably deserted to the enemy. That news had affected him deeply because he rather suspected the kind of danger his young friend would be facing.

Since he hadn't received any news from Canada, he had concluded that Louise had forgotten all about him. Reminding her of his existence was the last thing he would have done.

He fought in several battles where he distinguished himself for his bravery and sang-froid. After the war, the regiment was sent first to California and then to New Mexico. Duroc had risen through the ranks to the highest noncommissioned officer's rank. The army offered to send him to West Point so he could become a commissioned officer, but he had had enough of the military life.

Besides, he was already involved in some mining ventures. In his free time, he had studied mineralogy, and, having found an attractive investment, he had sent for the money he had deposited in New York and that, together with the savings he had put aside while he was in the army, had given him enough capital to make his first investments in a company founded to develop a gold and silver mine located not far from where the Fourteenth was billeted.

Several fortunate speculations had rapidly increased his capital so that we now find him, just a little more than a year after leaving the service, in possession of a small fortune valued at $50,000 in mining stocks highly rated on the market.

He no longer had relatives in Canada, but the love of country, so steadfast in the heart of Canadians, impelled him to go visit, at least, the beloved banks of the St. Lawrence now that he had the means to pay for an expensive trip. This feeling, which did him honor, was undoubtedly very compelling, but didn't his desire to see Louise, that Louise whom he had vainly tried to forget, also have something to do with this decision?

He had reasoned, based on the supposition that she had not answered his letter, that she had forgotten him and that she was married — of all this, he had managed to convince himself. And yet, he wanted to know for sure.

What if she had remained faithful to him?

That was more than he dared hope for.

Now that he was rich enough to not be ashamed of asking for her hand, he reproached himself for not writing her a second time, as he certainly would have if he could have foreseen that he would wake up one day a rich man.

Another issue made him want to see Canada again. He felt an overwhelming need to confound publicly and box the ears of the three scoundrels who, by stealing M. Latour's money, had separated him from Louise — probably forever. If Louise were married, as he was almost sure she was, he promised himself that he would move heaven and earth to make them pay for his lost happiness.

When he arrived in Montréal, he went to the Hotel Canada where, without revealing who he was, he inquired about Grippard, Bagoulard, and Bohémier. Even if those three had run into him, they wouldn't have recognized him. His torso was muscled; he sported a thick mustache and a long black beard reaching to his chest.

He learned some of the happenings that you, our readers, already know: Grippard was a member of Parliament in both Ottawa and Québec, and he had declared a spectacular and fraudulent bankruptcy. Bagoulard, already a member of the Legislative Assembly, was soliciting the votes of the people in the county having Pingreville as its county seat to represent them in the House of Commons; his chances of winning were good. Bohémier was in the hospital where his debauchery had put him for the twentieth time.

"Here's someone," thought Léon, "who has taken it upon himself to see to his own punishment for the wrongs he's done me. As for the two others, how is it possible for such scoundrels[2] to be entrusted with contributing to the governing of my country?"

He also learned that a large political rally was to be held in Pingreville, and that Bagoulard, who had the reputation of being the most popular and powerful orator in the region, was to deliver a speech which would surpass any discourse he had ever given.

"When is the rally?" Léon asked.

"Tomorrow," he was told. "The boat leaves at six in the evening and arrives in Pingreville at 10:00 p.m."

Duroc booked passage on board the steamboat *Montréal* and, during the trip, he learned about all the disasters that had befallen the Latour family. He was also told that Louise Latour, a veritable paragon of filial devotion, had refused all suitors who had come to court her, Bagoulard included, but it was rumored that, at her father's insistence, she was soon to marry the young politician. The marriage, it was said, would take place after the election.

"And to think," the informant added, "that the young lady has steadfastly refused to marry because she wanted to remain faithful to the memory of someone called Léon Duroc, a good-for-nothing, so they say, who went off to get himself killed in the War of Secession."

"And she loves this Bagoulard?" Léon asked.

"Apparently, since she's going to marry him — although the gossips say that she's accepting him only to prevent her poor old father, who has never been too bright, from going completely mad."

Since it was too late to visit old man Latour when the boat arrived in Pingreville, Duroc booked a room at the hotel. But he spent a sleepless night.

What should he do?

Should he go to M. Latour's first thing in the morning, or would it be better for him to wait for more information so as not to run the risk of being a spoilsport?

What if Louise loved Bagoulard?

Even if she did, should he let her marry a rogue like that without warning her?

On the other hand, would it seem right for him, as Bagoulard's rival, to come to Louise to denounce the man who had tried to steal her love away from him?

"Ah! Bagoulard," he said, gnashing his teeth, "I've quite a score to settle with you. Tomorrow you'll be delivering one of your most eloquent speeches, and Louise will be able to hear, see, and admire you from her window. As for me, lost in the crowd, I won't be lucky enough to attract even one of her glances. I'm not an orator. I'm a nobody, or rather, I'm a man whose reputation has been tarnished thanks to you and your accomplices. While you were studying in college and working in your lawyer's office, I had something quite different to do. Well, I'm going to unmask you. I'll watch for a chance to denounce you and I won't be afraid of getting up on the speaker's platform to tell everyone what you have done. When I've branded you in public for the shameless thief you are, I'll go see Louise, but not before."

CHAPTER LXIX

TWO BROTHERS IN ARMS

On the morning of the huge rally, a gentleman and lady arrived at M. Latour's asking to see Mlle. Louise. They were shown into the parlor where Louise soon joined them.

"M. Eugène Leduc?" said Louise, after hesitating for a moment.

"In person. Now, allow me to present my wife. Quite a long time ago, she saw me with M. Léon Duroc — when we were brothers in arms."

"I'm delighted to see you," said Louise, throwing her arms around the neck of the newcomer.

"I've often spoken to my wife about you and she didn't want to pass through Pingreville without coming to see you."

"Then please do us the favor of accepting our hospitality which I offer you wholeheartedly. We'll be able to see the rally from this window; it should be beginning any moment now."

"I'll leave you two together," said Eugène, "and I'm sure you won't miss me. Women always have secrets to share; that's probably why people assume they can't keep one. As for me, I protest against such slander. Women do know how to keep a secret. It's just that, for fear they might let it slip out, several of them sometimes get together to keep it safe."

"This time," said Hélène, "we'll do such a good job of keeping our secrets that you won't know a thing. But don't stay away too long. You'll be able to hear everything from here just as well as you can from out there."

"Just the time to chat for a bit with M. Latour whom I see over there in that group of voters."

Eugène went out and was moving toward the group he had just pointed out when a man placed a hand on his shoulder.

"Pardon me," he said, "but aren't you Eugène Leduc?"

"In person."[1]

"Then take a good look at me."

"Léon Duroc!" exclaimed Leduc, who started to embrace the stranger.

"Not here," said the other. "We are being watched and I have my reasons for not wanting to be recognized now. Come to the hotel. We can talk in my room."

"But what stroke of luck brings you here? We thought you were dead, we mourned you, and there's someone not too far from here who's still mourning you; and here you are, back from the grave, looking very mysterious; you look like a sapper with that beard covering your face."[2]

The two men worked their way toward the hotel.

"It's a very long story; and you must have lots of things to tell me too. When I registered, I didn't put down my real name, but this morning I saw the names of Eugène Leduc and Mme. Leduc on the register; you're married."

"Can you guess whom I married?"

"Well, I can't imagine."

"What? You predicted that I wouldn't go to France and that I'd marry Hélène Duchâtel, didn't you? Well, you need to know that your prediction has come true."

"My heartiest congratulations."

"And my prediction is about to come true also since here you are back again and Louise is still mourning your loss. Unless you are already married, but then again I don't think you have the look of a married man."

The two had arrived at Léon's room. They had closed the door and sat down to chat.

"Me, married!" said Léon. "You don't know me very well. But tell me, you just left M. Latour's — did you see Louise?"

"I just left her talking with my wife. Look here, Léon, here's a hug from both of us."

And the two friends embraced each other.

"How did you recognize me?" Eugène asked.

"I had seen your name in the register; if I hadn't, your blond beard and square shoulders would have thrown me off. But, speaking of the register, guess whose name I saw there, too? The name of a man I'm delighted to run into again — but for different reasons entirely."

"And his name is . . . ?"

"Charles Auguste Grippard."

"Well! Imagine that! It just so happens I have with me a document bearing his signature which you could find useful at the right time and place."

And Leduc opened his wallet and pulled out the admission of guilt he had extracted from Grippard thanks to the help of Brindamour and Bohémier.

"Why, this is wonderful! How in the devil did you ever manage to obtain such a priceless document?"

Eugène regaled Léon by telling him the story of the phantasmagoria and the astonishing effects it had had on the worthy M. Grippard.

"Now," Léon said, "I shall keep this document and use it to put Bagoulard on the spot, for I intend to unmask him publicly. I've promised myself I won't go to M. Latour's until I've proved that foul rascal — who dares think he's worthy of marrying

Louise — guilty of imposture and infamy!"

"No, leave the document with me. If need be, I'll read it myself in public, that is, unless M. Grippard refuses to corroborate the testimony you're going to give concerning Bagoulard, for that would be even better. Those two are political rivals and I think I can get him to make a verbal confession right in front of the crowd."

"Be careful. He could have you beaten up."

"Me? I'd bash his head in before he could give the signal. I want to go even further; I'm going to get him to insist that his party's speakers, because he isn't in the habit of speaking himself, accuse the government of forcing people to emigrate. Bagoulard will answer that only the riffraff is leaving — that's the usual retort.[3] That's when you'll interrupt him and he'll invite you to come up to the platform to debate the question. He frequently resorts to this tactic to silence the hecklers. Of course, you'll accept and, under the pretext of defending the Canadian emigrants to the United States, you'll denounce him. Does that suit you?"

"Perfectly."

"Now, while you're talking, I'll say to Grippard, 'Bagoulard is going to call Duroc a liar. If you don't say that Duroc is telling the truth, there's a certain document bearing your signature which will be read forthwith before this rally.' "

"Wonderful. Don't tell anyone that I'm here, except your wife, of course. Hug her for me and ask her to prepare Louise for the possibility of my return. See that you do that before I get up on the platform."

"Well, that's settled; everything's arranged. I'm going back to my wife — she must be wondering where on earth I am by now. I can't wait to tell the wonderful news of your return."

CHAPTER LXX

✤

EPILOGUE

Eugène and Léon carried out their plan of action to the letter. There was a packed crowd and the meeting was rather boisterous. It was easy to see that each of the two parties had organized its band of rowdies who were just waiting for the signal to hurl themselves at their adversaries. Grippard was the power behind the scenes for one of these groups, but he was far from suspecting that his own group would side with those who would accuse him of orchestrating a swindle along with Bagoulard. He was also far from thinking that he would provide the opportunity for that accusation and he was very far from expecting that he would be forced to come forward and admit his guilt. That, however, is just what happened.

Eugène found a way of saying within Grippard's hearing: "The speakers should be talking about emigration. Nothing is being done to keep people in this country, and that subject should be all the more interesting since several of us here are Canadians who have lived in the United States, and we would like to see men in public office take a little more interest than they do now in the class of people who are emigrating."

Grippard had hastened to tell his party's speakers about these comments and they had spared no pains in hurling every epithet they could think of at the government, which they accused of wanting to drive their native sons away and replace them with foreigners.

When Bagoulard began to speak, it was easy to see from the ripples passing through the crowd that everyone wanted to be where they could best see and hear the fiery orator. He was really a handsome sight when, transformed by the fervor of his delivery, he poured out in his sonorous and pleasing voice harmonious and lofty sentences inspired by his lively imagination.

He answered the speakers who had preceded him point by point. Everyone listened to him with fascination. Even those who did not approve were swept off their feet by the wave upon wave of his eloquence. They couldn't help but admire him. He had already had quite an effect on the crowd when he came to the subject of emigration.

Despite his talent, Bagoulard had one fault: going down the beaten path a little too much. Canadians who emigrated to the United States had long since been called riffraff in certain political circles. Bagoulard felt compelled to repeat that stupid characterization, that gratuitous insult hurled in the faces of people who were much more honest and law-abiding than he was himself. All of a sudden a voice rang out from the crowd.

"That's not true!"

"Mr. Chairman, I have interrupted no one and it is my wish not to be interrupted either."

"Then watch what you say about your betters."

All eyes turned toward Duroc, for he was the one who had just spoken, as the reader has no doubt guessed. However, seeing that he looked as though he was quite capable of defending himself, nobody dared to silence him.

"My friend," Bagoulard replied, "if you want to discuss the point with me, come up on the platform and you'll answer me from here."

"I accept your proposal," said Léon as he made his way to the platform, "but I resent your having the audacity to call me friend."

No one recognized Duroc, but their curiosity had been aroused. Everybody wanted to see how this stranger would acquit himself.

"You will please wait until I have finished speaking," Bagoulard began again.

"Pardon me, *Monsieur,* you have invited me and I have accepted. Now isn't the time to impose new conditions. Besides, I haven't a great deal to say and I won't take up much of your time."

"All right, speak then, but be quick about it."

"I'm not taking orders from you."

Léon took off his hat, greeted the chairman, and began to utter the following words: "Gentlemen, I may seem like a stranger among you, but six years ago I lived in your city. My name is Duroc and I've just come back from the United States."

Hearing this, a hundred or so villagers who had known Léon let out a frenzied hurrah and the rest of the crowd took up the cry without knowing why they did so. The townspeople now knew that two rivals in love were doing battle for the hand of the same woman.

Things were starting to get interesting. Murmurs ran through the crowd and people looked up to M. Latour's window where Louise and Mme. Leduc had just disappeared from view.

Bagoulard was aghast.

"Gentlemen," Léon continued, "I thank you for these expressions of sympathy. They prove that if the Canadian emigrant never forgets his country, those fortunate enough to remain by the beloved banks of the St. Lawrence don't forget those who have left either — even those who are rumored to be dead. I've just heard the speaker say that the Canadians who emigrate are vile rabble. That's not true, I tell you. I have lived in the United States, and I'm not scum. And what I'm saying about myself, I can say about practically every one of the Canadians living on the other side of the border.

"Among those of you listening to me in this intelligent crowd are a large number of men who, like me, have known the bitterness of exile, and I ask you, are they not all worthy, brave, and honest workers who would do honor to any nationality? Most of you, gentlemen, have sons, brothers, relatives in the United States, and I ask you, aren't those absent loved ones all very honorable people?

"And who are those slinging mud in the face of these honest craftsmen? In this instance, it is a man whose foul debauchery has become the talk of the most important city of our province. I've come to tell him so to his face; and that isn't all. I, who am speaking to you, why was I forced to become an expatriate? Was it because I was dishonest? Far from it; it was because I was the victim of a scam committed by this man who has just had the audacity to insult an entire population of hard-working people. Do you recognize me, Alphonse Bagoulard? Ah, what misery I have endured because of your misdeed. I was believed to be dead and I suffered for six long months from a chest wound.

"When your accomplice, M. Grippard, whom I see here, extorted $1,000 dollars belonging to my ex-employer from me, how much did he pay you and Bohémier to have you deny two days later that he had just borrowed that sum of money for a few hours? I was too honest to want M. Latour to suffer because of the blind confidence I had placed in M. Grippard and the two accomplices he had for witnesses. I would have gained nothing if I had taken him to court because you were all thick as thieves.

"I sold my life to pay that debt and I went to fight in Virginia where I almost lost my life. If I had stayed here and not paid the note, I would have been dishonored, and I didn't want to live without honor. Would you have done as much, you, the honest man who robs people in order to send them off to the United States and who then dares call them rabble in public? Just you dare repeat that insult and I'll hit you right here physically as I've just done morally.

"Gentlemen, please excuse me for this somewhat sharp outburst, but I couldn't contain myself. I'm not a public speaker, but I am an honest man — and that's worth a whole lot more. So, I'll conclude by summing up my thoughts thus: the Canadians who have emigrated to the U.S. are honest workers and those who denigrate them are the riffraff."

That impassioned speech was met with an enthusiastic hurrah. Grippard, believing that Léon had in his pocket the document Eugène had just told him about, rushed up to do some explaining, but Bagoulard didn't give him time. He categorically denied the facts that Duroc alleged, told how Duroc had attempted to commit suicide, and claimed that Léon had first spent M. Latour's money, and that he had then attempted to drown himself and, fearing arrest, had fled to the United States.

He then added, "That's how he thanks M. Grippard and myself for interceding on his behalf with the authorities so he wouldn't have to go to prison. M. Grippard is my political opponent. However, I'm sure he will be fair enough to acknowledge the truth of what I've just said."

"It's in his best interest to corroborate what you say," several voices cried out.

M. Grippard appeared on the platform but, contrary to what Bagoulard expected from him, he admitted that he had borrowed $1,000 from Léon in Bagoulard's and Bohémier's presence. The reader will undoubtedly remember that Grippard's affidavit also contained his admission that he had proposed that Duroc counterfeit M. Latour's signature. That explains why Grippard had preferred to make a verbal confession hoping that Duroc, out of gratitude for his good-faith effort, would allow him to hide part of the truth as long as he refuted Bagoulard on other counts.

"Only," he added in conclusion, "I did not intend have him lose that money. He left without a word and I have never had the opportunity to repay him. I am ready to give him my note for $1,000 plus interest. I just wanted to play a trick on him, but it almost had a tragic ending."

"Just like all your ploys," cried out M. Latour, who was in the crowd.

"Now, gentlemen," Duroc continued, "I hope you'll agree that I've convicted M. Bagoulard of fraud and lying. As for M. Grippard, I could complete his admission, but I will do nothing of the kind. You know enough about him to make it impossible for me to sully further his already tarnished reputation."

"Yes," interrupted Bagoulard, "but you conspire with him to lie about me."

That remark was answered by a resounding blow to Bagoulard's ear and cheek.

A general mêlée broke out in the crowd, resulting in a number of black eyes. The chairman declared the meeting closed and the crowd dispersed, very much enlightened about men in public office in general and Bagoulard in particular. A crowd of former acquaintances gathered around Duroc to congratulate him. M. Latour himself came up to shake his hand enthusiastically and invite him to come home with him. Duroc accepted eagerly, but first he excused himself so he could make himself presentable.

From her window, Louise had witnessed just about the entire incident. When Duroc had identified himself, she had withdrawn to hide her emotion, but, since joy isn't fatal, she had soon managed to calm herself enough to come back to her observation post.

Léon, accompanied by Leduc, went to get a shave so he could reappear before Louise just about as he was when they parted.

Returning to the hotel, he found two men waiting for him. They were the two seconds sent by Bagoulard to challenge him to a duel. He told them to make arrangements with Leduc and it was decided that the two of them would fight with pistols at fifteen paces. Bagoulard, who considered himself the injured party, would be the first to fire. The meeting was to take place the next day on a deserted island across from Pingreville.

With that matter settled, Duroc, anxious to see Louise again, went with Eugène to M. Latour's. Louise had taken great pains in choosing what to wear and she was ravishingly beautiful. It would be impossible to describe the lovers' delirious joy after such a long separation, so we'll let the reader imagine that touching scene — all the while recommending that the reader give it his all and not be afraid of exaggerating.

When he learned that Duroc was rich, M. Latour felt the last objection he might have had about giving him his daughter vanish entirely. It was decided the marriage would take place a few days later, since Duroc needed to return to New Mexico as soon as possible; his business affairs there demanded his presence. His intention was to make his fortune as quickly as possible and come back to live in Canada, but since that could take some time, it was decided that Louise and her father would go to live with him until he was ready to return.

The next day, two canoes crossed to the island which had been chosen as the scene for the duel. The combatants were positioned. Bagoulard was a bit nervous.

"You'd do well not to miss me," Léon said to him, "because I won't miss you. I warn you I'm a good shot."

Bagoulard took aim carefully before pulling the trigger. The bullet whistled by Léon's ear.

"A little too much to the left," Léon said. "It's astonishing how people seem to have it in for me on that side. And now, I'm going to kill you," he added with a fero-cious look; then, relenting: "Oh, no, I'm not as mean as all that, but I'm going to show you that I could kill you if I wanted to. You have a lock of hair there that bothered me yesterday during your oration. That lock is the cause of our quarrel. I'll get rid of it."

And he pulled the trigger.

"The lock of hair has now been removed. Now there's no more lock to infuriate me."

Indeed, the fascinating lock of hair to which Bagoulard owed so much of his oratorical successes had just fallen to the ground, mowed down by Léon's bullet.

Bagoulard lost his election. No matter how much he danced about, his lock was no longer there. Samson had been shorn of his hair and Bagoulard's eloquence was silenced for a while until another lock replaced the one left behind on the island.

What else is there to say? Eugène opened a store in the Eastern Townships. Duroc married Louise and left for New Mexico with his adored wife and father-in-law; there M. Latour died after having had the satisfaction of seeing his daughter as happy as anyone could hope to be in this world. There are no stories to tell about happy kings. The same can be said about happy couples. Suffice it to say that the Durocs came back to Canada, that they and the Leducs are there still; that all of them are in perfect health and completely satisfied with their lot in life. We would be tempted to add, as they do in fairy tales, that they lived happily ever after and that they had many children. But we must not get ahead of ourselves. The events of this story happened too recently for such a statement to seem plausible, and it would be absurd to spoil a story which is true for the most part with an unbelievable ending. In a forthcoming work, whose title has not yet been chosen, perhaps we'll give the reader further news about some of the characters who have played a part in this one.[1]

ONE CAME BACK: A NEW TRANSLATION AND NEW EDITION

A NOTE FROM THE TRANSLATORS

Rémi Tremblay loved language and *Un Revenant* showcases the full range of his linguistic talents: puns, wordplay, a poem, and English as spoken by Northerners, Southerners, soldiers in the field (including German and Irish recruits), and sailors. Using military terminology and word pictures of sights, feelings, and sounds, he makes life in camp, on the march, and in the battlefield come alive. Nor does he neglect life on the home front. Tremblay includes a rhymed sonnet written by a young lover and shows villains bantering as they plot to use the phantasmagoria. To all of this Tremblay also adds quotes in Latin and Italian.

Our challenge was to provide an English translation which can be read side by side with the French original without doing injustice to either version. The translation was in its final stages when Tremblay's own unpublished English draft came into our hands, thanks to Claire Quintal. We discovered that in some places our translations were the same; in others, however, we had found different solutions to express the same thought. Tremblay himself never did translate his poem; Margaret Langford provides a verse rendition in the text as well as a literal translation in the notes.

The present translation is the result of many ponderings, consultations, discussions, and revisions. Throughout the process, Tremblay's lively wit and intense interest in his own life and times as well as his regiment, the 14th U.S. Regulars, have inspired us to rise to the challenges he set before us. We hope that they have brought forth our own best knowledge of both English and French so that our translation will not only ring true, but also partake of the quality of the original. To do otherwise would have been tantamount to perpetuating the treason which translators so often have been accused of inflicting upon texts: *traduttore traditore.*

One Came Back, Un Revenant, and Back from the Grave

Tremblay never did publish the promised sequel to *Un Revenant*. However, the unpublished English translation of his work, now in the archives of Le centre de recherche et civilisation canadienne-française, Université d'Ottowa, testifies to his continued interest in the subject. Thanks to Claire Quintal, the Centre gave permission to the translators to examine and use Tremblay's typescript, which he intitled *Back from the Grave.* "Un revenant" is a ghost, someone who comes back after death. The present translators have chosen to emphasize the the fact that one out of so many soldiers did indeed come back from the war, and to leave aside reference to the grave. Profiting from the availability of the typescript and the line-by-line comparison which Dr. Quintal has made of *One Came Back* and *Back from the Grave,* the translators have chosen from time to time to adopt the Tremblay wording. Such instances are duly noted.

The 1980 re-edition of Tremblay's 1884 first edition contains no preface, notes, or other explanatory material, with the exception of a short biographical sketch on the jacket. The selected explanatory materials in this annotated translation are designed to place the work in the context of Rémi Tremblay's life and experience. A selective bibliography is provided below for readers seeking additional information on Tremblay and on Franco-Canadians and Franco-Americans and the Civil War.

THE 14TH REGULAR U.S. INFANTRY AND

RÉMI TREMBLAY'S WAR RECORD

Tremblay constantly refers to "his" regiment in *One Came Back*. The following correlates Tremblay's information on the Fourteenth with accounts by Dyer, Anderson, and the Fort Vancouver Historical Society.

The Fourteenth was organized by direction of the president on May 4, 1861, and confirmed by an act of Congress May 29, 1861. Its first general headquarters were in Fort Trumbull, Connecticut. The following provides an overview of the Fourteenth's service during the war and afterward:

May 1862 to 1864: the 14th is attached to the 1st Brigade, 2nd Division, 5th Army Corps, Army of the Potomac

March 1864 to April 1864: 4th Brigade, 1st Division, 5th Army Corps

April 1864 to June 1864: 1st Brigade, 1st Division, 5th Army Corps

June 1864 to November 1864: 1st Brigade, 2nd Division, 5th Army Corps

November 1864 to April 1865: Department of the East

April 1865 to June 1865: Provost Guard, Army of the Potomac

August 1865 to June 1866: Fort Vancouver, Washington

June 1866 to September 1866: San Francisco

September 1866: Arizona

Prior to its return to Fort Vancouver in 1884, the Fourteenth was frequently involved in actions concerning Native Americans in various parts of the West.

Military records show that Tremblay was assigned to Company F when he enlisted at Rouse's Point, New York, on November 7, 1863. The rolls list his occupation as baker. The following shows the Fourteenth's itinerary during his service:

November 7, 8: Advance to the line of the Rappahannock

November 26 to December 2: Mine run campaign

December 2 to May 3: Winter quarters; Rémi/Eugene's first "hike"

May 4 to June 12, 1864: The Rapidan campaign

    The Wilderness (May 5-7)

    Spotsylvania Courthouse (May 8-21)

    North Anna (May 22-26)

    Totopotomoy (May 28-31)

    Cold Harbor (June 1-12)

June 16 to November 2: Siege of Petersburg

    Mine explosion (July 30, Reserve) witnessed by Rémi/Eugène

    Weldon Railroad (August 18-21); Tremblay in Libby/or second "hike"

    Poplar Springs Church/Peebles' Farm (September 28-October 2)

Boydton Plank Road, Hatcher's Run (October 27-28); Tremblay in Libby
   prison or captured following Saltville★
November 1, 1864: The Fourteenth is ordered first to New York City, then to
   Elmira
March 1865: Rémi/Eugène released from Libby prison in a prisoner exchange
April 4, 1865: The 1Fourteenth arrives at City Point

★Tremblay refers to his experiences at Libby prison in *Un Revenant* (1884), in his
1885-1887 correspondence with Major Edmond Mallet concerning his (Rémi's)
desertion, and in his autobiography, *Pierre qui roule*. He also refers to his "hikes"
through Virginia and Kentucky. According to *Un Revenant,* the last "hike" ended with
his capture at Saltville in October. An August date for his capture is more consistent
with the six-month period that Tremblay and his biographers state he spent in prison.

In early September 1885, Tremblay and Narcisse Cyr engaged in a journalist's battle about Tremblay's war record. At this time, Tremblay was the editor of *L'Indépendant*
in Fall River, Massachusetts. Narcisse Cyr claimed in the Fall River *News* that Tremblay deserted from his regiment on August 20, 1864. Tremblay retorted, also in the
News, that "between the 20th of August and the 5th of February, 1865, I was not seen
within Federal lines for the excellent reason that the rebels had me in their power"
(undated copy of an article from the *News* in the Bibliothèque Mallet; Tremblay refers
to it in his September 15 letter to Mallet).

Undoubtedly, Reverend Cyr's published accusations, including those published in
the *News* article entitled "Hero or Deserter?" (same undated copy) inspired the Mallet correspondence. Mallet's letter of September 18, 1885, though sympathetic, warns
Tremblay of the dangers in his case. Deserters have never been amnestied. The government will still pay a bounty of $30 for any deserter apprehended. On the other
hand, he appears to accept Tremblay's contention that he deserted only after the war
was over (in 1865, not August 1864) when he comments that "your leaving after the
war does not excuse desertion."

ABBREVIATIONS

ACA: The Association Canado-American, Manchester, New Hampshire.

ACP: Army Commission and Personal File from the National Archives.

OR: *The War of the Rebellion: Official Records of the Union and Confederate Armies.*

NMDC: National Materials Development Center for French, Bedford, New Hampshire. The National Materials Development Center existed from 1975 to 1982. The Keene State College Mason Library has all of the Materials Development Center publications. However, the Franco-American Center/Centre Franco-Américain in Manchester is the official repository for these materials, including *L'Innocente victime* and *Un Revenant*. The center has copies of these two works, as well as others from the NMDC, available for purchase.

NOTES

Foreword

1 With over thirty years' experience writing and speaking on Franco-American culture, Julien Olivier has spent considerable time researching and reflecting on the migration issues. He notes that "numbers are uncertain and estimates vary considerably," that "no one kept track," and that "there was a constant back-and-forth movement across the border." Time periods, terminology (such as "Canadian" and "French-Canadian"), and areas where immigrants settled vary from researcher to researcher. Estimates on migration numbers range from 850,000 to 1,710,000. In Olivier's estimation, 1 to 1.5 million is the most reasonable migration figure for the period between 1880 and 1930. For further reading on the subject, he refers the reader to the work by Yolande Lavoie: *L'émigration des Canadiens aux Etats-Unis avant 1930*. According to Olivier, her publication is the most detailed and reliable source (Olivier, "Migration of French Canadians to the Northeast of the United States," *Le Forum,* vol. 29, 3, Sept. 2001, pp. 6, 32-33).

2 Tremblay's 1884 readers would have recognized his stock characters: the Latours, Bagoulard, Bohémier, Brindamour, and Grippard. Bagoulard is known for his oratory; "Bagoulard" recalls the expression "avoir du bagout" — to convince or dupe through fast talk. "Bagout"+"lard" would then mean "he who fattens himself by dispoiling others with his fast talk" — a pork-barrel politician. Moreover, the suffix "-ard" is pejorative. In partnership with Bagoulard, we find Grippard (who holds on to his own money) spending his investors' money freely while keeping his hands on his own. Their nefarious work is furthered by the wastrels Bohémier (the ne'er-do-well Bohemian) and his partner-in-crime, Brindamour (a bit of love, a love child).

Introduction

1 Quite evidently, Tremblay had an ear for languages and dialects. In *Un Revenant* he shows his alter ego Eugène passing as a Southerner by his speech, mocks a drunken officer's words as he exhorts his men, and records a German soldier's broken English. *Un Revenant* also reveals Tremblay's love of Latin quotations — a love no doubt fostered by his strong Catholic upbringing and by journalistic custom in Canada at that time. According to Marie-Louise Bonier, chronicler of the Franco-American community in Woonsocket, Rhode Island, Tremblay was an accomplished polyglot fluent in French, English, German, Spanish, Italian, and Hebrew.

2 Julie Lemery, third daughter of Augustin Lemery and Angèle Bélanger, belonged to one of the founding French-Canadian families of Woonsocket, Rhode Island. Like many of his compatriots, Lemery first came to the United States at the time of the Papineau Rebellion of 1837. After going back to Canada for a time, he returned in 1853 to settle permanently in the Woonsocket area. Bonier's genealogy of the

Lemery family includes a thumbnail biography of Tremblay.

Marie-Louise Bonier's overview of the Franco-American presence in Woonsocket, first appearing in French in 1920, is a comprehensive local history detailing the saga of Franco-Americans in Woonsocket from the first migrations in 1814-1815 to 1920. Her work contains fascinating entries not available elsewhere: genealogies of Woonsocket's first families, rare photos of Franco-American notables, as well as a list of Franco-Americans serving in the Civil War. The genealogical section duly notes Rémi Tremblay's marriage to Julie Lémery, descended from one of the founding families. A brief account of his war record appears in a footnote.

A tantalizing entry appears on the list of Franco-Americans from Woonsocket in the Civil War. Some soldiers enlisted using pseudonyms. One soldier is listed thus: Narcisse la Prairie (Rémi Tremblay). There is no footnote cross-referencing this information to the genealogical entry. Did Tremblay attempt to enlist under this name at age fourteen when he witnessed the Rhode Island Volunteers parading through the streets of Woonsocket? Was there another Rémi Tremblay living in Woonsocket at the time? Bonier does not say. Tremblay's own war record has him serving exclusively with the 14th U.S. Regulars.

Chapter I

1 The original French reads "toujours soucieux des intérêts de leurs commettants." Tremblay translates "ever sollicitous of the welfare of their constituents."

2 Undoubtedly contemporary readers appreciated Tremblay's references to specific Montréal streets and sites. The Faubourg Québec was a quarter known for its lowlife. The historical overview of famous Montreal streets in *Les Rues de Montréal* indicates that St. Denis was one of the favored residences of the elite in the late 1800s. *Le Red Light de Montréal* adds an interesting dimension. As innocent young Léon makes his way to the harbor, he moves into the heart of what was the Red Light district. By the middle of the nineteenth century, the port of Montréal was already a rowdy sailors' quarter. By the turn of the century, the intersection of Craig Street and Saint-Laurent was one of the most notorious corners in the town. Those seeking to retrace Léon's steps will find that the Rue Dorchester is now René-Levesque (Ville de Montréal, *Les Rues de Montréal,* Montreal: Méridien, 1995; Daniel Proulx, *Le Red Light de Montréal,* Montreal: VLB Editeur, 1997).

Chapter II

1 Throughout, *Un Revenant* reveals the impact of Tremblay's Catholic upbringing. We note the heavily religious nature of these early readings.

2 "Pingre," the adjective, means "stingy, miserly, or nigardly."

3 "Sic vos …" translates as "Do unto others as you would have others do unto you."

Chapter IV

1 Eugène is a young man desperately in love. The French original shows his sincere but not terribly artistic effort at writing a sonnet to his lady love. The translation attempts to capture these qualities in poetic language. The original reads as follows:

> Ce que je ne dirai jamais, pas même à toi,
> Louise, je l'inscris sur cette page blanche,
> Depuis longtemps, déjà, tu me remplis d'émoi
> Mais j'appelais ce trouble, amitié douce et franche.
>
> Hélas, c'était l'amour qui m'imposait sa loi.
> Malheureux, je rêvais! Je m'éveillai dimanche.
> Quand cet amour fatal, qui me remplit d'effroi,
> Vint fondre sur mon coeur ainsi qu'une avalanche.
>
> Ta richesse entre nous élève une barrière;
> Je suis pauvre et commence une triste carrière.
> Tu vis gaiment. Pourquoi viendrai je t'attrister? [sic]
>
> Je veux entretenir cette flamme insensée.
> Et, gardant mon secret au fond de ma pensée,
> T'adorer sans espoir et sans te consulter.

The literal prose translation reads:

> What I will never say, even to thee
> Louise, I write on this blank page,
> For a long time, already, you have filled me with emotion
> But I called this agitation sweet and open friendship.
>
> Alas, it was love that imposed its law on me.
> Wretched me, I was dreaming. I woke up on Sunday.
> Then that fatal love which filled me with fear
> Came swooping down to envelop me, like an avalanche.
>
> Your wealth raises a barrier between us.
> I'm poor and am beginning a dismal career.
> You live gaily. Why should I come to make you sad?
>
> I want to keep this insane passion.
> And, hiding my secret in my innermost thoughts,
> Love you without hope and without consulting thee.

Chapter VI

1 See Chapter XXX, Note 1, for information on Louis-Adélard Senécal, of whom Grippard is a caricature. Cyrille Felteau's description of Senécal's political life and financial ventures matches Tremblay's depiction of Grippard in every detail.

2 The expression appears in English in the French original.

3 The French original reads:
   "Toi tu as une mine patibulaire."
   "Pas Tibulle, hère…"
   Here Tremblay creates an extremely intricate play on words: "Patibulaire" — someone destined for the gallows; "mine" — looks; "hère" — usually used in French with "pauvre" — "poor wretch."

Chapter IX

1 In 1864, the Union Army was desperate for men. Casualties and desertions were high. Anderson reports in his history of the 14th Regulars that the regiment was severely depleted. Desertion numbers had run as high as seventy-two a month the preceding year. The total for that year was 439. Incentives for joining, unless the new recruit came in place of a conscripted soldier, were not as attractive as the volunteer incentives. He cites the government bounty for enlistment in the regular army at $200 — $500 less than Tremblay's figure. However, as bounty soldiers in a volunteer regiment, new recruits could expect from $1,000 to $2,000. A replacement in the regulars, like Léon, could have received a $1,000 bounty (Anderson, "The Fourteenth Regiment of Infantry" in Rodenbough and Haskin, *The Army of the United States,* p. 598). Tremblay says Léon enlisted for five years. Elsewhere he cites the same figure for Eugène's (his own) term of service. Keene State College professor emeritus James Smart, Civil War historian, notes that the term of enlistment for men in the regular army at this time was three years. (Professor Smart was one of the readers of this translation's first-draft version. His comments on historical matters have informed the work.) On Tremblay's own enlistment papers the printed word "three" is struck out and replaced by a "five" printed in ink above it in both the "Declaration of Recruit" and "Consent in Case of Minor" sections. Both Rémi and his "guardians" understood he was enlisting for five years (*Regular Army Enlistments,* 1863, vol. 57, entry 153, p. 211).

In Chapter XXXIX, Rémi refers to generous reinlistment terms being offered to men whose original three-year term of enlistment was about to be up. Moreover, the Mallet correspondence suggests that the army was not overly concerned about the whereabouts of Canadian soldiers. In these circumstances it does not seem terribly surprising that the Rouse's Point recruiters would alter a young boy's enlistment papers to show he was of age, fit to serve, and was agreeing to do so for five years.

Chapter X

1 Here Rémi begins the history of "his" regiment, the 14th U.S. Regulars, during the Civil War. A regiment had been designated as the Fourteenth on two previous occasions. Anderson tells us that this Fourteenth was organized under the President's Proclamation of May 4, 1861, and confirmed by an act of Congress on July 29, 1861. Its headquarters were first fixed at Fort Trumbull in Connecticut (Anderson, pp. 586, 588). Anderson corroborates Rémi's remarks on the regimental numbers in the Wilderness campaign. Toward the end of April, the Fourteenth had one battalion with approximately 550 men. Conscripts and convalescents helped fill the ranks (Anderson, p. 599).

2 Records show that the Fourteenth suffered the following casualties during the Battle of the Wilderness: out of 530 men engaged, 188 were listed as wounded and missing, representing 22.4% of the regimental force (Reese, *Sykes' Regular Infantry Division*, p. 309). The author notes that some regulars participating in the battle felt that the number killed was much greater, as many who fell wounded were subsequently burned to death (Reese, note 28, pp. 435-436). The overall casualties were appalling. Out of the 100,000 Federal troops, 2,246 were killed, 12,037 were wounded, and 3,383 were reported missing — a total of 17,666. The Confederates, with 60,000 troops, suffered approximately 7,500 casualties (Long, *The Civil War Day by Day,* p. 495).

3 A close approximation. According to the report of Lieutenant-Colonel Major I. Spaulding, Commander, and J.C. Duane, Chief Engineer, Army of the Potomac, a bridge over the Rappahannock located at the lower crossing, Fredericksburg, was completed by Major Brainerd's men on May 10, 1864. It measured 420 feet in length (OR, series I, vol. XXVI, part 1, p. 316).

Chapter XI

1 The original French reads "Pas et démarches." We have chosen to use Tremblay's title "Back and Forth."

2 Anderson reports that "during the winter of 1863-1864 it [the Fourteenth] was engaged in guarding the line of the Orange and Alexandria R.R. In this duty it had many conflicts with rebel raiders and bushwhackers" (Anderson, p. 599). Also, in a diary with entries from January through December 1864, Sergeant Burgess Ingersoll notes that on Monday, March 7, 1864, the Fourteenth moved from its former camp three miles away to Catlett's Station.

3 The original French reads "Elles se composaient de café, de sucre, de biscuits durs appelés *hard tacks,* et de lard salé."

4 Professor David Stowell, a historian specializing in the nineteenth century, has verified the realism of this account of army life found here and in the following pages. His comments on historical matters have informed the work.

5 The original French reads "ce qui faisait dire à Leduc que les armes blanches étaient dev-

enues noires." Could it be a play on words between white (the North) and black (the South)? Tremblay omits this line in his translation.

6 Anderson provides the following information on officers and men killed and wounded in battle. There were 516 enlisted men present when the regiment broke camp on May 3. "The following officers were present: Hudson, Keyes, Mille, Ilges, Burbank, Brady, C. McKibbin, Perry, Sinclair, Tom Collins, Broadhead, John Clay, Krause and Drake DeKay; Coppinger, Smedberg and Choisy were with the divison on staff duty." Before the month was over, 240 enlisted men were killed, wounded, and missing. As for the officers, Anderson's information combined with Reese's shows the following for the 1st Battalion, 14th U.S. Infantry (eight companies) at the beginning of Grant's campaign: Captain Edward M. Hudson (WIA Wilderness), Captain Hamlin W. Keyes (MW Spotsylvania), Captain David B. Mc Kibbin (POW Bethesda Church), Captain Horace K. Thatcher. (Tremblay used the spelling "McGibbon" but official records give the name as "McKibbin.")

   Wilderness and Spotsylvania:

   First Lieutenant Daniel Broadhead (also spelled Brodhead), Company B — wounded (Wilderness).

   Captain Sullivan W. Burbank, Company H — killed (Wilderness).

   Lieutenant Tom Collins — killed (Wilderness); his body, never found, was believed to be burned in forest fires.

   Captain Edward McK. Hudson — wounded (Wilderness).

   Lieutenant John K. Clay — killed (Spotsylvania).

   Captain Guido Ilges (Tremblay refers to him as Eiges), Company E.

   C. McKibbon.

   Captain David B. McKibbin.

   Captain Hamlin W. Keyes — mortally wounded (Spotsylvania).

   Captain James F. Millar, Company B.

   Lieutenant Sinclair — wounded (Spotsylvania).

   William R. Smedberg (Tremblay calls him Smithberg) wounded (Wilderness).

   First Lieutenant James W. Weir.

   Captain D.B. McKibbin assumed command of the regiment on May 18 (Anderson, pp. 600-601). He was reported POW at Bethesda Church on June 2.

Chapter XII

1 The description of the Leduc family journey matches the description Tremblay gives of his own family's journey from Woonsocket back to Canada in 1861 (*Pierre qui roule*, pp. 77-78).

2 A description of Tremblay's own journey when he enlisted in the Fourteenth.

3 Tremblay writes: "…where he had become thoroughly conversant with the language of the country owing to the necessity of speaking English and English only, supplemented by the reading of numerous novels bought at the sutler's."

Chapter XIII

1 Tremblay frequently reiterates his desire to fight on the side of the French. In the Foreign Legion? It would be difficult, if not impossible, for him to reach France at this time. However, Napoleon III has sent French troops under Maximilian's command to conquer Mexico. Rémi might indeed have been able to join the French army there.

2 John Singleton Mosby (1833-1916), the "Gray Ghost," was at this time harassing the encamped regulars as they waited to begin the spring campaign. His men slipped through Union lines in small groups in the dead of night, typically attacking trains and depots, and then vanished without a trace. He is said to have been the most effective partisan raider during the Civil War. His most frequently cited exploit was the capture of Brigadier General E. Stoughton and his men during the night of March 8, 1863, in Fairfax Courthouse, Virginia. Ramage describes this fascinating episode in "Capturing a Yankee General in Bed" (Ramage, pp. 58-76). An area in Northern Virginia between Alexandria and the Blue Ridge came to be known as "Mosby's Confederacy." He used surprise, fear, and rumors of his presence to make his small force seem omnipresent. For more on Mosby, see Ramage.

Chapter XIV

1 The French title reads "De Charybde en Scylla." Some manuscript readers preferred using the colloquial English "From the Fire back to the Frying Pan" in place of the allusion to Greek mythology. Tremblay chose the present title.

2 The original French reads "D'ailleurs j'ai là deux pistolets." French songwriter Gustave Nadeau (1820-1893) composed more than three hundred songs during his lifetime. In the original French, his name is spelled "Nadaud." Tremblay changes this to the accepted spelling "Nadeau" in his English translation.

3 Henry A. Wise, former governor of Virginia and one of Lee's generals, might be the model for young Wyse's father. However, photographs show him as a much younger man with short hair only touched with gray. The original French reads "plutôt grise que blanche." Tremblay's translation reads "whitish gray."

Chapter XV

1 The original French reads "Retour au regiment." Tremblay translates "Returned to Duty."

2 Sergeant Ingersoll shows the Fourteenth moving to Catlett's Station on March 7, 1864.

Chapter XVI

1 Once again, Tremblay refers to a five-year term of enlistment.

Chapter XVII

1 Tremblay uses the very same title.

2 Camp rations, according to Anderson, consisted of "coffee, hard tack, beef or bacon,

beans and rice." On the march, men frequently lacked adequate supplies of even these meager rations. The need for foraging is firmly rooted in the realities of war.

3   Did Tremblay share Eugène's talent for savate? His autobiography remains silent on this point. However, savate does offer advantages to the short, slight, and agile practitioner. Both Rémi and Eugène fit this profile. The lively fight descriptions do give both English boxing and savate moves, according to Peggy Partello, Keene State College librarian and boxing amateur.

Chapter XVIII

1   Here, as elsewhere, Rémi sees the French language and culture as providing a common bond among enemies. The young Canadians' rescue of Hélène (attributed to their French gallantry), earns them both a warm reception at the plantation. Hélène's father is a Louisiana plantation owner. Her knowledge of French will allow her to earn her living teaching in a college for women after the war. In so doing, she demonstrates the same praiseworthy characteristics as Louise, Eugène's faithful fiancée. Tremblay also notes that Eugène finds a friend and protector in French-speaking Colonel Prentice of the 7th Virginia Cavalry.

Chapter XX

1   See the chronology in the section above entitled "The 14th Regular U.S. Infantry and Rémi Tremblay's War Record."

2   The original French reads "continuait à foudroyer" (*Un Revenant*, p. 78).

Chapter XXI

1   The original French says "le commandant était gris comme cinq cents Polonais" ("the major was as drunk as five hundred Poles"). In his own translation, Tremblay also prefers "drunk as a lord."

2   Tremblay's admiration of Napoleon was typical of French Canadians as well as all French-speaking people everywhere in the world. Napoleon was renowned for his rousing exhortations to his troops. Elsewhere Tremblay refers to Napoleon (rather than Wellington) boots, and to his dream of going to fight with the army of Napoleon's descendant, Napoleon III, in Mexico.

3   The original French reads "J'ai envie de crier, à feu M. le rebelle de considérer ta balle comme non avenue."

Chapter XXII

1   See Note 6, Chapter XI for the listing of officers in the Fourteenth at the beginning of Grant's campaign. Here as elsewhere, Eugène finds himself in a predicament Tremblay himself experienced. Thanks to Tremblay's predilection for getting into trouble, we have ample information concerning his experiences at the Battle of Cold Harbor. In *Un Revenant* as well as his poem "Le Drapeau du 14e," dedi-

cated to Major Edmond Mallet, Tremblay captures the moment.

We might not know as much about Tremblay's participation in this battle had it not been for his concern about his desertion. In 1885, he sent a copies of *Un Revenant* and "Le Drapeau du 14e" to Mallet, for he looked to him to resolve his difficulties.

Tremblay might not have been so concerned were it not for his dispute with the Reverend Narcisse Cyr, which, in turn, coincided with these polarizing events: the battle mounted by the parishioners of Notre Dame de Lourdes in Fall River to continue the practice of having a French curé and French parish schools, the death of Louis Riel, and the visit of the "apostate" priest Charles Chiniquy. Tremblay's newly founded Independent championed these Franco-Canadian causes. The parishioners won the day. And Chiniquy, who came in search of converts, went away disappointed.

Cyr, claiming that Canadian schools provided inferior education, mounted a journalistic attack. Tremblay and *L'Indépendant* replied in kind – attacking Cyr both in English in the press and in his scathing French poem "Le Cyriade." Cyr responded by writing the War Department to obtain Tremblay's war record and threatening to have him arrested as a deserter. That did not happen.

Thanks to this spirited exchange, we have considerable background information on Tremblay's war experience.

First, the Battle of Cold Harbor. The scene Tremblay describes better fits the battle at Bethesda Church on June 2. "At 7:45 a.m. on June 2, Burnside received Meade's order to coordinate his movements with Warren's Vth Corps to his left. Meade wanted the IX Corps pulled back to a position north of Bethesda Church in order to cover the right of the V Corps. Then both corps would move closer to Cold Harbor protecting the vital right flank of the army from any Confederate attempts to turn the position" (Schroeder, *We Came to Fight,* pp. 125-139).

June 2 was a very hot day ending with rain in the evening. The attack was set for early in the day, but a variety of difficulties, including troop movements, ammunitions problems, and fatigue, caused a postponement until late in the afternoon. Tremblay's account captures the debacle: Federal lines overrun, men separated from their units, men disoriented in the woods, and attempts to rally and confront the enemy. In his diary, Sergeant Burgess Ingersoll refers to a group of twenty men of the Fourteenth being surrounded by the enemy. Some escape.

Thanks to Tremblay's poem as well as his correspondence with Mallet, we can identify some of the men present as the regimental flag is saved: Captain David B. McGibbon, First Lieutenant C. McGibbon, and Sergeant La Belle. In *Un Revenant* Leduc re-enacts the role of Sergeant La Belle; Eugène is, of course, Tremblay himself. Patrick Schroeder and Brian Pohanka, historians for the 5th New York (Veteran) Volunteer Infantry, confirm that their unit was present at Bethesda Church. In fact, arriving "tired and dusty" that morning, they had insisted on joining the fight. Tremblay describes the flight with the regimental flag through the woods toward a group of "our ZousZous" on a small hill. Patrick Schroeder shows the Zouaves' own attempts to rally shortly before Tremblay's men reach their position: "It was impossible to rally the regiment until the disorganized knots of men made it over a small creek and up a hill to safety with the main Federal line near Bethesda Church" (Schroeder, p. 131). "The 140th and 146th New York units were present as well—all units wearing the colorful Zouave garb" (Pohanka, Pohanka-Langford e-mail, September 17, 1999).

Major Mallet, to whom "Le Drapeau du 14e" was dedicated, seemed to have been quite pleased to receive copies of it as well as *Un Revenant*. In fact, Mallet appears to have been favorably disposed toward Tremblay. In their correspondence extending from 1885 to 1887, Mallet at first warns Temblay that bounty hunters can still receive $30 for turning in deserters. After investigating his case, Mallet informs him that a review by the authorities could very well end by his receiving a discharge "without character" (Mallet, October 2, 1885, Washington, D.C.). Rémi did not pursue this option. In all probability, his correspondence and seemingly cordial relationship with Mallet had already served its purpose. In *Un Revenant,* in his autobiography *Pierre qui roule,* and in his correspondence with Mallet and the Pension Record Department, he freely admitted deserting while simultaneously contending that extenuating circumstances should excuse this error. In any event, Tremblay lived in New England for several years after the war without being arrested (Mallet-Tremblay correspondence, 1885-1887).

Following the Civil War, Major Edmond Mallet was an Indian agent for the United States government. He would have been familiar with the Fourteenth's post-war activities. Anderson traces the fate of the Fourteenth after the Civil War (Anderson, pp. 604–609). Troops were sent first to New York, then to San Francisco, to Fort Vancouver, back to California, and then to Arizona. However, the headquarters remained at Fort Vancouver until June 1866, and then also moved to Arizona. In the reorganization of the army in 1869, the 45th Infantry and the Fourteenth were consolidated, at which time the new Fourteenth moved to Nashville, Tennessee. In April 1870, the regiment was transferred to Fort Randall, Dakota; in August to the Department of the Platte, with headquarters at Fort Sedgwick. In 1876, when the Sioux War broke out, companies C, B, and F were sent to join Crook's column. The regiment continued its participation in the Indian campaigns until the regimental headquarters was transferred back to the Vancouver Barracks, Washington Territory, in July 1884.

And Tremblay's war record? While the debate between Tremblay and Cyr is interesting to note, the Pension Record Department had the final word in its file #4294 1890. In short, the army still considered Tremblay a deserter, but only after his final escape while under escort to Fort Trumbull on May 11, 1865.

On March 17, 1890, Tremblay, now editor of *La Patrie,* wrote from Montreal to the U.S. War Department to request blank forms and instructions on how to proceed to remove charges of desertion under the act of March 2, 1889. On March 20, 1890, Assistant Adjutant General Arthur MacArthur writes, "You are requested to furnish this Office a statement of your whereabouts after your apprehension at New York City, when you were sent to Fort Trumbull, Conn., and the circumstances under which you left the service again."

In his reply to Arthur MacArthur, written on the *La Patrie* letterhead paper and dated April 1, 1890, Tremblay states his case as follows:

In answer to your letter dated March 29th 1890 and headed '4294 P.R.T, 1890. Subject: Removal of charge of desertion,' I beg to state as follows: When I was apprehended in New York City in the winter of 1865, I had in my possession an unexpired thirty day's furlough which I held from the military authorities at Camp Parole, Annapolis, Maryland, where I had previously arrived from Libby Prison. Had I had the presence of mind to show this document, I should not have been arrested. I was then suffering from dysentery and felt somewhat weak both in mind and body. I tore the furlough, instead of showing it, was sent to Fort Trumbull and to Annapolis a few weeks later. During the whole of my stay in the service after that, I was confined as a prisoner under the same charge or other the purport of which was never made known to me.

When Lincoln was assassinated and when Lee surrendered I was still in Camp Parole. As far as I can remember, orders came to discharge all volunteers and send the regulars to the headquarters of their respective regiments. Being still in the guardhouse, I was sent in charge of a cavalry sergeant, who had been provost-sergeant of the camp. Not knowing what were the charges against me and fearing the result of prolonged confinement pending a Court Martial, I managed to give him the slip at New London Conn. before he had a chance to deliver me over to the authorities at Fort Trumbull. This took place on or about the 8th day of May, 1865. I remember that I arrived in Canada on the 12th of May and I think it was four days after I had left my guard, whose name I believe was Jackson and whose rank was that of a sergeant in the volunteer cavalry. Such is the true statement of the facts which you have requested me to give you. Believe me.

> Yours very respectfully,
> Rémi Tremblay

A notation in the hand of Arthur MacArthur dated May 16, 1890, reads as follows:

Case of Rémi Tremblay
Co F 1st Batt 14 Inftry
Note on records in this case

'Charge of desertion of August 20. 1864 reversed; was captured at Weldon RR Va Aug 19. 1864, was paroled at Aikins Ldg Va Feby 5/65 reported at College Green Bcks Feb 7, 1865, admitted Hospital Feby 17. 1865 deserted from furlough [unreadable words] March 10, 1865. Confined in guard house Camp parole Wed March 18, 1865 for desertion; released March 23, 1865 reconfined April 7, 1865 for desertion, released and sent to Fort Trumbull Conn May 9. 1865 — failed to reach this place and escaped from guard while en route near New London Conn on or about May 11. 1865 and is a deserter from that date.'

See enclosed reports
Inform claimant

A MacArth
Assistant Adjutant General

On May 17, 1890, the Adjutant General's Office of the War Department sent the following form letter to Tremblay in Montreal. The sections in italics indicate the handwritten remarks applying to Tremblay which were placed in the blanks.

Sir

In reply to your application for removal of charge of desertion from record of your service in C F *1st Battalion 14th Infantry* you are respectfully informed that under existing laws the department is not empowered to take favorable action in the matter.

The records show that *Rémi Tremblay enlisted Nov 7 1863 for 5 years — was assigned to Co F 1st Batalion 14 Inftry, deserted while en route to Fort Trumbull New London Conn about May 11.1865 and this is still a desertion charge.*

The most that can be done for this man by this office is to issue a discharge certificate without character as of date and by reason of desertion, which action will not expunge the "fact" of desertion, but will close his connection with the military service.

If the man will accept such discharge certificate, his statement to that effect must be forwarded to this office.

Very respectfully,
Arthur MacArthur
Assistant Adjutant General

The records do not show that Tremblay chose to forward his statement. Whatever the case, it is clear that the U.S. Army was not interested in pursuing him or other deserters at this point.

2 These words, appearing in English in the French original, recall the first words of the Civil War song "The Battle Cry of Freedom" by George F. Root: "Yes, we'll rally round the flag, boys, we'll rally once again/Shouting the battle cry of Freedom."

3 The original French reads "Une batterie de 32 vint les appuyer" (*Un Revenant*, p. 92). Our translation agrees with Tremblay's.

Chapter XXIII

1 Tremblay's descriptions of bravery in battle bring new meaning to the high casualty figures. He shows us private soldiers walking casually back and forth from their rifle pits to bring provisions to their comrades, and officers standing erect in the line of fire as they address their men — actions putting them in harm's way.

2 In the French text the passage reads as follows: "Et l'ordre passait de bouche en bouche, mais des malins, après avoir transmis l'ordre, donnaient un coup de coude à leurs voisins et disaient:

_Blaze away.

Ce qui, dans les circonstances, auraient pu se traduire en Canadien par: *Envoyez-fort* (*Un Revenant*, p. 94).

3 The original French reads "où le reste de l'armée était déjà en ordre de marche" (*Un Revenant*, p. 94). Tremblay translates "where the remainder of the Potomac Army already stood in marching order."

4 The original French reads "son éternel cigar" (*Un Revenant*, p. 94). Tremblay translates "his irremovable and omnipresent cigar."

5 The original French reads "jeter ses chaussures" (*Un Revenant*, p. 95). Tremblay chooses "parting with his footwear."

Chapter XXIV

1 Evidently Tremblay can't resist refering to the traditional rivalry between the French Canadians and the Irish.

2 The French reads: "On causa des absents, sans oublier les absentes" (*Un Revenant*, p. 99).

3 Once again Tremblay displays his Biblical knowledge, referring to the Old Testament book Lamentations, as well as the Gospel quotation that a prophet has no honor in his own country.

4 A reference to Napoleon I, who frequently reminded his men that he himself had begun as a corporal. In Napoleon's times, soldiers demonstrating initiative and leadership potential were frequently promoted from the ranks.

5 Yet another instance where Tremblay justifies Eugène's and his desertion.

Chapter XXV

1 The original French uses both "lunette" and "jumelle" (*Un Revenant*, pp. 104–105). Tremblay translates "field-glass."

2 In the light of what is known about the Springfield, their goal is attainable. Under test conditions before the Springfield was adopted in 1861, a marksman fired off ten shots within five minutes at a target two feet square placed one hundred yards away. Six out of ten shots hit the target. Theoretically a skilled rifleman could load and shoot 120 times an hour. However, given the realities of the battlefield, together with admonitions to conserve ammunition, the soldiers in Eugène's rifle pit could find their goal challenging (William C. Davis, *Fighting Men of the Civil War*, pp. 55-58).

3 Horace K. Thatcher served with the Fourteenth from 1861 to 1865. He was dismissed following his court-martial for embezzlement. On the battlefield, he was apparently a brave and gallant officer respected by his men, as Tremblay indicates. We find him in the field in the following battles: Second Bull Run, Antietam, Fredericksville, Chancellorsville, Gettysburg, North Anna, Bethesda Church, and Weldon Railroad. He was commissioned brevet major for gallantry in action at North Anna and Bethesda Church.

Ironically, just before the gallant service which won him his promotion, he engaged in activities leading to his court-martial and discharge. From the end of March through the end of April 1864, he acted as disbursing officer in charge of paying volunteers in Indiana. In this capacity he embezzled $18,042. Thatcher signed the oath of office confirming his appointment as brevet major on December 13, 1864. He was brought before a general court-martial in Indianapolis, Indiana, on July 6, 1865, pursuant to Special Order No. 107, C.S. He was dishonorably discharged on December 23, 1865. The court judged it more prudent to discharge rather than imprison him. If imprisoned, he could not find the means to pay back the embezzled sum. There is no indication that any of the moneys were ever repaid. While he did try to have the judgment against him reversed and lay claim to the salary he would have otherwise received during 1865, his attempts were to no avail.

Subsequently, Thatcher enlisted in the 3rd Cavalry, where he held the rank of master sergeant from March 23, 1868, through 1869. Seemingly, embezzlement had become a habit. During a brief attempt at civilian life, his picture appeared on a wanted poster offering a $300 reward for his apprehension and an additional twenty-five cents on the dollar for any moneys recovered from his theft from the Adams Express Company, Louisville, Kentucky, on July 15, 1870. This episode could explain why he changed his name as he returned to the military life. From 1872 through 1874, using the name Edward K. Howard, he served with the rank of sergeant at West Point, New York. He died in 1877, leaving a widow and two children. Ellen Thatcher, a former school teacher, was apparently convinced that Thatcher was an innocent man, wrongly condemned by the military. Her petition to the military to release the salary withheld in 1865 was denied. At the time of her 1878 petition she had returned to teaching in the public schools to support herself and her children (Francis B. Heitman, *Historical Register and Dictionary of the*

United States Army, vol. 1, pp. 951-952; Reese, p. 174, 259; ACP file: Memorandum of papers in case of Horace K. Thatcher Late Capt. 14 Inf. with 865.A6P 7848).

Chapter XXVI

1 The original French, in keeping with Tremblay's love of irony, reads "aussi véridiques que flatteurs pour notre héros" (*Un Revenant,* p. 112).

2 "Steady habits" is Tremblay's wording.

Chapter XXIX

1 To date, research has not identified the source of this quote.

Chapter XXX

1 Tremblay presents Grippard as the epitome of the money-grabbing swindler mascarading as a respectable businessman. A stock character? Yes — yet in fleshing out Grippard's life, Tremblay apparently borrows details from the life of the well known contemporary entrepreneur and speculator Louis-Adélard Senécal. A bold investor, a man with his finger in many pies, he made and lost several fortunes. During the American Civil War, he made a fortune trading with the United States. By the end of the war he had a small flotilla of steam boats and barges on a regular route: Montreal, Sorel, and Whitehall "en passant par les Etats-Unis." His biographer, Cyrille Felteau, notes a particularly virulent attack against him appearing in Wilfrid Laurier's pamphlet "La caverne de quarante voleurs" (The Cave of the Forty Thieves). In this pamphlet, Laurier's caricature of Senécal explains his method of investing: "Je pose zéro … et je retiens tout" — "I invest nothing …and I keep all the profits" (Cyrille Felteau, "Portraits de Louis-Adélard Senécal et de William-Edmond Blumhart," in *Histoire de la Presse,* tome I, pp. 137-156).

2 Tremblay chooses "quack medicines" as his translation for "orviétan"(*Un Revenant,* p. 130).

Chapter XXXI

1 Dr. Frederick Wolf, Keene State College physics professor, Terry Borton of Magic Lantern Shows, and Mervyn Heard, doctoral candidate writing his dissertation on phantasmagoria, have all read Tremblay's phantasmagoria chapters with great appreciation. Heard's critique, excerpted below, provides a the definitive word on Bohémier's and Brindamour's experiments as shown here and in subsequent chapters.

"Thanks for letting me read the excerpt — very entertaining. I also note that the word 'revenant' is also the French word for ghost! However, I regret to say that the process described sounds somewhat far-fetched. It seems to me that what we have here is a mish-mash of ideas. Certainly most of the items of equipment mentioned were employed at one time or another in the cause of ghost projection —

but there are other elements which seem to defy the properties of light!..."

He goes on to list other problems: projecting an image on vapors from water scattered on a rug, unpressurized steam rising, phosphorous sending smoke into the air for more than a few seconds, phosphorus taking so long to slide down a piece of ice. Furthermore, he states:

"There is also the problem of the projection beam....If an angled mirror is used to convey a projected image after leaving the lens then there may be no noticeable generative rays. However, if — as suggested in this excerpt — the lens is contained within the tube, and there is no mirror beyond it, you would certainly be able to see the point of projection.

"So — my conclusion — Tremblay may have read about some of these things but not fully understood them. It certainly works well as a tall story though" (Heard-Langford e-mail, October 8, 1999).

2 Tremblay's translation, which we have followed here, is a nice way of indicating Brindamour's ignorance. In the exchange which follows, we have blended Tremblay's wording with ours.

Chapter XXXII

1 Trembly plays on the words "raw"(uncooked/unschooled) and "cooked" (cooked, seasoned, knowledgeable) in the original. "C'est toi qui es cru, et tu le seras toujours, parce que tu es un dur à cuire" (*Un Revenant* p. 139). Brindamour is both unschooled and untrained.

Chapter XXXIII

1 Aesculapius is the Roman god of medicine and healing.

Chapter XXXV

1 The play on words reads here is just about identical to the original.
    "Ce n'est pas le miroir qu'on vexe," dit Bohémier....
    "Mais non, c'est toi qu'on vexe, imbécile" (*Un Revenant*, p. 161).
In his translation, Tremblay simply passes over his own play on words.

2 Here Tremblay plays on the expressions "être en train de," to be in the process of, and "être en train," to be in good spirits, to be drunk (*Un Revenant*, pp. 161-162).

3 Research has not identified this song.

Chapter XXXVI

1 Tremblay's description suggests that he knew such a man. Research has not revealed his identity.

2 Hustings are political venues where campaign speeches are made.

3 The French reads "Il ne se doutait pas que la voie droite est la meilleure pour arriver lorsqu'on est doué comme il était d'un talent supérieur" (*Un Revenant*, p. 168).

4 The French reads "et faisait exécuter à la fameuse mèche une danse des plus fantastiques" (*Un Revenant,* p. 170).

Chapter XXXVII

1 Tremblay's description of the camp corresponds to descriptions given both in Anderson and Hardee's (Don Heitman. *Heitman's Simplified Hardee's and Skirmish Drill.* Indianapolis: Volunteer Publishing Company, 1990).

2 Professor James Smart takes exception to these numbers. *The Encyclopedia of the Civil War* cites the following figures for June 15, 1864: 10,000 men in Smith's advance guard; under 2,500 men in Beauregard's force defending the city. The same source shows Grant's army at nearly 125,000 and Lee's army at under 50,000 by late winter, 1865 (pp. 276-277). Long estimates more than 100,000 Federal troops against 50,000 Confederates (Long, p. 525).

3 A mortar known as the "Dictator" could shoot projectiles weighing two hundred pounds (Davis, p. 106).

Chapter XXXVIII

1 The mine explosion was an utter debacle. The explosion occurred at 4:45 a.m., killing an estimated 278 Confederates and creating a crater 170 feet long, sixty feet wide, and eighty feet deep. By 8:30 a.m. about 15,000 troops were engaged. Leadership was lacking: General James Ledlie, in command of the attack, and General Edward Ferrero, in command of the black division, sat drinking in a bombproof shelter while their troops were being slaughtered.

  By the time the Federals were ordered back in the early afternoon, approximately 5,500 men (4,000 Union, 1,500 Confederate) were dead or wounded (Long, p. 548; Reese, pp. 319-321; Richard J. Sommers, "Petersburg Besieged," in Davis, pp. 1059-1145).

2 Lower Canada is now Québec. Long before the Quiet Revolution, Tremblay advocated using French in his province. Upper Canada is now Ontario.

Chapter XXXIX

1 Tremblay uses "French furlough," an interesting contradiction in terms. A military leave can be legitimate or AWOL. A furlough is an official permission to be excused from duty. The soldiers were AWOL. We should note that the French refer to unofficial leave-taking as "filer à l'anglaise," while the English call it "taking French leave." The average numbers of deserters per month from May 1, 1863, to December 31, 1865, are as follows: 4,647 a month in 1863; 7,333 a month in 1864; 4,368 in 1865 (Long, p. 714).

2 Smedberg lost his right leg at the Battle of the Wilderness (Reese, p. 156). To date, research has not revealed the identity of Tremblay's Downer.

Chapter XL

1 The picture and caption on the wanted poster put out by the Adams Express Company in Louisville, Kentucky, on July 15, 1870, provide a description closely matching Tremblay's: "About five feet six inches high; age 30; straight and erect in his walk, sharp features, prominent, straight nose; black hair; black moustache, heavy; brown or dark eyes; false upper front teeth; dark skin; weight 120 or 140 lbs...." (ACP file: Memorandum of papers in case of Horace K. Thatcher Late Capt. 14 Inf. with 865.A6P 7848). It seems likely that Thatcher was older than the poster states. Also, Tremblay judged him to be a few inches taller.

Chapter XLI

1 John Tanner (1780–1846?) was born in Kentucky. When he was about nine years old, he was carried off and adopted by the Chippewa Indians, who called him Shaw-shaw-wa-be-na-se (the Falcon). Dr. Edwin James of Fort Brady took down his story, which was published as *A Narrative of the Captivity and Adventures of John Tanner (U.S. Interpreter at the Saut de Ste. Marie) During Thirty Years Residence Among the Indians in the Interior of North America,* New York: 1830. An English edition appeared in London in 1830; French and German translations came out in 1835 and 1840 respectively. James Macauley published his version of Tanner's story in *Grey Hawk; Life and Adventure Among the Red Indians,* London: 1883. Tanner's narrative tells how he acquired Indian skills, such as hunting, trapping, and the ability to survive for long periods of time with little or no food (Noah Story, ed. *The Oxford Companion to Canadian History and Literature,* p. 779).

2 A "blackleg" is a swindler, sharper, or professional gambler; the term also can refer to a scab or strikebreaker.

Chapter XLII

1 The original French reads "un simple couteau de poche." Tremblay uses the term "jackknife" in his English translation.

2 In the French folksong "Marlbrough s'en va-t-en guerre," the Duke of Marlborough's victory is turned into defeat and he dies. In actuality, this English general, ancestor of Winston Churchill, was victorious in the battles of Höchstädt, Ramillies, and Malplaquet. Though gravely wounded at Malplaquet in 1709, he did return home in triumph. It is said that the French composed this satirical folksong to express their vexation at his victory. However, it did not become popular until 1781, when Marie Antoinette and the royal court made it all the rage. The pertinent verses show a page coming to tell the Duchess about the Duke's death and burial.

> Monsieur d'Marlbrough est mort,
> Mironton, mironton, mirontaine,
> Monsieur d'Marlbrough est mort,
> Est mort et enterré.

L'ai vu porter en terre,
Mironton, mironton, mirontaine,
L'ai vu porter en terre,
Par quatre z'officiers.

L'un portait sa cuirasse,
Mironton, mironton, mirontaine,
L'un portait sa cuirasse,
L'autre son bouclier.

L'troisième portait son sabre,
Mironton, mironton, mirontaine,
L'troisième portait son sabre,
L'autre ne portait rien.

The English version reads as follows:

Monsieur Marlbrough is dead
tra la la tra la la tra la la
Monsieur Marlbrough is dead
He's dead and buried.

I saw him carried to his grave
tra la la tra la la tra la la
I saw him carried to his grave
By four officers.

One carried his breastplate
The other carried his shield
One carried his sword
The other carried nothing.

3 A Colonel Clarence Prentice did command the 7th Confederate Cavalry Battalion. Records show he would have been twenty-four years old in 1864 (Prichard, James, and Jeffrey C. Weaver, "The 7th Battalion Confederate Cavalry, Virginia," from the website ftp://ftp.rootsweb.com/pub/usgenweb/va/civilwar/va7th.txt).

Chapter XLIII

1 The title refers to the famous song "Un Canadien errant," written by M.-A. Gérin-Lajoie to commemorate the wanderings of patriots exiled following the Papineau Rebellion (1837-1838). It has since been sung to recall the wanderings of French Canadians and Franco-Americans at other times. The first verse reads as follows:

Un Canadien errant, banni de ses foyers,
Un Canadien errant, banni de ses foyers,
Parcourait en pleurant des pays étrangers.
Parcourait en pleurant des pays étrangers.

Chapter XLV

1   The original French reads "je monte à l'anglaise" (*Un Revenant,* p. 207).

Chapter XLVI

1   In the summary of Federal troop engagements for October 2, 1864, Long notes tersely, "A Federal expedition aimed at the salt-mining operations in southwest Virginia was repulsed at Saltville" (Long, p. 578). "Although John Hunt Morgan was killed on September 4, 1864, the remnants of his command were not defeated until December 3, 1864" (Long, p. 566, 605).
2   The French reads "fit un bon demi-arpent au trot" (*Un Revenant,* p. 218). Tremblay translates "broke into a trot which lasted him about thirty yards."

Chapter XLVII

1   The original French reads "Les étapes d'un prisonnier de guerre" (*Un Revenant,* p. 218). We have used Tremblay's translation here.

Chapter XLVIII

1   The Union army rolls list an officer named George C. Joslin, major in the 15th Massachusetts Volunteer Infantry Regiment. Taken prisoner on November 27, 1863, he was exchanged in August 1864 (Andrew F. Ford, *The Story of the Fifteenth Regiment Massachusetts Volunteer Infantry,* p. 4). Did Tremblay know Major Joslin? Had he met him during his first imprisonment? Before his wanderings through the hills of Virginia and Kentucky? Did he know he could safely "borrow" the name of an officer already exchanged?

Chapter XLIX

1   The original French reads "toutes les intempéries de la saison" (*Un Revenant,* p. 227). Tremblay translates this as "all the inclemencies of the weather."
2   The original French reads "Le descendant des races britanniques qu'il soit Anglais, Ecossais, Irlandais ou Américain se croit toujours pétri d'un limon supérieur à celui des autres hommes" (*Un Revenant,* p. 229). Tremblay omits the passage containing this remark in his translation.
3   Professor James Smart expresses skepticism about this episode.
4   Could these soldiers have been part of the group Benjamin F. Booth reports arriving at Salisbury on November 13, 1864? In his description of his stay in this prison, he notes, "Another lot of what they lovingly call 'fresh fish' (these are black 'bass')

arrived today. About 300 colored soldiers…and about 1200 or 1300 white soldiers were brought in to become the guests or victims of Major Gee and his butchers" (Benjamin F. Booth, *Dark Days of the Rebellion,* p. 116).

Booth's account of life in Libby and Salisbury prisons bears a striking resemblance to Tremblay's. Undoubtedly they were unaware of each other's narratives. Tremblay published his French-language account, *Un Revenant,* in 1884. Booth did not publish his grim tale until 1897 after waiting in vain to see if another author would attempt this daunting task. According to family legend, Booth used unsold copies of the work to fuel his woodstove. A new annotated edition by Steve Meyer brings Booth's valuable testimony to light today.

Benjamin F. Booth enlisted in the 22nd Iowa Infantry on August 18, 1862. He was twenty-five years old and in robust health at the time. He weighed eighty-one and a half pounds and was near death when released from Salisbury prison in March 1865. Known as "the reporter" of Salisbury by his fellow prisoners, he kept a meticulous record of his stay there. Captured at Cedar Creek on October 19, 1864, he spent the first days of his imprisonment at Libby before being transferred to Salisbury on November 3.

Both Tremblay and Booth describe the prison crowding, sparse rations, desperate attempts to keep warm, friendships, thievery, body vermin, and prison humor. Both give detailed descriptions of their journeys back to Union lines, the disastrous effect of good, wholesome food on starving men, their own emaciated condition, and the final scrubbing down they receive before they are allowed to be in contact with other men in camp. For those fascinated by Tremblay's eyewitness account, Booth provides a wonderful opportunity for additional reading.

5 The original French reads "croyons-nous" (*Un Revenant,* p. 231). Tremblay translates "if we are not mistaken."

Chapter L

1 The original French reads "un grand gaillard, type de commander de nègres" (*Un Revenant,* p. 232).

2 On November 14, 1864, Booth notes the prices posted by the door of the sutler's tent which had just opened for business that day in the Salisbury prison stockade:

Potatoes, per bushel	$40.00
Onions, per bushel	$50.00
Rice, per lb.	$2.00
Salt, per lb.	$1.00
Corn bread, per lb. loaf	$5.00
Black pepper, per oz.	$5.00
Sugar, per lb.	$1.00
Tobacco, per lb.	$5.00

Booth comments, "If we only had plenty of rebel scrip we might live like kings, but as we have not, I fear his majesty will do a slim trade" (Booth, p. 122). Did Tremblay perhaps intend the price of flour to read $80.00 a barrel?

Chapter LI

1 Booth, like Tremblay, has his own form of prison humor concerning body lice. On October 22, 1864, Booth is still in Libby prison. He observes: "I find it is in extremely dirty condition. Evidently the chambermaid forgot to bring her brooms....Then, that peculiar species of 'song birds,' or, more scientifically speaking, 'scratching birds,' known to the ornithology of southern prisons as 'Graybacks,' are very numerous and seem to be as voracious as the human 'graybacks' who robbed and insulted us with out let or hindrance. As between the two, the original 'Grayback' is very much more of a gentleman than his human counterfeit" (Booth, p. 63).

Chapter LII

1 The original French reads "son modeste repas" (*Un Revenant,* p. 242).
2 The original French reads "une palette ayant deux pouces de largeur" (*Un Revenant,* p. 243).
3 The original French reads "passer un quart d'heure auprès duquel le fameux quart d'heure de Rabelais n'était que de la St. Jean" (*Un Revenant,* p. 244).

Chapter LIII

1 The pun on the double meaning of the French "élargir" is omitted here. The original French chapter title reads "Elargis sur parole." Omitted portions read as follows in the original text: "Les prisonniers élargis sur parole (ceux qui sortaient des prisons du sud étaient si étroits qu'ils avaient grand besoin d'être *élargis*)" (*Un Revenant,* p. 247). "Large" in French means "wide." Of course, all the prisoners have become thin and emaciated from the meager rations they were given in prison. Thus the sense of the French chapter title is "released/*fattened up* on parole," and of the original text is "Those who were being released from Southern prisons were so thin that they very much needed to be *fattened up* while on parole."
2 Was there ice on the James at this time? Whatever the case, the dates Tremblay records here are in line with the Pension Department records of his service (see Chapter XXII, note 1). The *William Allison* and the *City of New York* were in use during the prisoner exchange at this time. Official military correspondence from February through March reveals references to "the steamer New York" (February 5 and February 13), "the steamer Allison" (February 16), and "the steamer William Allison (March 2) (OR, series II, vol. VIII, pp. 182, 217, 239, 333). R. Ould, agent of exchange, in his letter of February 16 to secretary of the navy S.R. Mallory, refers to the "steamers Allison and Schultz, now engaged almost daily in the transporta-

tion of prisoners...." Ould's letter to the secretary of war on March 5 refers to the difficulty of delivering prisoners when there are freshets (OR, series II, vol.VIII, p. 333).

3 Research has not as yet corroborated this happening.

4 *Furia francese* is an Italian expression used to describe the "fury" with which the French attacked Italian forces in Italy during the campaigns of Charles VIII in Italy during the years 1494-1495. As an autodidact, Tremblay seems compelled to display his knowledge of history and his command of his own mother tongue: hence the puns.

5 The original French reads "les fièvres remblantes" (*Un Revenant*, p. 251).

Chapter LIV

1 This incident corresponds to what Tremblay reports of his own actions (see Chapter XXII, note 1).

2 The original French reads "deux morveux." Tremblay translates as "two greenhorns" (*Un Revenant*, p. 254).

3 The original French reads "Demi-tour à droite!" Tremblay translates as "Attention! Right about face!" (*Un Revenant*, p. 255).

Chapter LV

1 The original French states that Brady was: "sous-assistant-adjutant général de la 1ère brigade de la 2ième division du 5ème corps d'armée" (*Un Revenant*, p. 260). Tremblay translates this as "acting assistant-adjutant-general."

Tremblay's description fits the profile of George Keyport Brady given in Heitman. A lieutenant as the Wilderness campaign began in 1864, he was promoted to captain in June 1864 and brevet major on August 18, 1864, for gallant service during the Battle of Weldon Railroad. He was regimental quartermaster from January 1, 1862 to June 10, 1864 (Heitman, vol. 1, p. 239).

2 The original French reads "un porte-cigare" (*Un Revenant*, p. 260). Tremblay translates as "a cigar holder."

3 The original French reads "malotrous" (*Un Revenant*, p. 261). Tremblay translates as "gang."

4 The original French reads "Le Yankee s'était mis en garde" (*Un Revenant*, p. 262).

Chapter LVI

1 Did Eugène/Rémi borrow the name of a soldier actually on the Union rolls? To date, research has not provided an answer to this question.

2 The original text reads "buen retiro" (*Un Revenant*, p.268).

3 The original French reads "il lui sembla que sa chute lui avait un tant soit peu rentré les membres dans le corps" (*Un Revenant*, p. 268).

Chapter LVII

1 Ellsworth was President Lincoln's personal friend. Twenty-four years of age, he cut a dashing figure. He was organizer of the 11th New York, also known as the First Fire Zouaves. Although Tremblay shows young Ellsworth dashing up the Marshall House stairs, other accounts show there were two others with him. After shooting Ellsworth, hotel keeper Jackson was immediately shot by Private Francis E. Brownell. The incident captured the imagination of both Northerners and Southerners (Long, pp. 78-79).

2 The French original provides readers with the French translation within the body of the text, immediately following the English lines: "Frappez, hommes libres pour la cause de l'Union. Ne rengainez plus vos épées, tant qu'il restera une bande de traîtres sur les rives de Columbia (Columbia se dit pour les Etats-Unis, comme Albion pour l'Angleterre)" (*Un Revenant*, p. 271).

3 The French original describes an engraving which shows Ellsworth carrying the flag under his arm while simultaneously trampling it under his feet. "Une gravure ... qui représentaient le colonel Ellsworth descendant un escalier, portant sous son bras le drapeau confédéré qu'il foulait aux pieds...." (*Un Revenant*, p. 271).

4 During the Civil War, the United States government raised money by extensive taxation, affixing stamps to just about every conceivable item that could be taxed. Undoubtedly Tremblay is making fun of this excessive taxation. According to Michael Mahler, in his introduction to *United States Civil War Revenue Stamp Taxes,* "On July 1, 1862, as part of a broad program of taxation designed to offset the costs of the Civil War, the United States Congress enacted an extensive schedule of stamp taxes on documents, patent medicines, perfumery and cosmetics, and playing cards, the duties to be paid by adhesive stamps affixed to the articles taxed, or by stamps imprinted directly on certain documents. Later this schedule was expanded to tax matches, photographs, and preserved foods as well. By the standards of the era, the revenue generated by these levies was impressive: at the time of their final repeal in 1883, Americans had paid over $210 million in stamp taxes, using an estimated eight billion stamps in the process. A delightful profusion of stamps was printed, 157 for use on documents and 584 more for proprietary articles.... (Michael Mahler, *United States Civil War Revenue Stamp Taxes.* Pacific Palisades: Castenholz and Sons Publishers, 1988.)

Chapter LVIII

1 Lee surrendered on April 9, 1865.

2 Research has not yet revealed the identity of this officer.

3 Tremblay has the guard calling Eugene a "marsouin," a porpoise (*Un Revenant*, p. 277). "Espèce de marousin" is a friendly epithet. Tremblay is continuing to display his knowledge of dialect.

4 Tremblay's original text provides both the English and the French translation.

"...*and don't you forget it.* (Et ne l'oublie pas)" (*Un Revenant,* p. 278).

5 The original French passage reads: "_Je ne dis pas le contraire. Vous ne semblez pas avoir peur de l'élément liquide. Ballotté par les flots tumultueux, le *man-of-war* (*man-of-war* est le terme usité pour *navire de guerre* dans la marine anglaise et américaine, sa traduction littérale est *homme de guerre*) remorquera le navire désemparé" (*Un Revenant,* p. 278).

6 The original shows the guard saying that he has a "sponge" in his throat: "J'ai une éponge dans la gorge aujourd'hui" (*Un Revenant,* p. 279). Tremblay translates literally. The present English translation uses the more common English idiom.

Chapter LXI

1 Farmers.

2 In the summer of 1865, more than a thousand volunteer officers attended a three-week training camp at Laprairie, on the south shore of the St. Lawrence just opposite the island of Montreal (George F. Stanley, *Canada's Soldiers,* 3rd ed., Toronto: Macmillan, 1974, p. 221; Desmond Morton, *A Military History of Canada,* 3rd ed., Toronto: McClelland & Stewart, 1992, p. 89).

Chapter LXII

1 The original French reads "avec les larmes dans la voix." Tremblay substitutes "eyes" for "voice" in his translation (*Un Revenant,* p. 296).

Chapter LXIV

1 Frequently French Canadians came to U.S. manufacturing cities to make the bricks used to build the factories where subsequent immigrants came to work. We find similar instances elsewhere in New England. Brickmakers came for this purpose from Canada to Suncook, New Hampshire, reports Robert "Steve" Langford. His Leblanc-Daneault family ancestors subsequently came to work in the mills and eventually settled in that same town.

2 The Fenian raids on Canada occurred from 1866 to 1871. The Fenians, a branch of the Irish Republican Brotherhood, founded March 17, 1858 by James Stephens, planned to seize Canada and use it as a bargaining chip to free Ireland from the British Empire. If this failed, as less idealistic members believed, the raids could start a war between Great Britain and the United States. In this event, surely large numbers of British regulars might well be sent to reinforce Canadian troops and this action, the Fenians hoped, would permit a successful Irish uprising. The Fenian army was plagued by difficulties from the beginning: lack of secrecy, small numbers of ill-equipped volunteers, and lack of standard uniforms. The troops themselves were an interesting mix of former Union and Confederate veterans and Irish patriots. The beginning of the end came for the Fenians when, on June 5, 1866, President Andrew Johnson declared that the U.S. Neutrality Laws of 1818 would be upheld. Henceforth the U.S. would not turn its back on Fenian border cross-

ings. Ironically, the raids provided a testing ground for the Canadian army and gave Canada itself a sense of its own strength. The raids began on June 2, 1866, when Colonel John O'Neil positioned his troops on Lime Ridge outside Ridgeway, Ontario. They came to a definitive end when he tried to start an uprising in Manitoba with a force consisting of only forty Irish Americans and Métis (P.G. Smith, "The Fenian Invasions of Canada," www.thehistorynet.com/MilitaryHistory/articles, pp. 1-6).

3 Between 1758 and 1858 no French ships docked in Québec. Ten years earlier, Eugène/Rémi would not have had this opportunity.

4 The original French reads "les parements de l'uniforme" (*Un Revenant*, p. 312).

Chapter LXVI

1 Cartouche and Mandrin were notorious eighteenth-century thieves. Cartouche, particularly renowned for his coach robberies, had a network of of accomplices throughout France. He was betrayed and sentenced to death on the wheel in 1721. Mandrin and his band of two hundred men specialized in smuggling taxable goods such as tobacco and silk into France. He was captured and condemned to death in 1755. Entaya, known as Baptiste Pierre, remains unidentified as of this writing. Presumably he was an equally notorious Canadian "thief" not in the style of Cartouche and Mandrin, but similar to Grippard.

2 Cyrille Felteau notes, "De 1880 à 1885, on le retrouve à la présidence de trois organisemes d'envergure: le Chemin de fer du Nord, La Compagnie de navigation du Richelieu et d'Ontario, enfin la Montréal City Passenger Railway (en quelque sorte, l'embryon de la CTCUM....) (*Histoire de la Presse,* tome I, p. 137).

Chapter LXVIII

1 The original French reads "Un revenant pour tout de bon" (*Un Revenant,* p. 332). Tremblay translates "Back from the Grave."

2 The original French reads "canailles" (*Un Revenant,* p. 334). Tremblay translates as "scoundrels."

Chapter LXIX

1 The original French uses both "Lui-même" and "C'est moi-même" (*Un Revenant,* p. 337, 338).

2 A sapper is a military engineer who specializes in fortifications and mines.

3 "Laissez-les partir, c'est la canaille qui s'en va" — a statement attributed to Sir George-Étienne Cartier, a French-Canadian statesman, politician, and lawyer (1814–1873). Frustrated by the massive migration to the United States, he might have stated the above in a moment of exasperation. It has, however, never been proved that he said this. He was forced to flee to the United States temporarily as a result of his involvement in the rebellion of 1837. He was elected to the Legisla-

tive Assembly in 1848 and enjoyed a brilliant political career, forming the Macdonald-Cartier ministry (1857-1862). He was the leading French-Canadian advocate of the Confederation. Tremblay, whose own family had emigrated, was clearly in sympathy with "la canaille" — in reality, impoverished farmers.

Chapter LXX
1 Tremblay never did write the promised sequel.

SELECTED FRANCO-AMERICAN CENTERS
AND INSTITUTES

La Bibliothèque Mallet, Union Saint-Jean-Baptiste, Woonsocket, Rhode Island

In 1908, one year after the death of Civil War hero Major Edmond Mallet, the Union Saint-Jean-Baptiste purchased his private collection from his widow. Expanded since that time, this 6,000-volume research facility houses genealogical reviews, out-of-circulation French-language newspapers, parish records, and one-of-a-kind photographs, in addition to Mallet's personal papers. The Mallet papers include his correspondence with Rémi Tremblay concerning the latter's attempt to clear his record of the charges of desertion.

Le Centre Franco-Américain/Franco-American Center, Manchester, New Hampshire

The center houses both a library and the Association Canado-Américaine museum. Its holdings total 30,000 French books. It is the largest research facility of its kind in New England. The center also offers for sale the remaining copies of the Franco-American classics series which were reprinted as part of the National Materials Development project.

Le Centre Franco-Américain/Franco-American Center, Orono, Maine

Founded in 1972 as the University of Maine Office of Franco-American affairs, it subsequently became the Franco-American Center. The center is dedicated to making the Franco-American population, identity, and history visible through seminars, workshops, conferences, and media efforts. The center is also the home of Le Forum, a vehicle of expression for Franco-Americans and those interested in them.

The Franco-American Women's Institute/ L'Institut des femmes franco-américaine, Brewer, Maine

Founded in 1997 to promote ethnic women's voices, the institute is also an archival site. Its website provides links to Franco-American and other Francophone sites. The institute welcomes inquiries and contributions for all Franco-Americans and all who are interested in them.

L'Institut français/French Institute, Assumption College, Worcester, Massachusetts

Founded in 1979, the institute is an academic research facility and a resource center for information about the Franco-Americans of New England, maintaining ties with similar research centers in France, Canada, and the United States. Throughout the years, it has organized colloquia and a variety of other cultural projects, and published books. Through its specialized research and extensive collection of Canadiana and Franco-Americana, available online within the Assumption College catalog, the French Institute seeks to increase awareness and promote knowledge of the French presence in North America.

BIBLIOGRAPHY

Rémi Tremblay and Franco-American Perspectives

Albert, R.S., ed. *A Franco-American Overview.* Vols. i–v. Cambridge, Massachusetts: The National Assessment and Dissemination Center for French, 1979.

Anctil, Pierre. *A Franco-American Bibliography: New England.* Bedford, New Hampshire: NMDC, 1979.

_____. "Du Quebec à la Nouvelle Angleterre." In *Le Magazine Ovo,* 1982, vol. 12, 46.

Bonier, Marie-Louise. *Début de la colonie franco-américaine de Woonsocket, Rhode Island.* Montréal-Manchester: Editions du 45e Parallele Nord, 1981.

_____. *The beginnings of the Franco-American colony in Woonsocket, Rhode Island par Mlle. Marie-Louise Bonier.* Translated and edited by Claire Quintal. Worcester, Massachusetts: Assumption College, Institut français, 1997.

Brault, Gérard J. *The French-Canadian Heritage in New England.* Hanover: The University Press of New England, 1986.

Chartier, Armand B. "Franco-American Literature: The New England Experience." In *Ethnic Perspectives in American Literature: Selected Essays on Their European Contribution,* edited by Robert Di Pietro and Edward Itkovic. New York: Modern Language Association of America, 1983.

_____. *Histoire des Franco-Américains de la Nouvelle Angleterre, 1775–1900.* Québec: Septentrium, 1991.

_____. *The Franco-Americans of New England: A History.* Translated by Robert J. Lemieux and Claire Quintal, revised and edited by Claire Quintal. Manchester and Worcester: ACA Assurance, 1999.

_____. *Littérature historique populaire Franco-Américaine.* Bedford: NMDC, 1981.

Chassé, Paul. "Rémi Tremblay." In *Les poètes Franco-Américains de la Nouvelle Angleterre 1875-1925.* Somersworth, New Hampshire: Manuscrit édition privée hors commerce, 1968.

Chodos, Robert and Eric Hamovich. *Québec and the American Dream.* Toronto: Between the Lines Press, 1991.

Courville, Serge and Normand Séguin. *Atlas historique du Québec.* Sainte-Foy, 1996.

Felteau, Cyrille. "Rémi Tremblay." In *Histoire de la Presse: Le Livre du peuple 1884-1916.* Tome i. Montréal: La Presse, 1983.

Mallet-Tremblay correspondence, 1885-1887; Bibliothèque Mallet, Union Saint-Jean-Baptiste, Woonsocket, Rhode Island.

National Materials Development Center Publications, 1975-1982.

Olivier, Julien. "Migration of French Canadians to the Northeast of the United States (New England and New York): What numbers and what do they reveal?" *Le Forum,* Sept. 2001, vol. 29, 3.

Publications of the French Institute, Worcester, Assumption College.

Quintal, Claire. *Steeples and Smokestacks: A Collection of Essays.* Worcester: Institut français, ACA, 1996.

Roby, Yves. *Les Franco-Americains de la Nouvelle-Angleterre.* Québec: Septentrion, 1999.

Rodrigue, B. *Tom Plant: The Making of a Franco-American Entrepreneur, 1859–1941.* New York and London: Garland, 1994.

Samson, Gary. *Emigration* (film). 1981

_____. *Milltown* (film). 1977.

_____. *World Within a World* (film). 1976.

_____. *World Within a World* (book). 1996.

_____. *Ulric Bourgeois: Photographe franco-américain, 1874-1963.*

Tremblay, Rémi. *Pierre qui roule.* Montréal: 1923.

Wade, Mason. *The French Canadians, 1760-1967.* Laurentian Library, no. 33, 1968, reprint; Toronto: MacMillan of Canada, 1975.

Weil, François. *Les Franco-Américains.* Paris: Delin, 1989.

Fiction

Beaugrand, Honoré de. *Jeanne la fileuse.* NMDC: 1980 (1878).

Lambert, Adélard. *L'Innocente victime.* NMDC: 1980 (1936).

Santerre, Richard R. *Anthologie de la littérature franco-américaine de la Nouvelle-Angleterre,* 9 vols. Bedford, New Hampshire: NMDC, 1980-81.

Tremblay, Rémi. *Un Revenant.* NMDC: 1980 (1884).

Critical Articles *on* Un Revenant

(Articles are listed in reverse chronological order.)

Langford, Margaret S. "Boys Into Men." *Le Forum,* May-June 2001, vol. 29, no. 2. Analyzes the hero's (Eugene/Rémi's) transformation in *Un Revenant.*

Brossard, Louis and Monique Lebrun-Brossard, "*Un Revenant,* roman historique et autobiographique?" *Le Forum,* September and December 1999, vol. 27, no. 5, 6; January-February 2000, vol. 28, no. 1.

Langford, Margaret S. "*One Came Back.*" *Le Forum,* January-February 1996, vol. 24, no. 2. Tremblay's "eyewitness journalism" approach to Civil War scenes.

Boivin, Aurélien. "*Un Revenant:* Episode de la guerre de sécession aux Etats-Unis, roman de Rémi Tremblay." In *Dictionnaire des oeuvres littéraires du Québec.* Montréal: Fides, 1980. Incisive analysis of *Un Revenant.* Criticizes Tremblay for following Eugene/Rémi's war experiences at the expense of the plot.

Santerre, Richard. "*Un Revenant.*" In *Le roman franco-américain en Nouvelle-Angleterre 1878-1943.* Boston College: Ph.D, 1974. Valuable critical insights by the NMDC researcher who subsequently oversaw the publication of *Un Revenant* as part of the NMDC Franco-American classics series.

Chassé, Paul. "*Un Revenant.*" In *Les poètes franco-américains de la Nouvelle-Angleterre 1875-1925*. Somersworth, New Hampshire: 1968. Definitive critical essay on *Un Revenant* up to that time. References previous criticism.

Civil War History

Anderson, Colonel Thomas M. "The Fourteenth Regiment of Infantry." In *The Army of the United States*, by Theodore F. Rodenbough and William L. Haskin. New York: 1896.

Association Canado-Américaine/Centre Franco-Américain Archives.

Bartlett, J.R. *The Literature of the Rebellion*. Westport: 1970.

Booth, Benjamin F. and Steve Meyer. *Dark Days of the Rebellion: Life in Southern Military Prisons*. Garrison, Indiana: Meyer Publication, 1995.

Botkin, Benjamin. *A Civil War Treasury of Tales, Legends and Folklore*. Lincoln: University of Nebraska Press, 1960 and 2000.

Britton, Wiley. *Memoirs of the Rebellion on the Border, 1863*. Lincoln: University of Nebraska Press, 1993 (1882).

Brown, Daniel P. *The Tragedy of Libby and Andersonville Prison Camps*. Ventura: Golden West Publications, 1980, 1988.

Campaigns of the Civil War. 8 vols. New York: T. Yoseloff, 1963.

Civil War Society. *Encyclopedia of the Civil War*. Princeton: The Philip Lief Group, 1994.

Conyngham, David Powell. *The Irish Brigade and Its Campaigns*. New York: Fordham Univeristy Press: 1994 (1861).

Davis, William C. and Bell I. Wiley. *The Photographic History of the Civil War: Vicksburg to Appomattox*. New York: Black Dog and Leventhal Publishers, 1994.

Davis, William C. *The Fighting Men of the Civil War*. New York: Smithmark, 1989.

Dean, Eric T., Jr. *Shook over Hell: Post-Traumatic Stress, Vietnam, and the Civil War*. Cambridge, Massachusetts: Harvard University Press, 1997.

Ford, Andrew F. *The Story of the Fifteenth Regiment Massachusetts Volunteer Infantry*. Clinton: Press of W.J. Clouter, 1898.

Fox, William F. *Regimental Losses in the American Civil War*. Albany: Albany Publication Company, 1889.

Geary, J.H. *We Need Men: The Union Draft in the Civil War*. Dekalb: Northern Illinois University Press, 1991.

Heitman, Francis B. *Historical Register and Dictionary of the United States Army*. 2 vols. Baltimore: Genealogical Publishing Co., 1994 (1903).

Hyman, Harold. *Heard 'Round the World: The Impact Abroad of the Civil War*. New York: Knopf, 1969, 1968.

Ingersoll, Burgess. *The Diary of Sergeant Ingersoll*. Entries from January through December 1864. Manuscript: The U.S. Army Institute of Military History.

Keene State College Civil War holdings.

Long, E.B. with Barbara Long. *The Civil War Day by Day*. New York: Da Capo Press,

1971.

Lonn, Ella. *Desertion during the Civil War.* Lincoln: University of Nebraska Press, 1998 (1928).

McPherson, J.M. *Battle Cry of Freedom: The Civil War Era.* New York: Oxford University Press, 1988.

_____. *Ordeal by Fire: The Civil War and Reconstruction.* Boston: McGraw-Hill, 2000.

New England Regional Library Consortium Civil War holdings. *The War of the Rebellion: Official Records of the Union and Confederate Armies.* 128 vols. Gettysburg: The National Historical Society, 1972; reprint of the 1880-1897 ed.

Ramage, James A. *Gray Ghost.* Lexington, Kentucky: University Press of Kentucky, 1999.

Reese, Timothy J. *Sykes' Regular Infantry Division, 1861-1864.* North Carolina and London: MacFarland and Company, 1990.

Regular Army Enlistments, National Archives.

Schroeder, Patrick A. *We Came to Fight: The History of the 5th New York Veteran Volunteer Infantry, Duryée's Zouaves (1863-1865).* Brockneal, Virginia: Patrick A. Schroeder Publications, 1998.

Thatcher, Horace K. "Memorandum of papers in case of Horace K. Thatcher, Late Capt. 14 Inf." ACP file, National Archives; with 865.A6P 7848.

Tremblay, Rémi. Pension Record Department File # 4294 1990, National Archives.

Walker, Mabel Gregory. *The Fenian Movement.* Colorado Springs: Ralph Myles Publisher, Inc., 1969.

Winks, R.H. *Canada and the United States: The Civil War Years.* Baltimore: Johns Hopkins Press, 1966.

Zuker, A.E. *The Forty-eighters: Political Refugees of the German Revolution of 1848.* New York: Russell and Russell (1967 c1950).

BIOGRAPHIES

Margaret S. Langford

Dr. Margaret S. Langford is a professor of French at Keene State College. She is co-founder and present co-chair of the "Pizza and Pedagogy" collaborative for language teachers in Southwestern New Hampshire. Her sabbatical leave projects in 1984 and 1992 focused on oral interviews and research on Franco-Americans. In 1999 her leave was devoted to *Un Revenant / One Came Back*. Since 1996 she has interwoven research, publications, and presentations on this work. Through small-grant sponsorship, she has brought Franco-American speakers, musicians, writers, and exhibits to the Keene State College campus from 1982 to the present. In 1992, the American Association of Academic Alliances honored her for outstanding contributions to the teaching and promotion of French as a second language. In 1994, the New Hampshire Association for the Teaching of Foreign Languages selected her as teacher of the year. In 1998, she received the New Hampshire Excellence in Education Award. She is a member of the American-Canadian French Cultural Commission in New Hampshire and of the French Institute at Assumption College, and is an incorporator of the Franco-American Centre in Manchester, New Hampshire.

Claire Quintal

Dr. Claire Quintal is the founding director emerita of the *Institut français* of Assumption College. Founded in 1979, the Institute, which has published the proceedings of its colloquia, launched in 1980, is considered to be the foremost research center on Franco-American history and culture. To date, sixteen volumes edited and/or translated by Claire Quintal have appeared. She was awarded the Legion of Honor and named an Officer of the National Order of Merit by the French Government. Québec honored her in 1980, naming her to the *Ordre des Francophones d'Amérique*. She is a member of the *Conseil de la Vie Française en Amérique* and chairs the American and Canadian French Cultural Exchange Commission of Massachusetts.

IMAGES FROM THE PAST

Publishing history in ways that help people see it for themselves

THE REAL WOODROW WILSON: AN INTERVIEW
WITH ARTHUR S. LINK, EDITOR OF THE WILSON PAPERS
By James Robert Carroll

Cold and unsmiling, idealistic but stubborn — these have been the popular images of Woodrow Wilson. In truth, he was a politician of considerable ability, an eloquent speaker, and a man capable of great warmth. A 1993 interview with Arthur S. Link, as he was concluding the 69th and final volume of the Wilson Papers after 35 years, reveals a fuller and more vivid picture of the president, and the compelling tale of Link's dogged perseverance, the joy of discovery, and marvelous luck. 28 illustrations. Chronology and bibliography. 5" x 7", 140 pages ISBN 1-884592-32-5 Cloth $19.50

THE QUOTABLE CALVIN COOLIDGE: SENSIBLE WORDS FOR A NEW CENTURY
By Peter Hannaford

Calvin Coolidge has long been dismissed as silent, and with little to say. A collection of over 250 quotations reveals the concise, direct, even eloquent way he stated his views on issues still relevant to the interests of contemporary Americans. The quotations, cited by date and circumstances, are organized alphabetically for use by speakers, writers, researchers, policy makers — in fact, any with an interest in American history. Also included are Milestones in Coolidge's life; a Selected Bibliography; and a listing of Coolidge Archives headed by the Calvin Coolidge Memorial Foundation in Plymouth Notch, Vermont. 5" x 7", 190 pages ISBN 1-884592-33-3 Cloth $19.50

WHITE FIRE
By Stuart Murray

In 1828, frontiersman Dirk Arendt is guiding an archaeological expedition in Zululand whose leader is an agent of a ruthless secret brotherhood seeking an ancient amulet now in the hands of Shaka, lord of the Zulu nation.

The amulet and its central Stone of White Fire has the power to reveal King Solomon's fabled diamond fields and gold mines, bringing great wisdom if used in the right way. If misused, it dooms its bearer to a life of torment.

Meanwhile the first Cape Colony pioneers journey northward into the wilderness in search of the Promised Land. The trekkers do not yet know it, but the land they intend to settle on is rich in the very wealth sought after by the secret brotherhood. 5 1/2" x 8 1/2", 325 pages ISBN 1-884592-25-2 Cloth $26.00

WASHINGTON'S FAREWELL TO HIS OFFICERS: AFTER VICTORY IN THE REVOLUTION
By Stuart Murray

In the sunlit Long Room of Fraunces Tavern, on a winter's day in New York City, 1783, George Washington's few remaining officers anxiously await his arrival. He has called them here to say goodbye — likely never to see them again. The British redcoats have sailed away, defeated in the Revolution. This moving incident, one almost forgotten in American history, was among the most telling and symbolic events of the War for Independence. As they anticipate their beloved general's arrival, the officers recall how their struggle for the sacred cause flickered, almost went out, then flared into final victory. In the story of Washington's Farewell are the memories of long-struggling patriots — the famous and the little-known—men committed heart and soul to the cause of American liberty: Knox, McDougall, Lamb, Hamilton, Steuben, Shaw, Humphreys, Varick, Burnett, Hull, Fish, Tallmadge, the Clintons, Van Cortlandt, Fraunces...heroes all. Index. Bibliography. 42 prints and maps.
5" x 7", 240 pages ISBN 10884592-20-1 Cloth $21.00

AMERICA'S SONG: THE STORY OF YANKEE DOODLE
By Stuart Murray

During the first uncertain hours of the Revolution, British redcoats sang "Yankee Doodle" as an insult to Americans — but when the rebels won astounding victories this song of insult was transformed to a song of triumph, eventually becoming "America's Song." This is the first complete chronicle of the story of "Yankee Doodle," perhaps the best-known tune in all the world. From its early days an ancient air for dancing, through the era of Dutch and Puritan colonial settlement, "Yankee Doodle" evolved during the French and Indian Wars and the American Revolution to become our most stirring anthem of liberty. Index. Bibliography. Illustrated with 37 prints and maps.
5" x 7", 248 pages ISBN 1-884592-18-X Cloth $21.00

RUDYARD KIPLING IN VERMONT: BIRTHPLACE OF THE JUNGLE BOOKS
By Stuart Murray

This book fills a gap in the biographical coverage of the important British author who is generally described as having lived only in India and England. It provides the missing links in the bittersweet story that haunts the portals of Naulakha, the distinctive shingle-style home built by Kipling and his American wife near Brattleboro, Vermont. Here the Kiplings lived for four years and the first two of their three children were born.
All but one of Kipling's major works stem from these years of rising success, happiness and productivity; but because of a feud with his American brother-in-law, Beatty, which was seized on by newspaper reporters eager to put a British celebrity in his place, the author and his family left their home in America forever in 1896.
6"x9"; 208 pages; Extensive index. Excerpts from Kipling poems, 21 historical photos; 6 book illustrations; and 7 sketches convey the mood of the times, character of the people, and style of Kipling's work.
6"x9" ISBN 1-884592-04-X Cloth $29.00
6"x9" ISBN 1-884592-05-8 Paperback $18.95

THE HONOR OF COMMAND: GEN. BURGOYNE'S SARATOGA CAMPAIGN
By Stuart Murray

Leaving Quebec in June, Burgoyne was confident in his ability to strike a decisive blow against the rebellion in the colonies. Instead, the stubborn rebels fought back, slowed his advance and inflicted irreplaceable losses, leading to his defeat and surrender at Saratoga on October 17, 1777 — an important turning point in the American Revolution. Burgoyne's point of view as the campaign progresses is expressed from his dispatches, addresses to his army, and exchanges with friends and fellow officers.; 33 prints and engravings, 8 maps, 10 sketches. Index
7"x10", 128 pages ISBN 1-884-592-03-1 Paperback $14.95

NORMAN ROCKWELL AT HOME IN VERMONT: THE ARLINGTON YEARS, 1939-1953
By Stuart Murray

Norman Rockwell painted some of his greatest works, including "The Four Freedoms" during the 15 years he and his family lived in Arlington, Vermont. Compared to his former home in the suburbs of New York City, it was "like living in another world," and completely transformed his already successful career as America's leading illustrator. For the first time he began to paint pictures that "grew out of the every day life of my neighbors."
32 historical photographs, 13 Rockwell paintings and sketches, and personal recollections. Index. Regional map, selected bibliography, and listing of area museums and exhibitions.
7"x10", 96 pages ISBN 1-884592-02-3 Paperback $14.95

THE ESSENTIAL GEORGE WASHINGTON:
TWO HUNDRED YEARS OF OBSERVATIONS ON THE MAN, MYTH AND PATRIOT
By Peter Hannaford

Why did Thomas Paine turn against him? Why did Elizabeth Powel call him "impudent"? What is the truth about the cherry tree story? What was his single most important quality? These and many more questions about the man called "the father of his country" are answered in this collection. The reader meets Washington's contemporaries, followed by famous Americans from the many decades between then and now and, finally, well-known modern-day Americans. Included are Benjamin Franklin, Thomas Jefferson, Abigail Adams, Parson Weems, Abraham Lincoln, Walt Whitman, Woodrow Wilson, Bob Dole, George McGovern, Eugene McCarthy, Letitia Baldrige, Newt Gingrich, Ronald Reagan — and many more. Read in small doses or straight through...either way, the book gives a full portrait of the man who — more than any other — made the United States of America possible. Over 60 prints and photographs.
5" x 7", 190 pages ISBN 1-884592-23-6 Cloth $19.50

LETTERS TO VERMONT VOLUMES I AND II: FROM HER CIVIL WAR SOLDIER CORRESPONDENTS TO THE HOME PRESS
Donald Wickman, Editor/Compiler

In their letters "To the Editor" of the *Rutland Herald,* young Vermont soldiers tell of fighting for the Union, galloping around Lee's army in Virginia, garrisoning the beleaguered defenses of Washington, D.C., and blunting Pickett's desperate charge at Gettysburg. One writer is captured, another serves as a prison camp guard, others are wounded — and one dies fighting in the horrific conflict in the Wilderness of Virginia. Biographical information for each writer (except one who remains an enigma) and supporting commentary on military affairs.

54 engravings and prints, 32 contemporary maps, 45 historical photographs. Extensive index.

Vol. 1, 6"x9", 251 pages ISBN 1-884592-10-4 Cloth $30.00
  ISBN 1-884592-11-2 Paper $19.95
Vol. 2, 6"x9", 265 pages ISBN 1-884592-16-3 Cloth $30.00
  ISBN 1-884592-17-1 Paper $19.95

ALLIGATORS ALWAYS DRESS FOR DINNER: AN ALPHABET BOOK OF VINTAGE PHOTOGRAPHS
By Linda Donigan and Michael Horwitz

A collection of late 19th- and early 20th-century images from around the world reproduced in rich duotone for children and all who love historical pictures. Each two-page spread offers a surprising visual treat: Beholding Beauty — a beautifully dressed and adorned Kikuyu couple; Fluted Fingers — a wandering Japanese Zen monk playing a bamboo recorder; and Working the Bandwagon — the Cole Brothers Band on an elaborate 1879 circus wagon. A-Z information pages with image details.

9 1/4"x9 3/4", 64 pages ISBN 1-884592-08-2 Cloth $25.00

REMEMBERING GRANDMA MOSES
By Beth Moses Hickok

Grandma Moses, a crusty, feisty, upstate New York farm wife and grandmother, as remembered in affectionate detail by Beth Moses Hickok, who married into the family at 22, and raised two of Grandma's granddaughters. Set in 1934, before the artist was "discovered", the book includes family snapshots, and photographs that evoke the landscape of Eagle Bridge, home for most of her century-plus life. Two portraits of Grandma Moses — a 1947 painting and a 1949 photograph, and nine historical photographs. On the cover is a rare colorful yarn painting given to the author as a wedding present.

6" x 9", 64 pages ISBN 1-884592-01-5 Paperback $12.95

REMAINS UNKNOWN
By Michael J. Caduto with 16 pencil sketches by Adelaide Murphy Tyrol

He somehow found his way to Vermont soon after the Mexican War. It was a long journey, the beginning of a private purgatory that lasted over 150 years. At last, with the help of friends he'd never met, he took the final steps in a quiet cemetery by the river on a sultry afternoon.

In this strange and haunting tale, based on a true story, the reader enters a world suspended between our earthly existence and the realm of the human spirit. A small community of people embarks on an adventure that compels them to bring the mysterious, mummified remains of one long dead to a resting place of peace and grace. With help from two distinct spiritual traditions, and a dose of healing humor in the face of grief, the journey unfolds with a sense of dignity and compassion.

5"x7", 80 pages ISBN 1-884592-24-4 Cloth $15.00

Available at your local bookstore or from Images from the Past, Inc.,

888-442-3204 for credit card orders;

PO Box 137, Bennington, VT 05201

with check or money order.

When ordering, please add $4.00 shipping and handling

for the first book and $1 for each additional.

(Add 5% sales tax for shipments to Vermont.)

www.ImagesfromthePast.com